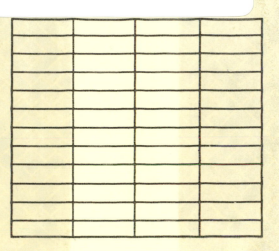

In search of a political philosophy

About the author

W.J. Stankiewicz is a political philosopher with broad interests in the social sciences. He was born in Warsaw in 1922 and educated in Poland and in the United Kingdom at the University of St Andrews and the London School of Economics and Political Science. In World War Two he served in the Polish Army-in-Exile in France (1940) and later with the 1st Polish Armoured Division – a component of the British Liberation Army – in the 1944–1945 campaign in France (Normandy), Belgium, Holland and Germany; and subsequently with the 2nd Polish Corps in Italy.

He has been a visiting post-doctoral fellow at the Center of International Studies at Princeton University, a Research Associate at the Mid-European Study Center in New York and an economist with the Government of Ontario in Canada. He has taught at the Polish University College in London and since 1957 at the University of British Columbia where he is Professor Emeritus of Political Science. He has lectured in approximately sixty universities on five continents.

The present volume, *In Search of a Political Philosophy*, consists of four treatises: a disquisition on conservatism, a dissection of liberalism, an indictment of socialism, and an obituary of Communism: it also contains a reappraisal of Western attitudes to the concept of ideology. Its publication marks the completion of the trilogy, *Relativism in Politics*.

Thus the main theme of Professor Stankiewicz's trilogy – relativism – has been extended to cover three areas of political theory: classical concepts (*Aspects of Political Theory*), theories of democracy (*Approaches to Democracy*) and political ideologies (the present volume).

Works by W.J. Stankiewicz

BOOKS

Institutional Changes in the Postwar Economy of Poland
(with J.M. Montias) (1955)
Politics and Religion in Seventeenth-Century France (1960)
Canada-U.S. Relations and Canadian Foreign Policy (1973)
*Aspects of Political Theory: Classical Concepts in an Age of
Relativism* (1976)
*Approaches to Democracy: Philosophy of Government at the Close
of the Twentieth Century* (1980)
*In Search of a Political Philosophy: Ideologies at the Close of the
Twentieth Century* (1993)

ANTHOLOGIES AND SYMPOSIA

*Political Thought Since World War Two: Critical and Inter-
pretive Essays* (1964)
The Living Name (1964)
Crisis in British Government: the Need for Reform (1967)
In Defense of Sovereignty (1969)
British Government in an Era of Reform (1976)
The Tradition of Polish Ideals (1981)

ESSAYS AND APHORISMS

*What is Behavioralism? Thoughts on the Crisis in the Social
Sciences* (1971)
Relativism: Thoughts and Aphorisms (1972)
A Guide to Democratic Jargon (1976)
Jottings (forthcoming)

In search of a political philosophy

Ideologies at the close of the twentieth century

W. J. Stankiewicz

London and New York

First published 1993
by Routledge
11 New Fetter Lane, London EC4P 4EE

Simultaneously published in the USA and Canada
by Routledge
29 West 35th Street, New York, NY 10001

Typeset in Baskerville by Ponting–Green Publishing Services,
Sunninghill, Berks

Printed and bound in Great Britain by Mackays of Chatham PLC,
Chatham, Kent

British Library Cataloguing-in-Publication Data

A catalogue record for this book is available from the British Library.

ISBN 0–415–08874–7

Library of Congress Cataloging in Publication Data

has been applied for.

ISBN 0–415–08874–7

To Marketa

Contents

Part II Empty liberalism

Preface

The present volume is a sequel to my *Approaches to Democracy* (Edward Arnold, London, 1980), which was a commentary on current ways of thinking about the democratic system and its values. Together with my earlier study *Aspects of Political Theory* (Collier Macmillan, London, 1976), which dealt with basic 'classical' concepts, the books form a trilogy under the general heading of *Relativism in Politics*. Each book may be read as an independent work. Conceptual affinity can also be traced to my critical symposium *In Defense of Sovereignty* (Oxford University Press, New York, 1969).

In Search of a Political Philosophy is an analysis of the assumptions – both conscious and unconscious – underlying the ideological thinking of the proponents and followers, and some theoreticians and critics, of the three democratic 'isms'; of their values; of the distinct nature of Marxist Communism – an all-devouring ideology; and of its impact on Western perceptions. It focuses on such questions as: (a) By what norms are political ideologies characterized and which of them are given precedents in some explicit or implicit hierarchy of norms? (b) How does a particular ideology view such issues as freedom and restraint, responsibility, equality, justice, power, authority, property, human nature and happiness? (c) What are the areas of ideological contiguity and those of mutual influence? (d) Where do the forces – both internal and external – which split Western societies become visible? (e) What are the sources of ideological incomprehension in our society? As in previous works, the concept of relativism serves as a unifying element in the analysis.

A new, simplified definition of ideology offered in the *Conclusion* reflects the author's concern with the role of 'mentalities' in ideological thinking, and with the functional nature of that process. It is offered together with the postulate that the concept of ideology ought to be 'repatriated' – an essentially voluntarist attitude.

In its early stages, the work on this book was supported by the Social Sciences and Humanities Research Council and the I.W. Killam Memorial Fund. I am indebted to both institutions for the Fellowships awarded to me. I am grateful to my friends R.C. Cooke and I.W. Peyman for their continuing interest and co-operation.

Some of the ideas developed in this volume were first voiced during my lecture tours in New Zealand, Australia, Southern Africa and India. The stimulus I received then from the audiences was all one could wish for.

W.J. STANKIEWICZ
University of British Columbia

Chapter 1

Introduction
Conceptual vagueness of political ideologies

In any discussion of political ideologies such as liberalism, socialism and conservatism, the respective adherents use normative terms to express their points of view. But these terms are almost always vague. Consider the following contemporary opinion: 'Socialism [to socialists] stands for the values of freedom, equality, community, brotherhood, social justice, the classless society, co-operation, progress, peace, prosperity, abundance, happiness – to mention just the most important ones.' But as its author, R.N. Berki, observes a few lines later, 'Who does *not* profess to believe in freedom, justice and prosperity? Who is not *against* oppression, misery and war?'[1] The same point is repeatedly made by philosophers. Thus Charles L. Stevenson says: 'Ethical terms are more than ambiguous; they are *vague.*'[2] Indeed, a whole school of philosophy has grown up which concerns itself solely with the clarification of such terms, not in the hope that we will then know what the terms mean – as empiricists, they have already decided that words do not have any meaning in terms of the empirical standards of truth – but only so that we will then be less likely to misunderstand each other. They promise us not so much the possibility of agreement as a clearer perception of disagreement.

Since a discussion of ideology must employ normative terms as if they had clear meanings, and since the apparent vagueness of the terms has been used as an argument that they cannot be clear unless we arbitrarily stipulate a meaning, something needs to be said about the vagueness in question.

Are the terms used in political theory and normative discussions more vague than other words we employ? Compare the length of the entries in a dictionary for such normative terms as 'cruelty' and 'murder' as opposed to those for 'table' or 'vessel'. Try to understand from the entries the meaning of the concepts involved and then decide which of the sets seems most vague. Oddly enough, it is the so-called empirically-based terms which are often more difficult to understand. A reader would not be able to classify accurately any specific article of furniture such as a table if he had nothing to guide him but the dictionary definition, whereas he would have a pretty good idea of what constituted 'cruelty'.

It is not correct to assume that if a term cannot be supported by empirical evidence, it must be vague. Yet the question of vagueness remains unanswered.

It must be admitted that in discussing liberalism, socialism and conservatism the normative terms are used in widely different senses and one cannot limit the meanings without being arbitrary. Consider a statement by a man who was born in a slum, worked his way through university and set up his own business: 'In this country we're all equal. I'm not going to have any socialist taxing me to death to support welfare louts.' We gather that in his own opinion the speaker is not a socialist and that 'equality' for him means that any normal person could go forth and do as he has done – that there is equality of opportunity and ability. We can also legitimately infer that for this man tax-supported welfare schemes are evidence of 'injustice'. Contrast this with another common line of thought: 'Some people are never going to make it in this world and we've got to take that into account. In a country as wealthy as ours there's no excuse for poverty. Government should prevent it. I've got no patience with rednecks who don't give a damn about their fellow-men'. It is not clear from this how the speaker would classify himself politically, but he would appear to think of the first speaker as an arch-conservative. He evidently considers his fellow-men to be naturally unequal in ability so that presumably he would regard 'equality of opportunity' as normatively unimportant. For him 'justice' obviously requires a sufficient redistribution of property to eliminate poverty but apparently does not call for equal distribution: he quite frankly assumes that inequality of some kind will always be characteristic of the human condition.

Each speaker is basically speaking of welfare – this is what their statements lead to. Yet implicit in each statement are normative concepts relating to such abstractions as 'justice' and 'equality', though neither even mentioned 'justice' and the man who mentioned 'equality' did not attempt to define it. What function would be served by first, demanding from each man definitions of these crucial terms and second, demanding that each use them in the same way? We have no difficulty in deciding how each is using the concepts within the context of 'welfare schemes'; there is also reason to believe that if the two were discussing the matter, they would have no difficulty in understanding each other despite the fact that the meaning they give to the normative terms is quite different. What then would we be seeking to do in asking for a definition? We would be asking them to state abstractly their position on all other questions besides the issue of welfare where the questions of justice and equality enter. What makes us think so? Because this is how we would test any definition they attempted. Suppose, for instance, that the man who, judging from his statement about welfare, appears to believe in equality of opportunity, were also to say that blacks should be given special consideration in job applications. This might well surprise us and we would be puzzled unless he was also willing to assert that equality of opportunity exists except for at least one racial minority. Is it not to avoid just this kind of misunderstanding based on our unawareness of qualification that leads us to demand definitions?

The really unreasonable part of demanding definitions is that we are in effect asking someone to present in an abstract formula all possible ways in which he personally uses a term. It is unlikely that this can be done by anyone, but this does not mean that the term is being used vaguely or inconsistently. We cannot make such judgements until we actually look at someone's usage. Even then, those unfamiliar with normative usage make such rather grotesque errors as that of interpreting a qualification based on the fact of there being other norms as an inconsistency: (for example, when those who assert that they believe in freedom of the press are charged with 'inconsistency' if they try to censor pornography).

More unreasonable still is the demand that we all agree to assign only one meaning to each normative term. Suppose we tried to make each of the two men who made a statement about welfare to agree to one definition for each of 'equality' and 'justice'. What we would in effect be asking is that each give up his argument, for the terms derive their meanings from the argument. Why should anyone be asked to do such a thing? What possible reason could there be for dismissing a rational argument without even considering it? The subjectivist school counters by saying that arguments are not rational at all: they are based on emotive terms with no fixed meaning. If so, how is it that an observer can extract those terms from the line of reasoning and indeed, at least with regard to 'justice', must do so, because the concept is not present except as a line of reasoning. It is clearly the reasoning that enables us to employ normative terms.

The multiple meanings of normative terms in political science are not really the problem they may at first sight appear to be – they reflect various possible lines of thought. They would become a problem if any one speaker used them inconsistently, but this would be the same as using rambling and inconsistent lines of reasoning.

In raising the issue of ideology with regard to liberal, conservative and socialist views an attempt will be made to discover whether each is characterized by a distinctive use of democratic norms. Three questions have to be asked. First, what argument or line of reasoning, which either explicitly or implicitly employs the term, is legitimate and convincing, and which ought to be rejected? Second, which of the norms are given precedence in some explicit or implicit hierarchy of norms? It is clear that each of the three 'isms' must subscribe to the democratic norms, but since a belief in democracy does not commit one to any statement about the importance to be placed on any of the norms, one is entirely free to rank them as one wishes; thus some see 'majority rule' as supremely important, whilst others would see nothing wrong with letting it become a mere ceremony. The ordering of norms proves to be the most distinctive feature of the difference between the three ideologies. Third, there is the question about the role of some norms that cannot be directly linked with democratic ideology and the response they receive from the three ideologies in question.

IDEOLOGY OR POLISOLOGY

The unsatisfactory nature of the term 'ideology' when applied to politics can best be shown by an example. Thus Noël O'Sullivan's definition of ideology leaves much to be desired: 'An ideology, unlike an attitude, requires a self-conscious attempt to provide an explicit and coherent theory of man, society, and the world.'[3]

We must allow him the parenthetic 'unlike an attitude' and that rather odd use of 'self-conscious', for he probably has in mind the psychological concept of 'conservative personality' and wishes to make clear that there is no connection between conservatism as an ideology and conservatism as a personality type. It is the essence of the definition that is troubling: 'a coherent theory of man, society and the world.' Include the 'world' in a definition of 'ideology' and we can say that 'science', 'philosophy' and 'religion' are ideologies, whereas what the political scientist wants to discuss are theories of man's relations with the State and society and/or normative systems governing these relations (which rest on – or presuppose – some theory of the 'nature' of man and society: that is, based on norms which are not purely arbitrary).

What marked the beginning of the notion of ideology? The need for 'ideologies' – as opposed to philosophies – did not arise until man decided that the 'self' ceases to exist at death and that no supernatural explanation of the origin of the universe or man is necessary. At first, the 'ideological' outlook was part of the philosophical and religious one. The affairs of this world become secondary – as do the norms governing them – if you assume that the 'self' continues in time and that life on earth is but a moment in the soul's history. Religious systems (and systems based on the assumption about the immortality of the soul) have always evolved an ideology when they have become dominant in a given society. Indeed, one way of distinguishing a genuine religion from a mere creed or sect is to see whether the system has incorporated an ideology. If it has not, it is and will remain a sort of part-time activity, something to be done on Sunday. But even when an ideology is incorporated, there remains a tension between the normative requirements of everyday life in society and those needed for the soul's welfare: no actual 'theocracy' is possible. A State can be dominated by the Church, but – the evidence of Calvin's 'parochial State' notwithstanding – it cannot operate on religious principles which presuppose that man and the State are both transitory and transitional. When a religion dominates a society it is forced to become 'worldly' and 'corrupt'; eventually those who are taught the original system of other-worldly norms come to feel that the Church must be 'reformed'.

Such problems would now be a matter of history if any modern ideology provided an adequate statement about man, the State and society. But this is not the case. Furthermore, if 'ideology' has come into its own – the very marked decline in the belief in 'soul' makes it theoretically possible for many people to substitute ideology for religion – the issue is far from being clarified; the conceptual vagueness has remained.

Many appear so eager to have religion replaced by ideology that they adopt credential systems – never intended to be ideologies – to serve an ideological function. The most notorious in our society is psychiatric theory which, based as it is on biological egoism, represents the individual as in conflict with the State and society. Thus, the presence of crime and mental disorder in individual behaviour is evidence of a 'sick society'; restrictions on the individual – especially on his biological drives, such as the sex drive – are regarded as evidence of 'oppression' by society. That political science does not effectively object to such an extension of a credential to an ideological system would suggest that it has not fully recognized the need for a central system of thought; we cannot simply make assumptions about man's nature and then take society and State as 'given'. There must be an adequate statement about man's nature and the consequent relations with his fellow-man, as well as about institutions necessary to this relationship. A theory of man's nature must be compatible with a theory of State and society.

To make this point clear, it seems advisable to consider substituting some other term for the misleading term 'ideology.' According to the etymology of the term, any system of ideas will suffice. But this is not correct. Religious creeds cannot function as 'ideologies', nor can psychological theories about the individual; as for theories about the universe, they are simply irrelevant. Perhaps a return to the ancient Greek view of the *polis* could lead us to a derived term like polisology to express what we want to say when we use the term ideology in political science.

KOLAKOWSKI'S VIEW OF THREE PERSUASIONS

It is in part the conceptual vagueness of the three ideologies that made Professor Leszek Kolakowski write a 'Credo': 'How to be a Conservative-Liberal-Socialist'.[4] If we summarize the beliefs which he attributes to conservatives, liberals and socialists, we can easily see why he thinks a man can be a conservative-liberal socialist. His statement can be paraphrased as follows: A conservative is: 1 A utilitarian who does not believe in perfectibility; 2 A sceptic; 3 Not a materialist determinist. A liberal is: 1 A Hobbesian who expands the concept of security but remains true to Hobbes's conception of man's relation to the sovereign power; 2 An adherent to the view that Hobbes's conception is necessary to progress; 3 An adherent to the view that the competitive implications of Hobbesian egoism are somehow mixed up with the Marxian idea of class conflict. A socialist believes: 1 That profit motive should not be the sole determinant of what is produced. 2 In something that will be explained below; 3 That arguments about the dangers of bureaucracy should not affect our opinions about the need for legislation.

As Kolakowski observes, these views are not mutually incompatible; one could therefore be a conservative-liberal socialist. But is it true that the beliefs are what he says – or at least implies – they are? Do they correspond to the beliefs we use to establish the three political persuasions, or are they the beliefs used by the followers of each ideology in recognizing one another? If they are, it is difficult to understand how people can be life-long conservatives, liberals or socialists, but not ideological mongrels.

There is something odd about Kolakowski's appraisal of our political 'Who's Who' which can be most clearly seen in the beliefs he attributes to the socialist. A democratic socialist would scarcely be able to recognize the views ascribed to him, but he may also be unable to follow 'Credo''s line of thought. Kolakowski's first point about socialist views seems designed to link with his first point about liberalism. By implying that it is impossible to understand what is said about socialist views on production, security and freedom without turning to what is said about 'liberals', he appears to be arranging his assertions so as to be able to make his summation on the unity of divergent views.

Kolakowski's second point about 'socialist' views (presumably democratic socialist) is very strange. As far as I can see, he says first, that socialists believe that inequality produces conflict; second, that they believe that non-socialists argue that a conflict-free society is impossible and deduce from this (a) that inequality is inevitable, and (b) that the profit motive is justified. Do democratic socialists reason in such a way? Outside the Marxian system of thought such analysis is not used. Democratic socialists – if they want to theorize – use the traditional techniques of logical analysis, not 'dialectic'. Kolakowski's third point – the one about bureaucracy – is also bizarre. He does not describe the views of democratic socialists who – not being continuously in power as under Communist régimes – do not find themselves required to defend bureaucracy.

An interesting aspect of Kolakowski's approach is that the values and beliefs he uses are not in our sense 'political'; they are not reflected in political thinking or the political process. Let us consider the difference between attributing an emphasis on equality to the socialist and attributing to non-socialists a view about the relation between equality and social conflict, as in the confusing argument 'deduced' in the second point about socialist beliefs above. Kolakowski is right about the relation between this view and socialism. It originated with Marx. He is also right in saying that this view is not at variance with the views held by conservatives and liberals. But why is the matter different when the view originated with a particular kind of socialism? The answer is that the members of Western democratic society have accepted the Marxian assumption but rejected the Marxian deductions, because in a democracy people do not know how to think dialectically.

Having had their attention drawn to the origin of the view in question and the fact that many non-socialists accept it, at least conservatives and liberals should reconsider its 'truth'. Democratic socialists are likely to do the same. But what if everyone should decide it is true? Does this require us to suppose that anyone who adheres to it is at least partly socialist? I think not. What matters is our response to the assumed fact. Does a common belief entail a common policy? Hence, are we to understand political divisions in terms of divergences of belief? This is a usual assumption that Kolakowski does not make. We should consider the possibility that policy differences reflect differences in norms, even though the underlying

assumptions are held in common (allowing for divergences of solution). The belief that inequality brings
conflict is one that crosses party lines; but it can also be
said that the response to the assumptions follows party
lines. Thus no conservative who holds to the third view
which Kolakowski attributes to conservatives (correctly, I
would say) would conclude that inequalities must therefore be eliminated as much as possible. It is likely, on the
other hand, that at least some of those who reject the
conservative view about materialist determinism would
advocate such a solution.

It is the interaction between beliefs held in common
and normative views not held in common that explains
policy differences: we will not understand what is happening politically if we focus all our attention on differences
in norms and beliefs. If we do the latter, there is no way of
understanding how we can agree to disagree.

Although Kolakowski has not accurately described the
views that characterize liberalism, conservatism and socialism as democratic ideologies, he has understood the
essential agreement.

He begins and ends his paper with a dismissal of the
Marxian prediction. He says in effect that class conflict
does not lead inevitably to revolution but only to policy
differences, as evidenced by party divisions. Although he
does not say so explicitly, he would presumably assent to
the proposition that beliefs held in common determine
social problems and normative views not held in common
determine policy differences; or to the view that norms
held in common determine what a social problem is,
whilst beliefs not held in common determine differences
in policy. He did not, I think, try to resolve differences or
to establish that they exist but to deny the Marxian view
that existing conflicts are irreconcilable and doom us to a
disintegration of the social fabric. This does not necessarily require him to be accurate in his attribution of
norms and beliefs. He need only show that we both agree
and disagree and that disagreements are not of the kind
conducive to class conflict. So long as we understand that
he was not attempting to define party differences but to

refute the view that disagreements in democratic society represent underlying and irreconcilable conflicts, he has done all that is necessary. At the same time, I believe that his method was unwise, for his inaccuracy about who holds which beliefs may lead some readers to dismiss his argument.

IDEOLOGY AND MIND

Is it possible to speak of a liberal (or, say, a conservative or democratic socialist) without a semantic designation like, say, liberal $_{BRITISH}$ or liberal $_{AMERICAN}$? If it is realized that transplanting the term liberal from the Eastern to the Western shores of the Atlantic has led to a reversal of the original meaning, can one avoid Jean François Revel's solution? He applies inverted commas when writing of the American brand of liberalism and conservatism (as opposed to the European and Latin-American brands, referred to without the inverted commas).[5] His is clearly a semantic device.

Although they are useful in certain circumstances, such devices can be avoided when we speak of a philosophic liberal mind (or conservative or socialist mind, as the case may be); that is, its essence, assumptions and motivations, rather than the activities of 'political man' – the political posturing of members of various persuasions, or party factionalism. Viewed in this light, problems of imprecise terminology or vagueness of subject-matter become more manageable. References to the 'isms' in everyday life comprise so many different attitudes, stances and traditions that unless there is a stable point of reference – the mind – the image of ideologies remains forever blurred.

Liberals, conservatives and socialists differ in kind from place to place and time to time. Thus the present meaning of 'liberal' in the USA is entirely different from that in Western Europe or South America. From a different perspective, a British liberal of today would probably regard a nineteenth-century liberal as a 'conservative' (perhaps even as 'undemocratic'), whereas a conservative of Burke's day would be unlikely to see himself as having much in common with a modern conservative. But here we are talking of externals, of 'style', as it were; we are merely saying that the style of the previous two centuries is not the style of this century. We are certainly not saying that, for instance, because styles change, we cannot define 'clothing' or that, because the style of liberalism has changed, there is no such thing as an 'essence' of liberalism.

The essence of liberalism (conservatism or socialism) lies in its ideology rather than in the attitude to particular issues. Issues change: universal public education or the *laissez-faire* policy are no longer questions of primary interest; nor are they helpful in distinguishing liberals from conservatives. Once they were of great interest and were used in public debates as if they expressed the 'essence' of some particular ideology. But they did not; they were ephemeral – matters of 'style'. The essence – what remains when one remembers that particular issues are always ephemeral (for they are meant to be solved) – lies in what is thought about man in relation to the State. It lies in 'ideology' and one's conceptions of human motivations.

Standard behavioural criteria (who votes for which party) give us no intelligible way of understanding the terms 'liberal', 'conservative', or 'socialist', whereas the concept of democratic ideology requires that such terms as 'right', 'left' and 'centre' make ideological sense. If they do not, democracy is but the political expression of relativism.

The actual situation, however, is perhaps not as bleak as the argument suggests, for we all seem capable of 'intuiting' the meaning of right and left wing, no matter what the behavioural patterns of the people involved. Margaret Thatcher of Great Britain, for instance, acknowledged that she and Ronald Reagan were of the same political persuasion, and Reagan seemed to recognize that the Canadian party headed by Brian Mulroney was 'conservative' (small 'c'). Indeed, the very fact that we can raise questions about the 'conservatism' of a Conservative – or the 'liberalism' of a Liberal – shows we are using ideological assumptions and contrasting them with behavioural criteria.

When behaviour is the issue, it is of interest to the political theorist to note that there are two kinds of behaviour. Referring to ideology, we speak of 'covert' behaviour – motivation – not 'overt' behaviour (to employ a distinction used in social psychology). 'Ideology' is what motivates, and so is any of the three 'isms'. This is why, within our terms of reference, there is no need to apply Alfred Korzybski's semantic $Adam_1$ and $Adam_2$. When using the terms 'liberal' and 'conservative' we are speaking of ideology, the behaviour of the mind: that is, motivation; whereas when speaking of Liberals and Conservatives we are referring to the 'overt' behaviour of $Adam_1$ and $Adam_2$.

Part I

Prudential conservatism

Chapter 2

Norms and relativism

CONSERVATISM, NORMS AND REASON

It is difficult to decide on the basis of ideological statements what a conservative is. Yet most of us on hearing
certain views about crime, welfare, immigration and 'undemocratic' régimes in other countries would not hesitate
to label them conservative. Thus the conservative interprets crime in terms of a normative breakdown; welfare is
to him at best an expedient rather than a social obligation;
immigration is something which must be subject to careful
control if it is not to be a 'threat to our way of life'; and
some undemocratic régimes are considered the best possible under the circumstances and therefore deserving
the support of a democratic government. What do these
views have in common that allows us to call them conservative? If they do not have anything in common, conservatism becomes a waste-basket concept to which all
non-liberal and non-socialist views are relegated – an
obviously unacceptable interpretation unless we can
argue that only liberal or socialist views are democratic.

Some people do in effect adopt this stance declaring
that all the above views are 'Fascist' or tainted with
Fascism: the view on crime is an argument for the 'police
State'; that on immigration is 'racist'; that on welfare
shows a lack of social conscience; and the view on
undemocratic régimes is the clearest proof of 'Fascism'.
It is argued that no democrat could possibly look with
favour on the military dictatorships currently supported

by democracies; hence the conservative cannot be very strongly committed to democratic principles if he is not eager to universalize the democratic way of life, but rather is prepared to tolerate dictatorships elsewhere provided they are not Communist. The conservative view is presented as undemocratic and expedient.

But it is precisely the conservative who emphasizes the traditional norms; he declares that it is adherence to concepts of right and wrong, good and bad that determines his position. Non-conservatives either set up a system of norms as the only valid set (the norms of democracy, socialism, science or Marxist-Communism) or they assert that all normative sets are a form of prejudice and that relativism is the only valid attitude. Hence democracy is 'valid' because it is a relativistic system, premised on making decisions by a show of hands, believing in acceptance of all points of view and based on the assumption that as we are all 'equal' no valid distinctions can be made between human beings.

To the conservative, democracy is false inasmuch as it is relativistic, and it is valid only inasmuch as its premises can be given a conceptual content. For him, the 'individualism' of democracy is a statement about the worth of the 'self' as a fundamental concept without which no other statement can be made. For him, for instance, 'equality' is the self's recognition of other 'selfs'. There is no possible way we can avoid solipsism, accept science, believe in democracy or any other system, unless we begin with a threefold conceptualization in which the 'self' recognizes other 'selfs' and distinguishes this set of entities from a world of non-selfs or 'its'. If we ignore this conceptualization we have to discard science as a methodology, for it is not based on a distinction between the perception by the self of an objective reality and the self's experiencing the objective reality, but on the assumption that perceptions of the 'self' can be checked against the perceptions of other selfs to arrive at a body of 'commonsense' information.[1]

It is not common for conservatives to analyse their position in this way. But if we look at the position of some

of those we acknowledge as 'conservative', beginning with
Edmund Burke – who raised the very issue of who is
conservative by setting himself, within a democratic framework, in opposition to those who insisted that 'democracy'
required a viewpoint strictly consistent with the norms of
democracy – we find that the conservative view is fundamentally different from the scientific. Human behaviour is
distinct from the behaviour of things (the 'its' of objective
reality); and the viewpoint parallelling conservatism is the
religious (rather than scientific) view of reality.

From the religious point of view, the 'self' is opposed to
the 'body' which somehow incorporates the 'self'. In
many religions this 'self' – defined as 'soul' – is conceived
of as transcending the death of the biological organism.
It may continue cyclically, being incorporated into other
organisms – as in Buddhism – or it may move into a
different sphere which in Christianity is called heaven,
hell or purgatory. The fate of the soul, however, while of
major consequence for believers in the particular religion, is outside the scope of our analysis.

What matters to both religious people and conservatives is that there is a 'self' distinct from the biological
organism. To both conservatives and religious people it is
not true that the determinants of behaviour are the biological drives of the organism (unless it happens to be a
'lower' organism that has not evolved a sense of self).
Although the conservative can make a stronger case for
his position than the determinist, validity is not the issue.
Whether 'special creation' or 'evolution' is assumed, the
concept of a 'self' transcending immediate circumstances
is biologically advantageous; if it can be shown that such a
sense of self has evolved, it can certainly be argued that it
has a biological advantage. Man has become the dominant
species because he has a sense of self transcending the
immediate circumstances; 'prudence' rather than 'impulse' motivates human beings.

Because of the primacy of the 'soul' or 'immortal self'
in religion, competition for goods and conflicts of interest
are seen as departures from the commitment to the
primacy of the soul, which by nature cannot be in conflict

with other souls. Hence the emphasis placed by all major religions on peace and charity. Accordingly, human relations should not be competitive or hostile, and the good society should so organize itself as to avoid conflict. Such is also the view of the conservative, who is prepared to support (as a means to this end) social arrangements not always acceptable to non-conservatives; if a class system reduces rivalries and conflicts, it is acceptable; if a measure of coercion is necessary against those disturbing public order – this, too, is acceptable.

It is on the issue of law and order that the conservative viewpoint is most strikingly at odds with the liberal and socialist attitudes. Both of the latter are likely to see conflict in society as a symptom of something wrong within the body politic rather than as something wrong in itself. They see the conservative insistence on law and order as an undemocratic adherence to coercion and a foolish attempt to suppress symptoms while disregarding the 'meaning' of disorder. The conservative's reply is that his adherence to democracy represents adherence to a system which is capable of solving social problems without public disorder; further, that anyone who argues that a breakdown in law and order is sometimes justifiable, cannot be genuinely committed to democracy as a system of government.

At this point the nature of the conservative's position becomes clearer. Although for him, as for the socialist and the liberal, man can be driven by inarticulated wants and passions, the conservative believes man 'should not' be so driven and certainly should not be encouraged by society to act in this way. Problems cannot be solved unless they are articulated. The 'good' society should not treat its members as if they were babies who can express needs only by squalling, leaving others to guess what is wrong. If some adult members of a democratic community are in fact incapable of expressing their wants, then the universal franchise of democracy must be modified; the 'equality' that the conservative recognizes is the seeming capacity of normal adults to know what they want and to express it verbally. If you argue that our motivations are subconscious and seldom expressible, democratic government becomes a mere form having no advantage over other systems. To a conservative, violence under a democracy is irrational.

The conservative position is most clearly manifest in the view that it is the total body of norms that must be brought to bear in decision-making; it can be seen in the readiness to 'muddle through' rather than follow strictly the logic of fundamental democratic principles (as the only ones relevant to democratic practice). Thus he is not moved by the argument that freedom of the press requires the total elimination of censorship; he believes that other norms apply as well: that there are such things as pornography, slander and misrepresentation; and that no valid decision can be made about censorship unless we consider other norms in addition to the democratic norm of 'freedom of the press.'

To the conservative, customary norms constitute a vast body of experience with human behaviour that we ignore only at our peril. This view has often been used to argue that the conservative is anti-rational, even anti-intellectual, preferring the security of what he knows to the logic of genuine moral principles, and further that he is not 'consistent'. In fact, while the liberal and the socialist characteristically attempt to reduce the norms of social life to those derivable from the set defining the system of government (thus making equality, freedom and rights the determining norms and leaving the rest to individual conscience), the views of the conservative are premised on broader principles. Can one at this stage draw any conclusion as to whether conservatism is an ideology? If an ideology is a body of norms and beliefs derived from a small set of assumed principles then conservatism is not an ideology, for it is precisely this attitude to norms that the conservative rejects. But if the adherent of an ideology must be inclined to 'intellectuality' and oppose the view that human behaviour is the product of unanalysable experiences and inarticulated feelings, then conservatism has a far greater claim to be called an ideology than either liberalism or socialism.

CONSERVATISM, NORMS AND RELATIVISM

Because norms are functional, enabling us to avoid trial-and-error learning with regard to human behaviour and to make decisions in terms of our 'self-other' conceptions rather than simply on the basis of biological impulses, relativism has not 'destroyed' norms, but has operated rather to disrupt both our systematization of norms and our efforts to arrive at some kind of natural law. To define norms as tastes or attitudes is to imply that it is a waste of time thinking about them. To assert that human behaviour is determined solely by biological drives is to put forward a 'natural law' of behaviour that excludes the need for reflection (reflection about motives becomes a rationalization). The same is true of social deterministic theory: establishing the 'causes' of norms is something a social scientist might undertake, yet the result will not be a validation of the norms but evidence of their irrelevance (and relativism).

Under relativism, the norms remain in the form of 'facts', whilst ethical systems ('hierarchies of values') become false and redundant.

The consequence can be seen in the shift of meaning of the Jesuit statement that 'the end justifies the means'. To Loyola, this meant that norms have a hierarchical order. The view that some norms are more important than others represented a tremendous advance over the traditional view that norms are 'separate absolutes' which are somehow equals and hence cause ethical dilemmas in situations where more than one norm applies. But if one denies the validity of any attempt to systematize norms, the assertion 'the end justifies the means' becomes the assertion that acceptance of a goal permits one to ignore any compunction one might have about the methods of attaining it. Thus if you believe that the union of Northern and Southern Ireland is a good and that violence will achieve this objective, you need not worry about traditional components of 'justice' such as innocence: let babies be killed by the bombs – if this is likely to induce a capitulation to demands. Violence and terrorism become

goods when normative systems are represented as irrational nonsense. What was once considered irrational is
now thought of as rational in the sense that the end
justifies the means.

Acceptance of particular norms is not enough. Norms
need to be systematized and if the given systematization –
the ideology – violates the principles of justice, it is false,
no matter how logical it may otherwise seem. It is important how one systematizes norms. The conservative, ever
since Burke had doubts about the French Revolution, has
denied that 'efficiency' and the 'logic' of excluding norms
from the system in order to attain an end is valid –
or essential – in making normative decisions. To him,
equally, a method of systematizing norms which is based
on excluding norms from the system is invalid – it is this
very attitude to norms which defines him ideologically.
Yet he is rather reluctant to label his outlook an ideology.
In general opinion, political 'ideology' has become restricted to the type of normative system which achieves
logical consistency by disregarding normative factors in
the means. (All that matters is the goal; achieving the
goal or striving in this direction 'justifies' the means.)

While denying that his views are 'ideological', a conservative will be more inclined to accept the label 'religious.' The distinction to him is not that an 'ideology'
deals with matters of man and the State and a religion
with man and God, but that followers of 'ideologies'
systematize norms in terms of the efficiency of norms,
whereas all religions deny that their normative systems
have such a basis.

Many conservatives are worried that they can agree with
others (non-conservatives) about goals and yet be opposed to most practical proposals for achieving them. For
this reason, many opponents see them as hypocrites who
are ready, for instance, to speak about the evils of poverty
but unwilling to adopt any practical measures. To be sure,
they raise many (too many, say their opponents) objections based on 'justice', while the issues seem so much
more clear cut to everyone else. Indeed, the concept of
justice appears central to conservative thinking. It is

tantamount to the systematization of norms that arranges them in a hierarchy in which anything that is a norm has validity. To non-conservatives 'justice' is the attainment by society of normative goals – the object of the good State. To the conservative, it is rather an operating system in which the attainment of the good never means disregarding norms. The kind of relativism the conservative is least likely to accept is one that defines the breaking of norms in terms of the end.

REASON, RELIGION AND MECHANISM

Clinton Rossiter, the American student of conservatism, writing in the 1950s, suggested twenty-one 'conservative principles'. Of these, number thirteen gives one pause: 'The fallibility and limited reach of human reason'.[2] If we are going to use attitudes to 'reason' as a criterion of conservatism, it would seem closer to the truth to think of the conservative as someone who objects to those who, while recognizing the limits of 'reason', deduce that it is fallible.

The issue is what Rossiter and other modern conservatives mean when they doubt 'reason' (as well as those who reject reason). We have a clue in Rossiter's strong emphasis on what most would call a 'religious' view. Thus in point (2) of his principles he speaks of a 'precious soul'; in (9) of 'duties'; in (11) of the 'sanctity of inherited institutions, values, symbols and rituals'; in (12) of the 'essential role of religious feeling'; in (17) of the 'wondrous, divinely ordained union of land, laws, customs'; and in (18) of 'reverence, contentment.' A great many conservatives would object to the way Rossiter formulates his view of conservatism: it certainly would not appeal to intellectuals, philosophers or the common man. Yet despite dissatisfaction with the formulation, most conservatives are likely to agree that its author was in the conservative tradition. The points he makes, though formulated in an anti-rational and non-philosophic way, have something in common.

Rossiter's image of the 'conservative tradition' is

coloured by 'religious' concepts and his statement of principles is not satisfactory: the implications of these concepts are vague; no clear definition of 'religion' emerges.

Suppose we try terms like mechanism and non-mechanism. Can we define conservatism with reference to the rejection of a mechanistic view of State and society – hence as a position that does not regard reason as 'fallible and limited' but rather as a technique for penetrating behind appearances and coping with theories for which some empirical evidence can be advanced (but which does not make us willing to surrender the body of human experience)?

The philosophic conservative would like the issue of mechanism put back where it belongs – a matter of academic debate – but the rise of the ideological State has both secularized and politicized ethics. Many conservatives – as well as others – are quite pleased by this development so long as the State permits non-secular ethical systems to operate freely (allows freedom of religion). For various reasons (such as the experience of the Wars of Religion, the fact that the premises of religious ethical systems are non-materialist) religious ethics are not an appropriate basis for State policy. But the politicizing of ethics is a different matter. Only relativists committed to the view that 'natural law' concepts of ethics are absurd can be pleased when the State defines itself as the source of social good (defined by its ideology), or as the agency by which the good is realized in action (as, for instance, as the enforcer of 'rights').

Behind disputes about relativism are assumptions about mechanism; behind the latter are assumptions about cause and effect. It is agreed that despite the philosophic difficulties Hume raised about the concept of 'cause', it is an indispensable tool of analysis, viz. that of 'reason'.

The matter on which we are not agreed is whether acceptance of cause-effect analysis entails 'determinism' – the view that there is but a single system of cause-effect and that there is no other factor operating in the universe as we know it: no chance, no free-will, no multiple systems of cause-effect, no God, nothing but this one system of cause-effect with neither beginning nor end (despite what the concept seems to imply about beginning and end).

Now there is nothing 'mystical', 'religious' or 'irrational' about doubting determinism and, particularly, the form of determinism – mechanism – which emphasizes the system's impersonality. Both 'reason' and empirical observation suggest that it is a serious mistake to move from the analysis of cause-effect to determinism. There is an unbridgeable gap between the two. Nonetheless, the rise of the ideological State shifted most people's thinking over from cause-effect to mechanism: we wanted to get rid of religious disputes by taking the concept of God (and religious ethics) out of politics, but in doing so we inadvertently got rid of 'reason', too.

The conservative objects to mechanism; if, like Rossiter, he is philosophically naïve, he may express his objection in what seem 'religious' and 'mystical' terms. It is unwise to do so. It is a mistake to think of this view as a belief in the 'fallibility and limited reach of reason.' The conservative would rather insist that his objection to mechanism is the product of 'reason' which has nothing to do with 'mysticism' or a reluctance to give up traditional ways of thinking.

CONSERVATISM, DEMOCRACY AND RELATIVISM

Inasmuch as the conservative adheres to the democratic system of government this is not because he derives it from 'first principles': 'that all men are equal and therefore . . .'. If he did that he would, like the liberals, make majority rule a primary norm of democracy, qualified perhaps by the principle of minority rights and further qualified by the principle of Sovereignty if he happened to be a rationalist. Ever since Burke reflected on the revolution in France, the conservative has shown a marked suspicion of such apparently logical deductions from first principles while insisting (inconsistently, according to opponents) that we must indeed reflect on what we advocate and not just act on what 'reason' demands. Yet it would be grotesque to deduce that the conservative does not believe in democracy. The main body of opinion warning against the perils of Communism and the implicit threat of tyranny in the expansion of governmental powers is that of conservatives: it is one of the ways in which we recognize who is conservative and who is not.

What, then, is the source of the conservative attachment to democracy? The answer lies in the conservative's very conservativism – his hostility to revolution as a device for attaining the good State. To him, democracy is the only system which allows orderly change and the rectification of the errors to which mankind is prone. His is a normative position unrecognized by his fellow-men: any act that is irreversible is by nature evil, even though its object is to solve problems. Thus, to a conservative the position of the Church on suicide is not an intrusion on private conscience but similar to the objection to murder: the less the possibility for changing your mind and reversing the act, the greater the degree of evil. To the conservative, a political system such as Communism was like suicide, for until 1989 it appeared irreversible (the Kerala case notwithstanding). This was why he dismissed as irrelevant the argument that if a Communist government has been chosen democratically, it must be recognized by all genuine democrats. To the conservative, the element of free will was negated by the Communist system's irreversibility and by the latter's essential evil. So very wrong is the irreversible to him that to prevent such social disaster he can countenance military dictatorships as expedients. They are expedients because they are not capable of indefinite continuance in time; they cannot ensure the continuation of the régime after the death or incapacitation of the ruling clique.

Even this qualification, however, troubles other adherents of the democratic position: the conservative's qualified commitment to democratic norms seems a lack of commitment – in fact a form of relativism which argues that the 'right' is simply the 'appropriate'. It is alleged that the conservative 'believes' in democracy only because his society has evolved a body of practices and institutions that make the concept of democracy an expression of the fact that such practices and institutions exist; further, that had his society moved in a different direction, the conservative would have accepted that different political order and even called it 'democracy' if his society had done so. Ironically, this is precisely the position the conservative opposes. He denies that the concept 'democracy' can be applied indiscriminately and asserts that democracy requires appropriate pre-existing social conditions. The fact that he does not suppose that the democratic practices and institutions of Britain, the USA or Canada can be superimposed on totally different cultures does not alter his basic view that it is norms and beliefs that matter: when these are respected, the society will be ready to evolve democratic institutions.

Let us see if it is possible to extract from conservative attitudes the fundamental conservative position about the nature of norms, bearing in mind that the charge is that the conservative unlike the socialist, shows no great interest in whether all mankind lives under democratic régimes exactly like his own. It is all very well to talk of 'irreversibility' but such a concept becomes a rationalization unless it can be argued that the conservative sees norms as determinants of behaviour and not vice versa, as in the materialist conception of history.

Unfortunately, in considering this issue, we cannot draw upon modern philosophic analysis: philosophic relativism today reminds one of Marxian determinism with the economic bias removed. Nor can we look to the democratic ideology of political scientists or religious apologists for an analysis of the fundamental issues. It is astonishing, for instance, that Christian apologists made no serious attempt to show that the historical relation between Christian norms and practices in Christian countries can be explained only in terms of the norms which historically preceded the practice: the northern barbarians – who are now Christian nations – were characterized by the glorification of war, slavery, the use of the ordeal to achieve justice, no real concept of guilt and innocence, no real sense of history or of norms other than customary practices. Yet today they are known for their belief in science, the rule of law (as opposed to custom) and democracy, and their opposition to torture, slavery, human sacrifice, etc. Most of these beliefs and values are direct expressions of Christian norms and all have a logical relation to them. We need only compare the history of non-Christian with Christian societies and consider that in a pre-relativist age the Christian societies forced non-Christian nations to abandon slavery, torture, infanticide, suttee, human sacrifice and so on to realize that the evidence is clear-cut and unmistakable. What matters in human behaviour is the norms – which cannot be derived from the actual practice at any particular time. Without the study of history – which is the expression of the norms and beliefs that set the course of historical developments – there is no possibility of understanding what is happening. The history of Christian nations provides the clearest example of the importance of norms in history. Yet the message of various interpretations is not unequivocal: Christianity, always focusing on the ideal, has emphasized its own failures at the expense of the facts about how far we have come from where we started. Consequently, the interpretation of history has been coloured by those who do not believe in history but only in 'situations' at a given point of time. Such points (which may be called 'behaviouralist points') are no help in the 'chicken or the egg' controversy over whether norms determine behaviour or vice versa: we are in effect asking a question about historical sequence while pretending that history is irrelevant.

Thus it does not seem possible to appeal to generally recognized historical facts in approaching the question of whether a conservative holds to the norms of democracy or just appeals to current practice when deciding what is 'democratic'. Another way of approaching the question is through the conservative's commitment to the premises of ethics: to a 'self' as distinct from all aspects of a total situation rather than as part of a continuum of inter-related cause-effects; to 'will' as a meaningful statement about 'causation' with regard to the self's behaviour; to 'reason' as a statement about the type of decisions which can be made by that 'will'. (To a relativist, 'self', 'will' and 'reason' have no significance in relation to human behaviour.)

What is certain about conservative ideology is the high importance placed on 'self', which has been demonstrated by the traditional emphasis on 'property' as a 'natural' rather than a legal concept. Characteristically, conservatives reject as 'undemocratic' those interpretations of 'equality' which logically require a redistribution of property. To them, the equalization of property would be the same as the abandonment of the 'self' as a concept along with that of 'property' – and hence an abandonment of the individualism that they regard as an essential democratic norm. Demands for property redistribution are consequently seen as attacks on 'liberty', even though others believe true 'liberty' is not possible without such equalization.

The consequence of this conservative insistence on 'self' is that equality has to be given a sense that is not incompatible with individualism; this appears to be done by means of the Kantian principle that no one should be treated as a means: we are all of equal worth. This hypothetic view – which does not appear to have been explicitly stated – must be deduced from the conservatives' rejection of 'majority rule' as allowing the overriding of the individual's rights. Thus the conservative ideology appears to be the only democratic view that does not represent 'liberty' as a 'golden mean' between the incompatible requirements of 'equality' and 'individualism' but instead attempts to make 'equality' an aspect of individualism.

Now if 'self' is a valid concept to the conservative, it follows that he must reject any determinist view of human behaviour. No matter what form determinism takes, the one concept totally incompatible with it is that of the 'self': under determinism, all change must be seen in terms of a continuum in which nothing has a sufficiently independent existence to have individuality.

Conservatives have taken a very strong stand against Marxian determinism as well as the social determinism of socialists (who might today be better understood as such rather than as economic determinists interested in property equalization). The conservative position on psychoanalysis – the other influential determinism in the modern world – is not so clear-cut, perhaps because the latter's adherents deliberately conceal its determinism in order to offer 'advice' (which presupposes that life is not determined).

However, the conservative insistence that 'punishment' is a valid response to crime and the equally strong conservative resistance to the idea that 'punishment' is always unjust because the behaviour was the product of circumstances beyond the individual's control, strongly suggest that the conservative naturally rejects determinism because the concept of 'self' is central to his ideology (determinism being an attack on 'self'). Nothing we know about socialists suggests that determinism is for them anything but the 'scientific' point of view. A socialist, for instance, told that his views on welfare legislation reflect determinism is not likely to be troubled: he may even see the connection as evidence of its 'truth'. To the conservative, however, the determinist-based views of the contemporary social sciences represent a threat to what he calls 'law and order'. He means by this a threat to norms, rather than – as critics charge – a threat to current laws. The conservative is too much committed to democracy ever to identify current laws with norms (though he is quite ready to change certain laws) and too much committed to the concept of norms as distinct from laws (he is convinced that some democratic laws violate normative principles) to be a relativist.

Chapter 3

'Progress' and change

From Burke's day to the present, conservatives – both as types of personality and as adherents of a political ideology – have been known for their resistance to change. Indeed, the resistance to change is so much more obvious than their ideological values (conservatives have some difficulty in explaining exactly what they wish to conserve) that many people are convinced that conservatives are not really *conservatives* in any meaningful sense but primarily opponents of change. Since Heraclitus' main views seem to have been accepted by modern science, the 'conservative' view appears unrealistic and decidedly unscientific: if all is in flux, resistance to change results in a maladjustment between the political order and social conditions. Consequently, 'social problems' are now seen as maladjustments between government and society; no matter what one's political ideology says about the State it is disregarded in favour of the 'scientific' view. When change is regarded as the essential character of reality and some people are known to resist change, it follows that at least one of the features of 'good' government is the ability to enforce change – to try to stop people from being 'conservatives'. If this requires an expansion of government powers, then both liberals and socialists are prepared to accept such a development with equanimity: it is 'scientific' and presumably good for us. Conservatives disagree: they are naturally not prepared to be coerced by their own government into a non-conservative position. Such action would be decidedly undemocratic.

The position of the conservative was much worse when 'change' and 'progress' were synonymous terms and whatever 'science' said and begot was assumed to be true and therefore good for us. Nowadays the popular attitude to science is changing. 'Progress' in the sense of change promoted by science is no longer a self-evident good. The idea that there is a good kind of conservatism as well as the traditional 'bad' kind (which entails resistance to change) has led to the coining of a new term – conservationism – to express the good side of resistance to change. At present, it has no application to social institutions – it is not a political concept – but the nature of language and ideas is such that it seems likely to promote a re-examination of conservatism and perhaps permit a clarification of what we have in mind when speaking of resistance to change as a good.

When a person cannot make intellectual distinctions (say between liberty and licence, socialism and Communism) in the way we make empirical distinctions (I mean *this*, not *that*), his opinion comes as an attitude of approval or disapproval explicable in terms of upbringing and constitution: 'conservatives' resist change and I – an individual – either agree or disagree. But if people are enabled to say clearly that some change is good and some bad, 'conservatism' is no longer a fixed opposition to change. With the two terms (conservatism and conservationism) we are forced to think about what it was formerly easy to assume was a general attitude – in order to reconsider it.

The problem with this approach is that the 'attitudinal' school which assumes that normative positions are attitudes of the 'pro' and 'con' kind – that the difference between, for instance, liberty and licence is a matter of approval and disapproval of the particular behaviour – is only too pleased to discover that at last we have produced a term that fits their theory: a 'conservationist' is one who approves of resistance to change and a 'conservative' one who disapproves of change. The attitudinal school works on the Freudian assumption that evolution made a mistake in developing the human brain; that the brain is functionless and biologically disadvantageous, for it leads to 'rationalizations' and confused thinking about our own motives (which in theory are the same as those guiding chipmunks: 'for' and 'against', according to experience with situations that satisfy or frustrate biological drives). The danger is that when we begin to use the term 'conservationist' in a political sense, the attitudinal school will have proof that they are right and that it is but a linguistic oddity that it took such a long time to develop a term expressing a 'pro' attitude to resistance to change.

Yet, for those who believe that the human brain is not a biological mistake and that the concepts it is developing are biologically advantageous in affecting our behaviour – the brain could not have evolved unless this were true – the formulation of the new concept (conservationist) is likely to alter everyone's attitude to conservatism. What is especially significant is that the new term has arisen among those who traditionally have been most opposed to conservatism: it is the younger people who now insist that not all change is good; they demand that the 'older and wiser' consider the idea, abandon their materialism and think of the future. Many today are returning to the concept that natural law demands that men adjust to nature rather than assume that somehow they will learn enough about the natural order to manipulate it to suit current wishes and impulses. The views are much too mystical and unformulated to constitute a 'philosophy' but there is a potential for rethinking what have long been tagged as 'attitudes'. Conservatism, if it ever was just an attitude, cannot remain one when the matter of distinguishing between good and bad arises. It can now be spoken of without immediately raising the 'pro' and 'con' issue.

Although social change is no longer identified with progress, a major obstacle to conservative thinking remains – our society's suspicion of thinking as such and especially of normative thinking. If norms are not concepts but attitudes, it follows that thinking about them produces only rationalizations of one's attitudes. According to this view, a conservative ideology would be a rationalization of a conservative attitude or reluctance both to face change and to modify the society and political structure to accord with change. The conservative, it has been said, does not approve of social experiment. This is a serious charge in a society that recognizes at least one value as being something more than an attitude – scientific methodology.

To a conservative, it is scarcely surprising that many scientists and social scientists are leftists who have supported the 'social experiment' of Communism. Though most of these scientists have by now recognized that the 'experiment' has failed and are no longer eager to try it in their own countries, nonetheless, as good scientists, some of them are still interested in seeing whether it might not work in other countries under somewhat different conditions. Such reasoning is alien to a conservative. To him 'social experimenting' of this kind is tantamount to trial-and-error learning in the very area where we have a better methodology – rational analysis of the norms and beliefs involved.

Until the development of our understanding of the modern principles of physics underlying the physical world, all scientific experiment was indeed trial-and-error learning. It was reasonable to mix together different substances to find out whether they would interact; however, to do so now would make no sense, not because we have tested all possible combinations but because we know from molecular theory that there are only certain possibilities. The conservative is convinced that similarly we have a fundamental knowledge about the social behaviour of human beings: that what we call norms constitute an accumulated body of information about human behaviour and its consequences. Thus such behaviour as sitting, jumping, sleeping is normatively ignored as inconsequential (except under special circumstances), whereas cruelty, stealing and murder are 'wrong' (except under special circumstances considered so exceptional that we have established formal procedures – courts of justice – to decide the issues).

The conservative is the first to recognize that some normative terms, like freedom, equality and justice, are concepts analogous to such fundamental principles as 'gravity' or the 'conservation of energy' (rather than to the experimentally-based generalization that an acid plus a base gives a salt plus water). He will argue that it is absurd to suppose we can find out the meaning of such terms by 'social experiment'. One will not learn anything new about 'freedom' by setting up a dictatorship and seeing what happens. The meaning of 'freedom' can only be determined by the scope allowed by the actual norms. To speak in this context about 'experiment' is to advocate trial and error in a situation where rational reflection is the only valid method.

Thus, a possible definition of 'conservative' is 'a person opposed to trial-and-error methods with regard to social and political institutions'. This is a positive (favourable) way of looking at conservatism. A negative way, though expressing the same idea, is 'a person opposed to social experiment'. This seems unfavourable and is so regarded because 'experiment' here is thought of and advocated as if it were identical with trial and error. Thus in the school system, slogans such as: 'experience is the best teacher', 'learn by doing', 'action now' and 'don't knock it if you haven't tried it' have been advocated since the radical sixties, so that it became commonplace for a government official to listen to a rational analysis of a proposed new programme and dismiss the consequent objections with 'Let's give it a try anyway'. It was evidently supposed that one really could not know whether a plan was feasible until it was actually put into operation and that objections based on analysis reflected a 'conservative' mind – an attitude standing in the way of 'progress'.

Perhaps no great harm is done when the loss involved by disregarding the conservative view is only time and money, though a common conservative objection to unrestrained government expenditure today is that we cannot afford social experiments costing hundreds of millions of dollars. But much more is involved when normative issues – which the conservative puts under the umbrella of 'freedom' – are disregarded. To the conservative, 'freedom' is the general principle or concept used when speaking about the particular norms of the society which are worth conserving. Conversely, to the 'liberal' it is the presence of these norms that raises the issue of 'freedom'.

Indeed, this appears to have been the issue when Max Eastman decided that he really was not a conservative, even though his editor, William F. Buckley Jr., was unable to see where he and Eastman differed on social issues.[3] The only apparent difference between them was that Eastman objected to the *National Review's* emphasis on norms. The difficulty was not, it should be noted, that Eastman's norms differed from Buckley's but that Eastman's attitude to norms, his – as it were – normative theory, did so. The point deserves attention. The main difference between the conservative and other democratic ideological positions is to be found in the normative theory held by conservatives rather than in major differences in the norms of the two groups.

An interesting feature of ethical theories is that no matter what the theory says about the nature of norms, the theory itself becomes a norm. Thus the relativist who argues that no customary norm is 'true' and no norm can be, subsequently employs his belief when making decisions about the teaching and enforcing of norms: the belief acts as a norm. In this way most of the major ethical theories refute themselves. (It is difficult to see, for instance, how the attitudinal school can maintain its position in view of the fact that for its members at least, one belief which is not an attitude acts as a norm.)

With regard to private behaviour, it hardly seems to matter what ethical theory one holds, for all the theories come round to the view that customary norms are for the most part valid: thus egoists, relativists, hedonists and advocates of natural law recognize most of them as prudential. One can tell the difference between selfishness and egoism, debauchery and hedonism because philosophic positions do not promote the type of behaviour which they are often used to describe – or to rationalize. The situation becomes different however when the issue is no longer one's personal behaviour but one's attitude towards the behaviour of others: what should the society's (and the State's) position be with regard to the norms? Plato did not write the *Republic* because he assumed no one can be even human outside the State, as some commentators suppose, but for the reason he gives: in the structure and policy of the State the fundamental ethical theory is writ large. Only there does it really matter what your theory is; only there can you discover what it is.

Buckley was unable to see how the views of Eastman, who had a long history as a socialist and liberal, differed from those expressed in the *National Review.* Eastman's current outlook did not seem to differ from his own. Nonetheless, Eastman resigned because he could not agree with the 'conservative' views of the journal. What did this mean, if in fact his own views were the same? Eastman explained to Buckley that the issue was the 'religious' slant of the *National Review.* Eastman, defining himself as a 'liberal', could not stomach the 'religion'. There Buckley left the matter, completely baffled, though he implied that Eastman was 'prejudiced'.

I suggest he was not so in any meaningful sense of this term: we cannot understand what happened by applying it. If, however, we recognize that the normative position of what we call religion is always some form of natural law theory, matters become clearer. A liberal cannot accept natural law theory: for him it so complicates the idea of 'liberty' that it becomes gibberish as a central political issue. The staunchest conservative has a concept of liberty as does any liberal who rejects natural law. But if you accept natural law, liberty is but one norm in a body of norms; you need a further theory explaining why this norm should be pre-eminent. The theory of natural law does not provide a method of ordering norms. It needs to be supplemented by a religion, ideology or philosophy.

Buckley's norms appeared to be the same as Eastman's; therefore, said Buckley (a conservative), they must both be conservative. Eastman disagreed because, he said, his attitude to the role of norms was different. He defined himself as a 'liberal' because he objected to the journal's (the *National Review's*) emphasis on the role of norms. In the past Eastman had been a Marxist who followed the Marxist norms and, in particular, accepted the views on social determinism. He broke with the Marxists over their normative views, but evidently did not change his views about determinism; for these reasons he defined himself as a liberal.

How would liberals define him? Most, of course, would see him as distinctly 'right wing', but they could hardly classify him as a non-liberal. There is no body of norms which clearly distinguishes liberals from conservatives – this is why many people deny that we can speak here of ideological distinctions. But if a man can himself distinguish between being a liberal and being a conservative despite normative identity with conservatives, what else can we call the difference except 'ideological' (especially when making the distinction involved a good deal of soul-searching and personal sacrifice, as it did in Eastman's case)? Would a classical liberal, aware of Eastman's attitude to norms, maintain it is not the liberal view?

It seems that John Stuart Mill would not. His notion of 'liberty' depended on the assumption that we do not know the truth; consequently, any action on the part of the State or society premised on the contrary assumption (that we do know the truth) must violate our liberty. This argument, which of course does not pretend to describe the whole of Mill's views on 'liberty', has acquired a much wider appeal today as the 'scientific' view; it has also been reinforced by relativism as well as by egoist psychological theories showing both the State and society as restrictive institutions. It is certainly held by a great many people; there seems to be no reason why its political expression should not be called the 'liberal' view. People calling themselves 'liberals' might see it as an incomplete statement of their views, but there is no evidence that they would reject it as unrelated. In fact, on the evidence of Eastman's withdrawal from the conservative ranks, it would seem to be fundamental. Despite his norms,

Eastman could not think of himself as a conservative, because the conservative view of norms, at least as expressed in the *National Review,* was not his.

The question remains whether the *National Review's* view of norms can be called 'conservative' or simply the views of a particular group of conservatives. A considerable number of people do not like the journal's particular normative positions, seeing some of them as merely reflections of the norms of the Catholic Church. Eastman emphasized this fact and tried to make it the central issue. But the Church itself is showing signs of being reluctant to propagate its particular norms, in part because of the peculiar meaning now given to 'tolerance' but more because the issue today is not which norms are valid but whether norms as such are. It is folly to try to argue for the validity of particular norms if those you are addressing regard norms as infringements on 'liberty' and errors inherited from the past. The real issue is whether we are to understand human behaviour in terms of determinism or free will. Only if one believes in the latter is it worthwhile to discuss human behaviour in normative terms. Now there is no question that there is a body of people who do believe that it is. Is there any reason why such people should not be called 'conservatives' when the issues discussed are political? Would those who hold such a view object? There is no evidence that they would. Indeed, the one essential characteristic of conservatives today is that they analyse issues normatively rather than in terms of determinism. Faced with social disorder of any kind, they first demand that it be stopped, rather than 'investigated' to determine the 'causes'. To them, analysis of possible determinism is a matter for the courts to determine, not an assumption for the State to act on when considering the meaning of 'liberty'.

The norms of the liberal and those of the conservative can be identical; yet, because the conservative thinks of human behaviour in terms of free will (rather than determinism), their respective political behaviour is quite different. Indeed, it is basically the twofold aspect of normative positions which accounts for the fact that socialists identify 'liberals' with 'conservatives' – their norms are often indistinguishable – whereas conservatives often equate 'liberals' with 'socialists' because their attitude to determinism is often identical and hence their policies are often indistinguishable from one another.

The division between those who hold to a determinist view of social problems and those who hold to a normativist one has important consequences for the stability of democratic governments. No matter who forms the government, a large body of people, both within and without the government, will consider its current policy wrong. To appeal to the democratic principle of majority rule will not ensure acceptance of the given policy. In an ideal democracy, the parties set forth platforms which some agree with and some do not, but which are nevertheless accepted: there is recognition that where disagreement exists there has to be a rule allowing action. This rule in a democracy is the majority principle. However, the principle of majority rule, to be workable, requires agreement that X should be done and also agreement that Y is the way to do it. There have always been disagreements about implementation but these were considered a minor aspect of the problem. They were settled by consultation with people who were not even members of the government; they were practical issues solvable by expertise; they were not considered normative issues which required a further opinion from the public or further debate within parliament. It was possible to view policy issues in this way because everyone believed that agreement on a goal entailed a general consensus that the implementation of policies involves purely practical matters to be handled by 'experts'. But when a society is divided primarily on the question of *how* problems are to be solved, the majority-rule principle gives an illusory way of achieving agreement. It solves but one aspect of the problem – what should be done – and leaves the main issue – how – outside the democratic process. As disagreement about the normative versus determinist view is dividing us, the 'how' has now become the central normative issue – yet this fact is being ignored. (Worse still, disagreement is dividing members of the government who are attempting to institute their agreed policy; they often do not seem to understand why they are in disagreement.)

Among those affected by this situation, socialists are the least prone to be internally divided. Their norms are consistent with social determinism: socialists are socialists because they are social determinists. Conservatives, while far from agreeing about the content of their norms, seem in general agreement about the role of norms in human behaviour and tend to act accordingly. Liberals tend to be determinists, but without being committed to determinism, as socialists are.

Chapter 4

Freedom and authority

FREEDOM, PSYCHOLOGICAL EGOISM AND CONSERVATISM

It is natural to expect the attitude of conservatives to be anti-socialist but not anti-social. To become anti-social, the conservative argument about individualism has to be interpreted as a statement about psychological egoism – the premise which can be traced to Hobbes and which is common to modern psychoanalysts. The latter begin with a hypothesis about the motivation of biological organisms, such as newborn babies – who appear to be a bundle of drives – and deduce from this the relations between adult human beings in a hypothetical state of nature. At this point psychoanalysts stop, content that their original hypothesis deals with 'natural law' and the 'ideal' freedom. Whether this freedom would be tolerable is not their concern: they are interested solely in individual patients and the problems their patients face as a result of not living under the hypothetical condition of 'freedom'.

Hobbes, however, was concerned with the social consequences of psychological egoism. He established that such a condition is psychologically intolerable, something all human beings – who operate on the hypothesis of psychological egoism – strive to avoid. He did it by emphasizing the need for a strong central government (or sovereignty). If we want to know whether conservatives advocate psychological egoism – are anti-social – we must begin at the point where Hobbes ended and ask what the conservative attitude to government is.

One of the generally accepted features of conservatism is its steadfast adherence to the need for government. Historically, conservatives resisted democracy when its defence was based on anarchistic principles. However, now that both liberals and democratic socialists conceive of government as a moral agency, conservatives are clearly distinguished by their resistance to this view. They want a strong government, but not very much of it. Indeed (if we disregard Hobbes), we may even confuse modern conservatism with classical liberalism, and think of political conservatives as psychological conservatives (or as 'liberals' who have not changed and do not want to). References to the *laissez-faire* ideology emanating from some conservatives today make it appear that they hold some nineteenth-century liberal views in this respect, but in fact the differences are very pronounced. To confuse modern conservatives with last century's liberals on this basis is to misunderstand conservatism and ignore the nature of the *laissez-faire* doctrine.

In the late eighteenth and early nineteenth centuries, science was seen as having proved that economic laws were such that social laws regulating the market place were contrary to man's interests and a restriction on freedom. Subsequently, despite humanitarian misgivings on the part of many who called economics a dismal science because of its inhuman requirements, the laws regulating prices, the purity of food, wages, etc. were dismantled. The results were socially and politically disastrous. What we now call Communism was one economist's response to the *laissez-faire* views of his colleagues.

Economic *laissez-faire* belongs to the past, despite occasional voices raised in its favour. One feels that its advocates are merely trying to rally opposition to legislation they dislike; knowing that by attacking a particular piece of unpalatable legislation they can hardly gain general support, they generalize their sense of grievance into a call for *laissez-faire*.

Modern *laissez-faire* is ethical rather than economic,

deriving from supposed 'natural laws' purportedly discovered by behaviourists and psychoanalysts. Consequently, we are getting rid of ethical legislation very
reluctantly (with misgivings similar to those which nineteenth-century dissentients had about abolishing humane
economic legislation). Evidently liberals have not learnt
from history: they tell us not to believe those who say that
freedom is served by abandoning legislation which conflicts with some natural law discovered by science (or
social science). But genuine science has no way of determining anything that can rightly be called natural law.

What is the conservative view of all this? The liberals'
view is clear: as science has shifted, so they have shifted,
but their views about the role of government have not.
They conceive of government as a secularized version of
the Church temporal, responsible for the maintenance
and propagation of a truth originating elsewhere (but
not, as with Communism, a doctrinal truth). The liberal's
truth is still in the process of being discovered by science.
Such a position is anathema to conservatives, who go back
to the Hobbesian conception of the State as a regulative
agency, though not a moral one. The State's laws will
conflict with some people's views on ethics; hence the
fewer laws the better. On the other hand, the recognition
of individual differences – tolerance – is part of the
regulative function of the State which is needed but
cannot be accomplished if the State acts as a moral
agency. According to the conservative, the laws which are
being discarded in our time as 'outmoded moral statements' should be re-examined (and re-instated as 'regulative'). The very failure to make the distinction (between
moral and regulative agency) puts freedom in jeopardy.

CONSERVATISM, AUTHORITY AND THE RULE
OF LAW

Placing, as he does, the emphasis on convention, the
conservative is regarded by non-conservatives as resisting
change – a view that puzzles him. Those who apply the
primary (dictionary) sense of conservative – 'disposed to

preserve existing institutions' – also think of the conservative as authoritarian, although to him, authority is society's agent for change, not for the status quo. He regards the absence of a legal agent for change as anarchistic – leaving society at the mercy of chance.

It is logical to view a conservative as an upholder of authority, for one of the primary functions of authority is to enforce the conventions, which according to the conservative are necessary to communal life. It is impossible even to play a game without an umpire or a book of rules to whose authority one can appeal. However, if one so limits the sense of authority it appears that conservatism does indeed mean resisting change. But in doing so we define authority in terms of convention: umpires and official rule books are regarded as different forms of the same thing.

The consequences are not acceptable to all conservatives. During a symposium on conservatism in 1980, one of the discussants (Tom Palmer, commenting on Shirley Robin Letwin's position) said 'Anything goes, so long as it proceeds along [sic!] predictable and established rules'.[4] Palmer justifiably raises an ethical objection to Dr. Letwin, because when using the concept of rule of law she has confused the 'conventional', which has a function, with the 'customary', which may be anything at all. However, Palmer has missed a key point about the relation of authority to convention: an authority is a convention capable not only of upholding existing conventions but having the right to introduce new ones as the need arises. If we do not feel the need for someone capable of doing this, a conservative can be defined simply as an upholder of the rule of law, ready to support anything if it is in accordance with the law and resisting all objections on the ground that the law is necessary and must not be changed.

One of the points which reflects prevalent confusion about conservatism refers to the attitude to law as contingent on the distinction between the lawmaker and the law. They have a good deal in common. Both, a set of official rules and an umpire, can be called 'authorities'. Both derive their authority from convention: we agree to acknowledge their authority because they serve a function. However, if we think of umpire and rule book as interchangeable (theoretically, in ideal conditions umpires would not be necessary if rule books were detailed enough),[5] the conservative's respect for convention would move him towards the totalitarian conception of the rule of law. Accordingly, one day our lives will be (or should be) so minutely circumscribed that we will not need an actual government: we will have moved from the view that 'all the world is a stage' to the view 'all the world is a game' in which each of us has an assigned position. But no one has ever described conservatives as holding this view. Conservatives do not believe in a totalitarian 'rule of law'.

The alternative, however, to the view that both official rules and umpire are called authorities is to see the umpire in terms of coercive power. In this interpretation, the umpire is himself bound by official rules but has the authority to penalize violations of official rules in order to maintain authority. This interpretation may in some respects be no better than the totalitarian. It would require an even minuter set of rules binding both umpire and participants, and imposing penalties for nonconformity. Such penalties would be particularly distasteful now when even the logic of systems of penalty – talion – has broken down.

Once upon a time, the logical penalty for violation of authority was exclusion: violate the rules of a game and you were 'benched'; violate those of etiquette and you were ostracized; violate the rules of public authority and you were ostracized in the classical Greek sense. As for the really outrageous violations, the guilty were permanently excluded – suffered the death penalty. Significantly, only in games do we maintain nowadays the logical penalty. Our social system of justice can no longer be a source of information to us about the nature of authority (nor can it say what logically follows from a failure to acknowledge it). Indeed, one way to recognize the conservative is by his belief that justice requires a system of logical penalties rather than some system of fines or other acknowledgement of the importance of the market-place in our lives. He still believes in ostracism and segregation in a way which shocks those who have stopped believing in what one may call social logic. He does not believe all people have a right to community just because they are alive. For him, membership in a community is a privilege that has to be earned.

To the conservative, umpire and rule book, though both 'authorities', are distinguishable in terms other than the umpire's possession of coercive power. Law itself is implicitly coercive: acknowledge the law and some penalty is necessarily attached to violations. If the rules are simply prudential – as it is supposed social rules 'should' be – the violation carries its own penalty without any necessary 'addition' by society. Try to violate gravity and you will break your leg or neck, depending on circumstances; violate conventions and – even without the umpire – the rules will necessarily prescribe a penalty, which you will have to accept if you want to continue playing; agree to the game and you agree to be coerced. If, then, the conservative believes in the rule of law – the authority of law – why is he so insistent that the rule of law and authority are necessarily different though related?

The answer lies in the fact that at least some conservatives (e.g. in Canada) call themselves progressive conservatives without any sense of contradiction. To understand this name means to understand the conservative ideal: authority is necessary because change is necessary and only what is adaptable – a government – has the required characteristics. To a conservative, an authority is a conventional device for adapting convention to a world in flux. The essential question is not whether we need the convention but the question of jurisdiction: when do we have 'too much' or 'too little' government? If liberals have been traditionally concerned with the question of 'too much' and socialists with 'too little' government, conservatives in one sense can be considered 'middle of the road': they debate both questions. Unfortunately, they fail to explain why they debate both sides; nor have they made it clear that they are discussing the jurisdiction of authority (not whether we need it or not). Hence we get such rather odd terms as 'left-wing' and 'right-wing' conservatives. If they are to be a viable political force, the first thing conservatives must do is to announce to the world that they do not question the need for authority but only the extent of its jurisdiction.

GOVERNMENTAL JURISDICTION AND FREEDOM

When speaking of governmental jurisdiction, whether there is too much government or too little, we are speaking of 'liberty' (or freedom). What strikes the conservatives about the continuing debate on freedom, is the absence of such associated concepts as 'independence' and 'responsibility', as well as the peculiar emphasis on rights, which makes talk of freedom imply a demand for a special kind of welfare to be distributed by the State to its citizens. The conservative does not like the concept of a welfare State and he objects to the kind of 'liberty' which is part of the distributed welfare. On this basis the conservative can assert that democratic governments have already exceeded their jurisdiction by allowing popular notions of liberty to prevail (and to define a concept that cannot be defined in terms of desire).

Let us consider first the disappearance of the concept 'independence' from the discussion of freedom. To the older generation, independence is still a meaningful concept: indeed many old people insist on retaining their independence, being self-sufficient and beholden to none – in a way that baffles social workers (who think they would be better off under professional supervision in a home, as some certainly would be if they had no conception of independence). Only two generations ago the conception was adhered to by virtually everyone in a democracy. Being an element of freedom, independence as a norm rested on the view that assistance of any kind creates an obligation which one might not like to incur. A right without a reciprocal obligation was unintelligible. To speak of being 'free' when one was in fact dependent on someone else's benevolence was absurd.

Now independence is often represented as incompatible with rights – generally believed to be the 'freedom' distributed by the State to the public as part of a general welfare policy. Social workers spend much time trying to convince elderly conservatives that they have a right to insist on public assistance; they have no such problem in propagating the liberal and socialist philosophy among non-conservatives.

The concept of freedom becomes purely egoistic when 'independence' is detached from it: ideal freedom is the state of an individual who has no responsibilities and accepts no obligations. Such a condition would be anarchistic; and if society is to remain viable, traditional individual responsibilities and obligations must be accepted by the State. Consequently, the State's jurisdiction now embraces the entire area of personal relations: the egoist concept of personal freedom requires it to do so. The conservative may protest that as a result we have lost our independence, but if he does so he is no longer speaking in terms intelligible to the prevailing opinion. Those he is arguing against derive their concept of freedom not from political philosophy but from psychological theory – psychological egoism – which they consider 'scientific' (and which defines the conservative's norms as outmoded and self-interested). As psychological egoists say, if all men are actuated by their biological drives, then what we call norms are but a reflection of our egoist impulses. Following this theory, people are led to accept the concepts of obligation and responsibility, which are clearly statements about one's relations with others and are (under egoism) not natural but merely conventional. Behaviourists – the theory imputes – have thus opened people's eyes to the deception practised on them by conservatives; the latter should have the good grace to give up their speculations on freedom that require the use of 'obligation' and 'responsibility' and let behaviourists guide democracy towards freedom in the scientific sense. If this means that the State acquires jurisdiction over all aspects of human relations, then this is progress.

In the face of this onslaught, conservatives, who speak

of such things as the undue growth of government, the expansion of the welfare State and the threat to freedom posed thereby, are preoccupied with mere symptoms. The issue of freedom remains beclouded because it is now generally regarded as a *social* problem – the problem of convincing the conservative-minded of the need to give up their views on independence and think in terms of the all-pervading issue of rights.

THE PARADOX OF 'TOO LITTLE GOVERNMENT'

The Hobbesian argument that the function of the State is to control the anarchistic tendency of unregulated egoism has been frequently interpreted as assigning the State absolute power. In fact, Hobbes's conception limited the State's jurisdiction to matters of law and order: matters of justice – questions of ethics – had to be decided by someone other than the sovereign power. They were beyond State jurisdiction.

This conception permitted the development of democracy and kept it from becoming totalitarian. The idea of the State as a non-ethical institution limited the State's jurisdiction by pointing to the maintenance of law and order as the overriding principle. (This took place even in those democratic nations which did not explicitly limit State jurisdiction by separating Church and State constitutionally.) Other conceptions of the good existed but had only a secondary claim to consideration: a State that did not control egoism – maintain law and order – ceased to be a State. Everybody but the conservatives want to make the State into some form of ethical institution. The consequences are either totalitarianism – as under Communism – or a steady return to anarchy, which in conservative opinion is the present tendency under democracy.

When the function of the State shifts from the maintenance of legal justice (the social conditions necessary to any other kind of justice) to the promotion of social justice (some ethical system), the importance of the State's essential function is reduced. From an ethical viewpoint it cannot be argued that arresting shoplifters is more important than eliminating poverty. Therefore, an ethically-based State will deal with what is considered the more important problem and neglect the less important. But the State should not be making ethical decisions of this kind. It is exceeding its jurisdiction and neglecting its real duty: because of its preoccupation with social justice, law and order are not being maintained.

Yet each time a conservative-minded government tries to reduce welfare expenditures in order to devote more attention to its main areas of jurisdiction (defence and legality), it is branded as immoral. The government's response to such a charge should be that the State is amoral, not immoral; that ethical questions are outside its jurisdiction; and that it will necessarily become oppressive if it tries to become a moral agent. The democratic State does not want ethics in the form of ideology forced on society by a government which thinks such coercion to be its primary duty.

Furthermore, the State's ability to enforce regulations is diminished if ethical questions are linked with the judicial process. 'Judge not that ye be not judged' may be a Christian virtue, as is the forgiveness of sin, but a legal system cannot be upheld on this basis. Yet there are indications that the ethical concepts of innocence have crept into our legal system, for determinist theories of causation (e.g. an unhappy childhood) are being used to prove legal innocence. The courts are approaching crime as if the issue were sin and the criminal courts were acting on behalf of the Recording Angel on the Day of Judgement. Needless to say, they should be doing nothing of the sort. Certainly, we need a concept of innocence in the law courts because each time an innocent man is declared guilty, the genuinely guilty is enabled to continue his criminal activity. But, for the same reason, we cannot allow the ethical concept of innocence based on deterministic assumptions to affect judicial innocence. If the present trend continues, the point will be reached where no one will ever be found guilty judicially: 'guilt' no longer seems to be a legal notion but essentially an ethical conception. The conservative is likely to conclude that we are not getting enough government because democratic governments are nowadays exceeding their jurisdiction. This paradox needs to be enshrined in a conservative manifesto.

FREEDOM AND AUTHORITY: THE PRUDENTIAL FRAMEWORK

From the days when Burke protested against revolutionary talk of 'rights' and 'liberty', the conservative has insisted that his idea of 'freedom' entails a prudential restriction on freedom. When the conservative attempts to explain his position to others he faces the issue of prudence – an integral part of conservative thinking.

At first, the problem seems reasonably clear: man's animal impulses (his 'hedonism') are in conflict with his sense of self-extending-in-time (his 'reason'). If I am hungry, what do I eat – or should I forgo the satisfaction of eating anything on prudential grounds despite the opportunity which may be there? Animals do not have this problem; they act on the basis of biological drive modified by experience. Not eating on the ground that they will become obese or that what they eat belongs to somebody else – and that respect for property ultimately serves self-interest – is beyond them.

If we kept the terms 'hedonism' and 'reason' out of the discussion perhaps it would be a good idea to use 'animalism' to refer to the view that the biological factors which guide (or even determine) animal behaviour also best serve man's interest. 'Prudence' would then refer to behaviour based on a concept of self extending in time and peculiar to man (the only species having such a concept). Within this framework there is still a great deal of scope for debate. Several questions arise. Are prudential principles the same as egoism? How do we reconcile 'prudence' and moral obligation, or are they not in conflict? Can the concept of self override our biological nature (or is Hume's argument about the emotional base of behaviour irrefutable)? The latter question is crucial to the conservative. There is no point in speaking about 'prudence' if we cannot act prudently. If Hume is correct, the conservative, whether he likes it or not, would have to say that the 'hedonist' conception of freedom based on individual desire is the only realistic one, although it is clearly imprudent and has been recognized as such ever since 'unenlightened' hedonism was shown to be contrary to 'true' principles of hedonism.

Since Hume's days, however, the way we look at the problem has changed completely. It can no longer be argued – as Hume did – that logically 'reason is the slave of the passions.' The theory of evolution establishes that the argument is fallacious: if man's capacity for 'reason' did not profoundly influence human behaviour, the human brain could not have evolved to the point it has. Why? In the first place, human beings are not just a degree or two more intelligent than other species in the way some animals are a little bit faster or stronger physically. Human beings are so many times more intelligent than other animals that they do not have any competitors of the kind accounting for evolution in general; with regard to intelligence, men are unique – are indeed the rational animals. The only way to account for this in terms of evolutionary theory is to adopt the view that the competitive advantage conferred by our intelligence is the capacity to behave 'prudently' – in terms of a self extending in time – as opposed to all other animals, who can act only in terms of their biological condition as affected by the immediate circumstances in which they find themselves at any point in time. A very complex brain is necessary to make very complex computations. One that is only a little better could not make the necessary computations or override biological impulses. Animals can make associations but they cannot act prudently for they lack both the complex brain and the sense of self extending in time on which prudence is based.

If Hume's argument was proved wrong by the theory of evolution, other theories were given a new basis. Thus the 'prudence' Hobbes used to explain the move from the state of nature to sovereignty could now be made a biological fact rather than a speculation which presupposes that reason can override biological nature. Burke's argument that we cannot speak of freedom outside of a prudentially established 'authority' and 'tradition' was also given a basis in man's nature. In consequence, a conservative ought to have been pleased by the advent of the theory of evolution. However, the construction placed on the findings of science has been exclusively in the hands of nonconservatives – liberals and radicals – who have drawn totally different conclusions. They have argued that evolution establishes determinism as a fact: we human beings, despite our sense of free will, are part of a universal system of cause-effect; hence insofar as freedom means anything, it refers to an inescapable desire to act in accordance with our biological impulses. 'Authority' represents a restraint on those natural desires which we might be able to justify rationally but which we cannot possibly expect to operate in the way Hobbes and Burke thought it could. Because of man's 'nature', we would not act prudentially.

The conservative who agrees with the above view is not conservative in the Burkean tradition. The view is based on 'liberal' assumptions about 'freedom' which have merely been coloured by a conservative respect for 'authority.' One of the tasks of modern conservatism is to get back to the central term 'prudence' – which under present conditions means to reappraise the significance of the theory of evolution.

FREEDOM AND AUTHORITY: BRITISH AND AMERICAN CONSERVATISMS

Roger Scruton gives the essence of the British view of political conservatism: 'In politics, the conservative attitude seeks above all for government and regards no citizen as possessed of a natural right that transcends his obligation to be ruled'.[6] Scruton recognizes that this immediately raises the question of freedom and that any definition given will be different from that applicable to American conservatives: 'The freedom that Englishmen esteem is not, and cannot be a special case of that freedom advocated by the American Republican Party.'[7]

The English conservative's stress on government derives from the rational principle of sovereignty and reflects a long tradition of emphasizing reason. To demonstrate that American conservatives differ, one must show that they place less emphasis on reason.[8]

Let us take the matter of customs or conventions. No American, no matter how conservative he is (as defined in the USA), really understands the kind of conservatism which accepts conventions (once they have been defined as such) as beyond criticism. He sees such an attitude as irrational. If he himself acknowledges the need for at least some conventions, he uses this to support his attacks on 'reason': some conventions, such as those that enable us to have language, he deems necessary; therefore, to his mind, 'reason' is revealed to have a shortcoming as a guide to 'oughts'.

This is a distinctively American view. It cannot be supported by appealing to Burke's views on 'tradition' and 'custom', as some American conservatives suppose. The British (and more broadly, the European) conservative does not focus on the arbitrariness of convention or custom and concludes that, at least sometimes, we must abandon rational analysis. He focuses on the function served; decides whether some rational principle or rule could better serve that function; and, if not, accepts the arbitrary convention as rational – because it is functional. The question of arbitrariness arises only after one accepts the function. Recognizing the latter is anything but an irrational process. It requires astute analysis. It is not a matter of opinion and cannot be left in the hands of the public.

What Americans, both conservatives and liberals, do not understand is that European respect for custom and authority has nothing to do with a frame of mind or difference in psychology. Essential to this respect, in a tradition going back to the scholastics, is an intellectualism that is anything but authoritarian. The need for authority is not questioned for it has a function: it is reason which has established this beyond question. Hence – so the argument goes – there can be no valid definition of freedom that rests on a denial of this premise. (If you think there can be, you are not using the political concept of 'liberty' but something else, such as the concept of free will or an assumption about man's egoism).

The problem with the word 'authoritarian' is of the same kind as in the case of 'freedom': the word has more than one meaning. In the European tradition, it refers to those people who accept authority as a rational principle necessary to life in society – hence requiring that the principle be acknowledged. Although such an 'authoritarian' will defend the principle of authority, he will not try to defend rationally any particular decree stemming from authority. He knows quite well that the action may be arbitrary, defensible only in terms of function. He does not want to be caught up in debates such as whether a non-arbitrary rule may or may not be possible. Irritating and irrelevant as such debates are, they reduce the effectiveness of authority. Nothing gets done when people debate issues of 'liberty' based on non-political concepts; in doing so they tend to forget the main issue: that the political concept of authority (essentially of sovereignty) is necessary to society's existence.

The American situation is different. Virtually all authoritarians are unaware that they are authoritarian for they look inward for their concept – to free will and a willingness to submit to 'authority' – not outward to a rationally established rule. Yet, to Americans, the actual 'authority' is defined by the statistical fact of acknowledging someone or something as an 'authority'. Understanding such statistical regularities – Charles Manson gathered a small cult around him, Billy Graham a larger one, and President Kennedy a still larger following – can focus on the personality of the followers (their authoritarian personalities) or the personality of the leader or 'authority' (the charisma). This kind of analysis of what 'authority' is can involve as many further steps as one cares to take.

The American conservative finds himself in a peculiar position with respect to his definition of authority and authoritarianism. The definition accords with the concept of 'liberty' as a matter of free choice and of democratic 'authority' as being the result of the will of the majority. But why should anyone who did not make that choice of 'authority' in the first place be required to submit to it? Any answer given to this question takes us back to pre-Hobbesian conceptions: you have to obey because obedience is part of the natural or civil order. But what happens then to the free will that defined the 'freedom' that defined the 'authority'? Are we not back to a medieval conception of authority in which the divine right of kings is replaced by 'majority rule'? Is it resistance to such an anomalous position that explains why Americans of both liberal and conservative persuasions place such an extraordinary emphasis on majority rule and, at the same time, quite clearly do not really want any kind of government?

COERCIVE POWER AND AUTHORITY

There is a tendency to overlook that power as a normative concept is important to conservative thinking. Conservatives deny that possession of coercive power is wrong: for example, that it is conducive to tyranny and conflict. The only 'authority' that to a conservative represents wrongful coercive power is a 'charismatic' authority – that which exists because some people are willing to follow a leader. Repeatedly, to be sure, charismatic leaders have advocated peaceful, non-coercive human relations: they do not need coercive power to exercise their authority. On the other hand, some of them, such as the 'Reverend' Jim Jones of the Guyana massacre and Charles Manson of the Sharon Tate killings, have been anything but peacefully inclined by nature: they appear to have been psychopaths, although habitually their ostensible message was: peace, love and non-coercion.

The respective attitudes of conservatives and liberals to charismatic authority (as exemplified by cult leaders) bring out their views on power. Liberals tend to see such authority as a key feature of the kind of society that ought to exist. Conservatives, whose tolerance is sometimes stretched to breaking point, find it hard to see how cults that have no real tenets, but only leaders, meet the normative requirement for freedom of thought and religion. Complete tolerance would mean disallowing criticism on the ground that attacks on charismatic authority constitute 'hatemongering', indistinguishable from racial and religious prejudice. It would encourage the view that the only legitimate authority is one that can exist in the absence of coercive power. This is precisely the view that the conservative adamantly opposes, for it undermines the existence of the kind of authority which makes possible both society and the family, on which the existence of human beings depends.

Consider, for instance, recent legislation, first passed by a liberal-socialist nation such as Sweden but now spreading to other countries, which prohibits the use of corporal punishment by parents. In theory, parental authority is still recognized, but since the means of asserting it have been taken away, one may well doubt whether the authority still exists. The concept of 'child abuse' now includes even reprimands. Furthermore, children in our society are actually encouraged by social workers (and similar experts on the nature and limits of authority) to complain about parental exercise of their authority. According to behavioural theory, the 'authority' of parents should rest on the children's willingness to grant it – or it should be charismatic. Anything else is tyranny. The same reasoning, of course, is applied to the government's authority over citizens: inasmuch as a government employs coercive power, it is exercising authority 'illegitimately'.

No one will object to the idea that the kind of coercive power possessed by authority has to be limited. But when no coercive power exists, authority disappears if what we consent to is not the concept of authority but the authority's decisions. Alternatively, authority may exist in a form of 'influential' (suggestive) authority, capable of answering that peculiarly modern question 'What shall I do now'? If authority has no coercive power and we have to consent to each decision made, 'authority' serves the function similar to that of parents who are willing to make suggestions only when the child asks what it should do.

If such an idea seems utterly bizarre, one should remember that this is how many people look on party platforms and how they feel parents should exercise authority when the child misbehaves: suggest an alternative way of behaving and wheedle them into it if you can. Anything else entails coercive power (defined as wrong). The model followed is that of charismatic authority.

To the conservative, an authority without coercive power – even latent – cannot serve its real function of maintaining law and order and enabling co-operative action. Even if everyone is willing to co-operate, someone has to give orders. It does not matter whether one begins with an egoist or altruist conception of man. If we are to benefit from communal life there has to be an authority who does more than suggest courses of action requiring our agreement. Consent to some end supplies no clue to the means: the mere fact, for example, that I agree to the building of a dam gives no clue as to what should be done next. Someone has to issue orders and enforce them.

The most disturbing consequence of any attempt to remove coercion from democratic society is a changed conception of freedom. Decisions based on 'desire' force us into a determinist framework, for it can be established that 'desires' are part of a cause-effect pattern, whereas this is not true of rational concepts which alone make the intuitive concept of free will meaningful.

If the only authority recognized is the new, 'suggestive' authority of democratic and charismatic leaders, these authorities become the only ones in society having free will. Everyone else is acting within a cause-effect framework. Part of the latter is the influence of the new kind of authority which cultivates techniques of representing its own interests as 'desirable' to others. The 'others', preoccupied with the satisfaction of desires, do not have the ability, or interest, to question what is happening.

Despite the absence of coercion, according to the conservative a society operating under such a system is not 'free'. It cannot be made free just by reintroducing coercion, but it can become free if coercion is recognized as a rationally-based concept justifying authority as an essential component of a social system. To a conservative mind, it is not a self-evident truth that the coercive power of authority proves that there is something wrong with it. What troubles the conservative is charismatic authority, which needs no coercive power and is neither rational nor social in any real sense. Rather it splits society into sects and factions.

Coercive power: liberal and conservative views

Though both liberals and conservatives stoutly maintain that they believe in minimum government, it is clear that the power of government has been steadily increasing for over a century. Is one to conclude that liberals and conservatives are hypocrites or that man does not have much control over the increasing complexity of 'government'? The issue would be much clearer if we stopped speaking about 'minimum government' and spoke instead of *minimum coercion* and the relationship between this concept and 'authority'. The question of whether one needs government or not does not divide liberals and conservatives.

As noted earlier, conservatives do not object to coercive power as such, for they see it as integral to civil authority. Influenced as they are by the fact of charismatic authority (which does not need coercive power to maintain a following), liberals are inclined to believe that coercive authority can be limited to temporary conditions, such as the state of war, or the very brief early period in one's life. They believe that coercive power should not be institutionalized because it need not be. To them, 'minimum coercion' represents the view that justifiable coercion is an exception to the general rule that there should ordinarily be no coercive power in a democracy and that, inasmuch as one can point to its institutionalized presence, this reveals undemocratic aspects of society.

Let us take as an example 'school bussing' in America,

which the conservative regards as an indefensible expansion of the coercive powers of government. The liberal will frankly admit that coercion is involved – he can hardly deny it – but will argue that it is temporary, functioning in an educative manner. Thus, once people had learned through association that blacks are not inferior members of society and once blacks have had the same opportunities as whites, the law will become a dead letter; in other words, it will cease to coerce.

To the conservative this view is very dangerous: it assumes man to be the creature of his environment, an irrational animal. If one assumes this, where does the concept of authority come from, according to which one can legitimately use coercive power provided it so manipulates matters that one day it will not be needed? In Walden II – his 'behaviouristic mod' version of a liberal society – Skinner proposed just such an arrangement. Like the cultists who thought of him as a 'guru' or charismatic leader, he overlooked Orwell's objection: mask the coercion and you mask authority and put it beyond the possibility of being objected to by those who have been manipulated into accepting it in the first place. It is nonetheless there, though in a form that those subject to it cannot imagine. It has been derationalized – and so have its coercive powers.

The conservative, unlike the liberal, does not want the appearance of coercion to be eliminated; he wants it to be clearly set forth. It is only the coercive power itself that is open to criticism. Most people, excluding anarchists, accept authority itself. But authority is both assigned and defined in terms of the coercive power which is permissible. To try to employ a kind of coercive power one does not have is to exceed one's authority.

Liberals are quite right in thinking that coercive power detached from authority is bully power that cannot be rationally justified. But when attached to authority it serves the essential role of defining the authority and clarifying its function. We 'consent' to authority as serving a function which is in our interest, although as individuals with a will of our own, we will not 'consent' to each decree unless threatened with a penalty for not doing so. If we insist that we are no longer really consenting while being coerced, we deny the function of authority to which in theory we had consented, or had acknowledged as rational.

Chapter 5

Prudence and politics

The touchstone of conservative thought has always been 'prudence', just as that of the liberal has been 'freedom' and of the socialist 'distributive justice'. To the conservative, prudence is the mid-term in a progression: rational-prudent-wise. Here 'rational' represents our minimum expectation for all human beings; 'prudent' denotes the product of an interaction between rationality and experience (children and subnormal adults cannot behave prudently); 'wisdom' is an exceptional quality we cannot normally expect because we do not know all the factors involved. Politically, this means that a conservative will not support any system of government predicated on the assumption that we can educate people to become 'philosopher-kings'. Plato was unquestionably not a conservative. Hobbes and Burke, who did not expect very much from the sovereign power, were conservatives. Hegel, who did expect a great deal, was not.

But it is not the modest expectations of Hobbes and Burke that define them as conservative. The defining concept is 'prudence' which is not just the mid-term in a progression (whose components are rather vague), but refers to behaviour in one's own interest and implies continuity in time. To the conservative, continuity – which in certain circumstances can be referred to as 'tradition'[9] – is central to the idea of government; he is in fact reluctant to define any actual political system as 'government' unless such a system has continuity in time and the means to ensure it.

As a normative principle, prudence – being based on the concept of self extending in time – is different from selfishness and the philosophy of selfishness – egoism – in which the 'self' spoken of is not necessarily conceptual but only the sum of desires which operate at a given point in time. Thus children characteristically act selfishly but seldom prudently: what looks like prudence is more often the timidity or wariness towards the unknown that is equally characteristic of animals. This point needs to be kept in mind when referring to prudence as typical of conservatives' official views. Many who recognize prudence as a conservative norm imagine that it entails a preference for the familiar and a fear of the unknown. People so predisposed can probably be called 'conservative', but they are the bane of Conservative parties: they help create an image of conservatives as being not prudent at all but ostriches who refuse to face social problems and the need to adapt to change.

Beginning with the assumption that 'conservatives' do not want change, critics deduce that the motivation is a satisfaction with things as they are; and, further, that such people must have a privileged position in society which they wish to preserve. But this reasoning is fallacious and its premises are false.

We must, of course, face the fact that prudence has traditionally been set in opposition to benevolence (the desire to do good): inasmuch as one acts benevolently, one does not act prudently. The consequence of this opposition is that the 'good' as conceived by ethical philosophers is represented as something no one would willingly undertake; hence the problem of 'obligation' and 'duty' becomes an ethical issue to be resolved: how can the good be represented as 'prudent' when it is not?

PRUDENTIALISM AND THE 'GOOD'

Conservatives maintain that there is something wrong with an ethical system (including ideologies) which asserts that there are goods which society must distribute. Indeed, what conservatives want to conserve is a valid conception of the 'good'. Accordingly, reasoning in terms of 'prudence' (acting in terms of a long-range self-interest whose nature is only partially determined by present circumstances) is one of the most useful ways of asserting this view without entangling oneself in questions such as whether there are any goods everyone should seek.

When Burke argued that supporters of the French Revolution were unpractical idealists who violated ethical considerations for the sake of their visions and yet did not himself present a clear ethical alternative, he did so in the name of 'the first of all virtues, prudence'. To Burke, the State is in no position to assert what the 'good' is, nor can the individual citizen do so. The nearest approach we can make is to recognize that biological impulse does not serve as a guide: we should act prudently rather than hedonistically; we should also not suppose that anyone – State or charismatic leader – knows. Although Burke did not say as much, his argument implies that the Hobbesian sovereign and even the Machiavellian prince – both of whom were required to act 'prudently' so as to remain in office – are far more trustworthy than an ideological sovereign that assumes to be acting in terms of a known good.

To act rationally we need to believe two things: first, that there is a good and second, that we do not know what this good is. If we deny there is a good – as the relativists do – we become hedonists and violate even commonsense prudence. Trying to solve these problems by representing an ideology as the good results in our getting a Fascist or Communist style of society in which some future hedonist condition is used to justify a present tyranny.

According to conservatives, in view of our limited knowledge the best we can do is to require that everyone – governed and government – act on the principle of prudence. If and when we reach such a state of enlightenment that we know the nature of the good, we will naturally expect both the government and individual citizen to be governed by the principle of the good. For the time being, 'prudence' is the only principle that includes those aspects of the good of which we are already sure; furthermore, it also frankly acknowledges its own limitations. The prudent are not saints, nor are they feckless hedonists, aimless relativists or ruthless idealists. This may sound like the Aristotelian 'golden mean' – and it certainly would not be difficult to represent Aristotle as a conservative – but it is not necessarily temperance that guides the conservative. Rather it is 'prudence': what seems best in the light of reason, experience and our recognition that we not only have a history but a future. In fact, 'prudentialists' is a word worth considering as a replacement for the misleading term 'conservatives.'

PRUDENCE AND PATERNALISM

So long as the 'good' is defined as the 'desired' and the latter 'explained' in terms of personal experience, problems of authority are limited to questions of what is politically and socially desirable (to maintain the relativistic conception of the good). For most people democracy is a political and social system designed to serve 'desire'.[10] Politically 'reason' is made the slave of passions.

When discussing the 'good' – and limiting our concern to the concept of 'desire' – it is clear that the desired and the desirable cannot be equated. To pretend that they are the same, means having to deal with some of the objections to Utilitarianism, for the equation of 'desired' and 'desirable' brings out some of the fundamental problems of hedonism: whose desire (desire for 'pleasure') are we talking about? Is it about the desires of some particular person, or about desires in general – the desirable? If the latter, how exactly did one derive it from the former? The desire theory of the 'good' may fit psychological perceptions but does not eliminate philosophical objections.

It is important to political theory, conceived as a 'pragmatic' philosophy, to assume that man's consciousness of his situation in respect to the universe – added to his self-awareness as a biological organism – is of consequence to his life in a community; furthermore, that this double awareness must have an impact on the process of theorizing itself. There is a wide difference between what I want to do (a) as a biological organism and (b) when I am conscious of my continuance in time. Hence the question: what do I do about the fact that 'unenlightened hedonism' – straightforward biological desire – is incompatible with my feeling of extending in time (implying that anything in accordance with an individual impulse or desire is 'not good for me')?

Our sense of a self extending in time requires us to reject the relativistic view (i.e. 'resolute' relativism which sees the desired and the desirable as the same thing) and represent the *desired* as what we are conscious of as animal beings, and the *desirable* as what we conceive of when considering the self over time.

If we speak in terms of desire, the desirable is the prudent. This reversal of relativism alters the conception of authority; for with the introduction of prudence it is no longer true that democratic authority must submit to 'public opinion', observe the majority rule principle, or in any other way act relativistically as desire theory maintains it 'should' (in order to be consistent with relativism).

The issue can be presented as a conservative 'threat' to 'democracy': if prudence is made a normative component of political authority (and self-interest seen as more important than desire), then government can override public opinion just as a prudent individual may ignore immediate impulse for the sake of long-range self-interest. Thus, according to this reasoning, the moment we accept prudence as a valid individual motivation, we are open to paternalism in government.

If we think in terms of 'threat', the conservative is someone who does not see any real threat in paternalism. Under this interpretation, the 'conservative' is just a particular type of personality. Underlying, however, the conservative attitude is a particular attitude to relativism: he regards it as philosophically unsound. His conservatism has a philosophic rather than personality basis. To the conservative, the desired and the desirable are not the same thing and cannot be made so just to accord with a relativist conception of democracy.

Nonetheless, we cannot ignore the popular suspicion

that the conservative talk about non-relativistic norms and the need for a meaningful concept of authority is a mere rationalization employed by a certain type of personality. Without question, a great many 'conservative personalities' – people who seem ready to submit to any authority that promises a social and normative order – are to be found in democratic conservative parties. The philosophic conservative's point, however, is that such people are as likely to be found in liberal, socialist or even Communist parties; they shift back and forth according to social circumstances and the prevailing ideological views. The philosophic conservative is much more steadfast in his loyalty, for it rests on an analysis of what is desirable rather than on 'desire', on prudence rather than policy and on an authority which has an intellectual rather than a charismatic base.

PRUDENCE, CONSERVATISM AND RELIGION

If conservatives make prudence a central concept, we would expect them to emphasize the prudential principle of the separation of Church and State and like liberals and socialists to be at best merely tolerant of religion. Although many conservative apologists have emphasized the importance of religion to the conservative attitude, it is not obviously true that conservatives are particularly well disposed towards 'religion' in general.

The evidence is, for instance, that conservatives must make a special effort and lecture themselves on tolerance when confronted with Zen Buddhism, the Hare Krishnas and Scientologists. If we are to associate religion and conservatism we have to speak of conservatism and orthodoxy; when we do so we are back to the general proposition that conservatives wish to 'conserve'.

On the other hand, the cult religions, which have proliferated under the 'tolerance' advocated by liberals, have an element in common not found in orthodoxy: an egocentrism so egregious that it encourages irrationalism. Unlike the faith important in orthodoxy (which some empiricists call 'irrational' because it goes beyond the evidence supplied by the senses), cultist religions begin with the individual's egoism and make it the basis of both the promise offered to the faithful and of the definition of 'faith'. Some – but not all – cultist religious speak of 'soul'. This 'soul', however, appears to be a sort of permanent ego which, properly cultivated, enables one to attain superiority in this life (make a virtue of 'pride', to use an orthodox term). Other cults do not link their teachings with the traditional religious concept of soul; e.g. in Scientology, the ego is all and it defines 'faith'. 'Faith' refers to such a confidence in one's own opinion that even commonsense is dismissed as an intrusion. Thus cultist faith is completely irrational and has little in common with orthodox faith, based on extrapolation (since the nature of the universe remains unknown).

To tolerate cultist faiths and religions, the conservative has to suppress his conservatism and become almost a liberal; egoism is what he sees as the essence of such faiths. The conservative supports orthodox religion because it is anti-egoist: its message is that the universe is not an impersonal mechanism and that it is a serious mistake for the individual to act as if it were. To act as if it did not matter how one behaves so long as one gets what one wants is most imprudent, says orthodoxy. The conservative concurs, adding that it is also socially irresponsible.

How can the conservative both emphasize prudence and attack egoism? So long as 'prudence' is defined purely in terms of the extension of self in time, there is conflict. But we do not normally conceive of 'prudence' as egoistic – as behaviour in the interest of a self in competition with other 'selfs'. Rather, 'prudence' implies the self's very necessary relations with other selfs: the egoist is seen as acting 'imprudently'. Every prudent man knows that a reputation for egoism is very disadvantageous. If prudence is virtue, egoism is folly. According to the religious view, it is a sin – pride – which is contrary to the cosmological order, a view that no conservative will oppose. We need, however, to be clear that the conservative view does not derive from religion. Many of the views represented as 'religious' are incompatible with conservatism; it is also conceivable for a conservative to be an atheist. A conservative, mindful, for example, of the wars of religion, is likely to be highly reluctant to identify a political ideology with any religious faith. At most, conservatives and the orthodox are 'fellow travellers'.

PRUDENCE AND THE CRIMINAL CODE

The view that a democratic government should not attempt to promote the public good by trying to serve as the rational factor in an irrational society – acting prudentially for the imprudent – raises the question of whether the function of government should be to make the citizen act prudently (responsibly) in his social relations. Theoretically, the criminal code is based on this assumption. As is generally known, however, its provisions are now legal fictions: 'life imprisonment', for instance, usually means about six to nine years. Although the judgement 'guilty' invariably means what it appears to mean, 'innocent' can mean anything from true innocence to acquittal owing to a misplaced comma in the indictment. A technical error can serve as a reason for declaring an accused person not guilty.

The criminal code is nowadays being incorporated into the welfare system. Many people are convinced that if a crime is committed, the government should compensate the victim rather than focus on apprehending the criminal. It seems to them that there is no longer much point in capturing criminals; it costs too much to do so and the process serves no clear function. The prudential principles on which it was once based – one got punished for crime – are almost non-functional.

If it is true that a democratic government must not try to act as the prudential factor in human behaviour but should rather encourage the citizen to act prudently, then can one consider as a corollary the view that a criminal code must be more punitive and set more restrictions on legal innocence than on guilt? A punitive code clearly operates on the assumption that human beings can act prudently. But is it also educational, demanding prudential behaviour from the citizen, not only from the criminally inclined? Does a genuine criminal code serve the primary function which the conservative expects from government, namely that of insisting on the citizen's prudence and responsibility? Is this why conservatives impatiently brush aside 'behaviouralist' statistics which suggest that punishment does not deter criminals? To the conservative, the statistics in question miss the point, for he does not believe it is the sanctions of the criminal code that keep him from crime. To him, the point is that the traditional approach of the code was premised on a human capacity to act prudently: its provisions served notice on the citizen that his society expected prudence. If one changes this view and makes the court system as 'understanding' as a social worker, government has to assume all the responsibility it once demanded from the citizen.[11]

No conservative wants or expects government, least of all democratic government, to interfere with our concepts of justice. To accord with the latter, the criminal code should make it transparently clear that prudential behaviour is expected from the citizens: the operating assumption of society. If in particular instances it can be established that those who are arraigned cannot in fact act prudently – because they are mentally deficient or insane – we do not need to amend the provisions of the criminal code. The traditional concept of 'innocence' was based on just such considerations. Now, through the influence of 'behaviouralist' assumptions, the courts are acting as if nobody could act prudently, all behaviour being determined by factors beyond the individual's control. If nobody can do so (act prudently), says the conservative, why expect the government to act this way? If one makes the courts as 'understanding' as they are, the government becomes a benevolent dictatorship arrived at by an electoral process, its benevolence extending to everyone except those who, being prudent, are the only ones able to pay the cost of such a government. Here it is not 'creeping socialism' and 'soak the rich' (or, rather, 'soak the prudent') schemes that encourage high taxation but plain economic facts consequent on the view that democratic government serves as the prudential factor in behaviour. Ironically, the only citizens who are ultimately able to bear the burden are the prudent, and they do so reluctantly, for they see such governments as adhering to a wholly alien ethical system. The way the criminal code is at present operating demonstrates this in a conspicuous manner.

DOES 'CONSERVATIVE PERSONALITY' MATTER?

'The main point I want to make about the theoretical interpretation of conservatism', says Professor Quinton, 'is . . . that in both its forms, religious and secular, it rests on a belief in the imperfection of human nature'.[12] This 'theoretical interpretation' is not a philosophic view, for it begs the question: whoever holds it professes to have a knowledge of the good and also a knowledge of factors in man's nature that make it impossible for him to attain the good even though he may know what it is.

There is no point in analyzing the 'imperfection' view, for it does not seem to be the outlook of many people.[13] It was important, however, in the seventeenth and eighteenth centuries, when the implications of the then new mechanist view of the universe led to a division between the optimists, who emphasized man's power over 'fate', assuming both a mechanist universe and free will in man, and the pessimists, who saw the potential for evil. What Quinton calls conservatism and literary critics call 'classicism' consisted of two factions: the pessimists on one side (Savile, Swift, Bolingbroke and Johnson) and the optimists (whom critics call Romantics) on the other. By Victorian times, a third position had been inaugurated, meliorism, introduced by George Eliot, who influenced J.S. Mill or was influenced by him. But what we are speaking of are literary movements, not conservatism – the political ideology.

One can understand why Quinton discusses 'conservatism' mainly in terms of literary personalities. Art has escaped the philosophic objections to absolutism in ethics because artists by their very nature present a subjective (relativist) point of view. This is why, nowadays, if one wants to see ethical issues discussed, one turns to literature, not philosophy. But it is not a satisfactory solution to the philosopher's irresponsibility, for the most one can get from *littérateurs* are *pensées* and maxims – no doubt worthy of our consideration but not of our intellectual commitment.

The difficulty with using non-philosophic sources is that we have no assured way of 'understanding' them as literary expressions of conservatism or anything else: we have no means of appraising them. (The same is true of approaching philosophic views – say Burke's – as if they were 'literature'.)

Consider Quinton's treatment of Burke's contention that 'The individual is foolish, the multitude, for the moment, is foolish. . .but the species is wise'.[14] What immediately strikes one is the parallel between this and Lincoln's saying 'You may deceive all the people part of the time, and part of the people all the time, but not all the people all the time'. The saying probably did not originate with Lincoln, who had a flair for the well-turned phrase but was not a man given to reflection. Is his aphorism a 'democratization' of an English conservative view? Does the American acceptance of it (as the ultimate defence of democratic government) explain why Americans are considered basically conservative?

The idea conveyed is that this particular way of defending democracy does not represent the 'people' as determining policy but only as capable of knowing – sometimes – when a government is not governing. At any time majority (and minority) opinion can be wrong; it is completely untrustworthy. Yet, in the long run, as Burke puts it 'The species is wise'. The views of those now dead as well as those now living are relevant to our views of good and bad. What matters to conservatives is man in time – not immediate circumstances – a position opposed by the relativists to whom only current opinions matter.

This is not, however, the construction which Quinton

places on Burke or on conservatism. Quinton asserts – does not argue but merely asserts – that what Burke means is that 'The best political knowledge. . . is collective and historical, to be found. . . in institutions which have survived successfully for a long time, modified to fit . . . changing circumstances'.[15] This is indeed a conservative viewpoint, an expression of a conservative mentality. As a human being, Burke felt this way – he had a conservative personality. But the issue for the political theorist is conservative thinking: how does one move from an outlook or viewpoint to some specific view about government's relations with the citizen such as that contained in Lincoln's statement? Are we to suppose that Lincoln was a more astute philosopher than Burke or that he understood Burke better than Quinton?

The point is that there are certainly conservative viewpoints, just as there are liberal and radical ones, that guide the individual in his daily life. When we think in terms of political theory we want to know the effect of such views on one's politics. Several questions arise. First: what do we expect from government? Second: when is the government 'wrong'? Third: when do we measure its performance against the 'will of the people' or against what 'science' shows to be the 'good'? The conservative answer to the last question is: 'Never'. The answer to the second question depends on whether we have been foolish enough to depart from conservative principles and institute a government supposedly based on the 'will of the people' or 'scientific principles'. The conservative answer to the first question is distinctly vague, something like: 'Not very much'. But whatever it may be, the point is that we are not speaking of political conservatism unless we try to relate a conservative personality to our expectations about governments. Quinton focuses on conservative personalities, Viereck exhibits a conservative viewpoint, but all these matters are outside the political theorist's immediate concern.

Chapter 6

The Burkean legacy

RADICALIZING BURKE'S CONSERVATISM

Conservatism differs from other political views in its reluctance to treat questions of 'justice' (or 'social problems' as one tends to say today) by pretending that such problems are new and require radically new approaches. A new normative system would require a new social and political structure – a revolution; but the conservative denies that any valid new normative system has been proposed: he is not open to the argument that innovative approaches to social problems are needed.

Confronted by changing conditions – such as a rising crime rate – the conservative advocates greater effort – increased enforcement and paying more attention to moral instruction in the school and home – rather than a new sociological approach to crime. He denies that the problem of crime is new. What is new is the abandonment by many of the conviction that morals matter and adoption of the view that it is sociological conditions which determine what we call morals. This kind of relativism does not allow us to have a concept of crime even while employing one: it poses the problem of crime in such a way that it appears insoluble and that it is unjust to try to solve it.

The very innovative approach which the conservative is called upon to make constitutes a normative revolution he cannot accept. The issue is not the philosophic validity of relativism or sociological evidence in favour of

Sumner's view that the 'mores' (the norms of society) can justify anything, for it is not the arbitrariness of norms but their function that matters. The 'keep to the right' traffic rule, for instance, is certainly arbitrary. But an arbitrary rule serves a non-arbitrary function. Hume, who raised insurmountable objections to traditional natural law, blandly observed that he forgot all speculations as soon as he left his study. Saying this, he implied that he was not a relativist: evidence for arbitrariness – the distinction, for instance, between murder and butchering animals for food – is not proof that norms are functionless. But if one accepts that function matters, it is possible both to argue that traditional conceptions of natural law are faulty and to act as if laws based on these conceptions were not invalid.

Burke was no doubt familiar with Hume's stance; he himself made relativism ideologically irrelevant. He also recognized that philosophic arguments are not applicable to everyday affairs. (Philosophic arguments for relativism, incidentally, are like those raising questions about causation; they are problems in epistemology with no bearing on the way we solve problems in science or ethics at the present time.) The real issue is that norms serve a function which can be established only by communal experience. This was Burke's view and it accurately reflected Hume's practice.

In essence, then, the classical conservative tradition with regard to normative change (justice) is that we are in no position to abandon the customary methodological approach, even though very serious questions can be raised against it. In Burke's day, as now, specific normative changes disguised under the concept of 'rights' were being introduced, but these changes involve issues that require separate discussion. Here we are discussing only the general question of the conservative attitude to change in the light of the Burkean maxim – or paradox – that 'a State without the means of some change is without the means of its conservation'.[16]

Now if we think of a State purely in terms of coercive power – as relativists are inclined to do – the statement appears much more paradoxical than it actually is: a totalitarian State of the kind set forth in *1984* quite clearly conserves itself by being able to resist change. However, both Burke and the revolutionaries were conducting their debate within the framework of 'justice': the State referred to was a *de jure* State with the emphasis on 'authority', not 'power'. The issue was: first, whether only a specific type of government – an elected one – is sufficiently open to change to retain authority; and second, if the answer is yes, is the nature of all other governments such that they become hopelessly corrupt, beyond all possibility of reform, because they by nature resist change and soon have no option – in order to maintain power – but to continue to resist change.

Burke's maxim summarizes his view that no State which has had *de jure* authority (with the exception of acknowledged tyrannies) can ever be said to be beyond reform, for the *de jure* State – no matter how arrived at – conserves itself through its capacity to adjust to changing social conditions. This view enables the conservative to use the term 'radical' as a reference to those who deny the proposition by insisting that if any reform is to occur it must be a root and branch one which 'eradicates' – or roots out – the source of corruption (always seen in terms of 'resistance to change'). To the radicals, all 'conservatives' are individuals who resist change.

Among the non-conservatives today there is a tendency to reinforce one's hostility to conservatism by arguing that Burke was clearly wrong about the *ancien régime* in France. The matter is of interest to the conservative for how can any one be so certain about a matter of historical interpretation? Certainly, there was a revolution, but is it certain that it was 'necessary'? Why have we taken Burke's view that 'a State without the means of some change is without the means of its conservation' as proof that the *ancien régime* was incapable of change? Burke, of course, did not take this view and argued against it. Yet, we are now in the curious position of using Burke's maxim as evidence that Burke was wrong (not about the maxim but about its application). If it is all a matter of the inter-

pretation of history, no harm is done. But the issue is
radicalism and revolution: the overthrow or repudiation
of a State, political order or ethical system if it does not
have a particular form or does not elevate certain principles called 'rights' to a supreme position in the normative system. Can we justify that?

The 'conservative' interpretation of the Burkean maxim
– 'a state without the means of change is without the
means of its conservation' – emphasizes the need for
continuity, for if we want to speak of 'change' there has to
be something that remains unchanged. Otherwise, we
would be dealing with Heraclitean flux – that all is change
– in which case there would be no point in discussing the
matter. To Burke it is the concept of 'State' (and human
society) that provides the necessary continuity, though
Burke insists that the State itself changes and has to have
the means to do so if it is not to be overthrown and
replaced by a new State or be incorporated into another.
If it does not have the means, it will vanish into the flux
from which 'the first of all virtues, prudence' rescued us.
Like Hobbes – whom he is obviously following in calling
prudence the first of all virtues (without prudence, in the
Hobbesian scheme there would be no move away from the
state of nature) – Burke made 'prudence' central to his
conception of the State. But unlike Hobbes, he attributed
this first of all virtues primarily to the sovereign power
(for Burke began where Hobbes left off) and in doing so
came remarkably close to a utilitarian point of view.

Burke's opponents (both in his day and now) deal with
the issue of change and continuity 'atomistically': what
remains constant in the midst of flux is the individual (if
we are speaking of human affairs) and atoms (if we are
speaking more generally of the matter); the State is an
illusion – an abstraction – which in order to exist must
change in accord with the 'nature' of its component parts.
Under this view, for example, a 'democratic' State would
still exist if the electorate voted for the introduction of
Communism. What happens afterwards does not concern
atomists, for it all lies in a misty and uncertain future:
such questions as 'what is the "nature" of the individual

members of society' or 'whether Communism might or might not be suitable', remain unexamined.

According to atomistic conceptions, it is best to focus on empirical facts – what is 'now' – and leave philosophy and political theory to mystics. All that matters is that even conservatives have said that a State must change. Prudence, after all, is merely a passion which is not nearly so compelling as an organism or so specific as a 'right': conservatives are indeed too vague in their insistence on 'prudence' as the first of all virtues. Burke's definition of law as 'beneficence acting by rule'[17] (a distinctly utilitarian definition) is seen as a nineteenth-century liberalism which current 'atomism' has superseded: it is 'rights' that matter. Rights are 'scientific' – even under relativism – because they are atomistic. Thus contemporary opponents of the conservatives assert that the latter do not understand the 'scientific' attitude towards the Burkean maxim about change and the concept of the State. They profess that the 'radical' or atomistic view claims 'rights' to be elemental and the 'conservative' view of the State to have been outmoded by 'science'. In short, Burke 'did not know' what he was talking about and his 'wrong' interpretation of the historical facts about the French Revolution 'proves it'.

THE CONSERVATIVE VIEW OF 'RIGHTS'

The question of rights and their role in the 'good state' to which Burke addressed himself remains today one of the central ethical questions facing political theory. In Burke's day, the revolutionaries who justified opposition to the State in the name of 'human rights', used some kind of natural law theory and 'reason' to support their views but were opposed by Burke on the grounds that the rights 'in proportion as they are metaphysically true . . . are morally and politically false'.[18] Thus Burke did not attack the postulated rights but the way they were applied politically. His stance, which remains the conservative position, allows a corollary: the less one is responsible for maintaining moral and political truth, the more rights one can propose. Thus far from being a set of minimum requirements for social and political life, the UN Universal Declaration of Human Rights goes far beyond the rights found in any State. 'Idealists', of course, can come up with even longer lists and frequently do so.

The present emphasis on 'rights' seems curious when taken in conjunction with the widespread acceptance of relativism. Why should anyone familiar with the relativist position want to enshrine certain norms in a legal document and so transform these norms into artificial absolutes binding on the very State that enforces them?

The intellectual situation in Burke's day may throw some light on the question. Then, as now, the Church – the traditional source of ethical authority – was in hopeless disarray. Intellectuals – the kind of persons who spoke of 'rights' – did not as a rule look any more to the Church for guidance although the Church had traditionally exercised some restraint on the absoluteness of sovereigns. It was not that intellectuals desired absolute 'freedom' from the 'arbitrary', including arbitrary ethics. The moral and political issue then (as it is again now) was that men no longer have a concept of ethical authority and no conceivable way of getting one, though they have ways of arriving at political authority. But we must have some concept of right and wrong. Only non-intellectuals think relativism means that there is no such thing as right and wrong in any meaningful sense. The intellectual's view of relativism implies an absence of ethical authority. 'Rights' are what remains politically when ethical authority has vanished.

The problem is that the 'rights' do not function in the absence of an ethical authority capable of systematizing rights and responsible for ultimate decisions: 'in proportion as they are metaphysically true' they are 'morally and politically false'. A list of rights is as useless as a list of sins. It is not true that human beings disagree about the content of normative lists: we disagree about the way we systematize them. Is abortion 'murder' or is it merely 'birth control'? Is the prohibition against cruelty a notch higher or a notch lower than the prohibition against murder in a normative hierarchy (the question of euthanasia)? Most of us are agreed on what should be on the list, but we are not agreed on how to systematize the normative items because we cannot imagine how to arrive at an ethical authority capable of doing so. What we need is a theory of ethical sovereignty parallel to that of political sovereignty.

Burke, of course, did not supply one: no political philosopher ever did. What he did was to argue that in the absence of ethical authority: first, the 'law' should be considered as – and judged in the light of – 'beneficence acting by rule'; and second, the sovereign power itself, in deciding what 'beneficence' is, should use what in effect are utilitarian standards: 'Political reason is a computing principle'.[19] In other words, Burke was definitely not arguing for submission to the decrees of the sovereign no matter what was decreed; nor that the sovereign power always knows best; nor (as many have maintained) that tradition must be upheld at all costs. To Burke, 'rights' are meaningful: the citizen can question the 'beneficence' of the sovereign power in their light. What he cannot do is argue that any particular instance of violation of the rights is *ipso facto* proof of a lack of 'beneficence'.

According to Burke, it is impossible to decide moral and political issues in terms of any single rule. What matters is the 'computing principle' which constitutes 'political reason'. In the absence of ethical authority we are forced to put our trust in the latter. If 'political reason' – or even our trust in it – breaks down, we are doomed. In Burke's day it was merely trust that was breaking down. In our day, under the onslaught of a revived interest in 'rights', political reason is on the wane. It disturbs the modern conservative that democracies are now in an even worse plight that the eighteenth-century monarchies were.

BURKE: FREEDOM, RIGHTS AND LIBERAL ROMANTICISM

The difficulty in giving due weight in our time to what

Burke said about 'freedom' and 'rights' is that he was an orator as well as a philosopher. Traditionally, only sophists have employed rhetoric as part of their resources. Burke's style weighs against him, and his very success – the peroration of his speech on the impeachment of Warren Hastings was once part of standard English courses – has made him seem especially reprehensible to an age which values 'objectivity' and has no real place for grace in respect to style (or anything else, for that matter).

To be sure, Burke's opponents also used rhetoric – but defended its use in terms of apprehending reality and disseminating truth. Preoccupied with 'freedom' and 'rights' as they were, the Romantics argued that rhetoric and imagination are the prerogative of poets: anyone else who employs them – the sophists of yesterday and advertisers of today – must be trying to deceive rather than enlighten.

The point that Burke, although a very strong opponent of the 'unexamined existence' characteristic of Romanticism, was himself part of the general trend in the Romantic movement – a trend evident in the late eighteenth century – has already been made by a biographer of Burke, Sir Philip Magnus. He defended the 'bunkum and romantic nonsense' of the passage in the *Reflections* that extolled Marie Antoinette by observing that it 'marks almost such a landmark in English prose as the publication by Wordsworth and Coleridge of *Lyrical Ballads* in 1797 is generally said to do in our poetry: the Romantic movement in English literature had begun'.[20] Yet the passage defended by Magnus in terms of Romanticism is an example of tawdry formal rhetoric, far beneath Burke's usual practice and not necessarily characteristic of the movement. To focus on the stylistic features of Romanticism would be to miss the point. The issue between Burke and the Romantics which also separates him from many of our contemporaries, is the Romanticist conception of 'freedom' in terms of human desire and the attitude to society and government seen as an unwarranted infringement on that 'natural' freedom.

When Burke asserts that 'government is a contrivance

of human wisdom to provide for human wants', Romantics listen, albeit unwillingly. They have heard the argument before and reject it as the self-serving opinion of those who have a vested interest in the status quo. But when Burke goes on to say that among the 'wants' provided for is 'restraint upon their passions', Romantics (and their modern descendants) simply laugh. They see Burke as contradicting himself: We want 'freedom', they say, not restraints, and there is no conceivable way of legitimately representing a desire for 'freedom' as a desire for restraint. Thus words are rhetorically twisted and their sense confused.

Psychoanalysis – perhaps the most widely used modern ethico-psychological system – rests on a similar view. It assumes that there is a conflict between the requirements of the 'superego' (the product for the most part of civilisation) and the 'id' (our primitive biological being). What is implied by 'maladjustment' provides empirical evidence that Burke is wrong to assert that restraint can be found among our 'wants'. Although there is a popular notion that the psychoanalytic view is in some way 'scientific', it derives from the Romanticist belief that we need neither society nor government. A further derivative is the concept of a 'natural' or basic definition of 'freedom' as an expression of the desire to fulfil our desires unimpeded by anything. In this light, Burke's ideas are labelled 'wrong': his wrongness is presented as reflecting a defence of vested interests that ever since his day has been called 'conservatism', an ideology set in opposition to liberal Romanticism (now just plain liberalism).

The fact that all domesticated species except man can be found in a feral state – that is, are known to be able to survive in the wild – provides evidence against the Romanticist notion that once past infancy we can rely on our biological nature to supply the information needed for survival – as well as all about the 'good' – and therefore need no help from society. (The enduring attraction of the Tarzan stories is an indication that many people feel that it is perfectly possible to live outside society and benefit from the experience, provided one is fortunate enough to meet with either a motherly ape, as baby Tarzan did, or a good-natured she-wolf, as did Romulus and Remus.) But when conceiving 'freedom' in terms of a hypothetical psychological condition in which the individual is unaffected by societal notions of good and bad, the Romanticist was not going by what common sense, reason or empirical evidence showed. English Romantics, for instance, did not attempt to provide evidence for their idea of freedom: the notion was basically a reaction to something they disliked within their own society rather than a reasoned proposition. The culprit was the mechanistic view which seventeenth- and eighteenth-century science put forward as the finest product of reason. It had no place for love, poetry, religion, beauty or compassion, but seemed able to make so strong a case for itself that it could only be rejected out of hand by those who felt in their very core that mechanism was wrong. Against 'reason' one erects 'imagination' and 'feeling'.

What is conjured up in this situation is the age-old dispute between the relative claims of 'intuition' as opposed to 'analysis' as a source of truth, a dispute in which the political issues of 'government' and 'freedom' do not really belong. The Romantics, however, did not think so – and still do not. They saw themselves as opposing the concepts of authority and authoritarianism put forward in the guise of government and social order; they were ready to define 'freedom' with reference to their intuitive feeling that their right to independence and individuality was threatened. To desire restraint on desire, as Burke said? Sophistry!

Burke's view is an expansion of Hobbes's conception of man as having in a state of nature such a plethora of desires that no community is viable without some constraint put on its members. The issue of happiness – what we really want when we have an indefinite number of wants – is put aside by Hobbes as he attends to the issue of constraint and its necessity to community and develops his theory of sovereignty. To Burke, the issue was central, for it was being used by the Romantics to define 'freedom': we want to satisfy our desires, they said, and we do not want *any* constraint, even if the consequences are a threat to the community. This is an extreme Romanticist position. Following Mill's *modus vivendi* conception of freedom, most modern liberals accept restraints that are necessary to community. Few, if any, however, accept Burke's view that we not only want the constraint Hobbes argued for but also a constraint on our very desires. Would Hobbes have ever argued, as Burke does, that 'the inclinations of men should frequently be thwarted, their will controlled and their passions brought into subjection . . . by a power out of themselves'?[21]

We need to remember that Burke is not arguing that for our own good our passions need to be restrained. Many have argued for this view: all hedonist theorists offer variations on it. Burke goes much further. He argues that this is what we want, rather than what someone else thinks is good for us. He also puts the issue in a way that must raise the hackles of every romantic liberal: 'the restraints on men, as well as their liberties, are to be reckoned among their rights'.[22] This statement is clearly meant to dumbfound the opposition.

It is interesting that the UN Universal Declaration of Human Rights seems to agree with Burke. Thus, Article 26 contains a compulsory right – the right to education. Although one suspects that there are a number of other rights in general usage – for example, the compulsory right to be free of certain diseases, such as smallpox – the point is that our conception of freedom being what it is, most people greet the idea of compulsory rights with incredulity. Most insist that by definition 'freedom' entails the absence of constraint; some even argue for the absence of influence: never advise or act as mentor to anyone since it could reduce his 'freedom'.

The ramifications of Burke's position on freedom – his advancing so far beyond Hobbes in the name of freedom rather than security – cannot be explored here, though we might note that if it is true that we do desire restraints on our desires, then certain psychological problems in regard to the social contract vanish. Thus, if one of our desires is the curtailment of our desires, the view that the contract considered as historical must have occurred during a fleeting moment in time when reason out-weighed passion, is no longer a telling objection. In fact, it is only the Romanticist conception of 'freedom' that has made the social contract seem psychologically improbable. If we do not have to believe in that conception, we are freer to believe in the contract.

The main political issues today, however, concern rights rather than contractualism. We begin with government as a premise of our existence – accept the contract, in effect – but challenge the actual process of government in terms of 'rights', which we seemingly multiply in accordance with our desires (rather than arrive at them by a process of analysis). It is clear from the 'activism' associated with modern conceptions of rights – as based on a hypothetic 'right' to coerce even a democratic government – that 'rights' and action in their support have virtually re-placed discussions of liberty. This decidedly anti-intel-lectual development reflects precisely the Romanticist indifference to self-analysis and reflection on the human condition, the indifference to which Burke was so op-posed. Talk of 'rights' rather than 'freedom' or 'liberty' allows a focusing on action as opposed to intellect and makes an organized response by government very dif-ficult. It is much easier to give in to demonstrations in support of women's rights, native rights or prisoners' rights since as a rule no genuine intellectual or rational challenge has been issued. Consequently, the govern-ment can either use the police to break up the demon-stration and appear undemocratic (because such be-haviour on the part of authority violates the rights of freedom of speech and peaceful assembly) or yield to the demands, no matter how unfair. Thus our society faces dilemmas about 'liberty' with regard to what are special interest groups that no definition of democracy requires the government to grapple with, but which cannot be ignored when 'freedom' has been defined as linked to desire – and when desire is obviously present.

There are also implications for political theory. The issue here is a mistaken concept of freedom as a 'natural' desire to fulfil one's desires. The idea that we are not free when the government yields to our demands if those demands cannot be fitted into a rational framework – some concept of 'justice' rather than 'desire' – completely alters the image of democracy as 'rule' (or desires) of the people. It requires the current thinking on rights to be reappraised in more traditional terms.

Ultimately the question is whether one regards democracy as an ideology – an expression or realization of norms – or as anti-normative, with 'rights' considered milestones on the road to relativism, even though they draw on natural law tradition and seem objective rather than subjective.

Burke opposed a concept of rights that is subjective (and as such an attack on tradition); he also opposed democracy when it is represented as a denial of the need for authority and tradition. The two go together: a false concept of democracy (democracy as anarchism) gives a false concept of rights (rights as desire); a false concept of rights (as self-interest and consequently factionalism of social units) gives a false concept of democracy (as factionalized interest groups). It is the latter view that some of the modern readers of Burke uphold and which is used against them as illustrating their 'denial' of rights. Burke himself insisted that he did not deny the concept of rights but rather was among its foremost supporters. What he objected to – what modern conservatives also object to – is the use of 'rights' as a reference to individual desires. The term 'rights' is essentially political. It must not be confused with questions of 'right'. 'Right' and 'wrong' exist apart from society. 'Rights' presuppose a political order and must be treated within its framework.

WHAT CONSERVATIVES TRY TO CONSERVE

The problem in understanding Burke is that of understanding conservatives and conservatism in general: what is a conservative trying to conserve?

The hostile answer is 'the status quo'. Although undoubtedly there are people whose 'conservatism' is indeed a resistance to change, Burke's conservatism is of a different kind. He claims that 'Liberties and the restrictions vary with times and circumstances and . . . cannot be settled upon any abstract rule'.[23] Although this may sound like relativism, Burke's views – and those of conservatism in general are decidedly not relativistic. They rest on the assumption that there is something worth conserving: the body of information about human relations set forth in the law. Burke, like other conservatives, rejects the idea that mankind would be better off if, somehow, we were 'free' to do as we please within, say, the *modus vivendi* limits that Mill acknowledged as necessary to a communal life.

Both liberalism and conservatism are not mere names of factions within a democratic ideology but constitute fundamental propositions that make liberal and conservative minds recognizable even when we are not talking about political matters. Burke is a 'conservative' because his arguments rest on the proposition that society and government are not mere conveniences but are essential to human existence. This is why he asserts that 'men have no right to what is not reasonable and to what is not for their benefit'[24] and is scornful of the liberal argument that we all have the right to go to hell in our own way. Like conservatives in general Burke holds that human beings simply would not exist if they had some natural right to ignore commonsense.

The liberal perspective, on the other hand, is basically the Romantic view of society and government as an infringement on natural freedom. As such, liberalism is fundamentally negative, even though it is not anti-social. It wants to get rid of, or at least lessen, the force of the very institutions – law and tradition – that the conservative values. Democracy serves to hold the liberal and conservative tradition in a dynamic equilibrium: it prevents liberals from being revolutionaries of the kind Burke opposed; and it precludes conservatives from becoming radical.

Chapter 7

The nature of government

FROM A PRAGMATIC TO A PRINCIPLE-ORIENTED GOVERNMENT

An absence of principle is an absence of direction. We accept this view easily with regard to the individual; when we do not call those without principle 'unprincipled', we call them 'drifters', or – more sympathetically – 'happy-go-lucky.' Although we resist the idea that a government that lacks principle might be 'happy-go-lucky', we hide this meaning from ourselves by calling such a government 'pragmatic', as if this were a practical and commonsense way for a government to be.

Why are the consequences of a lack of principle in government usually ignored nowadays in the sense that societies refuse to face them? The answer is provided by the question: how could a government of principle govern democratically in a multi-cultured society with conflicting systems of values? Whose principles will be followed? In a democratic State, the device of 'party platforms' is used in the hope of solving the problem, but the device evades the real issue. Governments which base policy on party platforms are nonetheless drifting.

All democratic political parties have platforms which reputedly allow the public to make a choice and thus obtain a government that will carry out their will. Incidentally, empirical studies can demonstrate that this is not exactly the case. But the crux of the matter lies elsewhere. The real problem with party platforms as an expression of 'principle' is that at most they express desires of the kind that motivate the happy-go-lucky, are designed to appeal to desires, not interests, and change from election to election, as particular issues attract attention.

The problem with attempting to make any other kind of appeal is that for some two centuries our basic assumption about human nature has been that man is not a rational being, but rather acts on the same type of motivation as all other animals. (If this were in fact so, we would be unable to distinguish the happy-go-lucky from other people, the principled from the unprincipled, etc.)

It is an article of democratic faith that accepting the irrationalist view of man is the only way to avoid imposing norms on a society which has a great many conflicting norms. To appeal to popular desires and avoid the question of norms is tantamount to being 'democratic'. 'Platforms' do this and statements of principle do not: a party with principle must be labelled undemocratic.

This, of course, poses a problem for people of principle, who appear to be in the majority. For whom are they going to vote? If the issue were just a matter of having a normative order, most voters would be satisfied with the argument that a democratic government must respect the norms of the community – not take a stand about which are better or best. The issue is that a government is not really governing if it operates pragmatically, for this is the happy-go-lucky attitude of the drifter. No one wants such a government.

In what way can a conservative government be principle-oriented? There are two ways for the conservatives to approach the problem. One is to include a demand for less government in the party platform. When such conservatives attain power, however, they discover that they really cannot do much about the size of government. Many of the government agencies which they had thought could be dispensed with, are found to have a necessary function.

The other approach is to accept as a matter of principle that no government should try to act as a 'prudential factor' in human affairs. To follow the latter (to assume that the government must play a prudential role) is ethically wrong. It strikes at the heart of the ethical behaviour which makes us consider the consequences of our actions. If we do not do that, if – like children – we are irresponsible, someone has to look after us. This is what some people expect of a 'responsible' government. But according to the conservative view, to expect such action from the government tends to produce the opposite result. In short, it is morally wrong – unprincipled – for a government to allow itself to be called 'responsible' when, in fact, it encourages irresponsibility in the community.

However, as conservative governments have discovered, it is difficult for a responsible government to dismantle the body of regulations created by democratic authorities to replace the prudential factor which is now lacking in individual behaviour. 'Desire' theory has operated for so long that many people in our society do not know how to act prudently. To abandon the legislation designed to replace prudence would mean to bring in chaos. What a conservative government can do is to attack those theories of ethics – comprised under the term 'relativism' – which encourage the happy-go-lucky approach to life, e.g. naïve ethical views based on unenlightened hedonism.

This is not tantamount to projecting a dogmatic ideology. A government which attacks the views which prevent ethical analysis performs a function similar to that ascribed to it by Hobbes – of providing the conditions for normative behaviour. This is essentially what a 'minimum' government is.

The importance of this consideration to conservatism is that at one stroke the problem of drift is removed from government. We worry about the lack of direction from government because we have come to expect the administration to give direction to a society that is drifting. So many decisions have now been assigned to government – which we as individuals ought to be making – that no government can cope with them systematically. Democratic governments drift with the tide of events because democratic societies do likewise.

AUTHORITY, PROGRESS AND THE RETURN TO FIRST PRINCIPLES

Ever since the Greeks classified 'government' into types, one of which was 'tyranny', the history of civilization has been split into 'East' and 'West' with the West moving in the direction of what we call 'progress' and the East reflecting flux and change. (To the Asians, the latter was so inconsequential that they made no serious effort to record it.) Government in the East was as a rule whimsical: what happened depended on the chance factors that determined the ruler's personality – not on some concept of 'authority'. Without a clear way of defining the responsible exercise of power, history simply repeated itself and the day came when the backward and primitive Europeans caught up with and surpassed the Asians. At the time of European 'imperialist' expansion into Asia, we found the civilizations there in what appeared to be the same state as in the days of Alexander of Macedon.

The fact that the direction we imposed on change – the one we call 'progress' – and the concept we used to achieve it – 'authority' – are now both considered arbitrary and scientifically indefensible concepts, may suggest that the day of Western civilization has now passed and that 'tyranny', Oriental despotism and historical stagnation are what we can expect if we do not return to first principles.

At present, only the 'conservative' appears to believe that there are any such principles and that they are necessary to directional change – progress. Most people, however – and some of them call themselves 'conservative' – think that uniting 'conservatism' and 'progress' is a verbal trick designed to make conservative resistance to change palatable to those who value change. The conservative objects only to directionless change and arbitrariness. In order to make his position clear we need to return to the concept of tyranny and its relation to 'authority'.

The question of when authority is tyranny and when it is not has been investigated by political thinkers since the rise of modern democracy. It determines party allegiance within democratic society and may even cause one to abandon democratic ideology altogether and opt for a different conception of government.

Outside the Greek tradition of reason – which in practice, until recently, meant beyond the influence of Christianity (which incorporated Greek thought into the Hebraic-based theology) – there was no conception of legitimacy. A sovereign could be recognized as having personal characteristics that made his reign disastrous, but there was no conceptual basis, no institutional structure and no political tradition for mounting an effective opposition. Asians responded 'fatalistically' to what we would call tyrannical régimes; they had no way of defining a government as tyrannical. The presence of a sovereign power constituted government – which ended the matter.

Instead of beginning, as in the Western tradition, with a concept of authority (which has 'obedience' as its correlative), the Asian tradition begins with 'obedience' or submission and leaves to fate or chance the nature of the 'authority' one is required to obey. (The same principle applied wherever what we call 'authority' existed, as in the family. There were no restrictions on the power of a father over the members of his family. He had absolute power stemming from the norm of 'obedience'.) One could only hope for the best and resign oneself to the worst. The norm that one began with did not allow anything else.

If this view of the relation between 'obedience' and 'authority' were confined to old Asia (modern Asia has now absorbed a good deal of Western tradition) there would be little reason for mentioning it at all. But it was also a part of pre-Christian European tradition; moreover, when the Hebraic element is stressed more heavily than the Greek element in Christianity, it becomes a part of the Christian tradition as well.

A great many people who profess to be 'conservatives' and 'fundamentalist' Christians derive their idea of authority from the norm of obedience. Quite correctly, they argue that obedience – or submission to authority – is essential to a normative order. They do not realize that as they begin with obedience rather than authority, they undermine the concept of law and order which they think they are upholding. Their essential irrationalism can be seen in the emphasis they place on the coercive factor when fostering obedience. To them, application of the tag 'Spare the rod and spoil the child' promotes obedience, which promotes respect for 'authority', which in turn promotes law and order. Yet Western political theory defines 'authority' in such a way that coercion is usually unnecessary: it is reserved for periods (childhood) and personalities (irrationalists and egoists) who do not believe in the rational tradition. 'Conservatives' who emphasize coercion are certainly not conserving our central tradition but something essentially alien.

'Progressive' Conservatives think that the future of civilization depends on such clarification. To them, an emphasis on coerced obedience entails the legitimation of 'tyranny' which, in the nationalist tradition, is defined as an illegitimate form of government. A 'tyrant', specifically, is someone who exercises authority without respect for its function of supplying the conditions for a normative order. A tyrant treats his power – which is the result of his having authority – as a piece of good fortune or the acknowledgement of a natural superiority which enables him to exercise his will effortlessly and fulfil his desires. He is an egoistic hedonist. A society which endorses a philosophy like this is likely to fall victim to government by 'tyrants'. Such a society has no real future, for it has no direction. No matter how its government is arrived at – whether by hereditary rule or an electoral system – it will not progress but will merely adapt to conditions as they arise. 'Progressive' Conservatives think that current attitudes to norms and authority presage a bleak future for civilization. They also believe that to speak of 'liberty' and 'democracy' is not a defence, nor speaking of 'law and order' a solution.

CONSERVATISM AND MAN'S INNER LIFE

Although many conservatives are likely to disagree with George Will on specifics of government policy for a democratic government, all will agree with the fundamental thesis of his *Statecraft as Soulcraft* (1983). What matters according to him is the inner life of man – a repudiation of Justice Frankfurter's view that 'the law is concerned with external behaviour, not the inner life of man'.[25]

In one sense, of course, Frankfurter is right: the law is not concerned with the inner life of man because it does not know what is going on inside him, nor would it know how to influence him even if it did. Furthermore, even if it did know and could influence him, the fundamental principle of the separation of Church and State would still require a democratic State to avoid legislating on such matters.

Both liberals and conservatives agree on this issue. They are also agreed that, in another sense, the law is very much concerned with the inner life of man: 'intention' – not just consequences (external behaviour) – has always been central to our conception of justice. At this point, however, initiated by the liberal-utilitarian tradition, a parting of the ways between liberal and conservative thinking begins.

Utilitarianism was at first welcomed by both Whigs and Tories (the names then given to the liberals and conservatives respectively) for it was the first – or so it seemed – political philosophy that supplied a domestic policy consistent with the separation of Church and State. Until then, differences in successive democratic governments were mainly characterized by variations in foreign policy. Hence historians are quite justified in discussing pre-Victorian government exclusively in terms of war and domestic policy with reference to the financing of wars. Utilitarianism made it possible to speak of genuine domestic policy.

Utilitarianism, however, seems only to have maintained the separation of Church and State by refusing to enforce traditional religious conceptions of good and bad. (Or, if one thinks of the principle of the separation of Church and State in terms of the tolerance by the State of differences in ethical views, Utilitarianism introduced an illusion of a continuing separation.) It brought in a new ethical system based on hedonism. As this became apparent to its opponents, who rejected such a philosophy, the distinction between liberals and conservatives began to take shape. Conservative resistance to innovations in ethical conceptions supplied the common view that conservatives were opposed to change; their insistence on 'morality' as hitherto conceived suggested that 'conservatives' were especially religious. No definite ideology, however, that can be called conservatism developed until liberal Utilitarianism began to incorporate conceptions of materialist determinism under the influence of Marxist theory. It is the rejection of this combination that now characterizes the conservative.

Materialist determination of values does not follow from Utilitarianism. It will not be found in Bentham or Mill, who were primarily interested in promoting conditions conducive to the greatest happiness of the greatest number. But since it is the *conditions* for this that are promoted, the view that all conceptions of the good are based on material conditions is congenial to a utilitarian: it supplies an argument against the conservative opponents of utilitarian-based government policies. Conservatives are thus defined as having a vested interest in the *status quo*; their arguments based on the violation of 'liberty' or any other normative view are reflections of vested interests.

Such a high-handed dismissal of the significance of what goes on in the human mind is entirely unacceptable to conservatives. Hence their rejection of the liberal view that one should make changes in social conditions not for the sake of 'justice' or 'happiness', but in the expectation that social problems will be thereby solved. The conservatives believe that solutions to social problems – essentially derived from faulty ethical views – cannot be found in manipulation of the environment.

Certainly, says the conservative, let us supply decent living conditions for all – as through slum clearance programmes – but let us not suppose that slums have much to do with being a criminal. Poverty and crime are not necessarily related. If the immediate social problem is crime in the streets, to reduce expenditure on city police in order to increase spending on housing and slum clearance is tantamount to misdirection of our efforts. Such a policy has not worked: the evidence is unequivocal. Yet governments keep on doing it, they keep on increasing welfare payments so that all citizens will approach a middle-class income. In consequence, according to the present liberal-determinist view, all will acquire middle-class ethics. But such thinking is wrong, the conservative avers: it is not middle-class living standards that create middle-class ethics but *vice versa*. The evidence can be found in the history of the rise of a middle class. It developed from the poor who acquired a middle-class income by means of thrift, temperance and industry. One cannot acquire such virtues by being given money.

Liberals reject this view as being an argument for indifference to the fate of the poor. They point out that thrift, temperance and industry have not improved the lot of most of the world's poor; they explain that the poor may all have these virtues simply because they cannot afford to do anything else. But this argument is an evasion of what the conservative is arguing for and against. The uncharitable view that the poor are responsible for their own condition is nineteenth-century *laissez-faireism* characteristic of Victorian liberals, not modern conservatives, who have no objection to improving the lot of anyone but who object to the liberal assumption that ameliorating material conditions somehow enhances the inner life of man. To the conservative, liberalism today is the assertion that man has no significant inner being, no genuine individuality, but as a creature of his environment can be 'improved' by changing the social conditions under which he is brought up. Traditional liberalism is being abandoned for an alien ideology that has broken with customary Western conceptions of man's nature. Thus, in many respects, the modern conservative resembles a pre-twentieth century liberal; but this is so because liberals have repudiated the beliefs they once shared with conservatives. Reluctance to change with the times, incidentally (usually imputed to conservatives), has nothing to do with their position in this matter. This reluctance is based on known facts about the relation between the 'inner life' of man and his behaviour. Despite what Frankfurter said, it does matter what the law's views on this question are.

THE DILEMMA OF CONSERVATISM

The resistance of the political conservative to being identified with people opposed to change raises the question of the conservative attitude to the thinking that produces such identification. The matter is that of the conservative attitude to associationist psychology[26] and the empiricist tradition with which it is linked. To what extent can the conservative be thought of as holding to the older tradition that human thought is characterized by 'logic', not the chance associations that Pavlov reputedly demonstrated as characteristic of animals? If the conservative can be so characterized, we have an explanation of the very strong objection of conservatives to views about the materialist determination of behaviour, whether Marxist or not.

The conservative does not believe that it is the government's duty to manipulate the human environment so as to improve man's morals. He does not believe that human character is determined by environment. To him, over-extended welfare schemes waste money and enlarge the powers of government until a point is reached where it no longer makes sense to distinguish between a democratic and a totalitarian system.

Let us return to Pavlov, who was the first to subject associationist psychology to experimental methodology. Ever since the empiricists rejected rationalism, most people had simply made the same assumption as empiricists – that associationist psychology is a self-evident truth; consequently, that our notions of cause–effect, or good and bad are simply associations of ideas arrived at by chance experience. In his conditioned response experiments, Pavlov tested the theory by eliminating the chance factor. What did he discover? A view seems to prevail that he found associationist theory to be correct, but this is not so. It is not true that all dogs can be conditioned: only 'obedient' dogs, those willing to be conditioned, can be. But this should hardly come as a surprise. Everyone familiar with the training of animals and the education of humans knows that it matters whether the subject is willing to cooperate. Thus it is almost impossible to train cats to do anything, not because they are stupid but because they do not care what human beings want. Dogs are in general much more willing to please and are therefore readily conditioned; however, as Pavlov discovered, some of them display the same independent spirit as cats and cannot be conditioned. In the behaviour of higher animals, there is an element of will, willingness and wilfulness that throws grave doubt on associationist theory.

If this were not what Pavlov discovered, his experiments would have little bearing on human behaviour. If he had discovered that associationist theory is correct, we would be confronted by an insoluble mystery: what is the point of human intelligence? If human beings and all other animals are simply conditioned by chance experiences, why does our species need so large a brain? How did it evolve and what functions does it serve? Indeed, under associationist psychology, the evolution of the massive human brain would be disadvantageous. The greater memory it permits would make us less and less able to cope with reality as past experiences accumulated. It would have so 'conditioned' us that we would no longer be able to respond to current circumstances. Far from being the most adaptable of species, we would be the most rigid and 'unrealistic' of all animals.

It can hardly be argued of course that conservatives have necessarily read through and reflected on Pavlov. Nevertheless it can be said that they reject the associationist theory that he was testing, for associationism implies that what we call logic is an artificial system; what we call morals are chance associations; and what is important in matters of government is the attention it gives to improving the human environment. Thus to some conservatives nowadays it may be difficult to distinguish between democratic political parties because in practice the latter hold to the irrationalist position of associationist psychology. In a sense, then, political conservatives, when rejecting as 'undemocratic' all government policy based on the assumption of materialist determination, behave in an 'ultra-conservative' way: they hold an eighteenth-century view of 'reason'.

The problem of a conservative is to define his position in an intelligible way. What is conservative policy on the role of government? Conservatives speak of a return to traditional values, the need for law and order and a reduction in government powers – but how can such views be translated into specific policies? How can a democratic government urge a return to traditional values when everything in a democratic society seems to point in the opposite direction? The difficulties in devising a programme suitable for a conservative party are very serious indeed.

When analysing the conservative position one may in effect be arguing that a genuine conservative party is not possible. Such a view is close to Scruton's assertion (arrived at from a different angle) that 'there is no general politics of conservatism' and that 'The forms of conservatism will be as varied as the forms of the social order'.[27] This view, however, differs from his second 'axiom' that conservatism engages with the surface of things, unless we speak of the manifestations of conservatism in party allegiance, the attempt of the conservative to make his presence felt in the community. No doubt responsible conservatives feel this to be part of their duty, but when they try to make their presence felt, they also feel they are not really attending to fundamental issues: they are engaged with 'the surface of things'. 'Real' conservatism is much deeper than conservative politics.

Empty liberalism

Chapter 8

The liberal tradition

AUTHORITY, AUTHORITARIANISM AND SCEPTICISM

Political theory is distinguished from philosophy by the limitations not of its subject-matter but of its possible ethical positions. Just as what we call science cannot adopt Berkeley's idealism and still remain science, so political theory – no matter how sceptical of claims to authority – cannot adopt relativism or anarchism of any kind and remain political theory. The ethical philosopher's concept of 'freedom' is excluded because the political philosopher (political theorist) is dealing with man in society, not man in relation to the cosmos. No one, unless he is willing to make completely unwarranted assumptions about human nature, can escape the theorist's view that when speaking about man in society we must begin with the concept of authority, rather than freedom. When the political theorist deals with 'liberty', a term he might well insist is peculiar to his field, the meaning he assigns to it and the justification for it which he advances must be made consistent with facts related to sovereignty and authority.

The political theorist's premise is not simply an assumption, as in the case of the premises of empiricism and causality in science, but rests on contractualism. Those who are hostile to political theory invariably represent the latter as mere legalistic casuistry. Yet social contract arguments are not legalistic: they do not begin with

'Given a contract' or 'Here is the evidence that a contract exists, even though no one can produce the document'. All legalism that can be imputed derives from statements like 'Given the cogency of the argument that man is not law-abiding by nature but needs to be in order to coexist with his fellows'.

The 'authority' in contract theory is usually a 'supreme authority' or sovereign power. It is essentially different from what emerges from psychological theories of dominance-submission or aggression-coercion which attempt to explain social order without introducing the concept of authority in any meaningful sense. Theories of this type are popular because they allow one to think of 'freedom' in egoistic terms. It is precisely the consciousness of inescapable egoism that makes the political theorist adamant about contractualism. With this in mind, let us examine the question of the bearing of J.S. Mill's essay *On Liberty* (1859) on political theory.

What the modern political theorist would like to derive from Mill is a supplement to Hobbes. Under Hobbesian theory, there is no real way for the citizen to be critical of the sovereign's performance: the citizen not only has to submit to authority but in effect has to become an authoritarian himself. He has to accept and promote the 'authority' of the sovereign, even when the sovereign is tyrannical. Hobbes failed to define the difference between 'sovereignty' and 'tyranny'; what was needed was a clear-cut way of knowing when the sovereign was tyrannical. Mill's solution was to extend the scepticism about the validity of knowledge to the sovereign's commands and the influence of society. We need arguments against authoritarianism based on the view that the acknowledgement of authority by a moral and law-abiding citizen implies that he believes in the moral nature of the social and political authority. Mill's essay *On Liberty* is a classic in its presentation of these objections. But, the political theorist would ask, what about authority itself? Mill repeatedly refers to the need for authority.

At times, he does so in a way that would curl the hair of modern liberals, as when he states that a certain level of civilisation and individual development is necessary before one can begin speaking of 'freedom'. Nowhere does he reconcile his admission of the need for authority with his criticism of authoritarianism.

One obvious beginning would be to argue that the authority of the sovereign power is limited to the function it serves, and that acknowledgement of that function, though it entails obedience, does not entail the assumption that the sovereign power is right. Authoritarianism and obedience are totally different concepts. Mill set out to attack public authoritarianism and its exultation over mindless obedience, and to expose its dangers, without even raising the question of any actual relation between authoritarianism and respect for authority.

There is something peculiarly naïve in the 'ought' element of Mill's arguments that conventional views of right and wrong should not be used to coerce people into conformity and that the individual ought to resist such pressures. Questions arise as to how such a psychological change can be brought about and whether it really is something to be advocated even if one could imagine a way of inducing it. What happens to 'authority' if people stop being 'authoritarian'? Since Mill's conception of 'liberty' is a psychological change presented in the form of an 'ought', let us look at contractualism in terms of psychology.

All contractual theory is based on the hypothesis of 'prudence' as a factor in normal adult behaviour. (Although men do not necessarily always act in their own interest, their failure to do so is a frequent cause of regret.) Using the concept of psychology, rather than 'natural law', contractual theory rests on the view that men want to act in their own self-interest, know that they often do not, and accordingly acknowledge the 'authority' of someone or something that can make them conform to long-range self-interest rather than to immediate desire. Basically, then, the theory is an explanation of one aspect of human psychology – the fact that normal human beings do not feel unfree when they realize that some types of behaviour are not permitted, nor feel like this when on prudential grounds they themselves restrain an impulse. The coercive power of authority can operate only so long as human beings are prudent: the habitual criminal is not coercible because he is not prudent.

The problem with contractual theory based on psychology is that prudence clearly has to be taught. Children are not prudent by nature and have to be subjected to the authority of their parents – an authority that does not rest on a rational respect for authority as such, but on coercion and enforcement of obedience. The evidence is that if they are not subjected to the rational exercise of such authority (that is, if they are indulged, neglected or tyrannized), then as adults they neither behave prudently nor respect authority in the contractual sense. Instead, they develop a concept of 'freedom' which is tantamount to unenlightened hedonism. In the absence of initial rational authority, the type of prudence that is necessary to the concept of sovereignty apparently does not develop.

Mill's conception of liberty, being that of a philosopher working within a democratic framework, sought to include the concept of 'freedom' based on hedonism and on prudential theory. He began, like Hobbes, with the individual but made no assumptions about human nature. In keeping with the empiricist tradition, he accepted as a fact that some people are unenlightened hedonists and some are not; like the empiricists, he doubted whether one could make valid moral judgement about a given situation. He ended by being a sceptic who argued for the institutionalization of scepticism in the conception of 'liberty'. Could he have had the slightest inkling that a society which is prepared to follow him closely will inadvertently promote authoritarianism?

What is disturbing is that those who advocate freedom in an absolute sense – through anarchism, relativism or scepticism – ignore the fact that rules, and an authority that imposes them, serve a useful function. So long as the latter is fulfilled, it does not matter whether the rules are arbitrary or not. If, for instance, one discovers that keeping to the right on the roads is an arbitrary rule, then so long as one is satisfied that this rule has a function, nothing whatsoever has been established with regard to freedom. Nor has anything been revealed in regard to freedom by establishing that a particular person does not wish to observe the given rule.

The modern political theorist's idea of liberty implies an awareness of function rather than concern with 'arbitrariness'; his discussion of freedom is not based on an objection to the arbitrariness of rules and similar matters. Does an acknowledgement of such a position mean making a step towards authoritarianism an uncritical acceptance of the decrees of authority, and acceptance as 'authorities' of those who have no genuine claim to their position? Obviously not. There is no relation between recognizing the function of authority and being uncritical: the opposite is the case. Those who respect authority do so because they are aware of its function. They strongly object to the irrationalism of those who are so unanalytical, so preoccupied with an unimpeded fulfilment of their desires that they do not stop to think what will happen to them if they are allowed to follow such inclinations. They become true authoritarians. Authoritarianism arises from an inability to be critical. In a curious way Mill's scepticism (advocated as 'freedom') promotes it.

J.S. Mill's Scepticism

There are two kinds of liberals, neither of whom understands the other. First of all, there are those who think of 'liberty' as a good in itself and as an observable condition of State and society, ideally anarchist but in practice falling short of it. Then there are those who think of liberty as a means towards some other good. Mill belongs to the second group. In his case the good in question is 'truth' or 'knowledge', each of which is thought of as good because of its effect on man's condition as a member of society (as promoting 'progress'). In his view what mainly decides whether a State is liberal are the opportunities it offers for scepticism as a basis for action.

Is there any relation between the scepticism that Mill felt to be good for us and authoritarianism in the sense of a willing submission to what is regarded as 'authoritative', even though the latter may have no relation whatsoever to anything the political theorist calls 'authority'? This is a question for political theorists because of the obvious potential for authoritarianism of this kind to conflict with what is 'official' (defined as the position of legitimate political authority).

At this juncture, the liberal view that political authority should not have official views – that the liberal State should not be ideological – will not be examined. What will be discussed is the question the liberal philosopher raises of scepticism as a good, with an absence of it regarded as an indication of something 'illiberal'.

The question Mill's position raises is axiological: assuming scepticism is possible, is it good for us? Further, are we going to define a liberal State on the basis of the possibilities the State offers for acting in accordance with the principle of scepticism?

The first objection the political theorist must raise is that in the hands of amateurs, scepticism ceases to be a philosophic tool and becomes mistrust of authority. The latter is the natural posture of an egoist. On the assumption that everyone is an egoist, no one can be trusted. The teacher, for instance may say that education is an act of benevolence and the government may stoutly maintain that it does its best to promote the public good, but under an egoist assumption such affirmations are not to be trusted: they are acts of deception. Philosophic scepticism does not operate on this assumption at all (unless one equates it with cynicism); obviously only philosophers understand the very difficult epistemological questions on which it is based. Everyone else is apt to reduce it to cynicism and relativism which, if generally held, can make a liberal State unworkable.

Mill could be a sceptic and still respect authority but no adolescent can. The 'scepticism' of schoolchildren, which used to be called 'cheek', prevents them from getting a proper education where they think of teachers' pronouncements as 'propaganda', as in the once popular song 'Another Brick in the Wall'. A consequence of Mill's conception of liberty has been a mistrust of education, which to him was a primary goal, and a mistrust of 'authority' in general.

This mistrust, however, has not lessened the authoritarianism that so deeply troubled Mill. The trouble with scepticism, at least in non-philosophical hands, is that it supplies no methodology on which to base doubts. If one does not know how to analyse an assertion in terms of its external and internal consistency, one has no real way of recognizing truth. A person with such a limitation cannot fail to become an authoritarian of the kind Mill most deplored. People whose main interests do not call for the use of logical analysis – as in the case of many of those preoccupied with the arts – are particularly susceptible to the most transparent charlatanry in the realm of ideas. Cultists of various kinds draw on the 'arty-crafty' for their support. Many of the 'radical chic' come from their ranks. Such people have no idea that they are authoritarian. They take pride in being sceptics; but this means only that they reject orthodoxy of all kinds. This is not the result Mill hoped for from a liberal society.

MODUS VIVENDI ETHICS

Mill's discussion of freedom is an attempt to arrive at what can be called *modus vivendi* ethics. Unlike many liberals today, he uses the concept of freedom in conjunction with Utilitarianism to modify the tendency of that philosophy to sacrifice the individual to the interests of society. Mill defends 'liberty' as necessary to 'progress' – a utilitarian argument – and, having put forward this view, discusses Utilitarianism as if it meant the greatest good of the individual for the greatest number of individuals.

The problems confronting our society would be markedly different if Mill had kept to what he said in the first paragraph was the subject of his essay *On Liberty* – 'The nature and limits of the power which can be legitimately exercised by society over the individual'.[1] In the second paragraph he shifts to the view that there has been an historical 'struggle between liberty and authority'. Rather than seeing 'liberty' as some kind of restriction on the exercise of authority, he sets the two concepts against one another. This opposition of liberty to authority still characterizes liberal thinking.

By introducing the concept of the 'sovereign individual', Mill ensures that logically there has to be almost an irreconcilable conflict. Given this concept, submission to authority has to be voluntary and 'authority' loses the 'power of the sword' which advocates of the social contract have argued is essential to any meaningful concept of authority. What are the consequences for social relations of the interaction between 'sovereign individuals'?

In defining 'liberty' in terms of sovereign individuals interacting with one another, Mill recognized that these sovereign powers have to arrive at some kind of *modus vivendi*: some principles which they acknowledge as the minimum necessary for social life. In Mill's view, political theory deals with *modus vivendi* ethics and any attempt to go beyond such ethics infringes on liberty. He argues repeatedly that we can advise or exhort others when we feel they are not acting in their own interest or in accord with ethical principles: in a free society that is the most we can do.

Such a view limits our sense of responsibility to that behaviour of others that we can establish as affecting others adversely. Thus if someone wishes to commit suicide, as a 'sovereign individual' he has a right to do so. This view of human relations undermines the concept of fraternity. In what way does a community exist if it is none of our concern what happens to our fellow men so long as they do not injure us? Under such a view of 'freedom', how is it possible to foster even a sense of parental responsibility for children? If one argues, as Mill does, that those who beget children are necessarily required to nurture them, at what point can the individual assert he is now a sovereign being?

Before Mill, such questions were looked at from the

opposite point of view: at what point does the authority of parent over child stop and that of State over citizen begin? As such, it could be given a legal form; constitutions set limits on the authority of the State and law defined the age at which one could legitimately assert one's freedom from the authority of one's parents. If one begins, however, with 'freedom', despite the fact that as individuals human beings are biologically dependent – not free – there does not seem any logical way to set forth in law what is present from birth. If we begin with freedom, we no longer know how to demand it, whereas if we begin with the fact that we are not free, we can at least conceive of setting limits to others' authority over us.

It can be argued that *modus vivendi* ethics, as conceived by Mill, has no real place for social 'responsibility', even though it is difficult to see how the authority he at least tacitly acknowledges as a part of his ethics could operate unless those endowed with authority had a sense of responsibility. In other words, contractual theory creates two ethical problems: one is so to limit authority that its effect is to improve rather than worsen man's condition (the issue of 'liberty'); the other is to ensure that authority will in fact fulfil its function (be responsible). But Mill does not merely neglect the issue of social 'responsibility': he denies its ethical validity.

THE MILLIAN LEGACY

The impact of John Stuart Mill's legacy is such that nowadays one is likely to look at the history of political theory in terms of a conflict between the concepts of authority and freedom, and of a steady progression towards the latter, culminating in Mill's work *On Liberty*. Thus the Greeks shifted their sights from authoritarianism to a rational appraisal of tradition; Christian theologians mediated between conflicting claims to authority; contractualists endeavoured to justify political authority; and liberal democratic thinkers in the early modern age set limits to what could validly constitute such authority. In the light of this progression, Mill set forth the proposition that the principal issue has always been liberty, not authority.

The widespread acceptance of this view marks the revolution in thinking about relations between man and the State, and man and society, as envisaged by Mill. Before his time, democratic political parties in Britain were simply factions – Whigs and Tories taking a 'yes' or 'no' position with regard to particular proposals. After his time, political parties became ideologized, taking opposing views about 'liberty' and 'authority', but both leaning increasingly towards 'liberty' as the central concept.

Prior to Mill, it had been argued that acknowledgement of a sovereign power was a necessary condition for attaining the good as understood by the citizen and ensuring that his conception of that good was rationally based. When tempted to act on the basis of immediate desire and personal advantage, the possibility of punishment forced in certain cases a reconsideration of impulse as a guide to action. Within the State, even a tyrannical one, citizens are disciplined in the direction of prudentially-based behaviour, away from animal impulses.

In this situation, 'freedom' emerges as an intelligible but highly indefinite concept: human beings have personal desires the satisfaction of which, when not hindered by others, gives them a sense of being 'free'; they also have other desires that are restricted (and acknowledged by men as legitimately so), which fact gives them a sense of 'responsibility' (definable as constituting a sense of 'mature freedom'). Man's sense of responsibility raises the question of the responsibility held by authority (and its 'freedom'). No one has supplied the sovereign power with what the sovereign power has given to citizens. This Mill sought to do. As he worked within the democratic framework, he assigned ultimate authority to those who acknowledge authority. He spoke of the 'sovereignty of the individual' even though anyone who recognizes the authority conferred on government is clearly not sovereign. Speaking about the 'sovereignty of the individual' entails a return to a pre-contractual conception. In a sense, Hobbes also began with sovereign individuals.

Mill, nonetheless, is a revolutionary thinker because he changed the type of questions asked. Prior to him the crucial question was: 'Why is the coercion of authority not a restriction on freedom?' or 'What is the nature of the obligation we feel to acknowledge authority?' Now the question becomes: 'What is the jurisdiction of authority?' or, 'What decrees of authority do we have to respect?'

This is a dangerous question to ask now, when it is by no means certain that the answer to the first question has been universally accepted. Mill is a Utopian in that he presupposes an acceptance of contractualist arguments for authority, though not for sovereignty. Contractualism derives authority from sovereignty, but Mill thought that 'responsible' people did not question the obligation to respect authority (a Utopian view) and that consequently one could speak of the 'sovereignty of the individual' and be understood not to mean that individuals were asserting or could assert independence from authority. In his view, they were only asserting limits to the jurisdiction of authority.

Speaking about freedom in terms of a 'sovereign individual', however, puts authority and liberty into opposition, so that the acknowledgement of authority is no longer a condition for liberty, as under contractualism, but is itself a restraint on freedom. A serious conceptual problem now arises. Only responsible individuals – those who acknowledge the need for authority – can insist that they are 'sovereign individuals' and as such can insist that no other authority is sovereign. They do not know what limits they are seeking to impose; they only know that they should impose them because they are sovereign themselves. 'Freedom' thus becomes a resistance to authority.

Mill's conception of 'liberty' as suspicion of authority makes it necessary nowadays to use different arguments when defending democracy. Liberty has no necessary connection with the method of arriving at a government; nor does it give any real clue to the government about the policy to be pursued. In Mill's day, progress in social legislation suffered some setbacks because liberals saw it as transgressing the bounds of what a government can legitimately do. Today, a good deal of social legislation is being imposed because liberals assert that legislating on such matters is a necessary function of government. The content of the concept of liberty has not been clarified. Mill assigned to 'sovereign individuals' – not by any means everybody – the right to demand that in enacting and enforcing legislation authority employ a concept of liberty. Yet he left the definition of liberty in the hands of those whom he envisaged to be not the actual legislators and who are not even an identifiable body. (One has no idea who these 'sovereign individuals' are except from the negative standpoint: namely, that they are not children, possibly not primitives, etc.)

The difficulties created by Mill's liberal legacy are formidable. It is perhaps not surprising that the most serious, that of identifying the sovereign individual, has in our age been simplified by asserting that 'freedom' means doing as one pleases without regard to responsibility. But this is certainly not what Mill advocated. His 'sovereign individual' is not sovereign until he becomes responsible, just as in contractual theory a sovereign power that is not responsible does not retain sovereignty. Although Mill specifically rejected contractual theory, it was the contractual argument for sovereignty that he used in developing his concept of a 'sovereign individual'.

The Contract as Stage

Mill is often taken to be advocating sovereignty of the individual as the end to be achieved by the norm 'liberty', whereas the direction of his argument shows that the conception of sovereignty is, as in Hobbes, his premise. As a sceptic, Mill did not profess to be able to advise about ends but only processes: 'liberty' is to the attainment of the good as the scientific method is to knowledge. Neither 'liberty' nor 'science' is to him an intrinsic good.

How significant is the distinction between a social

methodology for arriving at normative truths and a scientific methodology for reaching truths about objective reality? The distinction can be used to separate Mill from the social Darwinists who thought of human beings as part of a single overall process subject to scientific laws; according to them, the scientific method was to be applied to the analysis of human behaviour and the 'good' determined as a sub-variety of scientific truth. Mill, trained from boyhood in philosophy, knew that it is impossible to arrive at meaningful 'oughts' in this way, no matter how certain one is of 'what is'. A different methodology is needed. Mill's conception of 'liberty' is just such an assertion.

Although social Darwinists are now in disrepute, their methodology has prevailed; it is what some now call 'scientism', others behaviouralism. Mill's 'liberty', once a manifestation of scepticism about traditional values, has itself become a traditional value – the view that the individual citizen 'ought' to be sovereign and that if this is not the case, we are not free.

Mill's 'sovereign individual' is not something that arose with the origin of man as a species. In his very first sentence, Mill specifically denies that he is speaking about 'the so-called Liberty of the Will'. Rather, it is related to 'the stage of progress into which the more civilized portion of the species has now entered'. Mill rejected the contractual theory, which he interpreted as an argument for obligation in general, rather than for a specific kind of obligation; he accepted, however, the latter as marking a 'stage of progress'. Thus the concept of stage is essential to Mill's body of ideas because it represents his oblique – not acknowledged – acceptance of contractualism as an argument for the necessity of authority (though not sovereignty).

Mill was not a relativist but a sceptic: the two terms must not be confused. Relativists are sure that they know the ultimate nature of the good; they seek to derive the content of 'good' from the conditions within society at a given time; and they expect science to provide the necessary information. Mill did not believe any of this and evidently hoped that the concept of liberty would hinder the propagation of such views. In fact, it has not done so but instead has been used to reinforce them: posterity has denied any link between the concept of liberty and contractualism, as it rejected the concept of stage. It has also represented Mill as an imperfect social Darwinist.

THE MILLIAN TRADITION AND MODERN LIBERALISM

Since Mill has long been a very popular philosopher in the English-speaking world (selections from *On Liberty* being part of many secondary school English courses), and because he sees authority and liberty as being in conflict, it is tempting to attribute some of the rather confused popular views about liberty to his influence. Mill acknowledges that authority is not a necessary evil but a good (as in the authority exercised by parents over their children), but because he rejected contractualism, he could not state clearly why it is so (in the way the contractualists can); hence he could not make it clear that authority and liberty are two 'goods' on a continuum. In the absence of the contract theory, the opposition of authority and liberty makes authority a kind of evil that citizens want to reduce in order to have more of the good, namely more liberty.

One contemporary liberal philosopher, Rawls, has set himself the task of restating the contractualist argument in a liberal framework, although he refrained from making a case for 'authority'. He has forgotten that the immediate problem for anyone reviving contractualism is to argue that authority is integral to the concept of liberty. Professor Rawls's task is a very ambitious one – that of constructing a liberal philosophy, or concept of the good, with 'liberty' as its premise. His book *A Theory of Justice*, is formidably long because, among other things, it is an argument for a particular ethical system rather than, as in the case of Mill's essay, a discussion of an ethical problem within an existing ethical system. Rawls wants to bypass what he calls 'the dispute about the meaning of liberty' and 'assume that liberty can always be explained by a reference to three items: the agents who are free, the restrictions or limitations which they are free from and what it is that they are free to do or not to do'.[2] For Rawls, liberty provides an approach to a conceptual framework within which ethical problems can be discussed and a system arrived at. For Mill, the system – Utilitarianism – already existed and the problem was to give the concept of liberty a significant role. However, the idea of the sovereign individual, which Mill used as a premise for his concept of liberty, is incompatible with Utilitarianism as traditionally understood. Anyone who begins with 'liberty' has to establish a new framework compatible with 'liberty' as a premise and Utilitarianism as a system. This is what Rawls attempts to do.

Power to Relativism

The primary change from the nineteenth-century to modern liberalism (as can be seen in Rawls) is that 'liberty' is no longer regarded as a problem within an ethical system but as a philosophical concept which helps to prove that ethical problems exist. Rawls, like Mill, is not a relativist. Although they differ on the matter of contractualism, there is a clear link between Rawls's attempt to arrive at a theory of justice and Mill's which was to give more weight to the individual within a system of justice (one that made the interests of the individual insignificant as compared with those of the 'greatest number').

Like Plato, Mill endeavoured to set up the social conditions that would enable men to be 'free' (arrive at the truth); but, unlike him, he looked for a particular normative concept, liberty, to accomplish this end. Clearly, such a view was not relativist. Mill's arguments, such as that we do not know the truth, may only make it *appear* that he was in favour of relativism as the essential liberal viewpoint. From here, it is only one step to acknowledging that the claims of authority – when admitting the cogency of contractualism – are tantamount to a denial of liberty. Among modern liberals, Rawls who does not support such views, is rather an exception. The question now is : can relativists who think of themselves as within the liberal tradition be called true liberals or have they moved off in a wholly new direction?

In raising the question one must distinguish between two issues: the anarchistic consequences and anarchism. The latter is a political ideology because its postulates about man's nature (and the nature of authority) are such that specific political action is possible or even necessary. Relativism makes no assumption about man's nature but only about the nature of his normative views. According to relativists, one's beliefs about the good are arrived at and imposed on men arbitrarily – and so is any concept of the good. There is no valid concept of the good in the sense there is one of the truth. To relativist liberals, Mill's argument in favour of liberty is unsound: they do not belong to the 'classical' Millian tradition. What can now be said about the anarchistic implications of such liberalism and to what extent are we talking about actual political behaviour labelled 'liberal' when speaking of relativism?

Relativism, as relativists point out, does not prevent people from having a conception of the good or from banding together with those of similar inclinations. What is seldom if ever admitted is that when they do band together it is not for company's sake but to impose their conceptions of the good on others. Many liberals seem to believe that in a free society we should be free to coerce one another (either by pressure to conform or through prohibitions imposed by laws and regulations), but that we should also – as a corollary – be free to resist such coercion. This is a far cry from J.S. Mill, but it is also a far cry from the anarchy of Hobbes's 'state of nature'; it also bears no relation to anarchism as an ideology.

Believing as they do that all conceptions of the good are arbitrary, relativist liberals acknowledge the contractualist view that a conception of the good, if it is to be more than a wistful yearning, can be realized only through coercion. But they differ from the contractualists by denying the State its monopoly of coercive power. In consequence, the relativist liberal not only sees no inconsistency in electing a government and then demonstrating against its policies, but thinks of such behaviour as the only one compatible with liberty: 'We do not know the good', he says, 'but we do know that our feelings about it can only be satisfied by political activism'. It appears that the issue is not 'Power to the People' but 'Power to Relativism'.

Chapter 9

The liberal mosaic

DISAPPEARANCE OF RESPONSIBILITY AS A COMPONENT OF LIBERTY

In J.S. Mill's day, the liberal creed could be stated rather simply: the promotion of individualism (the concept of 'rights') so as to prevent the Utilitarianism advocated as government policy from becoming a tyranny of the majority or a benevolent dictatorship indifferent to the welfare of the citizen as an individual. There was no necessary relation between the liberal ideology and democratic government. Although Mill himself advocated the extension of the franchise, his views about 'democracy' and those about 'liberty' were independent of one another. A non-liberal democracy and a liberal non-democracy were not for him self-contradictory; whether he thought a liberal democracy was the best form of government remains a matter of conjecture.

L.T. Hobhouse's interpretation of liberalism [1911] is quite definite on this issue: 'democracy. . . is the necessary basis of the Liberal idea'.[3] Although all liberals today would subscribe to this position, probably no one who considers himself a liberal would be prepared to say, as Hobhouse does, that 'if the elementary rights are to be secured for all it may be that a semi-despotic system like that of some of our Crown colonies is the best that can be devised'.[4] Today, it is the 'conservative' who believes that the preservation of rights in general is more important that the particular right to participate in the electoral process, at least with regard to the situation in some other part of the world.

This difference of viewpoint can be traced to the fact that in Hobhouse's day the extension of the franchise was hotly debated in Britain. Everyone was familiar with the question of responsibility: 'In considering whether any class or sex or race should be brought into the circle of enfranchisement, the determining consideration is the response which that class or sex or race would be likely to make to the trust'. Hobhouse held that opponents of the extension 'forget that. . . enfranchisement itself may be precisely the stimulus needed to awaken interest and. . . are apt to overlook the. . . danger of leaving a section of the community outside the circle of civic responsibility'.[5]

Liberals seem to have forgotten the question of responsibility which was so important to Hobhouse and the early liberals. This question remains fundamental for conservatives, who still, for instance, object to the welfare schemes of liberals and socialists, on account of the diminished sense of responsibility that such schemes cause or are said to cause. Hobhouse saw a unity of purpose in the aims of liberals and socialists[6] without realizing that this would lead to the disappearance of the Liberal Party in Britain. Once the issue of 'responsibility' becomes obscure, a grave difficulty in distinguishing between liberals and democratic socialists will be encountered in other countries.

Today, the concept of responsibility is unintelligible to many people except as a reference to some contractual obligation – the duties of an office. 'Freedom' for them consists in not having imposed on them responsibilities, such as those of marriage and ensuring the welfare of one's children. What used to be the individual's responsibility – even 'independence' in the sense of being self-supporting – is now considered the responsibility of the State. If it were possible for the State to assume all responsibilities, the main issue with regard to the difference between liberal and conservative views would be whether paternalism is compatible with democracy. The State, of course, cannot take on such an all-embracing task. We do not know how to maintain full employment; and we know that a guaranteed wage is not economically feasible unless there is almost full employment. As for the State taking over the full education of children – including the moulding of their moral character – there is a solid body of conservative opposition that is not likely to be overridden. On the issue of responsibility, conservatives and liberals are in irreconcilable conflict.

Being saddled by responsibilities imposed by liberal notions of personal irresponsibility (called 'freedom') no government knows how to accept them. But the problem tends to solve itself. Governments cannot make adequate welfare payments to all who need them and national economies may end by returning to a pre-liberal condition. Thus, when statistics show an enormous growth in the 'service industry', one sees a return to small-business enterprises. Since there is now less employment to be found among large-scale employers and the welfare service supplies little more than subsistence, individuals venture into business for themselves. Whether they like it or not, the old notion of 'independence' is being revived because the State cannot afford to be paternalistic. The concept, however, of 'independence' is only one aspect of responsibility. It is not possible to have a meaningful discussion of responsibility if one party to the debate thinks of 'liberty' in terms of the fulfilment of desire. In our days, 'responsibility' has disappeared from the liberal conception of democratic choice and has been replaced by the 'right' to follow desire. Hence objections to civil rights movements on the grounds that they are egoistic in tendency and totally lacking in responsibility are no longer intelligible to the liberal. To him, the ability to fulfil one's desires is freedom.

SENTIMENTAL LIBERALISM

If we want to know what happened to nineteenth-century liberalism – why even Mill in presenting a philosophical statement of its principle (Utilitarianism) could not bring himself to apply it rigorously – we should consult

Dickens's *Hard Times*. The book shows Utilitarianism as heartless and lacking in respect for sentiment.

In the English-speaking world, sentiment tends to override intellectual consistency: the more rational an ideology appears, the more suspect it is. When Hobhouse said 'Great changes are not caused by ideas alone. . . The passions of men must be aroused',[7] he was not simply referring to Hume's view that 'reason is the slave of the passions', but also had in mind the English mistrust of ideas unmodified by 'passions' (so well expressed by the peculiar English word 'sentiment', a feeling put forward as if it were an ethical principle). Thus Hobhouse affirms that 'those who effect a revolution . . . have need of a social theory', but he immediately adds that 'theory emerges from the practical needs which they feel'[8] so that 'theory' is made to accord with feelings and practical needs rather than the dictates of reason. English political theory often comes close to what in other parts of the world would be called 'policy'. How confusing this may be can be seen in Hobhouse's discussion of what he calls 'the heart of Liberalism' – a phrase that is significantly ambiguous in that it combines heart in the sense of 'essence' and heart as 'kindly feelings'.

Hobhouse asserts that 'Mill brings us close to the heart of Liberalism' in representing liberty as 'no mere formula of law, or of the restriction of law'.[9] If this is so, one can say that the current liberal emphasis on 'rights' that must be enshrined in law does not accord with the liberal tradition as Hobhouse understood it.

'Nor does liberty rest on self-assertion' says Hobhouse, continuing his negative definition of the heart of liberalism. Here Hobhouse breaks with Mill, who emphasized individualism as a counter to the strong tendency of Utilitarianism to submerge the individual in the interest of the greatest good to the greatest number.

On this point, current liberalism seems to reflect some of the ideas of both Mill and Hobhouse. In other words, there is no settled view about the importance of the individual in relation to the collectivity; this despite the fact that the emphasis on 'rights' suggests a consciousness among liberals that the individual is threatened by the collectivity when liberty is considered as not 'opposed to discipline, to organization, to strenuous conviction as to what is true and just' (which was Hobhouse's view).

Putting forward a view that Mill would have repudiated, Hobhouse seems to resist the relativism that Mill's scepticism encouraged. Hobhouse's attitude is necessary if liberals are to have a social policy; but having such a policy leads to an interference with the individual's liberty in a way strongly objected to by Mill. This is made very clear by Hobhouse's approach to tolerance.

In his assertion that 'The Liberal does not meet opinions which he conceives to be false with toleration' Hobhouse reaffirms the 'strenuous conviction' of liberals. He also reverses Mill's scepticism: 'He [the liberal] is always ready to put his own convictions to the proof, not because he doubts them, but because he believes in them'.[10] The consequence is activism: a liberal in the Hobhousian sense can act on his beliefs, whereas Mill's liberal is someone who tries to prevent others from acting on theirs. Inasmuch as modern liberals are social reformers, they derive their views from Hobhouse rather than Mill.

This twofold tradition poses a problem with regard to the concept of 'tolerance'. Its meaning is clear so long as one is a sceptic, but it ceases to be so when one becomes a social activist with 'strenuous convictions'. How is tolerance to be manifest and why should it be? Hobhouse does not say. He may not agree with what Mill had to say about tolerance, but at least we know what his position was. The same cannot be said about liberals today, for there is more than one liberal tradition on this matter. The tradition stemming from Hobhouse is more sentimental than conceptual. The liberal's 'heart' tells him that tolerance is a good thing and that social activism is also, but what is actually believed is not clear.[11]

LIBERALISM OR LIBERALISMS?

Though Professor Cranston admits that the word liberal 'is much newer [to Britain] than the political theory it stands for', it is 'the meaning of the word "liberal" in the English usage of the British Isles' which he first proposes to examine.[12] This position accords with, as he puts it, 'the lesson of the first great English liberal philosopher, Locke [who said]: "It is impossible to speak clearly and distinctly of our knowledge . . . without considering first the nature, use and significance of language."'[13] The word came into English in the early nineteenth century from the Spanish 'liberales', who 'stood for the Lockean principles of constitutional monarchy and parliamentary government'. It was applied to their opponents by British Tories to suggest that 'these politicians were un-English or akin to those of the continent'. The liberals 'were proud to admit that they believed in freedom', by which they meant 'freedom from the constraints of the state'. 'In other words', Cranston continues, 'English liberalism is the doctrine of the minimal state'. Although the ideal is as old as Periclean Athens, the English tradition is 'peculiarly national'. 'Most English liberals . . . have wanted to minimize the power of representative governments no less than that of other sorts of government'. They favoured widening the suffrage: one of the reasons for this was 'their belief . . . that the more democratically a government was chosen, the more moderate it would be'.[14]

Essentially, Cranston sees English liberalism as a remarkably unified point of view with specific content and distinct from both continental liberalisms – not unified in their political perspectives – and American liberalism, which has no clear content.

'To write about liberalism in more than a domestic context', says Cranston, 'one must write about liberalisms'.[15] He points out that the meaning given to liberty by Hobbes differs markedly from that of Locke or Mill. Unless one can establish that those who made liberty a central value can unify and integrate various past and present concepts of liberty in the domestic context, there will, even domestically, be more than one liberalism.

After inveighing against arbitrary stipulations masquerading as 'real' meanings, Cranston asserts, as was said earlier, that by 'freedom' the English liberal means 'freedom from the constraints of the state'. Aware that this is not what Mill meant, he uses his stipulation to criticize English liberals (with the exception of John Stuart Mill) for having 'failed to see the importance of constraints *other* than those imposed by the state'.[16] In other words, the methods of linguistic analysis by which he is influenced in his study have not prevented him from assigning a meaning to a concept and then examining the historical facts in terms of his own idea of what the meaning 'ought' to be. It led him to begin rather late in the English history of the concept 'liberal' (as late as the nineteenth century, when as a specific political term it was adopted from Spain), to work back to cover its early history and then forward again to twentieth century developments.

In analysing French *libéralisme* Cranston finds it necessary to coin terms to cover 'two distinct political theories . . . (a) Lockean liberalism and (b) *étatiste* liberalism',[17] the first deriving of course from Locke, the second from Rousseau. French Lockean liberalism differs from the English in making a constitutional settlement on Lockean lines the end, whereas English liberals see it as the beginning. *Etatiste* liberalism has a more positive conception of 'liberty', requiring the individual to rule himself rather than just avoid being ruled by others and 'urges the individual to make the state his own'[18] (a view, incidentally, that seems to have profoundly affected liberals in both the USA and Canada).

In Germany, in Cranston's account, liberalism also had a strong positive element through the influence of German metaphysicians, but for historical reasons it became allied with nationalism and disintegrated in the face of men skilled in *Realpolitik*, like Bismarck. German nationalism became permanent and liberalism disappeared. Although Cranston deals rather summarily with American liberalism, arguing that there the word liberal has few of the laudatory connotations which it has in Britain, he nonetheless accurately captures its essence. Following the argument of Vernon Louis Parrington (*Main Currents of American Thought*, 1927), he says that in the nineteenth-century USA there were two rival philosophies called liberal, one deriving from the *laissez-faire* English tradition, the other from the humanitarianism of the French enlightenment; in practice, the former tradition predominated. In the twentieth century, the word became tinged with radicalism. In the USA there is a tendency to identify liberalism with democracy (to substitute for the word democratic what the English would call 'liberal') in a rather vague way so that 'liberalism' is a 'wishy-washy', even pejorative term.

What does this all amount to? Cranston's observations about the liberal tradition are very helpful. By demonstrating the different meanings of liberalism he establishes that lying at the core of liberalism is its vagueness – a characteristic, incidentally, which is still clearly manifest three decades after the publication of his book *Freedom.* (Even in Britain the specific 'freedom from the constraints of the state' is distinctly vague about what is to be done about specific issues.)

On the other hand, the methodology he claims to have used is not the one he uses. He has employed historical analysis in arriving at an understanding of what liberalism has meant, but he professes to have followed the analysis of usage to which linguistic philosophers adhere. Since the words liberal and liberalism (as derived from '*liberales*') did not come into use in modern political history until a late stage, one could fault his professed methodology for clouding his contribution.

In his book on freedom, Cranston recognizes the shortcomings of his treatment of what others have called 'liberalism'. It is the absence of the concept of responsibility which shows that what he is really discussing is verbal usage. Most writers, particularly the liberals, have in fact discussed 'freedom' as if they did not need to deal with 'responsibility', but it is the duty of the political theorist to draw their attention to this matter (as Cranston himself acknowledges in the introductory note to the second edition of his work).

The analysis of usage as an approach to conceptual analysis is the only one open to empiricists who feel uncomfortable because logical positivists have dismissed non-empirical concepts as figments of the imagination. If you analyse usage, you are analysing what members of your society think; you are also analysing a major source of breakdowns in communication. (We have to use a limited number of verbal symbols to refer to wholly different thoughts.) If, under empirical assumptions, you analyse a concept, the latter has no referent in objective reality: you are talking only about the working of your own mind. Biologists can pay no attention whatsoever to usage when defining 'fruit' or 'fish' since they are speaking of genetic relations established by empirical evidence, not popular usage; but a political theorist cannot ignore usage and still make a useful statement about the conceptions of liberty and liberalism.

The problem with linguistic analysis is that it is seldom clear whether one is speaking of usage – the meanings assigned to symbols – or about concepts that, because of our limited linguistic resources, have to be expressed by a very limited number of symbols. The two are very different endeavours and it is easy to confuse them. Professor Cranston is a conceptualist who in this case merely happens to employ the methods of linguistic philosophy. The latter are not essential to his position.

JURISTIC LIBERALISM AND THE LIBERAL-DEMOCRATIC TRADITION: THE AMERICAN SOLUTION

Modern American liberalism is characterized by the conviction that the USA was 'born liberal'.[19] Whereas Burke founded his conservatism on tradition, American liberals base their liberalism on a lack of it. They see any departure from what happens when a State has to establish a tradition (a constitution) as a retreat from liberalism and even democracy. They regard the terms 'liberal' and 'democratic' as interchangeable and see the 'conservative' as 'un-American', a proponent of the Burkean rather than the American (Lockean) tradition.

This view makes the Constitution a far more restrictive conception than the rule of law – the entire body of judicial decisions – that characterizes parliamentary democracies. It also poses exceptional difficulties with regard to what can be called ethical anarchism. The latter implies that since we have no assured basis for our ethical judgements, the liberal-democratic State must not legislate on ethical issues; moreover, it must insist that its citizens be 'tolerant'.

Hobbes himself, of course, considered the sovereign power to be above the restraints of moral law and is seen by some as the first 'liberal'.[20] However, this view puts a liberal jurist like Professor Dworkin in a rather awkward position. As a jurist, he is aware that the law cannot be relativistic and still command respect, but he also knows that the law in effect legislates morality because it is based on it. Thus he says 'The Court. . . does not cite statutes, but it does appeal to principles of justice and policy'[21] and he raises the point of the 'individual's political and moral obligation to obey judge-made law'.[22] As a liberal, Walter Berns sees this, and indeed the whole of Dworkin's *Taking Rights Seriously*, as a 'book that takes the Constitution frivolously',[23] even though, as another member of the symposium *Liberalism Reconsidered* Mark Sagoff, observes, 'Dworkin . . . argues that . . . liberals require that the structure of social institutions be neutral on what he calls the question of the good life'.[24]

We have here the essence of the liberal problem where it touches on ethical anarchism. Dworkin recognizes the fundamental need for the sovereign power to remain neutral with regard to ethical disputes. This, of course, is not an exclusively 'liberal' view at all but a fundamental part of political theory. It is absurd to call Hobbes the first 'liberal', as Berns does, simply because Hobbes supplied a theory which entailed the separation of Church and State. Everyone except those unfamiliar with Western political thought is agreed on this principle. But Dworkin – a juristic liberal – recognizes that if we do not acknowledge limits to neutrality, we are bound to advocate ethical anarchism (the condition we hoped to avoid by acknowledging the jurisdiction of the State in societal matters). A wholly neutral sovereign would be like an umpire who is indifferent to everything that happens on a playing field except fist fights. He would have abandoned the central function of making and enforcing law.

There is a long tradition in Western thought that one cannot legislate morality (the most common example of this tradition is the history of Prohibition in the USA with its socially disastrous consequences). The view that one cannot do so, because legislation will not be effective, may reflect the 'ought not' position which derives from the separation of Church and State. Yet there are many instances of ethical changes following legislative changes, such as altered public attitudes to the use of opium as a result of legislation introduced at the turn of the twentieth century. Indeed, there is a school of thought – internalized law theory – which infers *all* moral views from legal ones. This view – as any natural law theorist or anthropologist will argue – is not complete, nor can it logically be so, as long as making law is a function of the sovereign power.

Liberalism has traditionally coped with this problem by setting stringent limits to the making of laws. Thus it has come perilously close to an anarchistic idea of freedom. Moral anarchism (relativism) makes it unclear whether one is advocating political anarchism.

The issue has never been cleared up. Mill did not support anarchism; but because of his scepticism and the consequent relativism one cannot be sure what legislation he would, or would not, have supported. This has long been the problem with liberal parties: their policy tended to be unclear until they acquired one from the socialists. Dworkin offers a solution by abandoning relativism. Summarizing the position he has taken throughout his essays in *Taking Rights Seriously*, he says 'It is no longer so clear that either common sense or realism supports the objection that there can be no right answer.'[25] By acknowledging that there are right answers and that the liberal knows them, Dworkin assumes a position that is different from J.S. Mill's.

It seems necessary for Dworkin (a juristic liberal) to adopt a view which, on the face of it, conflicts with the very neutrality that he expects from the State.

Dworkin puts the issue in terms of 'Two competing pictures of the foundation of liberalism. The first – liberalism based on neutrality – supposes that the fundamental structuring principle of liberalism is that the government should be neutral in matters of personal morality. . . The second picture – liberalism based on equality. . . supposes that the liberal's emphasis on neutrality in personal morality is not the source but rather one consequence of a prior and more general commitment to equality'.[26]

Dworkin rejects scepticism 'because if the moral majority is wrong, and each person should be free to choose personal ideas for himself, then this is surely because the choice of one life over another is a matter of supreme importance, not because it is of no importance at all'.[27] Mill would deny that his own scepticism had such a basis. He would say that it may be quite true that there are ethical absolutes, but the essential point is that one does not know what they are. He would, however, agree with Dworkin that the liberal State leaves the question 'What sort of life should I, as an individual, lead?' in the hands of the individual.

Nonetheless, the real test of any political theory is not the restrictions placed on its ethical jurisdiction but what it says about the making of positive law. Here, Dworkin agrees with Mill that the liberal-democratic State does not attempt to interfere with the ethical conceptions of its citizens. As Sagoff says 'Why should liberals go to such lengths to discount moral and aesthetic judgments, in short, public values, when one might think these belonged at the heart of political discussion? An answer may be found in the liberal contractarian tradition, which provides a logical and historical basis for the view that the government should ignore or somehow discount the other-regarding or impersonal preferences of the citizenry. According to the contractarian tradition, people do not associate politically to debate, construct, and act upon conceptions of the good society; they form governments to protect and to promote the personal interests they already have'.[28]

The liberal tradition that Sagoff has in mind is clearly Lockean: American liberals see it as the foundation of their democracy, while British liberalism is Millian rather than contractarian. Despite historically different philosophical origins, the two liberalisms are now united by their Utilitarian attitude. Except for a few die-hard democrats, liberals in both countries see Utilitarianism as the principle they expect the government to follow. It is true that now and then cries for 'Power to the people!' and 'majority rule' – together with assertions of 'equality' – come from liberal circles; but democratic government and universal adult franchise have existed long enough for the use of such slogans to be tantamount to a rejection of the government's policy rather than a recommendation of new policy. (No one, incidentally, knows what to do when such slogans are voiced, except when they refer to foreign States such as South Africa. They are a demand for a relativist philosophy which is incapable of providing any guidance for domestic policy.)

This leaves us with Utilitarianism as a source of policy; but if Utilitarianism is something that only the government can understand, its policies become inherently paternalistic. As Sagoff observes, 'We cannot avoid paternalism with respect to future generations'.[29]

To escape this problem and return to something like Mill's respect for individuality, Sagoff argues for what are rational ethical judgements: 'To treat a person with respect and concern. . . is at least to treat him. . . as capable of making or supporting policy choices on the basis of good reasons and not merely arbitrary wants. Insofar as an individual grounds his choices on reasons. . . he recognizes. . . their validity. . . for all members of the community. . . These reasons. . . demand to be recognized, considered and understood by others, particularly by those who in making public policy are supposed to be responsive to them'.[30] This is essentially Mill's view of responsible human beings. Sagoff uses it to distinguish between liberals, socialists and conservatives: 'Socialists and conservatives have well-worked-out dialectical and historical arguments – full of theories or explanations, as it were – of public virtue and of the good society. The liberal, on the contrary, has no such worked-out theory but proceeds by a *via negativa* to describe what a good society does *not* do'.[31] Such negatives, of course, imply positive judgement, but they are used only for the purpose of limiting the jurisdiction of government. Democratic government is represented as Utilitarian in policy but prevented from becoming paternalistic or exceeding its jurisdiction by a responsible, non-relativist individual. This is a recent development in liberal thinking, though it is one with which Mill would not disagree. But what kind of positive law would such a government support?

COERCIVE LIBERALISM

Although political parties calling themselves 'conservative' have been a constant feature of modern parliamentary democracy, yet this fact has been accompanied by a remarkable inability to formulate precisely the underlying norms of the movement. The reason is that 'conservative' norms reflect the whole body of values and recognize that society's norms are not arbitrary restraints on freedom but the embodiment of man's accumulated experience. Those who try to reduce them to a set of fixed principles, reputedly underlying the totality of experience, are bound to go wrong.

The only evidence for the soundness of the conservative position is that parliamentary democracy does in fact work, although it may not have a 'constitution'. So in effect does the democratic legal system which asserts that the law has a remedy for every wrong; this despite the fact that there is no lawyer or judge who could point to the actual law or laws providing the remedy before the latter is discovered. What parliamentary democracy and law do is to operate on the totality of norms, as Burke, the first to set forth the idea, boldly declared.

This idea is incomprehensible to liberals as well as to many conservatives. American conservatives, for instance, can hardly accept it because they are raised to believe that their Constitution – not norms in general – sets forth the basic principles of their society. Consequently, liberals – and many conservatives influenced by the American system – are preoccupied with 'bills of rights', whose object is to limit human behaviour by imposing legal sanctions for the 'wrong' kind of conduct. This they call 'freedom'.

It may seem odd that liberals could move from the principle that the least government is the best, to organized efforts to establish specific laws covering every aspect of human behaviour. Such a stance, incidentally, became the best alternative for liberals when Mill argued that one of the greatest threats to freedom is the coercive power of public opinion (in other words, of customary norms). Mill saw the acceptance of these norms as an unreflecting adherence to custom (which it often is); he considered democratically constituted laws to be more rational, more open to criticism, as well as subject to change (as indeed they are). If one believes in reason and the democratic legislative process, it is self-evident that only those norms that have been subject to such a process should have any coercive effect. Everything else is a purely private matter. Democratic society should mind its own business.

The effect of 'liberalizing' society by denying the justifiability of customary norms (until scrutinized by the legislative process) is to make government coercive. It also makes coercion the essential force in human society. It is true that reason still has a significant place in human conduct – it reputedly operates during the legislative process – but it is not a component of everyday human relations. These are based on personal attitudes, tastes and feelings, just as the psychoanalytic school says. Thus the liberal view fosters a suspicion of society, one's fellow-men and their motives, and a remarkably uncritical attitude towards the increasingly coercive powers of democratic government. This is interpreted as evidence of its ethical direction.

According to the traditional view of ethics, only the egoistically anti-social people need be coerced. When a person's behaviour is based on awareness that socially-imposed sanctions make unethical behaviour imprudent, the result is unfreedom; the more frequently people find themselves coerced, the less free they are. It does not matter if the coercive laws are themselves the product of rational analysis and can be rationally defended. The point is that society has to contend with both – the forces which promote resistance to the reputedly rational laws and the forces that create the laws. When society acquires such a schizophrenic image, 'government' is given an aura of rationality. This is a dangerous position because those who feel it to be true can see themselves as an élite who are the more ethical and rational the more they insist on increasing the coerciveness of government.

LIBERALISM, JUSTICE AND THE TWO-PRONGED DEFENCE OF DEMOCRACY

The liberal is so suspicious of 'government' that he is inclined to insist on a twofold process to preserve democracy – a democratically elected government without permanent tenure and a constitutionally independent judiciary which follows the principles that would preserve liberty even if the government were not democratic.

Under present democratic law it would be impossible for any democratic government to get rid of dissidents by locking them up as criminals or madmen, as can be done under Communism. But the system of justice which prevents the government from abusing the law appears to prevent society from coping with crime and insanity. Every time legal reform is urged, the cry of 'police State' is raised, for liberals insist that all our present restrictions on the policing of society are necessary not simply to justice but also to democracy. When the matter of modifying the restrictions is raised, the liberal does not speak in terms of 'law and order' but of 'democracy.' He not only implies, but usually declares, that the advocates of law and order are undemocratic and that if they had their way one would be living under a tyranny.

The liberal argument that the system of justice is one of democracy's main defences against tyranny can be challenged. There is clear historical evidence that a tyrant

usually has no problem in coping with a formally independent judiciary. (How effective was the resistance of the
German courts to Hitler?) If a major change occurs in a
society's normative system, as it certainly does when
acceptance of democratic norms shifts to acceptance of a
dictatorship, it is naïve to suppose that the legal system
will continue to operate as if nothing had changed. There
is no need for a two- or multi-pronged defence of democracy. Those who insist on strict adherence to secondary
elements such as the majority rule, no matter what the
consequences, or the full set of legal restrictions on the
activities of the police, regardless of the situation, are
likely to bring about the collapse of democracy as a viable
system of government.

The liberals' position is that certain practices which
through a slow process have become institutionalized in
democracies are now essential to democracy; the majority
rule and the elaborate controls on the judicial process
which were not present in the past are necessary now.
Psychologically this view is understandable. To abandon
it may be tantamount to asserting that the whole effort
was wasted and that liberalism is misguided. But it is
doubtful whether the practices would have been institutionalized at all if they did not serve a democratic function. The questions that now arise are: does a re-examination of the need for these practices represent a retreat
from liberalism and democracy? Does insistence on the
necessity for these practices possibly reflect a misunderstanding of democracy? 'Justice' is now often seen as a
focal point of liberals. Is there something called 'democratic justice', as distinct from 'justice'? Should the 'democratic' aspect of justice be emphasized? Liberals may have
good reasons for thinking so.

Even if 'justice' referred exclusively to legal procedures, there would certainly be a democratic, as opposed to an instrumentalist, form of it: one could understand that democracy needs its special *modus operandi*. But
justice transcends the application of rules and principles
to practices: it has a spiritual value.

Democracy (largely because of its derivation from

Christianity) is the only political system which asserts the worth of both the individual and the community. As a consequence its system of justice is traditionally concerned with ensuring that the innocent are never punished and that the guilty always are. So long as one keeps in mind that it is the democratic norms that lead to this view of justice, the legal system can cope with crime. It has been able to do so in the past. However, if one shifts the balance in favour of the individual, as liberals do, and regards the judiciary as an independent system set up to protect the individual against the oppression of society, democracy breaks down (together with the system that enforces justice and the norms that define it).

Unrestrained individualism or egoism is not a part of democratic ideology. Democracy asserts that both the sense of the 'self' and of 'other' are fundamental and interrelated concepts which find expression in the norms of individualism and equality. To see the judicial system as designed to protect and promote only the self and the 'rights' of the individual is to allow the sense of community to disintegrate. If the legal system is to serve as a defence of egoism, a device for protecting the individual, it cannot perform its basic function but conceivably begins to cooperate with the egoist against the community. This situation has led to increasing protests that the judicial system no longer cares about the victims of crime but only about the 'rights' of the criminal.

We do not need a 'twofold' defence of democracy, a concomitant of the liberal concept of justice, for the consequence of such a defence is an imbalance of norms. The danger in the liberal concept of justice is that society will react against this concept with the view that all that matters is law and order. Liberals, of course, maintain that it is precisely this danger that makes them insist that democratic justice demands a preoccupation with the individual's rights. But it is not true that the law either protects or oppresses the individual, any more than that democracy insists on equality at the expense of the individual or ignores equality in order to ensure the rights of the individual. Democracy requires the conceptual balance of 'self' and 'other' that each person must make in order to be sane: the balance of egoism and altruism, of prudence and hedonism, of the materialistic and spiritual that has constituted the central problem of ethics from the time when men first began thinking about the 'good'. None of us knows what the 'golden mean' is. Yet to suppose that 'justice' requires a weighting of the legal system in favour of the self against society, or that (in reaction to this liberal view of what democracy needs) one should let society override the individual – is false. Neither position is democratic or just.

LIBERALISM AS A FRAME OF MIND

An important aspect of the changing nature of liberalism is that 'liberty' is no longer thought of as an 'if-then' logical proposition. Under the latter, we either defend the 'if' on the grounds of consistency with some concept of freedom or, as with Utilitarianism, defend the 'then' on utilitarian grounds and justify the 'if' as conducive to it. Under the new concept, nothing whatsoever need follow: we are dealing solely with symbolic behaviour. Certain types of behaviour (such as the English use of masculine pronouns normally suggesting a common gender but resented by the feminists as 'sexist') is said to imply a non-liberal attitude. The argument is that this attitude, as manifest in customary behaviour and social institutions, must be changed: the consequences apparently do not matter. In effect, rational behaviour does not matter.[32]

In these conditions, it is hard for non-liberals to understand what modern liberalism is about. Why should a 'peace march' be liberal? Why 'women's lib.' (or 'feminism') and what does it entail? Why opposition to capital punishment? Why petitions against the policy of some foreign governments which cannot possibly affect these policies? Briefly, why is symbolic behaviour so important that any questioning of the consequences is dismissed as 'illiberal'?

It was psychoanalysis which first made symbols crucial to the understanding of human behaviour. Its methodology consists of the analysis of the symbols reputedly found in dreams, unwitting behaviour (such as 'body language') and 'accidents' (such as slips of the tongue). Psychoanalysts evolved this method because of their assumption about human motivations: our 'intentions' are considered an unreliable reflection of the actual motivations. The latter are unconscious, especially if they happen to be at odds with what society says they 'ought' to be.

It might be expected that such a view would have little appeal to anyone except the arty-crafty set, who seized on it as a justification of the artist's perspective on life. Until the rise of psychoanalysis, artists had no way of justifying their fictions and images except in terms of entertainment and pleasures added to 'truth'. The Romantics, with their doctrine of 'imagination', made the artist less dependent on conventional opinion; yet they were unable to justify their medium of communication until the Freudians asserted that their images and myths expressed man's underlying motivations.

There is however an ethical theory, Utilitarianism, which also finds psychoanalysis congenial. Like the latter, it considers 'intention' irrelevant. What matters is the consequences of one's behaviour. If you want to justify the omission of intent from the concept of the good, you need a psychological theory. From the earliest days of psychoanalysis, liberals like Bertrand Russell have been its strong advocates although its premises make conception of rational behaviour rather doubtful. Where psychoanalysis has a strong hold on popular conceptions of human motivations, 'liberalism' has become a frame of mind, reluctant to engage in a rational analysis of premises and consequences but emphatic about the importance of symbolic behaviour. To a liberal, whether a 'demonstration' influences government policy matters less than showing one's 'dissent'. Pursuing such action 'individualizes'; it also purportedly shows one's adherence to the liberal tradition.

Individualism, Individuality and Civil Rights

'An important first step in any discussion of political obligation' says Carole Pateman, 'is . . . the need for a theoretical attention to abstract individualism. This is especially necessary because of the tendency of political theorists uncritically to accept the liberal-democratic State as "given"'.[33] Pateman sees the liberal-democratic State as maintaining the status quo and argues that 'if the political practice of voting is . . . to enable citizens to order their political as well as social lives for themselves, then citizens must be able to decide when to assume an obligation and their own judgement must decide its content. Participatory democratic voting allows them to do these things'.[34]

The 'abstract individualism' to which Pateman refers is, as she puts it, 'an abstraction from social reality'. It is that 'of the capitalist, market economy and the liberal-democratic state and the postulated characteristics are those of the inhabitants of such a society'. And further on: 'If the individual is seen in the abstract, in complete isolation from other beings, then all "his" [sic!] judgements and actions are based solely on his own subjective viewpoint . . . That is to say, the individual's reasoning will be entirely self-interested'.[35]

It does not, of course, follow that the conceptual isolation of one member of a class from others entails that motivation must be egoistic. What is apparent here is the influence of C.B. Macpherson on Pateman's views which, however, is not our concern. The issue is that Pateman's views can be seen as a reflection of current liberal thinking: specifically, of liberalism as a state of mind.

The way we think of 'individualism' is crucial in this context. If the term is used interchangeably with that of 'individuality' – as Pateman and many liberals seem to do – confusion must follow. What, exactly, is being advocated?

Individuality refers to the fact that chance factors of biology and experience make each member of the human species unique in a way no other species is. One can, of course, treat this fact as a value – something to be preserved at all costs – and argue that conventionality and imposed conformity are a violation of the value 'individualism'. This seems to be what some liberals are doing today: the fact of individuality becomes for them equivalent to the norm of individualism. But this is not the norm as understood by conservatives.

To the conservatives an imposed standard, say a common language or conformity with certain rules, has no effect on respect for the individual's worth; furthermore, in their eyes no one's 'freedom' is impaired by the existence of rules and conventions, provided they are functionally justified and prize individualism in the traditional sense. Thus they do not face the problems of the liberals with regard to liberty which are posed by the need for rules and conventions.

This difference has led to many disputes between the two groups. Yet the liberal-democratic State has as a rule provided a framework for possible accommodation. Thus a shift from conservative to liberal government, or *vice versa*, does not in principle involve repealing the previous administration's legislation. Disagreements are not fundamental because the framework under which the legislation is enacted prevents irreconcilable stances. This is in fact the 'status quo' which, according to Pateman, is maintained by the liberal-democratic State and which she feels ought to be changed. But how can one reasonably object to the fact that liberals and conservatives can live together, and what kind of future can one expect under 'participatory democracy'?

It may be helpful to consider the concept of civil rights which both persuasions have always regarded as central to individualism. From the liberal viewpoint, 'rights' have prevented the conservatives from promoting law, order and convention at the expense of the individual; from the conservative viewpoint, they have prevented the liberal from turning the State into a sort of gigantic termite colony in which all men work for each other but to no meaningful end. There has been no close agreement about what one's 'rights' are, but there has been common agreement that the concept exists and that is meaningful.

Now, if one questions 'abstract individualism', it is 'rights' as traditionally conceived that are being disputed: in the past, both liberals and conservatives have always assigned rights to individuals instead of deriving them from what people say they want. 'Rights' were not thought of in terms of desires, but as conditions which 'ought' to exist irrespective of one's tastes. Thus, in a liberal-democratic State it does not matter whether the citizen wants to vote. But he has a right to do so and the reasons, unconnected with tastes or desires, can be supplied by political theory.

If 'individualism' (the value) refers to individuality, the very attempt to preserve 'freedom' by the traditional means of assigning rights becomes 'illiberal'. Under the new conception, one's 'rights' are what one demands, not what one is assigned. It also becomes essential for democracy to be 'participatory' and that there be a strong element of confrontation in democratic processes. 'Rights' must be demanded because they exist only as demands.

Viewed in this light, modern liberalism appears as a frame of mind rather than a set of principles. A liberal can have no idea what to support: he must await the turn of events and act accordingly. Consequently, there is no way of predicting future liberal policies.

The Liberal-Conservative Mind

It is easy to argue that liberalism has long been a frame of mind. Mill's argument for liberty was an argument for scepticism as an appropriate political philosophy. Under democratic conditions this led to such resistance to government that, as Hobhouse observed, by the end of the nineteenth century liberalism had ceased to function as a political force in the form originally advocated by J.S. Mill. As a frame of mind, however, it seemed so essentially democratic, tolerant and well-meaning, that the liberal-minded, like Hobhouse himself, tried to keep the liberal attitude alive by adopting those policies from socialist thinkers that could be incorporated into the liberal framework of 'tolerance'. However, his 'frame of mind'

approach, which lacked ideological commitment, ultimately produced the modern politics of confrontation.
Pateman, who espouses this type of politics, allocates the
content of 'rights' to those who make demands on government and society. This, incidentally is a position which,
although consistent with Mill's view that individual conscience must be the final determinant of right and wrong,
is hardly consistent with the need for a *modus vivendi* that
constrained everything Mill had to say about the nature
of the good.

If one says that liberalism is a frame of mind rather
than an ideological commitment, can the same be said of
conservatism?

Like Mill, Lincoln Allison in our day focuses his attention on a person's attitude to ethical views rather than the
particular beliefs he should hold: 'The main point' . . .
[he says] 'has been to stress how difficult it is to have a
coherent and developed moral sense, to be able to make
judgements which are substantive, in the knowledge that
other people will make different judgements'. This sounds
like a quotation from *On Liberty*, yet it would be hard to
say that it is not a 'conservative' view. Indeed, Allison goes
on to define it as specifically 'conservative': 'It is perfectly
possible to have such a sense while being a socialist . . . but
it is, perhaps, more difficult. It is far easier if one is a
person of independent judgement, though firmly rooted
in a particular culture and with realistic horizons: in
other words a conservative'.[36]

The problem with such a view is not whether it is more
appropriate to call it 'liberal' rather than 'conservative'
but that it makes one unfit for coping with ideological
views. Thus Allison, speaking of totalitarianism, refers to
it as if it were 'an aspect of the life of the mind', a matter
of simply being wrong-headed. Whereupon he says:
'Totalitarianism is bad and should be avoided, but that is
to be done by judgement and courage and a sense of
humour rather than by political theory'.[37] [*sic!*] Does this
mean that we should have laughed when the USSR in-
vaded Czechoslovakia in 1968 or Afghanistan in 1979 and
perhaps be quietly amused by Communist propaganda?

Whatever the answer, this stance is neither politic nor political. Can it possibly be argued that it is within the mainstream of democratic thinking?

To answer this question, let us return to my earlier concern[38] that the unresolved issues in religious controversies eventually reappear in the form of ideological disputes, as secular interests become paramount. What are these unresolved issues?

According to the historian, Roland Bainton, there were three intellectual elements involved in religious persecution: the belief that one was right; that the issues were important; and that coercion was effective in resolving them.[39] What has happened to these elements, now that 'ideology' has replaced 'faith' as a central concern?

The question of truth of belief poses few social and political problems: it has been 'solved' by detaching belief from behaviour. Despite evidence to the contrary, the consensus is that what we believe does not affect what we do. Following Hume, motivation is said to be unrelated to our conceptions of true and false. This being so, we can all confidently be tolerant of any belief and its propagation; disputes over religious beliefs were 'misguided' because by nature the beliefs were not 'important' – they had no consequences.

The above view disposes of both ideology and faith, not to mention the entire body of historical evidence that beliefs profoundly affect behaviour. It would be patently absurd to say that, for instance, Christianity has had no effect on history: it must have played a role in incorporating 'tolerance' into democratic thinking. It also seems evident from Allison's position that one cannot say that 'conservatives' typically deny it. There is evidence that conservatives in the USA do feel that beliefs matter and hence look with suspicion upon Marxist teachers in the schools; but there is no clear-cut liberal-conservative division in this matter. Tolerance is an important concept in democratic thinking and not many are willing to hack away at one of its props.

The second issue raised by Bainton, that of 'importance', is only partly 'solved' today by the general proposition about beliefs. Some of our beliefs – those about 'good' and 'right' – are by definition statements about behaviour: it is quite possible to believe that propositions about geocentric or solar-centric revolution have no real effect on behaviour, while holding that 'ought' and value statements most certainly do. Thus Mill's argument for a tolerance based on scepticism – that we cannot be sure about the 'truth' of those 'oughts' – is based on the evidence that ethical beliefs by their nature affect behaviour.

The solution to this issue adopted by many liberals is to include relativism in their 'frame of mind': statements about 'oughts' cannot be said to be either true or false. Therefore, although 'important', they are subject to the first argument for 'tolerance': that we cannot be sure we are right. If we are to believe Allison, this is also a conservative view; but if we follow Buckley, it is not. It seems that so far as conservatives are concerned, the issue is not settled.

What of the third issue – coercion as an effective way of bringing about the good society? Pateman clearly argues for this by advocating confrontation. Allison speaks against it by urging what can be called 'gentlemanliness'. If, however, one is to judge from liberal activism (which has now replaced Mill's *laissez-faire* views), liberalism is opposed to conservatism as a result of its belief that coercive laws, like the enforced bussing of school children, will bring about the 'right' attitudes of tolerance within society. (Conservatives, on the other hand, have a strong tendency to believe that coercion should be limited to enforcing a *modus vivendi* – that it is legitimate to coerce criminals but not those who are simply 'misguided'.) What is particularly disheartening is that although these issues have been examined before and we have been explicitly warned that they will recur, we have still not recognized the need to learn from history.

Liberalism versus Conservatism

The liberal values freedom from any interference by government or society which cannot be established as necessary to a *modus vivendi*. The 'value' of the restrictions is determined by the value assigned to life in a community as opposed to living in isolation.

The conservative focuses on what is secondary to the liberal – the social relations between human beings – and emphasizes 'responsibility'. To a conservative, it makes no sense to speak of 'freedom' as if 'responsibility' were an entirely separate issue. He believes the two issues cannot be considered independently and then united because of the need for some kind of *modus vivendi*: the fact that the latter has been achieved and that we are living in a society is more important than the conjecture that a more 'liberal' society is possible. The burden of proof that a better society is attainable rests upon the idealists, but they had best use 'reason' rather than political activism to make their point. Conservatives have no desire to experiment.

Now Allison believes that our *modus vivendi* is not to be cast aside lightly – in this sense he is in the Burke tradition – but he has also adopted Mill's scepticism about the arbitrary nature of traditional concepts and values. A conservative would argue that arbitrariness, and the question whether norms should be observed, are different things. The real issue to him is the functionality of norms: he cannot accept an individual's doubts about the truth of what is called the good. Conservatives believe in 'minimum government' or 'freedom of thought' for different reasons than liberals do. Liberals today are sceptical about normative order (except for norms which are consistent with their scepticism, such as tolerance) whereas conservatives regard scepticism about values as politically irrelevant: one cannot be a sceptic and still think of a *modus vivendi* as a central issue.

LIBERALISM AS MODERNIZED HEDONISM

The essential timelessness and pertinence of Kenneth Minogue's approach to the understanding of liberalism are immediately apparent to the reader of his book *The Liberal Mind*. He asserts that 'a need is an imperative form of desire'[40] and, with reference to Epicureanism, that the maximization of the satisfaction of desires led to the minimizing of desires. In such statements there is no attempt to discover what usage says about the distinction between needs and desires or what history says about Epicureanism and its peculiar relation to Puritanism. There is rather the reflection of a mind that is 'rational' in the sense understood before the word became the handmaid of empiricism.

In Professor Minogue's view it is necessary, at least initially, to assume that liberalism is a single entity. 'Nevertheless,' he says, 'it is important to distinguish between "classical liberalism" and "modern liberalism", since the former was far more radically individualist that the latter'.[41] To him, liberalism is clearly an ideology when the latter is defined as a 'set of ideas whose primary coherence results. . . from some external cause. . . some mood, vision, or emotion'.[42] Thus the liberal mind rests on a mood, vision or emotion.

Under liberalism, man is seen as a creature of desires; further, each desire creates a policy. This is not to say, however, that reason has no place in liberalism, for – as Minogue observes – 'reason is one of the totems of the liberal movement'; but this reason 'explores the logic of policies'[43] which, according to Minogue's analysis, are related to desire rather than some rational conception. It results in 'a disposition to subject everything to critical enquiry and to take nothing on trust from authorities' which is 'sometimes called rationalism'. But 'to call it rationalism falsely suggests that free criticism is spun out of the. . . faculty of reason'. Minogue suggests that it may suitably be called libertarianism: one of the two components of liberalism.

The other is 'the search for harmony, the pursuit of happiness and the doctrine of progress'. 'None of these', says Minogue 'is libertarian, and each may be directly hostile to the critical spirit. . . [which] disrupts harmonies, causes a good deal of direct unhappiness, and may or may not seem progressive. The only way in which libertarianism can be harmonized with these other elements of liberalism is by. . . making an act of faith to the effect that in the long run the products of the critical spirit will increase the amount of happiness.[44] He calls this the salvationist element. In liberalism both elements must be present. 'Here', says Minogue, 'is one of the marks of ideology, that of internal incoherence. For liberals are simultaneously to be found praising variety and indeed eccentricity of opinion and behaviour; and gnawing industriously away at the many sources of variety in an attempt to provide every man. . . with the conditions of a good life'.[45]

Minogue's objection to liberalism is not that it is ideological. Indeed, he argues for the need for faith and knows that it would be inconsistent to attack liberalism on the ground that it entails faith. His own 'faith' is that 'there exists something which we may call the moral life';[46] he objects to liberalism as being 'antipathetic to. . . traditional moral rules' and as having 'attempted to rationalize these rules by constructing a generalized policy adapted to the character of natural man'.[47] The liberal view as such takes us back to what Minogue began with: 'Man is seen as a creature of desires. And each desire creates a policy'.[48]

The gist of Minogue's objection to liberalism is his disapproval of hedonism. To him, liberalism appears as a modern version of hedonism. This accounts for the ideology's multiple forms and directions as well as for its underlying unity.

His stance implies rejection of the view that not only can human behaviour be best understood in terms of desires but that such cognizance is our only realistic end: unlike other animals, human beings are in the wretched position of being aware that their desires are ephemeral. Desires, of course, die with us, but we cannot realistically do anything about it, as for instance by developing a new conception of our position in the cosmos, such as that promulgated by the major religions. Briefly, the argument is that liberalism has the obvious shortcomings of hedonism: despite its basis in desire, it is not what we desire from a philosophy because it makes the fulfilment of desire futile and human awareness of life meaningless. As a philosophical position, it does not make sense; but it is also not suitable to the present situation. Classical hedonism was the philosophy of a leisure class. To be practicable, the conception still requires the presupposition of leisure.

What will a liberal say to such an argument? If he does not reject it, he cannot of course be 'liberal'. But is it really possible for many people today to reconsider liberalism? To do so is tantamount to reflecting not only on the 'ism' but on the 'self': any change is bound to be very slow. Minogue certainly does not try to force the issue. After all, despite his own outlook, he does not take a very strong stand against the liberal ideology and he ends on a note which is neither despairing nor optimistic: 'We will not affect the fate of truth by making resolutions to face the facts and exhorting others to do likewise; but we may affect the fate by trying to understand why such resolutions fail'.[49] A liberal can begin with this view and in time it may have an effect.

LIBERALISM, HEDONISM AND ELEUTHEROMANIA

The hypothesis that the concept of desire – if it includes both biological drives and learned associations – adequately explains animal behaviour (other than that of the species *homo sapiens*) and that consequently the concepts of 'mind' or 'reason' are needed when referring to such behaviour, is highly plausible. It is not that we cannot find evidence of rational behaviour in animals – they learn that from experience. When we say that animals do not have 'reason', we mean that we can adequately explain their behaviour by means of the concept of desire. For them, 'desire' is a reliable guide to survival or, if such a term can be applied, to 'happiness'.

It is the grave problems one encounters in applying a similar line of thought to human behaviour that help to account for the persistence of the view that mankind is a special creation. Physical similarities between man and animals have been observed from the early days of human reflection. The mental differences plus the unmistakable evidence that when man treats his desires as reliable guides to behaviour he defeats himself (and is anything but 'happy') encourage a conviction that we are somehow a very special kind of animal. No matter how we refine the 'desire theory' – and elaborate on 'hedonism' – it does not work as a reliable guide to human behaviour. Insofar as human beings are concerned, its premises are wrong. The pleasure-pain principle of hedonism is an attempt to adapt the cause-effect concept to biological behaviour: the result is an irreconcilable conflict with 'reason' and 'will' – necessary concepts when one deals with human behaviour.

Such questions would be 'only philosophic' and 'academic', quite unknown in everyday life, if it had not been for the public debates about Darwinian theory. If we evolved from lower species, then surely the desire that motivates and guides other animals must serve as an equally reliable guide for human beings, so that we can see restrictions on desires as restraints on freedom and happiness. In other words, 'science' has now defined 'freedom' for us and established it as essential to our well-being. After decades of debate, the issue is closed.

Among liberals today this view is widespread. It plays, however, no part in the liberal tradition that goes back to Locke and Mill. There are traces of it in Hume ('reason is the slave of passion'); hence there is a tendency to classify Hume as belonging to that tradition, though it is mainly his views on 'desire theory' that put him there. If he were really a liberal in the modern sense, he would probably have developed his psychological theory into a political statement about liberty.

It is true that 'liberty' perceived as unenlightened hedonism is directly opposed to the Utilitarian hedonism advocated by Mill. The clue to conceptual continuity is not hedonism but rather Mill's conception of 'liberty' as fostering the Utilitarianism which promoted the common good. What Mill advocated was freedom of thought and a degree of freedom of behaviour that would enable men to arrive at the information about the consequences of human behaviour (which in turn would make it possible to act in accordance with Utilitarian principles). He wanted less guessing and conventionality and more science. For him, liberty was a utilitarian tool, a means to an end, rather than an end in itself. Applied utilitarianism was the end: just what this entailed was not clear. It was something to be discovered; most certainly it could not be defined as liberty there and then. 'Liberty' and 'utilitarianism' were not interchangeable.

Mill's conception of the role of liberty with regard to 'progress' encouraged the view that one can look to 'science' for a sound basis of values (even though Mill himself was cognizant of the 'is-ought' problem in the matter of values). Although today liberals reject Utilitarianism, they think of themselves as following the liberal tradition – relying on 'science', rather than 'authority', for statements about the good. Since Darwin, they think of 'science' as having established that to be allowed to follow desire determines 'happiness', defines 'freedom', and makes the latter the central good. The implication is that first, everyone ought to be a liberal; second, that everyone holding some such conception of the good is a 'liberal'.

This view cannot be called unenlightened hedonism, as it does not maintain that we need not think about what we desire and can ignore the lessons of experience, but it can be called 'eleutheromania'. This word was once a psychiatric term, which expressed a mad desire for freedom. If applied to politics, it would refer to a citizen's attitude towards questioning government policy and resisting legal restrictions on his behaviour. As a concept of freedom derived from the 'desire theory', it is essentially egoistic and irrational. As a norm, it is irrational, first because no valid norm can violate the principle that one must never make an exception of the self, which is being precisely what egoists do; and second because, as Hobbes pointed out, any conception of freedom based on egoism is not in anyone's interest. Such 'freedom' is what egoists seek to avoid rather than attain; it is an argument for an anarchy and violates self-interest. Furthermore, to maintain that the above arguments are irrelevant because we have to follow desire theory (that it is a statement about what we do, not about an 'ought') is to reveal the irrational nature of such a concept of freedom. I suggest that advocacy of it is better called eleutheromania than liberalism.

Nowadays, one finds psychoanalysts rather than political theorists promoting the new concept of freedom. They advocate seeking 'freedom' – through, say, divorce – as a solution to problems arising from a sense of responsibility, formerly a concomitant of freedom. In the 1960's, they were openly behind the hippie 'mind-expansion' experiments with drugs; they applauded dropping out of the 'rat race' of earning a living and acquiring an education. Such a conception of freedom has the consequence of making it impossible to define 'insanity'. If 'freedom' justifies believing and doing anything, then who can be called 'crazy' and what possible justification can there be for questioning or in any way interfering with beliefs and behaviour?

THE EMPTINESS OF LIBERALISM

Liberalism has always faced the problem of showing that it has a positive content. So long as it speaks only of freedom from particular evils, conservatives can agree and incorporate such views into their own policies. There is nothing inherently 'liberal' in wanting to be free from social evils. But unless there is some positive content to one's idea of 'freedom', some values one holds and wants to promote, the concept is vacuous and loses ground to conservatism. Under such conditions conservatism also becomes vague; when social ills are remedied, it tends to be satisfied with things as they are. In such circumstances, socialists are right to speak of the 'old-line parties' as if there were no real difference between them.

Challenged by the socialists, conservatives have at least made a start with stating what they believe should be conserved: they pointed to the logical link between self and property, which implies a more general proposition that valid norms have a logic transcending mere social convenience and personal inclination. Uncertain though the actual content of conservatism may be, a positive commitment exists that goes far beyond resistance to change.

The liberal, however, cannot make this kind of commitment and still remain a liberal. When he tries to give a positive content to liberty – a freedom to be or do something – he has to derive the content from outside liberalism. (He must look for coincidences between the inherent negativism of liberalism and some negative elements in other systems which have positive undertones.)

Arguing from a conjectural natural equality, socialists see the actual distribution of qualities according to bell-shaped curves as an aberration which has been introduced by society but has to be remedied even at the cost of coercive action by the State. Thus liberals, while objecting to coercion as inherently contrary to freedom, are ready to make it a part of the ideology of liberty. The result is a confusing statement: liberty means something when it is 'negative', and it means something when it is a 'positive' assertion about natural equality; but what does it mean when both assertions are made simultaneously?

There is no evidence that liberals are concerned with this dilemma. Professing views about equality that do not derive from classical liberalism – which focused on the dangers of coercion – they hope that 'commonsense' adjustments can be made, or that if given political power, they will manage to avoid antagonizing too many members of the electorate. Both conservatives and socialists naturally regard this as cynical – an absence of genuine philosophy.

The suspicion that liberals have become intellectual opportunists ready to promote at any given moment whatever is represented as a good by a sufficient number of the electorate is confirmed by the incompatibility between their relativism and their attitude towards the distribution of goods. Pointing to changes in the distribution of wealth, education, health care, etc. as evidence of the influence and inherent rightness of their ideology, liberals have made the distribution of goods as central to liberalism as it is to socialism. At the same time, they have used relativist views about the good to argue against coercion, thus employing the classical liberal view about negative liberty (freedom from coercion). The difficulty, of course, is that a relativist should be indifferent to distributive justice: if one cannot define something as a good, it certainly does not matter how it is distributed. Distributive justice is important only to non-relativists.

Mill understood this problem clearly. Distributive justice was crucial to his Utilitarian view of liberty; inasmuch as we can say there is a continuity in the liberal tradition, one must look to the concept of distributive justice rather than to 'liberty'. Mill, however, was not a relativist but a sceptic: we do not know what the good is until, through trial and error, we discover it by uncovering consequences. Hence we need 'liberty' in a negative sense, as a freedom from coercion, especially with reference to conceptions of what the good is. Until we learn this, we cannot employ the State in the service of distributive justice: the millenium has to be indefinitely postponed.

This, however, is not current liberalism. Liberals want to introduce distributive justice right now. They say they can redistribute property (the 'good' of the property-self conjunction) without infringing on freedom because the connection between property and the 'self' is a legal fiction that can be changed by altering the law. They have to redistribute this good to fulfil the requirements of distributive justice. In short, liberals try to combine a relativist conception of the good with a non-relativist conception of distributive justice. Although this is logically impossible, liberals do not recognize the impossibility. Liberalism meant something to Mill: even its 'negativism' held out the promise of progress in ethical understanding; now the desire to make it more than negative has made it vacuous. Neither the negative nor the positive elements make sense when represented as part of a single ideology.

Chapter 10

Distributive justice

DISTRIBUTIVE JUSTICE AS A LIBERAL PRINCIPLE

Although the idea of distributive justice was implicit in Utilitarianism – the greatest good ('happiness') of the greatest number – Mill did not promote it. Unlike Bentham, he did not believe that philosophic radicalism could define the good itself. He was a sceptic to whom the principal problem was to arrive at a conception of the good.

When one considers the position of a modern liberal theorist, such as Rawls, or the less philosophic views of liberal parties, it is clear that they have returned to the question of distributive justice, often at the expense of the Millian 'sovereign individual'. Thus the liberals who advocate integrated schools and legal penalties against 'exclusive' neighbourhoods see themselves as improving the distribution of goods rather than restricting 'liberty' and, in doing so, conforming to a fundamental liberal principle. Mill would disagree with their views as encouraging coercion of the individual in the name of a good which is by no means assuredly an absolute. Have today's liberals abandoned liberty (as understood by Mill) and returned to a utilitarian principle because Mill's scepticism is no longer functionally necessary to Utilitarianism?

It seems that they have, but not because they are less sceptical than Mill about our conceptions of the good. It is possible to employ the utilitarian principle of distributive justice if the good is conceived of subjectively:

enforced integration of schools, for instance, conforms to distributive justice when the good is subjective and does not violate 'liberty'. Under such a conception, the 'liberty' referred to is a lesser subjective good which is necessarily overridden by the utilitarian principle.

In this return to Utilitarianism Mill's conception of liberty is not ignored. When one acknowledges that the good is being defined subjectively, there is a great danger in assigning to the State and society the task of distribution. The old 'tyranny of the majority' comes to the fore again. This problem, however, can be bypassed if what is distributed is the means to the good as ultimately defined by the individual, that is, if the emphasis is on income – the medium of exchange which allows one to purchase (distribute for oneself) what constitutes the good. Thus the danger of having a central power determining the good is mitigated. If income, rather than property, is distributed according to utilitarian principles, one escapes the State-capitalism of Communist systems as well as the fiction that one day the State will wither away and all people will be equal. 'Equality' is not a necessary part of distributive justice. Hence the liberal State is thought of now as a system of income redistribution by means of a graduated income tax, welfare schemes giving money to those who lack it, and elaborate State-supported pension and insurance schemes in which no one asks how the money is spent by recipients. What is being distributed is the means to purchase the 'good' as perceived by the individual. Under relativism, only the individual can know the good and the only distributable goods are those that can be bought. This is a thoroughly materialistic conception which does not even have an assured place for education as a good. It leads to a situation in which, to mention one misuse of the system, there is seemingly no way of preventing welfare recipients from getting drunk on welfare money.

A major problem introduced by distributive justice is that its requirements are in conflict with the concept of charity, acknowledged as central in traditional ethical views. Nowhere is this clearer than in the attitudes adopted towards unemployment and its effects. Before Utilitarianism shifted men's attention from intention to the effect of human behaviour, it was generally believed that one could not speak about ethical goals without mentioning 'benevolence' and 'malevolence'. Consequently, the good in an ethical sense was to be found only in human behaviour (provided theological conceptions were disregarded). Hence when 'will' is not attributed to the State – as in all non-Hegelian views – the 'good' State is one that provides the conditions for the development and exercise of the necessary ethical attitude. If distributive justice is a meaningful concept, it has to arise from 'benevolence', unless it can be shown that it is part of the condition for developing ethical views – whereupon of course, like 'security' it becomes part of something the State has to provide. Early 'classical' contractualists argued for 'security'; it can be argued that Rawls has turned his attention to distributive justice as another contractual component.

Let us now take one particular issue, unemployment, and see how the concept of distributive justice conflicts with the ethical attitude of benevolence or charity as a response to the situation.

Unemployment (and its consequence, poverty) has long been regarded as a proper object of charity. This was so only to the extent that it was seen as a misfortune beyond the individual's control. The wilfully idle, since the Elizabethan days labelled 'sturdy beggars', were considered rogues taking advantage of charity and making the charitable uncertain of their own impulses. As a result, they were treated very uncharitably – an attitude which was regarded by some, notably the Fabian socialists, as evidence of Western society's hostility to the poor and of its general ruthlessness. But on the whole, the evidence about human relations in Victorian England shows that people were very much concerned with the condition of the 'deserving poor'.

It is not our concern to determine whether private charity can function as efficiently as State welfare schemes with regard to unemployment. This is an ethical question whose answer is weighted in favour of pragmatism. The immediate issue is the effect of 'distributive justice' on men's attitude to unemployment and what the 'good' State should do about it. The immediate effect is that the problem of distinguishing between the 'sturdy beggars' and 'deserving poor' vanishes. No one need decide whether the unemployed are at fault, for distributive justice establishes a new 'right' – the right to employment – and compensation to those who are deprived of it by economic conditions or personal factors. What is in fact provided is a 'guaranteed income'.

In short, the logic of distributive justice operates as follows: begin with a utilitarian emphasis on distributive justice and define unemployment as beyond individual control; one then arrives at the concept of a guaranteed income as a new 'right' that the just society must provide. When the UN Universal Declaration of Human Rights was drawn up in 1948, the 'right to work' was enshrined (Article 23) although no known society knew how to implement it. If the Charter were being drafted today, a 'guaranteed income' would replace that right as being closer to the requirements of distributive justice. Conservative critics of the United Nations are often hostile to it not simply because the organization has become a forum for Marxists, but because it has always been a forum for liberalism treated as if it were the only possible ethical position.

DISTRIBUTIVE JUSTICE: COMPETITION AND CO-OPERATION

For Professor Rawls, as for Mill, the existence of inequalities is not *prima facie* evidence of injustice or lack of liberty. When speaking of justice, Rawls says at the beginning of his treatise: 'There is no injustice in the greater benefits earned by a few provided that the situation of persons not so fortunate is thereby improved'.[50]

Such a view is the only one consistent with a contractual theory that establishes a rule of law. To insist on 'equality' would be incompatible with 'authority' of any kind, either that of an administrator of 'law' or the 'authority' of both laws and norms which necessarily override individual conceptions of the good. (They exclude relativism as a possible normative view for a member of society.)

To Rawls, the contract itself is 'the intuitive idea that. . . everyone's well-being depends upon a scheme of co-operation'[51]; that is, juristic conceptions are excluded and no assumptions about human nature are made. The issue here is our recognition of the need to co-operate despite our varying interests; the existence of an actual contract or constitution is academic.

So far, only part of Rawls's fundamental proposition has been mentioned. He also says that 'since everyone's well-being depends upon a scheme of co-operation. . . the division should be such as to draw forth the willing co-operation of everyone'. Taking the traditional contractual position, he goes one step further to speak of distributive justice as part of the 'contract'. He introduces the concept of 'distributive justice', which not everyone will acknowledge as an intuitive truth: 'a conception of justice that nullifies the accidents of natural endowment'. Not everyone will agree that the cosmos is 'unjust' because of natural differences in men's native endowments (such as superior strength, intelligence, beauty, etc.) Many will feel that attempts to flatten out bell-shaped curves of the distribution of goods are doomed to failure. Some are inclined to think that a more realistic approach for society to adopt towards such inequalities is the traditional Christian view that those who possess natural advantages suffer from the sin of pride if they imagine they 'deserve' them; and that those who resent the superiority of others suffer from the sin of envy. In other words, it is man's attitude to the distribution of goods that is at fault, not the way they are distributed.

Yet there is little doubt that Rawls expresses current liberal views when he asserts that the very conception of a social contract entails a belief that one should, as far as possible, nullify the 'accidents of natural endowments'. In this, he and other liberals break completely with Mill, who emphasized 'liberty'; Mill expected that the entire society would benefit if people with natural gifts, such as high intelligence or imaginative insight, were made free to develop them without conventional restraints.

'Intuitively', says Rawls, 'the most obvious injustice of the system of natural liberty is that it permits distributive shares to be improperly influenced by these factors [natural talents and abilities] so arbitrary from a moral point of view. The liberal interpretation. . . tries to correct for this by adding to the requirement of careers open to talent the further condition of the principle of fair equality of opportunity'.[52] In the end, however, the Rawlsian social context is in fact open to competition, although he himself claims that co-operation is the basic element. Yet one looks in vain for a discussion of the competitive element, so important to his discourse on distributive justice.

Are men competitive by nature or are the conditions of society such that one is forced to assume competition?

Hobbes saw men as competitive by nature because of their natural egoism; consequently, his social contract emphasized the 'sword' as essential to social order. This view is not shared by Rawls for he admits that he has no 'theory of punishment' and that he has said very little about punishment, although it is 'part of the theory of justice'.[53] Are we to suppose that competition arises only within a social context? If so, would it not have been better to imagine a non-competitive society that does not need a concept of distributive justice to mitigate the 'unjust' consequences of natural inequalities that serve competitive ends? What we find in Rawls does not help us to come to any decision on this issue.

Non-competitive societies have certainly existed. It has often been observed that our IQ tests cannot be applied to other societies because the latter disapprove of competition, especially where the object is to determine inherent differences in natural ability. Such societies look on competitiveness and co-operation as incompatible. To be sure, prior to the Reformation this view was characteristic of Western civilization as well. Although inequalities were acknowledged, they were thought to encourage the practice of *noblesse oblige* rather than their use as weapons in a competitive struggle to be softened by a sense of distributive justice. Modern liberals seem confused about their premises. Do they recognize that competitiveness and co-operation are incompatible? These two concepts cannot be made compatible by the device of distributive justice which strives to make the competition more equitable (less obviously favourable to those of superior natural ability).

It is easy enough to argue that a concept of distributive justice which attempts to make competition 'fair' (a matter of equal opportunity) is doomed to failure and is not compatible with the accepted system of values. There are also other objections. There is a conceptual error involved – an attempt to make competition a form of co-operation, as if it were a contest or game in which there is no trophy or prize to be won but only a sporting spirit to be displayed. However, all arguments for competition rest on the view that such good as it produces arises from the desire for the advantages to be gained by the winner. Consequently, making the advantages uncertain or non-existent by means of 'distributive justice' removes the inducement to compete without in any way encouraging co-operation. If, as Rawls says, acknowledgement of the need for co-operation represents an intuitive contract, one needs a clearer statement about the relationship between co-operation and competition than that provided by 'distributive justice'.

INDIVIDUALITY, INDIVIDUALISM AND DISTRIBUTIVE JUSTICE

An obvious definition of political science is that it deals with the relations between the individual and the State. Political theory is the justification of these relations – not through 'rationalization' but in such a way that the citizen recognizes a sense of obligation to the State and ordinarily need not be coerced into acknowledging sovereignty, while the sovereign power understands the nature of its office and as a rule will not behave tyrannically. It comes as a surprise to read in a study of liberalism by Gerald F. Gaus that the 'core' of modern liberal theory 'lies in what a social psychologist, Zevedei Barbu, has called the balancing of two conceptions of individuality'. 'According to Barbu', Gaus continues, 'in the uniquely democratic personality the individual sees himself both as a unique manifestation of humanity, an end in himself, and as a member of a group'.[54] It has escaped Gaus's notice that of course such a view is the 'core' of liberal theory, as it is of any other political theory, and one can only wonder at his supposition that it derives from the insight of a single (however eminent) modern psychologist.

What is particularly troubling about Gaus's statement is his assumption that the opinion of a social psychologist provides a new insight on which political views can be founded, and that because the statement is about individuality it is of special importance to liberals. He fails to understand that the issue – important to political theory – is not a psychological concept of individuality but a normative concept of 'individualism' – respect for individuality.[55] The fact that 'individuals' exist does not provide an argument for liberals any more than the fact of the existence of governments provides an argument for tyrants. Inasmuch as liberals think of themselves as respecting 'individuality' in a way that democratic thinkers do not (sentiment liberalism), they have to provide an argument for showing this respect, not in support of the fact that there are individuals. There are several ways in which this can be achieved.

To convert the fact of individuality into the norm of individualism (the assertion that individuality or 'self' must be respected) requires some premise about 'self' or individuality that represents it as inviolable. Hobbesian contractualism did this and provided the first source for the defence of individualism: our very egoism (sense of self extending in time) gives rise to State and society when we are able to conceive of a means to enjoy the benefits without surrendering our egoism. It is true that

the means – a sovereign power – can then in theory
ignore the value men place on themselves. In reality, it
cannot do so because it continues to exist as a sovereign
power only so long as it fulfils its function of providing
security for egoists – which in effect amounts to acknowledging individualism.

A second source of respect for the individual is the
theological view that each man has worth because he has
a unique 'soul'. Just as human beings are not cogs in a
cosmic machine, they 'ought' not to be treated as cogs in
a social or political one. A State or society that treats its
members as mere units is incompatible with the theological conception of man in the universe.

A third method, popular among relativists, is to affirm
that the political ideology is of such a nature, e.g. democratic, that respect for the individual is part of the 'rule
of law'.

The 'rule of law' view of individualism is as sturdy a
defence as the other views (egoist and theological) so long
as individualism is embodied in a constitution and departures from tradition are resisted, or so long as everyone is
conservative. However, the last defence of this position
was that of Burke. Since his day 'tradition' has been seen
as an obstacle to 'progress'; law, convention and norms
have been regarded as adjustments to particular social
conditions. Consequently, constitutionalism is viewed as a
preference for tradition that keeps us from being 'realistic' about social problems which arise from changing
conditions. (A liberal, incidentally, is likely to say that
there is a conservative personality but not a conservative
ideology based on respect for the individual.)

What exactly is the liberal position with regard to
'individualism'? If Gaus's study is representative, the
answer must be that the question does not really interest
liberal thinkers. One does not know whether Gaus even
recognizes that the fact of individuality is not the same as
the norm of individualism.

When discussing an ideology, such as liberalism, it
does not matter what stress is put on particular *facts* if
they are not integrated with the ideological position in

question. (Otherwise there is a danger in emphasizing different facts at each subsequent discussion.) One needs to know why the facts of individuality are emphasized by liberals. Except for his initial proposition that liberals stress the problem of the relation between the individual and the community, Gaus makes little effort to explain why this is so. He apparently overlooks that first, it is precisely this issue that constitutes political theory; and second, that it is the particular answer we give that determines whether we are classified as democrats, anarchists or totalitarians.

Gaus is vaguely aware of the problem: 'But. . . if Marx and the anarchists are modern liberals according to my thesis, something is clearly wrong'. Basically, however, this does not trouble him. 'The conclusion', he says, 'is not at all as absurd as it might first appear'. The reason why he feels it is not absurd is that 'Modern liberalism is not characterized here simply by an attempt to reconcile individuality and sociability but in addition by (i) the form that reconciliation takes and (ii) the way in which the theory of human nature is used to justify liberal-democratic institutions'.[56] In other words, it is not absurd to see Marx as a liberal so long as one recognizes he is only a 'thin' liberal (Gaus's term for his basic proposition about liberalism).

Thin or not, the problem is not that of 'fattening up' the concept of liberalism by speaking of norms of reconciliation between individuality and sociability or justifying the emphasis on individuality by means of a theory of human nature, but that of justifying a norm. Why is individuality emphasized? Why adopt the theory of human nature that is advanced in the book? How does one move from an assumed fact about human nature to what is clearly a normative position? What exactly is to keep a liberal from deciding that the 'thin' liberalism of Marx is superior to the fattened-up one? As was mentioned earlier, there are at least three bases for defending the conservative position on individualism: egoism, theology and the rule of law. Liberal thinkers should supply at least one for their position if we are to be assured that they will remain 'fat' liberals and not turn into 'thin' ones when circumstances change.

People who respect individuality (theoretically adhere to the norm of individualism), but do not have a normative theory in support of this attitude, have difficulty in demonstrating their respect – of establishing that they are true liberals. There is a tendency to solve this by means of the concept of distributive justice, which has become central to liberal theory.

Broadly speaking, there are three ways of thinking about distributive justice. First, one can say with Aristotle that when goods are fairly distributed, justice exists. This sounds vacuous – a mere truism – but in fact it directs our attention to justice as the central ethical concept in political theory and sets itself in opposition to the view that justice is served when goods are equally distributed (something Rawls should have kept in mind). The second way is to argue that justice exists when goods are equally distributed. According to Descartes – who I believe was joking – the only good that is equally distributed is commonsense: everyone is satisfied with the amount he has and is satisfied no one else has more. The problem with attempting to distribute other goods in an equally satisfactory fashion is that not all of them are distributable; hence one has to introduce the idea of 'compensation'. This is what Rawls does: the 'under-privileged' have to be compensated by the just society because no one can distribute all goods equally. The third way of viewing distributive justice is to argue that when goods are equally distributed, the conditions for a just society exist – a rule of law becomes possible – but that equality of distribution does not constitute 'justice'. It is only one of the conditions for it.

Although this last attempt to combine the first two views supplies no clear way to make policy decisions, it helps to understand why a good deal of liberal thinking seems so vague. Unlike socialists, liberals are not satisfied that equality of distribution amounts to justice. At the back of their minds they have some further conception of justice whose exact nature they cannot define. The problem is that in making distributive justice a manifestation of their respect for individuality as well as failing to recognize that there is more than one concept of distributive justice (and that at least one of them – equal distribution – is anti-individualist), modern liberals have taken up a very vague position indeed.

RIGHT AND RIGHTS: THE JUST DISTRIBUTION OF THE UNDISTRIBUTABLE

A difficulty that Rawls poses for those who want to label him as a liberal philosopher *par excellence* is that he does not employ the term 'rights' which in our time has become the touchstone of liberals. The word is not listed in the index to his book. Yet the concept is implicit in the very distinction Rawls makes between his own views and those of the utilitarians. Thus he says: 'In utilitarianism the satisfaction of any desire has some value in itself which must be taken into account in deciding what is right'.[57] Then he asserts: 'In justice as fairness, on the other hand, persons accept in advance a principle of equal liberty and. . . agree, therefore, to conform their conceptions of their good to what the principles of justice require, or at least not to press claims which directly violate them. . . in justice as fairness one does not take men's propensities and inclinations as given. . . and then seek the best way to fulfill them. Rather, their desires and aspirations are restricted from the outset by the principles of justice. . . We can express this by saying that. . . the concept of right is prior to that of the good'.[58]

There are very marked differences in the way philosophers distinguish between right and good, and our problems in relating these meanings to the way right and good are used in everyday language. Rawls's position as a liberal would be clearer if he had presented his point of view in terms of 'rights' – goods to which one can assert a claim – rather than as a distinction between right and good held together by a concept of fairness.

Indeed, it is the liberal talk of 'rights' – of what the State must offer – that most puzzles non-liberals and makes it difficult to arrive at a consensus. Normally, what is fair is open to debate; yet 'rights' are represented by the liberals as something already decided upon – note the Rawlsian 'restrictions from the outset' – and to be instituted without any real debate when a liberal party attains power. No doubt this is the reason why Rawls, as a philosopher, ignores the very real problem which the expansion of the concept of 'rights' has introduced into the democratic process and chooses instead to justify the liberal line of thought that gave rise to new 'rights'. The degree to which his analysis reflects that of other liberals remains debatable when the presentation is in terms of a principle of justice which from the 'outset' restricts desires and aspirations. Is his analysis descriptive rather than prescriptive? Is he, or is he not, speaking about 'rights'?

As a description of the liberal view, Rawls's conception of distributive justice is most interesting to non-liberals when he applies it to the distribution of goods that cannot be distributed in the way property can. The opportunity to be well-educated, for instance, can be provided for everyone simply by subsidizing higher education. But the good we really wish to have distributed is 'being well-educated' which is not something that can be distributed equally, no matter how much money is spent on education. Too much depends on the individual's native intelligence, personal values and interests for any system of public education to achieve equality of distribution. What does the liberal do about the distribution of goods which do not have the characteristics of property that can be 'given' to others? After all, most of our goods are of this nature. If the liberal cannot arrive at an answer to the problem of distribution, he becomes indistinguishable from a socialist: he has to limit himself to the distribution of what is distributable, namely, property.

Rawls is most provocative not when he defends 'justice as fairness' as a general proposition, but when he touches on specific problems of the distribution of goods that are not really distributable. Only by suggesting some feasible way of doing so could the liberal concept of justice be made to seem a practical position to adopt. Using the specific example of education, let us see what Rawls has to say about this central issue.

There are in his book only three references to education, yet they tell us much about the liberal view and explain what many people regard as incomprehensible liberal attitudes. In the only developed reference to education, Rawls says: 'The difference principle would allocate resources in education, say, so as to improve the long-term expectations of the least favored. If this end is attained by giving more attention to the better endowed, it is permissible; otherwise not. And in making this decision, the value of education should not be assessed only in terms of economic efficiency and social welfare'.[59]

Rawls's position is likely to appear so startling to non-liberals that it may be misread. It may be reinterpreted to fit Mill's views on education as promoting progress and consequently requiring an emphasis on originality of thought and freedom from conventional viewpoints. Thus, one could ignore the condition of the 'If this end is attained by' so as to emphasize the 'more attention to the better endowed', since in the Millian tradition it would seem to be those who are better endowed who can best promote 'the long-term expectations of the least favoured'; that is Mill's 'liberty' was not egalitarian-based but utilitarian. Rawls's real meaning is established by a concept of equality: 'The idea is to redress the bias of contingencies in the direction of equality. In pursuit of this principle greater resources might be spent on the education of the less rather than the more intelligent'.[60] This means that more attention to the better endowed is 'permissible' if they are being trained as teachers of the less intelligent, but not if they are being 'educated' simply for the sake of 'economic efficiency and social welfare'. In Rawls's view, 'justice as fairness' requires society to consider the 'unjust' distribution of goods in nature as something to be redressed by liberals.

Can the practical outcome of such views be assessed? While Western democracies spend their resources on educating people to educate the least educable, the Communists carry on the 'élitist' views similar to those of J.S.

Mill. Hence, despite the obvious superiority of the Western world in creating and distributing goods, current liberal notions of justice might enable a totalitarian ideology to catch up and rival 'capitalism'. Education based on current liberal views of redress for natural inequalities is defeating democracies by insisting on the misapplication of their resources in the name of 'justice'. It seems that Rawls means what he says when he asserts that 'in justice as fairness the concept of right is prior to that of the good'.

DISTRIBUTIVE JUSTICE AND THE LIBERAL TRADITION OF A MINIMAL STATE

When Mill ideologized democratic political parties by providing a liberal philosophy for Whigs, he did not change the democratic consensus that permitted Her Majesty's government to have a 'loyal opposition'. Both conservatives and liberals retained a belief in minimal government and each defined 'liberty' in its terms, no matter what disagreements they might have with regard to particular policies. Liberal views about 'distributive justice', however, necessarily shifted the emphasis from restrictions on the State's jurisdiction over the citizen to his 'rights' – the demands or claims that the citizen could make upon the State. This required the expansion of State powers in a way that not all liberals and no conservative could accept.

The liberal party of Mill's time tended to split into liberals and democratic socialists. Members of these groups at that time would hardly have been able to distinguish one from another were it not for the liberal tradition of a minimal State – the basic source of the definition of 'liberty'. Nowadays, Robert Nozick, unlike Rawls, is prepared to revive the tradition of a minimal State and thus make Conservatives and Liberals again the central democratic parties. (His views are not, however, more congenial to conservatives than those of Rawls, for his arguments are not consonant with the conservative philosophy.)

The liberal tradition has been so strong in democracies that even conservatives are likely to forget that arguments for the minimal State take two basic forms. In the tradition stemming from Mill, both the State and society, though necessary to the individual's welfare, pose a threat to individualism which the liberal State strives to reduce. The ideal is the minimal State consistent with the government's ability to perform its functions, so that even when these functions are enlarged by the concept of the citizen's rights, the concept of a minimal State remains an ideal. Liberals, as a rule, feel no inconsistency in both arguing for the welfare State that requires extensive interference in the life of the citizen and voicing a deep suspicion of any State interference in private behaviour.

Conservatives, however, are aware of this inconsistency. Their traditional views about minimal government rest on the separation of Church and State. The authority of the State is by definition limited to that which must be rendered unto Caesar. What cannot be tolerated is a transference of moral authority to the State by the device of representing ethical issues as 'rights' of the citizen which are decided upon by the citizen and demanded from the State. Such a device transfers all essential ethical authority to the State and citizen but no one who is aware of the lessons of history can countenance such a marked change in ethical stance. To the conservative, Caesar has no moral authority.

With this in mind, let us look at Nozick's *Anarchy, State and Utopia*. Nozick's view is that 'Individuals have rights. . . so strong and far-reaching . . . that they raise the question of what, if anything, the state and its officials may do. . . Our main conclusions. . . are that a minimal state, limited to the narrow functions of protection against force, theft, fraud, enforcement of contracts, and so on, is justified; that any more extensive state will violate persons' rights'.[61]

Most conservatives reading this are likely to regard Professor Nozick as a conservative; so are most liberals, for the passage certainly does not reflect current liberal thinking. What is much more representative of modern

liberalism is Rawls's concept of distributive justice. But
Nozick's attribution of 'rights' to the individual such that
'I treat seriously the anarchist claim that. . . the state. . . . is
intrinsically immoral'[62] differs from other liberal views
only in that Nozick doubts the State can maintain anything other than 'negative liberties' (can only protect) – a
function which, according to him, the State arrived at
through a natural process of historical development.
Although this very limited function is compatible with
conservatism, no conservative can accept the ethical
premises – that what is ethical is determined by the
'rights' a citizen can assert against the State.

From the conservative point of view, a concept of
ethical authority is just as necessary as one of political
authority. The basic reason for this is the plain biological
fact that human beings evolved under authority, not just
under 'society', and cannot exist without it. Those who
doubt this proposition need only look at the evidence of
neglected and spoilt children, who have, of course, been
nurtured by society, but have not had the advantage of
being subject to authority. Far from showing the benefits
Mill attributed to such a 'liberal' upbringing, or being in
the forefront of innovation, such children are typically
exploiters of their society and usually have to be confined
as criminals or supported on welfare.

It seems that *homo sapiens* is the only animal that cannot
trust his biological impulses as guides to behaviour, or
even such modifications of instinct as he may pick up
from observing his fellow-men. Someone has to insist that
human beings control their impulses for their own sake.
This is what every responsible parent recognizes. In fact,
one defines parental 'neglect' and 'irresponsibility' by
reference to the absence of such insistence on authority.
The conservative claims that it is misguided to derive a
concept of 'liberty', plus an ethical code, from what
amounts to neglect justified by the supposition that men
can rely on their biological impulses to achieve 'happiness'. The known facts are against this type of 'liberalism'. Nozick is clearly heading in the wrong direction.

So long as discussion is limited to questions of political

authority, the above liberal view hardly matters, since there is general agreement that such authority is necessary. Anarchism today is peculiar to thoroughgoing antirationalists. But Nozick is obviously not one of them. His argument is that a State would arise from anarchy anyway: the question is therefore academic. The issue is liberalism, as can be gleaned from Nozick's *opus*.

The evidence is to be found in his argument for political authority proffered in the absence of one for moral authority: Church and State are separated intellectually (not just politically). But, the conservative would contend, one obviously cannot separate the two authorities intellectually. If it is both possible and necessary to argue for political authority, why cannot the same argument be used to support ethical authority? The two arguments should certainly not coincide: there were enough problems when Church and State turned out to be the same. But if one is prepared to plead for political authority, why stop at a point at which we need it for ethical reasons (to maintain 'rights') but do not need some kind of ethical authority establishing the 'rights' which the political authority preserves?

Unlike today's relativists who have revived both the concept of customary ethics and the view 'whatever is, is right', Nozick is willing to consider ethical issues as encompassing more than *modus vivendi* ethics. Thus a section of his chapter on 'Moral Constraints and the State' raises the issue of our treatment of animals. Ethically, it begins with the postulate 'Animals count for something',[63] which is not saying very much. Nor does what follows, for Nozick simply proceeds, à la Socrates, to raise questions based on the above postulate. He makes no attempt to clarify our ethical thinking or bring us closer to an understanding of why we should have a political authority but not an ethical one. Indeed he leaves one with the impression that ethical views cause problems and that men would be much happier if they did not think about such things. This view, however, may not be as applicable to Nozick as it is to others: it comes very close to the position held by a great many liberals.

Like the assassin's wife in Conrad's *The Secret Agent*, liberals appear to believe that most matters are best not looked into too deeply.

Chapter 11

Equality of opportunity: a liberal shibboleth

EQUALITY OF OPPORTUNITY AS JUSTICE

The principle of equality of opportunity may appear to be one of the least controversial among the various 'freedoms' or specific constitutional requirements that liberals expect of the good society. The immediate objection to, for instance, 'equality before the law' is that it is a demand to disregard the problems of responsibility – to treat children, the insane and mentally deficient as if their condition were not relevant. Equality of opportunity seems to be a matter of social prudence, of ensuring that the available labour resources are utilized to the best advantage, possibly following Saint-Simon's tag 'From each according to his power'. As such, it is no more a specifically democratic good than the market economy. Yet, historically, equality of opportunity has been represented as one of the goods provided by democratic rather than class-based societies. The common objection to class and caste is that they reduce or eliminate equality of opportunity and are good neither for the individual nor for society. Perhaps the principle is not as much a good as it first appears. Why have not all States promoted it as a primary principle? Why, in fact, has the traditional State been class-based and in effect reduced equality of opportunity?

The answer is that it is a principle of egoism which, if made central or left uncontrolled, would destroy the sense of community, the norm 'fraternity'. No one needs,

or presses for, 'equality of opportunity' unless the conditions one faces are competitive; for a competition is not
fair if the contestants do not have an equal chance of
winning. (This may require an adjustment of conditions –
that one horse carry a greater weight – that in other
circumstances would be an unjust interference with the
effort to attain a goal.) When conditions are non-
competitive, it does not make sense to speak of 'equality
of opportunity'. Rather one speaks of the desirability of
the goal and possibly of ways in which others might help
one attain it.

The presupposition in any discussion of the equality of
opportunity principle is competition for goods; the
assumption is egoistic individualism, not fraternity. If the
principle is demanded by 'justice', and since class or caste
reduces such equality, then 'justice' demands the elimination of restrictions and the weighting of circumstances in
favour of the less privileged. This is why Rawls speaks of
'justice' in terms of 'fairness': he is speaking about competitive existence.

Now one can arrive at such a view (Rawls does not) by
postulating the literal equality of man and assuming that
if it were not for class and social conventions, all men
would in fact be equal. But if a society attempted to act on
such a principle, it would be abandoning all sense of
community and committing itself to Hobbes's 'state of
nature'. Neither the State nor the community would
exist. Equality of opportunity could not operate as a
social norm unless linked with a counterbalance, such as
fraternity. This Rawls attempts to do.

Rawls recognizes of course that men are not literally
equal and that, as a principle of social order, 'justice'
must take this into account when equality of opportunity
is discussed. Thus, he rejects the argument from egoism
that 'justice' demands literal equality of opportunity:
'Undeserved inequalities call for redress, and since inequalities of birth and natural endowment are undeserved, these inequalities are to be somehow compensated for'.[64] Naturally, if we are to agree to such a
limitation on our own opportunities, we must have a

sense of fraternity. Rawls, while aware that 'The ideal of fraternity is sometimes thought to involve ties of sentiment and feeling which it is unreasonable to expect',[65] nonetheless introduces it into his theory of justice under the guise of the 'difference principle'. ('The idea of not wanting to have greater advantages unless this is to the benefit of others who are less well off'.[66]) Although he supports his analysis by arguing that such a feeling actually exists among members of the traditional family, he does not note that the latter has been breaking down; and that one of the obvious reasons for this is precisely the presence of the egoistic individualism that he wishes to modify by means of a sense of fraternity.

In fact our society rewards egoistic individualism, calling it 'equality of opportunity'. Although, in order to hold society together, we try to pretend that the principle demands the Rawlsian redress of inequalities, we are aware of a basic conceptual weakness. In effect when the State weights the competition for goods by giving special assistance to the 'underprivileged', it is acting as if it were the source of the sense of community. If the State goes, so will the community. This is now the liberal viewpoint. But a democratic State is in a bad way when it assumes that this way of thinking represents a factual truth. In all viable States, it is necessary for a sense of community to exist prior to the State. When this is not the case, when the sovereign power decides what the community is and what it needs, some form of tyranny is present.

Many argue that democratic governments are becoming increasingly coercive, forcing people to do for the sake of the community what they really do not want to do. Rawls contends that men would do voluntarily what they are now being coerced to do, if they gave the matter careful thought; furthermore, because of the need for a sense of community, a reasonable man would *modify* his demand for equality.

Such an attitude must presuppose an initial desire for equality of opportunity. But why should one suppose that such a desire represents man's nature, that men begin with a concept appropriate to egoism and then, recognizing it must be modified if the sense of community is to be retained, allow themselves to be coerced into the modification on the ground that prudence demands it? Such a view reverses the actual situation: men recognize that the good of the State demands equality of opportunity but they also recognize that such an equality is for the individual's good only if the situation is competitive and one feels equal to the competition. There is no evidence that man wants to compete rather than co-operate.

To recapitulate: what is Rawls's solution? Basically it is to redefine 'equality of opportunity' in such a way that it incorporates a sense of fraternity. One doubts that conceptual and normative problems can be solved in this way. There is a limit to the meaning of any concept which has a meaning: one can hardly solve problems by an ingenious reasoning which makes both X and not-X parts of the same concept and hope that some process of education will induce people to accept the result as a norm. Ultimately, norms are but special types of belief (about behaviour and its consequences); if they do not make sense, nobody, no matter how willing, can really believe in them and act accordingly.

EQUALITY OF OPPORTUNITY: FURTHER RESERVATIONS

To focus on inequalities in human beings – the facts about IQ, health, physical strength, etc. – is to pay inadequate attention to the fundamental equality: the basis for making human beings members of the same class. The sin of pride has long been recognized as socially disruptive, the basis of class conflict. Democracy offered a 'solution': a refusal to acknowledge the 'misfocusing' of attention as politically or legally relevant. Thus in private life men could be as snooty as they liked towards those they regarded as inferior, but they would not get any support for their attitude from society. This was an early approach to what 'liberal democracy' meant; it was a politically naïve view, for it gave free rein to socially disruptive attitudes. What is currently offered as a

solution is to attack the assumed basis of these attitudes –
by reducing the differences between human beings.

In the days of Fabian socialism it was felt that a redistribution of property would achieve this. It was rightly
recognized that disparities in property have much to do
with men's attitudes to each other; that while they can
feel sympathy for the disabled and imbecile – be ready to
acknowledge common humanity – it is difficult for them
to feel the same way towards a sturdy beggar. In the West,
the latter has always been the object of restrictive legislation. However, a little reflection shows that if one got
rid of sturdy beggars by redistributing property, the
process would have to be continuous so long as there
were people willing to have their lowly status.

An emphasis on equality of opportunity is a tacit
admission that inequality of property will always be with
us; that social effort should be directed towards promoting the kind of equality that enables human beings to
achieve their own goals.

As Walter Kaufmann rightly observes, this is completely
unattainable: 'An equal distribution is no guarantee of
justice'.[67] An attempt even to approximate the necessary
conditions would be extremely disruptive socially. Unfortunately, this kind of argument has no effect on those
who maintain that one should strive to attain the ideal.
To Kaufmann, equality of opportunity is either a 'hollow
cliché' (unrealizable) or a 'pernicious goal' (socially
disruptive).[68] Those who hold to it as a norm will argue
that first, since it is unrealizable, its perniciousness as a
goal will not be realized; second, that an approximation is
better than the present situation. Kaufmann's criticism
would have been strengthened if he had voiced a fundamental objection to 'equality of opportunity' as a norm.

A possible objection is that the principle 'equality of
opportunity' reflects only a slight shift from the naïve
assumption that the goal of democratic society is literal
equality; that the desired Utopia, instead of being equality
of circumstance, is a kind of *inequality* that ensues when
each man has been given 'equality of opportunity'.

A shift of meaning of this type enables a millionaire to

look with equanimity upon the concept of equality: it does not require him to give up his wealth in order to be democratic. But it also goes directly against the Fabian recognition of the role of property in human relations. If Henry Ford's sons can keep their property, what possible social arrangements would give the child of a welfare recipient equality of opportunity? The concept of equality of opportunity may be said to 'solve' the disruptive effects of a demand for actual equalization of property. But, while allowing those who promote it to dissociate themselves from communistic norms, it leaves them with a confused and fragmentary programme.

The central problem, normatively speaking, is that as a concept 'equality of opportunity' is now operating in a way that hinders a reappraisal of the norm 'equality'. Thinking in terms of 'equality of opportunity' as a good prevents one from discussing inequalities in democratic society in terms of 'pride'.

In a world where men are manifestly unequal and co-operative effort depends on inequalities (the division of labour and the nature of bureaucratic structure pre-suppose and require inequality) the norm 'equality' poses immense problems. One cannot help wishing to return to the early view that the issue is not the fact of inequality but rather that of 'pride' – the dissociation of some individuals from the community on the basis of their actual or assumed superiority. The materialist con-ception, however, of values, the assumption that the actual inequalities 'cause' a dissociation from or indiffer-ence to one's fellow-men forces us to debate the issue from a false position (which all parties to the debate must know to be such). This is like addressing an audience that cannot be told directly what the real issue is because it will sound 'undemocratic'.

EQUALITY OF OPPORTUNITY AS AN ALTERNATIVE TO SOCIALISM

If 'equality', the general concept, refers to man's relation-ship with his fellow-men, 'equality of opportunity' refers to man's relation to goods: it requires equal access to goods rather than the socialistic equality of distribution. There is, therefore, no necessary connection between the concept of equality (as a reference to human relations) and that of either access to goods or that of sharing them, unless goods can be shown to affect human relations. They are, of course, known to do so. Property, for instance, is so closely linked with the 'self' that an unequal distribution among those who are completely 'equal' as individuals (for example, identical twins) would create very marked differences in their relations with each other.

Since democracy is concerned with human relations in this world, it has been argued that the general concept of equality requires equality of distribution. Thus all problems of equality arising from the enhancement of self consequent on property accumulation would be resolved. Civilized man would have the same kind of equality as exists in primitive nomadic tribes whose need for mobility makes large differences in property a burden rather than an advantage. Civilization, however, rests on the possibility of accumulating property. The attitudes required are prudence and providence. Trying to solve the problems of equality by redistributing property would mean giving up too much.

It is the above consideration that made the principle of 'equality of opportunity' appear the democratic solution to the problems created by the effects of inequalities of property distribution on human relations. The solution seems 'democratic' because it presupposes individualism, which equality of distribution ignores. Instead of assuming that all goods have intrinsic worth, that it is a self-evident truth that all men desire the same goods and therefore the available supply should be equally shared, the principle (equality of opportunity) makes the decision about the good a matter of personal choice. If someone happens to prefer reading Shakespeare to watching a hockey game, or prefers a hamburger to caviare, it is not democratic to insist that the State should make everyone read Shakespeare and share caviare. It is not the democratic State's business to define the good and distribute it equally. Instead, let the individual define the good for himself and the State provide the kind of equality consistent with this view: that is, equality of access or, as it is usually termed, 'equality of opportunity'.

As the democratic ideology emphasizes both equality and individualism, one would expect 'equality of opportunity' to have been its central concept for a long time. One reason why it was neglected in the past is that the concept permits a ruthlessness which is inconsistent with the sense of community necessary to a State. Thus a successful businessman might argue that since by definition a democratic State allows equal opportunity, the poor must be poor because they are either not interested in striving to get ahead or unwilling to acquire the skill and experience necessary for success. Many examples of 'from rags to riches' were put forward in support of this view. It was rather common during the depression of the 1930s and was effectively ridiculed by the cynical observation that in the USA even the poorest man could set himself up in competition with General Motors. Equality of distribution seemed then more humane and realistic than such absurd interpretations of equality of opportunity; indeed it seemed a necessary precondition for genuine equality of opportunity, for it can be argued that only if everyone starts from the same basis one can speak of a genuine principle. Until the mid-twentieth century equality of opportunity seemed too relativistic to be fully acceptable: if each man is allowed to determine for himself what the good is, one implies that this kind of self-determination defines the nature of the good. Equality of distribution appeared more consistent with society's conception of the good. It was not believed that decisions regarding the latter should be left entirely to the individual and that in this matter democratic society should act only as an umpire ensuring fair play.

In our time, the kind of relativism which makes the individual and his tastes the touchstone of the good became very strong. Consequently, it became more common to interpret the meaning of both 'equality' and 'freedom' with reference to the principle of equality of opportunity. Liberals virtually define themselves as such by voicing the principle; some conservatives are attracted to it, although they may strongly object to the inherent relativism which makes it an attractive concept to others. The explanation for such an alliance is that emphasis on equality of opportunity reduces the emphasis on equality of distribution. If the issue of equality is made a matter of access to goods rather than of their possession, one no longer need fear socialistic welfare schemes which distribute the benefits of property throughout the community. It seems that some protagonists emphasise equality of opportunity because it is consistent with relativism, whilst others do so because it is an alternative to socialism.

EQUALITY OF OPPORTUNITY: A CAVEAT

What has been largely ignored by democratic theory is the potential for absolutism in the concept of 'equality of opportunity'.[69] Emphasizing the normative quality of the latter, democratic societies are running the danger of having to suffer from their erroneous assumptions. They avoid analysing the norm anew while waiting for the lesson from experience alone. Since the norm has a potential for tyranny, this may be very risky. Those who learn from experience politically, learn too late for the information to be useful to them, no matter how enlightening it may be to others.

The problem is that modern Western society adheres to an irrational view that the 'cause' of human behaviour is environmental conditions interacting with biology. Consequently, any change that is normatively good requires encouragement of the conditions that beget the norm. This view may be called a Big Brother's view of the good: someone knows, or people agree, that something is the good, but it cannot be rationally analysed.

Equality of opportunity can be regarded as one of these self-evident or accepted truths in a democratic society.

There is a looming potential for tyranny in any 'self-evident' truth which is supposed to be a central good. Under the assumption of irrationalism, equality of opportunity has a potential for something worse, totalitarianism. It demands that the State interfere in the areas that democracy itself defines as private and that the objections to such interference be overridden as mere prejudice.

The threat should be described in terms broader than those of Yves Simon, who argued that creating the conditions for equality of opportunity will lead to absolutism.[70] Simon was merely drawing attention to a special case of the need to balance the requirements of equality against those of individualism or freedom inherent in democratic ideology. This has been done for decades and democratic society will continue doing so, provided it retains a rational view of norms and behaviour. But this capacity to ward off totalitarianism is lost when norms are considered a mere 'superstructure' and man a mainly irrational being. When the latter views are adopted and 'equality of opportunity' is employed as a good, it becomes the duty of the democratic State to interfere with the individual, a way unthinkable to classical democratic theorists.

The democratic State today excludes the inculcation of norms (as mere 'prejudices') from its own system of public education but, as the theory of man's irrationalism requires, it takes steps to have 'environment' determine normative attitudes. Its major efforts are limited to 'problem individuals' and 'problem families'. Thus juvenile delinquents are sent off to holiday camps, so that the natural environment will 'reform' them, apparently in the way Wordsworth supposed 'Nature' operated. The treatment of 'problem families' provides an even better clue to what one may expect from irrationalism which operates under the concept of 'equality of opportunity'. Social workers are assigned to guide such families in all decision-making. Families are moved into subsidized housing; middle-class norms are presumed to evolve spontaneously from the new environment. But this does not happen, as anyone who believes that norms are rational concepts based on centuries of experience would expect. The direction taken by the liberal society is so to manipulate the environment that opportunities exist for all. The horror is that it can be argued – and is being argued – that when acting this way one does not violate human freedom; the individual is not coerced at all; it is merely the environment that is modified, so that the issue of 'freedom' does not arise. In the last analysis, it is the irrational view of human behaviour current today which holds the threat of totalitarianism.

Chapter 12

Liberal liberty and liberal rights

A NOTE ON TABULATIONS OF FREEDOM AND LIBERTY

Are tabulations of definitions of freedom (and/or liberty) useful apart from fulfilling the desire of scholars to establish typologies and presumably order their own thoughts? As Herbert Muller reminds us, an exhaustive historical survey of the variant meanings of freedom was conducted by Mortimer J. Adler and his colleagues. The meanings were reduced to three basic definitions: that of natural freedom of self-determination – 'the ability of a man to change his own character creatively by deciding for himself what he shall do or become'; that of acquired freedom of self-perfection – 'the ability of a man through acquired virtue or wisdom to will or live as he ought in conformity to the normal law'; and circumstantial freedom of self-realiz-ation – 'the ability of a man under favourable circum-stances to act as he wishes for his own good as he sees it'.[71] It would be presumptuous to claim that these findings were 'wrong' or 'faulty'. A comment, however, relating the three conceptions of freedom as a good to other con-ceptions of the good is certainly in order. Freedom as a good arises when there is a conflict about the meaning of the good between the individual and an authority or power which he cannot hope to escape or replace by representing himself as the only 'genuine' authority. (In the twentieth century, incidentally, some naïve liberals have acted as if the latter were possible).

Beginning with 'natural freedom of self-determination', the term has its roots in Rousseau's views on 'natural liberty' and man's 'unqualified right to lay hands on all that tempts him'.[72] It is an expression of Wordsworthian romanticism: 'Nature never did betray those who truly love her'. It seems to convey that man, like other animals, can trust his desires, inclinations or whatever determines the feeling that under the circumstances what one does is the 'right' or 'best' thing to do. Ethically, this view gave us 'unenlightened hedonism': our desires, our own impulses are an adequate guide to the 'good'. Epistemologically, it leads to the narrower thesis of empiricism: we can trust the evidence of our senses to supply us with the only kind of 'truth' open to us. Rather than 'natural', one is tempted to call it naïve or unenlightened freedom.

The freedom called 'circumstantial freedom of self-realization' in Adler (usually referred to as 'self-development') seems to parallel the modifications of unenlightened hedonism which historically were given such names as Epicureanism and Stoicism. The concept of freedom here takes into account the difference between 'maturity' and 'immaturity', or the notion that we cannot rely on our biological nature but, as individuals and societies, are for a considerable period of time subject to the authority of others. Both Mill's ideas on freedom and his liberalism were of this type; that he put them forward as relevant to mid-Victorian society reflects the astonishing presumptuousness of Victorian England rather than his philosophic conviction.

The problem with the Millian concept is that it does not entail a time schedule. When is anyone or any society 'mature' enough to be in a position to demand legitimately the 'freedom' which will enable him (it) to develop further? Hence there can be said to be the third type of freedom designated by Adler as 'acquired freedom of self-perfection' (usually called 'self-realization'). Instead of setting a timetable for freedom, a transcendental goal above and beyond time is set: it is the individual himself who decides whether he is mature or not. This seems to constitute a modern liberal view of the grounds for 'freedom' as a value. 'Doing your own thing' is the popular way of expressing it but since no one but the individual sets the standards, the view comes down to the same situation as is present under unenlightened hedonism. Except for one crucial point: this time round no objections can be raised, for the criterion of good lies within the individual. The view appears to be a normative version of solipsism.

Liberty

A failure to consider that 'liberty' is a political norm which cannot be discussed without reference to other concepts of political theory can lead to disappointing results. Thus a sociological argument such as John Hall's mixes up questions of freedom – as in his 'first component of liberty', which discusses some material conditions for liberty – with actual political issues, as in his 'second component' ('negative liberty'). He then splits off conceptually the related components of liberty, in particular, his 'final component' (control of government by the governed).[73]

DEFINING LIBERTY IN AN IDEOLOGICAL CONTEXT

Discussing liberal political views poses a special problem for the political theorist because the term 'liberal' is not restricted to ideological issues. The term is often referred to a psychological characteristic which has normative implications: open-mindedness, tolerance, generosity. 'Liberal' appears then to be a reflection of an intellectual trait which few people would care to disown. For the same reason, liberals are confident that all thinking people are liberal. No doubt they are if one deals with the realm of psychology; but they are certainly not if one speaks of ideology.

The significance of the wide meaning given to the term 'liberal' comes into focus with the realization of a peculiar development in twentieth-century liberalism which is present in E.F. Carritt's definition of liberty as 'the power of doing what one would choose without interference by other persons' actions'.[74]

Though most people (including Carritt, who offers it only as a 'preliminary' definition) probably recognize that such a definition needs qualification so as to enable human beings to live together – it needs to be supplemented with a social contract theory – it is doubtful whether many students of political theory have been unduly perturbed by its unsatisfactory nature. The definition is about a psychological issue (frustration) and is not quite relevant to a democratic situation. Although it makes no direct attack on what J.S. Mill said, it represents an abandonment of his position. Since these points are closely related, we will consider them together.

Before the rise of modern democracy (ideological democracy), 'liberty' as a concept was a wish for freedom from 'tyranny' or arbitrariness in the exercise of power. There is no evidence that at this early stage any serious argument was made for the absence of government and for claiming that such an absence would lead to freedom: anarchism is a late development in political thought. On the other hand, there has been a very clear desire to have government without the possibility of its becoming a tyranny. Thus, when we assert that 'liberty' is central to political theory, we assume that our theories of government should ensure that a government does not become a tyranny; we want our concept of government to entail 'liberty'.

Hobbes's *Leviathan* did not do this. Although it did not entail tyranny, contrary to what some critics have argued, it did not ensure that the sovereign might not become tyrannical towards at least some members of the State. The only 'solution' offered was a dilemma: put up with the present misery or return to a condition just as bad, perhaps even worse. (At one time, everyone seemed to recognize this: objections to Hobbes did not take an anti-contractualist form but reflected attempts to modify contractualist theory in the direction of 'liberty'.) The problem posed by the need felt for government, coupled with a fear of tyranny, was theoretically solved by liberal democracy. Democracy controls 'tyranny' or arbitrary coerciveness, not 'government' or the group of legislators who govern without reference to the electors' desires. Thus modern democracy accords with the requirements of Hobbesian sovereignty but excludes its potential for tyranny. (It also accords with the 'rule of law', which in Britain is often identified with a social contract.)

Mill seems to have recognized this situation as setting the framework for a discussion of 'liberty': the issue under democratic conditions is no longer tyranny; if we want to say something new, we have to move on. He himself moved on to questions of psychological liberty – what one might call the conditions necessary for 'freedom of the mind'. This is an important question when we ask what the point of freedom is (in the sense of 'freedom of speech', 'freedom of assembly', etc.). Mill shifted the discussion of liberty from questions of government legislation and coercion to factors impinging on the human mind, ranging from political to psychological issues.

Although Mill's discussion of liberty may at times be confusing, his intentions are not. What he had to say about liberty can only be understood within his ethical utilitarian framework. Bentham's Utilitarianism entailed relativization of norms and a shift of the unit of moral worth from the individual to a larger entity, such as society, the State or even that abstract body 'mankind'. Mill seemed not to mind the relativization of political norms – unlike modern liberals, for instance, he had no objection to despotism *per se* – but he did object to the shift made by Utilitarianism away from the individual as the unit of moral value. Consequently his discussion of liberty attempted to restore the place of the individual in the traditional European scheme. It also showed his desire to get rid of Utilitarianism's potential for upholding a 'tyranny of the majority', in which the actual majority might have no say as to what was being done in their name. Outside this framework, Mill's talk of liberty sounds like an obtuse argument for anarchism as a political system and egoism as a social system.

Some modern conservatives clearly understand this. Thus George Will looks to Burke and comments approvingly on his view that '"Government is a contrivance of human wisdom to provide for human wants," with these wants containing "a sufficient restraint upon their passions"'.[75] Modern liberals are likely so to define 'liberty' that the ideas of Burke and his followers on this issue appear mistaken. (Note, for instance Professor D.D. Raphael's assertion that 'Freedom means the absence of restraint' followed by his argument that 'Self-direction, choosing for yourself, is far preferable to having decisions made for you. . . This is why liberty is valued'.[76])

Such views do not constitute a mere difference in viewpoint of the kind that enables adherents of liberalism and conservatism to coexist as fellow democrats. To the modern conservative like George Will, human nature is such that we see nothing wrong in the fact that obedience is required; on the other hand, the modern liberal maintains that there is something in human nature that induces us to resist authority, guidance and restraint. To the liberal, liberty is a natural good because it is a natural inclination to follow 'desire'. (Thus, as quoted earlier, Carritt defines 'liberty' as 'the power of doing what one would choose without interference by other persons' actions' and, like other liberals, sees no need to argue that such definition is about a 'good'; he assumes he has defined a natural impulse.)

If to follow desire is desirable, it is odd that until this century political theorists were unaware of it. One would suppose, for instance, that all contractual arguments would have included some device to overcome man's 'natural' resistance to authority as well as to particular rules. It would also be hard to understand how civilization could possibly have developed if we had all been naturally determined to act according to our own lights. Why does history not reveal constant and determined resistance to authority, simply because authority exists?

It is possible to extract from Mill a formulation almost identical to that of Carritt, Raphael and others. Thus Mill says: 'The only freedom which deserves the name, is that of pursuing our own good in our own way'. He, however, immediately sets his statement into a utilitarian framework: 'Mankind are greater gainers by suffering each other to live as seems good to themselves, than by compelling each to live as seems good to the rest'.[77] (If we were analysing Mill, we would ask how he could know such a thing.) The issue here is the consequence of isolating Mill's respect for the individual from his recognition that the individual cannot – and must not – be isolated from some social and political order. We cannot have a society of egoists, nor can we have a political system like anarchism, yet this is what we are advocating if we talk of 'freedom' as an absence of restraints on our desires.

Before considering how Carritt's definition of liberty could be amended, we must be clear that our concern is with an aspect of ideology, not with natural law; that the point of reference is life in a State rather than in a wider construct of the universe (with 'freedom' as a good). The problem boils down to the function of 'liberty' in an ideological system like democracy. Whatever the definition of liberty, it must not be about the individual outside of society; nor must it use an ideological concept like equality to disguise its concern with isolated individuals, as in Mill's analysis. As a political idea, liberty must be related to such concepts as authority, sovereignty, obedience and political obligation. If it is not, or if the relationship is not self-evident, the definition lies outside the sphere of political philosophy. Whatever definition of liberty is reached, its role as a political concept is to set limits to the authority which contractualism creates but does not limit. There has to be 'authority' because it cannot sensibly be argued that we would be better off if we knew only what we happen to learn through personal experience. For this reason, in order to analyse liberty we must concern ourselves with the 'proper' operation of authority, not with its absence.

As a political concept, liberty is likely to be as difficult to define as the 'good', for it is the good conceived within a framework of coerced obedience – which is the opposite of what we usually think of as moral or ethical freedom. Each of us is born into a State which limits our choices because that is the reason for its existence. Any argument for political freedom implies that the condition thereby created is a good – is contracted for – no matter how inadequate or paradoxical the result.

Carritt and other modern liberals, who try to dispose of the paradox, do so by getting rid of the 'contractual' argument – known to all rational human beings – that authority and its coercion are good for us. The liberals err on the side of oversimplification: if political freedom entails a paradox, they seem to believe, then one should shift to a discussion of moral freedom, which is merely about choice and the 'wrongness' of restraints placed on it. But what is one to do with arguments that human beings cannot exist without authority and coercion? Forget them and contemplate the pure beauty of 'ideal' freedom?

Such views do not promote liberty, for they ignore the political issue: given coercive authority, to what restraints can it be subjected so that it will serve its function without becoming tyrannical (consistent with democracy)? These are the implications of the political (or ideological) concept of liberty, as opposed to other kinds.

POLITICAL THEORY AND METAPHYSICS: FREEDOM AND LIBERTY AS DISTINCT ISSUES

Drawing a clear distinction between 'freedom' and 'liberty' may be long overdue. The fact that it is customary for theorists to use the two terms interchangeably does not make the task easy. Nor does the legacy of J.S. Mill.

It should be noted that the very first sentence of Mill's *On Liberty* at least implies that 'liberty' and 'freedom' are distinct issues: 'The subject of this Essay is not the so-called Liberty of the Will', he says. But he also refers to 'free will' as 'liberty'; thus whatever the subject of his essay was, Mill would not use the resources of the English language to help clarify matters.

If we start by stipulating that 'liberty' is what concerns

political theorists and 'freedom' is the term referring to what lies outside politics, we face an immediate difficulty, since in English specific liberties, such as freedom of speech or freedom of thought are also called 'freedoms'. There seems good reason to retain the usage rather than try to change it, for such 'freedoms' are goods primarily because they are linked with questions of free will rather than with one's political and social relations. (Thus Mill's own discussion of freedom of speech, thought and conscience is premised on free will in general. He makes no attempt to establish a utilitarian case for such freedom (or freedoms) but bases his argument on 'truth', which is a good only insofar as we are not part of a determinist system [insofar as we have free will].)

Despite this caveat, a deliberate effort to restrict the term 'liberty' to some relation between an individual and a coercive (or potentially coercive) power would greatly clarify our understanding of fundamental political concepts. Even the very general notion of 'some relation' would eliminate a good deal of confusion; the political scientist's concept of 'liberty' cannot be defined outside a political setting and then somehow be attached to it by a metaphysical glue: it has to be about the relationship to the body politic, not about a hypothetical, non-political situation.

Today, in the post-Darwinian era, political theorists must be especially careful – and 'realistic' – in their discussions of liberty. They cannot, for instance, postulate a Hobbesian 'state of nature' that is non-social; hence they cannot found a definition of liberty (or freedom) on a statement about that condition. As a species, man is biologically committed to life in a community; therefore it makes no sense to refer to conditions necessary to community as 'restraints' on 'freedom'. Yet some of the contractualists' assumptions are of value to the modern theorist grappling with the concept of liberty. We will return to this issue presently.

Unfortunately, a good deal of what Mill had to say about 'liberty' was premised on a non-Darwinian postulate. When judging the situation, one should remember the relevant publication date (1859 for both *On Liberty* and *The Origin of Species*). Modern liberals seem to forget this: they act as though Mill's views had a sort of perennial truth abstracted from a biological reality which is now an accepted premise. They still act in a way in which Mill could be justified in acting. To him, there was a kind of 'freedom' which can be postulated about the individual and which uses Utilitarianism as a sort of metaphysical 'glue' with which to attach the concept of individual freedom to reality. Liberals today call this hypothetical, pre-Darwinian condition 'liberty', although we know that it could never have existed.

The modern theorist's necessary postulate that what he has to say about 'liberty' is distinct from everything that has previously been said about 'freedom', makes it especially important to distinguish 'liberty' from 'freedom'. But if he begins with the view that he is not speaking of a 'state of nature' that could not have existed, what exactly is he talking about, and what makes it a good? How can a post-Darwinian and post-Millian theorist define liberty as a good? How can some relationship become clear and good? Conceptually, he deals with the stance understood by the early contractualists. Amazingly enough, long before Darwin, they argued that man must be subject to restraint, and that the 'must' is an 'ought': it is 'good' that one be subject to restraint, that we recognize this, and that if we do not, we can and ought to be coerced into compliance. (This revision of Hobbes's 'Covenant without the sword . . .' although generally observed as fact, needs to be specifically expressed. Jurists should note it. It is of considerable importance to law and order as well as to notions of liberty.)

To the theorist dealing with 'liberty', the freedom of man under authority is not unqualified: he is not 'absolutely' free. This is not understood by the Romanticists to whom life in accordance with nature is a natural good (man in such conditions being not subject to authority). But we cannot avoid assuming original 'unfreedom' as the premise about the human condition. The discussion of liberty must be premised on an assumption that, logically, we have never existed in a state of nature; moreover, that such a state is not the 'ideal' we strive for when speaking of 'liberty'.

Does 'liberty' have theoretical significance and deserve definition? I believe new attempts at a definition should be made and that the debate should continue, Karl Popper notwithstanding.[78]

'Liberty' matters to the political theorist (and to others, one hopes) because being about man in society it raises questions about the jurisdiction of what (or who) is acknowledged to have a right to coerce. 'Freedom' raises an important question about determinism which must be taken into account if 'liberty' is to make sense.[79] But 'liberty' also poses an 'ought' question: voluntarily or involuntarily, what are the conditions under which it can be said to be 'good' that one individual submits to – or resists – coercion by society and authority in general?

Part of the answer is present in contractual theory. It is not true, it said, that coercion is wrong by definition, or that 'good' in the abstract – 'freedom' or 'liberty' – is violated by the fact of life in society. This was a remarkable insight, considering that contractual theory developed before the Darwinian argument that human beings cannot exist outside society.

Given that as individuals we cannot exist outside society and that we are necessarily subject to law, what does 'liberty' mean? Can it refer to something more specific than 'some relationship'? It can do so if we see it contractually, or in a way which Mill resisted.[80] If it is true that man cannot live outside society, 'liberty' has to be about this very situation rather than about some unwilling accommodation, a *modus vivendi* forced on us by the condition of life in a community. The views of modern liberals derived from Mill trivialize liberty because they assume that although man is a social animal, he is unwillingly so: we would all rather be Robinson Crusoes and derive our concept of liberty from this desire.

But the evidence of history is against this diagnosis. 'Liberty' became a value after contractualism provided an argument against the Robinson Crusoe hypothesis. The concept of liberty had better not be a norm that somehow 'denies' or 'refutes' contractualism, but rather what history shows it to be: an attempt to limit normatively the authority of a sovereign power as argued for by contractualism.

Having said that as individuals men cannot exist outside society, one must add: nor can they exist outside international society. No full theory of liberty can be formulated without considering international relations, especially the aggressive, domineering, 'imperialist' behaviour of some States towards their neighbours (and even more distant States). There is no meeting of political philosophy and the theory of international relations on the issue of liberty because while the former operates within the realm of established concepts without due regard to foreign experience – presumably coming from the areas of no paramount importance – the latter's orientation is towards the present: it avoids both philosophical arguments and historical concerns. Consequently, the almost forgotten definition of liberty in terms of independence is neglected by contemporary political theory. Yet in the words of John Plamenatz, 'Independence has been valued and alien rule resented by many more people than have aspired to democracy and individual freedom'.[81]

LIBERTY AS INDEPENDENCE

At the beginning of his discussion of 'Negative Liberty' (chapter 6 of *The Notion of the State*) d'Entrèves observes that for both Hobbes and Machiavelli, 'Liberty' referred primarily to 'independence': 'For Hobbes the "liberty of the Commonwealth" consists. . . in its independence. Machiavelli, too, when speaking of political liberty (*vivere libero, stato libero*), seems to have this meaning especially in mind. Liberty was to him primarily the absence of foreign rule, and only secondarily opposition to tyranny'.[82]

This point is of major importance to political theory for the following reasons.

First, it may lead to our discovering new roots of nationalism. The term 'nationalism' and its sense of 'devotion to one's nation' and 'a policy of national independence' was first recorded as late as 1844. The prevailing view is that nationalism developed under the influence of the Romantics who introduced the notion of a 'folk': its place in political theory has been uncertain. If the ideas of Hobbes and Machiavelli in this respect are to be taken seriously – as they are in other respects – this view will have to be revised.

Second, it links 'nationalism' to 'sovereignty'. D'Entrèves' point about Hobbes and Machiavelli brings out the question of who should govern as determined by those who are to be governed. Such an argument makes 'nationalism' a logical aspect of sovereignty rather than an invention of the nineteenth-century Romantics. It also explains why Woodrow Wilson's 'self-determination' was a logical response to the political situation after World War I.

Third, it reclaims for the notion of liberty the dimension attributed to it by the two classics and which, although subsequently supported by historically verifiable perceptions, was largely ignored by Western political theorists. Thus the link between the concept of negative liberty and independence is revived only occasionally (as in wartime) and is treated very superficially. On the whole, political theorists have lost sight of 'independence' as the core of 'liberty'. Unfortunately, the issue was never developed by modern contractualists; 'independence' has been outside their frame of reference. The results are: (a) ambiguous definitions of imperialism (b) imprecise formulations of political freedom (c) uncertainty about what to do with the concept of 'rights' in relation to 'obligation' (duty).

In analysing liberty we must go beyond the contractualist tradition which looks at the State as if it existed in a vacuum, as if international relations were of no consequence to the citizen and his relationship to the political authority. Yet political freedom (liberty) has both 'internal' and 'external' dimensions. Focusing on the latter brings in international interactions and power politics; focusing on the former emphasizes the objectives of national wills – men's aspirations as citizens and patriots.

The notion that liberty has an external dimension implies independent nationhood, freedom for a nation to cultivate a way of life and develop itself undeterred by foreign interference, not to speak of foreign domination. The meaning of 'liberty as independence' becomes strikingly clear when a country falls victim to foreign aggression and is deprived of freedom. Its citizens' aspirations become focused on self-rule and independence. Here the example of Poland is particularly relevant. Having until recently been deprived of true independence for almost two centuries (except for the interwar period 1918–1939), the Polish nation has premised its conception of liberty on the ending of foreign domination.

To sum up: as d'Entrèves has reminded us, the concept of independence is part of the classic discussions of political liberty. The point made by Hobbes and Machiavelli ought to be resurrected as part of the tradition of political thought that was meant to be anything but parochial. The growth of modern nation-states has made Machiavelli's ideas topical again. The rise of twentieth-century totalitarian States playing havoc with the national wills of their neighbours has not been sufficiently 'internalized' by Western political theory – despite voluminous discussions of the 'isms' – to make the discussion of liberty universally applicable and historically relevant. Most of the writings that have emerged from the recent Anglophone tradition have ethnocentric blinkers. Today, Carritt's definition of liberty reads like an ivory-tower exercise. The factor of independence – crucial to the national psyche of peoples behind what used to be called the Iron Curtain – has not been integrated into Western analyses of liberty. Its reabsorption would be a step away from intellectual isolationism and a recognition of a universe of ideas, historical events and political realities which continue to exist outside the national boundaries and semantic reaches of the Western Academe.

HUMAN RIGHTS AND LIBERAL RIGHTS

The 'rights' which are now to the fore in democratic societies differ markedly from the 'rights' referred to in that celebrated document of our time, the Universal Declaration of Human Rights.[83] 'Women's rights', 'black rights', 'prisoners' rights', 'animal rights' and other special rights – which are not even alluded to in the UN Declaration – come to most people's minds when the issue of rights is raised. In our analysis of liberty, the distinction between universal and special 'liberal' rights must be kept in mind.

Any attempt to define the content of liberty in terms of rights – as is done by those who advocate special rights – seems to focus on the groups of people who are deprived of 'freedom' as measured by the notion of equality. Insofar as the distribution of goods can be shown to be unequal with regard to distinguishable groups or classes such as women, natives and blacks, what is perceived is that they lack 'freedom', although the rest of society is apparently free. Liberty is then determined by the society's general economic and social conditions. The weakness of this approach to questions of liberty and rights is that it promotes disunity in society. Although democratic society is tolerant in the sense of acknowledging pluralistic differences in cultural traditions as valid (tolerable), it cannot tolerate the use of such differences to promote social conflict – factionalism.

What the issues raised by rights groups have in common is that they are not based on what is primarily right, but on the fact that in a democratic society – whether what is demanded can be called 'just' or not – a concerted pressing of demands is usually politically effective. Most rights movements seem factionalist and are the political equivalent of labour unions; but instead of uniting their members in order to coerce an employer, they unite their followers for the purpose of coercing democratic governments by discrediting them. (No matter how outrageous the demand, governmental indifference to such a demand – or its outright rejection – becomes 'evidence' that the government is 'undemocratic'.)

Obviously, such consequences are important to democratic theory. In the past, factions or single-issue movements were looked upon with so much suspicion that their very existence as legal entities had to be incorporated into the notion of the 'rights of man'. This was the case with the right of assembly and association. Historically, this right came into being at the time when the sovereign power was defined as 'above' factions. 'Tolerance' was an attribute of the *de jure* sovereign. Its correlative – the duty of those who have the 'right' to assembly – was that they would not behave as 'factions'; that is, would not try to coerce or even influence the sovereign power into violating the principle of being 'above' factions. Under contractualism, there could not be 'factional rights' within a society having a *de jure* sovereign. The existence of such 'rights' would be evidence that the so-called sovereign power was not sovereign in a *de jure* sense (whatever the position might be in a *de facto* sense).

We have now reached a paradoxical situation in which the aim of 'rights' groups is to coerce the government and society into believing that if coercion is successful the result will be 'democratic', but 'undemocratic' if the coercion is unsuccessful.

Rights are democratic issues not because democratic societies are 'free' – allowing people to express some inner urge – but because, having adopted a relativist way of conceiving of ethical issues, they have created a problem for themselves; they now need a democratic way to get rid of relativism. The choices to be made are so important that they cannot be left to a relativistic practice such as the majority rule. In other words, the concept of 'rights' turns out to be a sort of 'derelativization' device – a device peculiar to democracy, which created the problem in the first place. (We are 'democratic' not because we allow the question of rights to be discussed but because we created the issue by seemingly arguing that there are no absolutes such as 'rights'.) The conception of human rights today (as distinct from the factional rights of 'rightist' groups) is an attempt to assert, even in a world where relativism is the mode, that there are absolutes.

The concept of rights in the sense of some kind of normative absolutes above and beyond mere desires is essential to the defence of democracy. Thus, if 'desire' and its satisfaction is the good, on what grounds can it be said that the desire of the many – democracy – is superior to that of the few or one? In other words, on the basis of desire theory, is it possible to object to Thrasymachus's view that the good is the will of the stronger, or even possible to distinguish his view from that of democracy as the expression of 'will'?

To recapitulate: 'rights' represent the assertion of absolutes, not the absoluteness of desires (as they are for factional 'rightist' groups) and insofar as they are justifiable, they are justifications of democracy itself. If 'rights' did not exist, if all norms were relativist, there would be no possible way of justifying democracy as we understand it, as an ideology or a statement about absolutes. Those who believe in such absolutes are highly suspicious of liberals whom they regard as 'factionalists'.

Part III

Hedonistic socialism

Chapter 13

What is socialism?

The view that socialism is a form of secularized Christianity has been so long advocated by socialists that it hardly seems worth serious examination. At best it means no more than asserting that norms have a history; at worst no more than a propaganda device designed to lure politically uncommitted Christians into taking political action. But because there is a clear connection between modern democracy and the Protestant Reformation and because socialism is one form of democratic belief, it would be unreasonable to dismiss the idea. Perhaps one should bear in mind that today the majority of church-going Christians tend to be conservative rather than socialist and that they tend to view those members of the Church who are socialists as 'heretics', as indeed they certainly would be if socialism were secularized Christianity.

In our time religion has declined as an ideology in the philosophic sense. Its cosmology is now often derided and its assertion about the self's continuance in time (the immortality of the soul) is generally doubted, so that the Church's normative restrictions on sensual and materialistic behaviour are viewed with suspicion. Nonetheless, the Church remains a powerful force because it is now the only organized body holding beliefs firmly founded on respect for the individual and our capacity for free will. All other statements – those made by the social sciences, Marxism and Freudianism – are deterministic; consequently, anyone who considers his own intuitive sense of self in their light is unable to account for what he himself feels to be fundamentally true. However convincing the deterministic statements may seem (since they are made on the basis of reasoning from empirical evidence), they leave out of account the agents actually doing the reasoning – and hence remain unsatisfactory. On the other hand, no matter how questionable some of the statements of the Church may seem, its fundamental propositions about the self retain their force. So long as the Church remains the only body insisting on the fact of self and free will it will remain a major influence on human thought. Consequently, it will be tempting for the Church to secularize its position by abandoning its theology and the norms derived from the immortality of the soul and focusing on what theology says about human relations in this world.

Of the four basic tendencies of socialism mentioned in a popular text on socialism (R.N. Berki's), two – egalitarianism and moralism – are clearly derived from Christianity. The first, egalitarianism, is conceptually democratic rather than exclusively socialistic; it would seem related to the Protestant view that we must seek our own salvation and are in effect in a contest for salvation and therefore 'equal': the contest is not rigged. Berki, however, ignores the fact that egalitarianism is democratic rather than purely socialist and argues that the concept of egalitarianism, which he calls the '*classical* principle of socialism', must logically lead to the conception of community: 'to be truly equal with your fellows in the community you must . . . stop being self-regarding . . . . It means consciously accepting that self-transcendence is the truest form of self-realization, "membership" of the community the highest form of distinction. Egalitarianism thus expresses the aspiration for a return to a "public" or communal way of life'.[1]

It does not of course do anything of the sort when it derives from the individualism inherent in Christianity – an individualism which Gibbon saw as one of the principal causes of the decline and fall of the Roman Empire because it destroyed the sense of community. It is true that communalism has repeatedly arisen under Christianity. Under Catholicism, the various religious orders began as communalists whose members themselves owned no property; Shakers, Quakers and others tried the experiment again and again under Protestantism. The relation between property and the self is so clear that if one denies the importance of the self now – in this world – it follows that a rejection of personal property constitutes a rejection of this world. But this is not tantamount to rejecting self in favour of the community on the ground that we are all in some way 'equal'. If one goes one step further one can find that non-Christian totalitarian socialism – Communism – constitutes a denial of individualism and an assertion of equality through the abolition of private property (ostensibly the main source of inequality). Secularize Christianity and you are still left with the original individualism and hence a deep respect for property as the main manifestation of that individualism. Secularized Christianity is markedly capitalistic. Such was R.H. Tawney's message.

Berki's assertion that socialist egalitarianism 'culminates' in communalism certainly does not enable us to understand the platforms of any recognized democratic socialist parties. As a rule, they do not advocate any such thing or foresee it as an ideal. Opponents occasionally charge them with holding this view, arguing that what is advocated is a termite view of society in which no one has any individuality but all are workers for the mysterious 'society' whose members are mere organic components. This view may properly be attributed to some Communists and those influenced by egalitarianism divorced from individualism (who are bound to reject the Christian tradition of individualism as well as Christianity itself). To adopt a determinist point of view, to see the 'self' as conditioned by society and hence as having no real existence – leads to regarding communalism as the ideal solution to the problem of inequality. The only people tempted towards such an ideal today are those who have been influenced by determinist viewpoints, like the misguided souls who tried the Walden II experiment in the

USA. Socialist parties are not so unrealistic; they recognize the hopelessness of utopianism: it would exclude 'reform'. To advocate the social reform designated to promote such a communal State would inevitably raise the spectre of revolution and conflict.

Although Berki speaks of moralism as the Christian aspect of socialism, in his discussion of the logical consequence of egalitarianism he says that 'the common ownership of goods becomes a total value, an end in itself: nothing should be allowed to stand between the single individual and his community. . . . The egalitarian sees relentless struggle between [rich and poor] with no quarter given or asked for'.[2] This, too, is not a description of the democratic socialist position. When Berki says the egalitarian 'sees relentless struggle . . . with no quarter given' he is advocating Marxist-derived views, not the socialism of secularized Christianity typical of Western democracies. Indeed a major distinction between socialism and Communism is the issue of conflict (and revolution). Although the determinist views of the social sciences have represented conflict as inherent in the human condition, democratic socialism sees violence as a symptom of something wrong in society but remediable without conflict – something that draws attention to the existence of a social problem that must be eliminated by social action. It regards violence as evidence of an illness of the social body rather than a condition that must exist so long as inequality exists.

This interpretation of violence in democratic societies is not limited to socialists. Many liberals and conservatives hold similar views, as one would expect since the norm against violence derives from Christianity. Where socialists and conservatives differ is in the type of response advocated: socialism, being more thoroughly secularized than either liberalism or conservatism disallows responses based on norms and will. (Thus to a conservative insistence on law and order and a return to ethics appear the only realistic courses of action.) As a result, socialism has adopted the relativist viewpoint that behaviour is traceable not to norms but to conditions in society apart from the norms. The socialist sees the norms as guides to social action but not to individual behaviour. In this he differs markedly from the conservative.

EQUALITY, PROPERTY AND WELFARE

What can be called the suppositional or conditional view of equality – the proposition that men would be 'equal' if social conditioning and accidents of upbringing did not interfere with this hypothetic equality – is not confined to socialists (and Communists). Some liberals and conservatives are also inclined to believe it. We know this from the wide appeal of Watsonian behaviourism in the 1920s and its revival under B.F. Skinner in the 1950s, despite the fact that its fallacies had been thoroughly exposed. We know it also from the attacks on the concept of the intelligence quotient (IQ) and some related problems, especially the question of genetic inheritance of intelligence – the theory that was advocated by Francis Galton at the beginning of the century and is now undergoing a remarkable revival.[3] Yet members of democratic society in general want to believe the behaviourist proposition that a normal human being can be 'conditioned' to be anything – soldier, sailor, doctor, lawyer, beggar, thief; they do not want to believe that there are inherited intellectual differences that profoundly affect one's behaviour and position in society. Such people would like to derive the democratic 'ought' of 'equality' from a hypothetic 'is'; for if this can be done, one can then define 'justice' and 'democratic society' and have a clear programme of action: inasmuch as humans are in fact equal and society enables them to achieve what they desire, such a society is 'just' and 'democratic'.

Given this proposition, there is one clear and unmistakable source of inequality: the distribution of property. In the market economies of the modern world money can buy so many different goods that we have virtually reversed the Christian view that 'love of money is the root of all evil'. Most people are quite certain that to possess wealth is to possess all possible goods; they ignore warnings from various quarters that this is decidedly not true. They believe that 'every man has his price' and therefore that being able to pay the price means having power over others.

Indeed, it is quite likely that a fairly large number of conservatives think that, if it were possible to distribute property equally and maintain an equal distribution without affecting individualism as a norm, all problems that are solvable by human effort would be solved. No conservative, however, believes this can be done. He is too conscious of the relation between self and property (having usually inherited his property or acquired it by his own efforts) to suppose that 'equality' could be achieved by a redistribution of property without sacrificing 'individualism' and 'freedom'. At one time this position put him in opposition to the 'socialist' who might either argue that 'individualism' and 'freedom' are illusions where marked inequalities of property exist, or that what we call 'individualism' and 'freedom' are simply other ways of saying that one believes in inequality and not in the brotherhood of man and communalism. This position, however, has now become peculiar to the more radical trends of 'socialism'. The democratic socialist is prone to recognize that 'individualism' and 'freedom' are necessary components of democratic beliefs and that consequently any scheme designed to achieve equality at their expense cannot be called democratic, no matter how it is implemented, whether by revolution or evolution.

What is the evidence for such an assertion? The answer is that democratic socialist parties have shifted from advocating State ownership of the means of production as a primary goal to advocating State welfare schemes whose object is not to equalize property ownership but to achieve as much of the good possible under equality of distribution as is consistent with the existence of private property (as a primary good). This is not to say that socialists have reasoned out and developed the implications of their views on the welfare State, or even begun with first principles, any more than liberals or conservatives have done.

Characteristic of democratic thinking since the eighteenth century has been its concentration on specific 'problems' which are defined as much by the customary norms of the community as by the logic of democratic norms. What we call 'democratic behaviour' is strongly pragmatic and what we call 'democratic theory' constitutes deductions about the assumptions being made and analysis of possible consequences for fundamental democratic norms – if specific solutions to social problems are instituted. There is no such thing as democratic orthodoxy. With this caveat in mind, let us try to understand why socialists now think of the welfare State as the epitome of democracy and why there is a marked resistance to this view.

Fabian socialists, by their advocacy of gradualism, successfully countered the objection to violence characteristic of democratic thought derived from Christianity (though the type of society the Fabians advocated did not differ from that envisaged by the Marxists, who saw the conflict as inescapable). However, the Fabians were never able to argue convincingly that the so-called Protestant work ethic would be retained and their influence was limited. Their opponents objected that if property were equally distributed, no one would work unless compelled to: the best one could expect under Utopian socialist egalitarianism would be a beehive-type society, which, considering Bernard Mandeville's criticism (in his *The Fable of the Bees*, 1714), would not even be a prosperous beehive.

By calling the work ethic 'Protestant', we represent it as a matter of sectarian belief and thus dispensable when religion decays, but the only real connection (between work ethic and Protestantism) is verbal: Luther redefined 'vocation' so as to make labour as much a 'calling' as the priesthood. To Luther everyone was a labourer in the vineyards of the Lord provided he had faith. Apart from this view, work is an extrinsic value, a means to an end where property can be accumulated. Briefly, the connecting link is not between work ethic and Christianity but between work ethic and property as a value.

Fabian socialism, then, was seen as an unrealistic solution to the problem of egalitarianism where property is a value. Fabians were quite unable to get around the fact that if property is a value, so is work as long as it enables one to accumulate property; when it does not, it ceases to be a value and consequently society must either make compulsory all those activities that were formerly voluntary or live off its accumulated resources until they are exhausted.

Utopian or not, the very advocacy of equality of distribution presupposed an inherent 'natural' equality which had formerly existed and would come into being again if everyone started life with the same advantages. If one assumes differences in ability and interests such that some might be more capable of accumulating property (and some more interested in doing so), it no longer follows that equality of distribution is either just or practicable. Indeed, insistence on equality of distribution becomes equivalent to insistence on property as the central value and goal in life – a view, incidentally, more characteristic of conservatives, who derive the value of property from the emphasis they place on 'individualism', with property and self inextricably linked.

No socialist will agree to this 'natural law' view of property, of course. It places too many obstacles in the path of any interference with property. To the socialists (and many liberals) property is a legal fiction whose content and very existence depend on what the State says – the classical example being the abolition of slavery by law, that is, the total abolition of one form of property. This approach can easily lead to the view that only 'due process of law' keeps the democratic State from making general dramatic changes in the content of 'property'. To Fabian socialists the view of property as a legal fiction had revolutionary potential. But nowadays the socialists' focus is different. The emphasis is on the wise and just handling of the national income by the State (through suitable fiscal and economic policy) so that even those who lack the foresight, prudence, competence or any other qualities necessary to gain and spend wisely will be provided for as if they had those qualities. The democratic socialist nowadays does not base his views so much on a hypothetical original equality, which he would seek to restore by redistributing property, but on the fact of inequality whose effects he seeks to mitigate by State welfare or fiscal and economic policy in the interest of the community. To be sure, the concept of hypothetical equality has not disappeared from socialist arguments. This can be seen from the emphasis placed on those welfare schemes which seek to alter the living environment of the poor – through, for instance, subsidized housing and recreational facilities – rather than providing additional income or mitigating the effects of unwise expenditure. (The assumption behind this kind of welfare scheme is still the old view that if social conditions were equal, social conditioning would be equal and then – and only then – equality of opportunity would prevail.) It is this kind of welfare scheme that baffles and disturbs conservatives, many of whom are unable to afford homes equivalent to subsidized housing and are often outraged by the rapidity with which the subsidized houses are allowed to deteriorate into slums.

Few seem to realize that socialist interpretations of egalitarianism have led to social determinism. It is this view of human behaviour, as determined by irrational factors in the environment, which sets socialists apart from liberals and conservatives. The socialist no longer professes to know just what factors need to be changed, he is no longer convinced that property equalization is the required panacea, but he has faith in modern behaviourist science and 'social experiment' (along Skinner's lines) – a faith which adherents of other persuasions find incomprehensible.

SOCIALISM AND DETERMINISM

The durability of various socialist ideologies in the face of history and political theory, especially their enduring appeal to 'intellectuals', is best understood today in terms of the appeal to determinism. To many thinking people, no matter what practical and theoretical objections are raised against the particular forms of socialism, the belief that social problems are soluble only by manipulation of social conditions remains the 'scientific' view. When socialists say they are offering a scientific solution to problems, they are not using a figure of speech or 'emotive' language to influence others. They are advocating the views advanced in the social sciences; if these views frequently parallel Marxian views it is because both the Marxist theory and the social sciences work with the same deterministic assumptions.

Social scientists nowadays are convinced that the theory of evolution has established as a 'fact' that man is part of a deterministic system. Hence if a 'scientific' statement is to be made about ideology affecting behaviour, the effect must be traced to actual material conditions. The resulting statement need not be the same as a Marxist one, but the lines of thought will often coincide, especially with regard to the relations between individual and community. Although each point of view professes to respect the individual, the assumption about the nature of the individual as a personality is such that he vanishes into the community: under determinism, the individual as a personality is the product of social conditions.

But if socialism appeals to man's intellect by virtue of being 'scientific', it also appeals to his sloth and passivity.

All credential systems, including socialism, are very demanding of time and effort. To be sure, the true believer in socialism has to practise his belief: he must be an activist. It is puzzling, however, that anyone who believes in activism should promote a view which encourages a peculiar sort of passivity. Since socialist intellectuals assume that the impulse to change comes from 'society' (or the environment), they make the individual 'responsible' for his condition only in a very limited way. (Some argue that because the passivity of the 'oppressed' is also a product of social conditions, the true socialist must demand 'rights', even when those who supposedly have these rights do not recognize them.) To those who only intend to follow their inclinations, the view that social conditions account for most of their problems and that it would be useless to do anything other than demand that 'society' remedy them, may appear highly attractive. People of this persuasion fall into the deterministic trap.

The fundamental appeal of socialism rests on the assumed validity of environmental determinism. If one denies the autonomy of the individual, if everyone is the product of his environment, then the solution to social problems lies with 'society': thus in North America, neither native Indians nor welfare cases are responsible for their condition. They are evidence of something having gone wrong somewhere.

Where does it all lead to? If one questions any particular point in the argument: whether human beings are biologically 'equal' (in the sense of having 'identical' characteristics) or questions the incapacity of the individual to make choices – then the case for socialism is no longer self-evident. But it is pointless to raise such questions when the social sciences refuse to consider such possibilities. In order to be scientific, the social sciences have to assume the identical nature of the factors they are studying: in this instance, the equality of human beings. They must assume that the causal factors which operate in the physical sciences operate in their own field as well, thus maintaining a continuum between the physical, biological and social sciences. In order to be 'objective', they have to reject the traditional views about norms. The social sciences are in fact socialist sciences and socialism is really a form of scientism.

SOCIALISM AND RELATIVISM

There can be little doubt that democratic ideology has a high relativist potential: the principle of 'tolerance', as popularly understood, comes very close to being a demand that one make no judgement about the views and behaviour of others; the principle of 'equality' seems hardly tenable unless one decides that the inequalities we perceive are merely non-qualitative differences because 'there exist no genuine qualitative differences'. The principle of 'majority rule' can be seen as a demand that one ignore reason and decide issues on the basis of attitude, taste and personal interest.

Yet not all those prepared to subscribe to democracy are necessarily ready to accept relativism. A conservative, for instance, virtually defines himself as such by his rejection of relativism: customary norms are what he is basically interested in conserving. He finds it impossible to believe that everyone on earth throughout known history has been wrong about anything so fundamental as the concepts which define relations between human beings and that it does not really matter what these relations are or how we behave. Thus, the conservative sees majority rule as a principle of last resort: it can be applied only when all available information has been used and neither the closest reasoning nor the most cogent arguments can produce agreement. Under no circumstances is it to be the principle of first resort ('all in favour of lynching say aye'), for this is pure relativism.

For the conservative, tolerance is a principle of social harmony rather than of relativism or, as with some liberals, that of scepticism. Whereas John Stuart Mill argued that we cannot be sufficiently assured of truth to be in any position to suppress what we regard as false, the conservative is more likely to hold the much narrower view that tolerance requires first, that we as individuals avoid unnecessary conflicts of opinion and second, that the government remain above and outside all such normative conflicts. Indeed, to a conservative the entry of government into an undecided normative conflict is evidence that it is exceeding its authority.

On the third major element in democracy relating to relativism, the conservative also takes a non-relativist stand: 'equality' for him does not require the elimination of qualitative judgements of behaviour and performance. (Exactly what it does mean for him will be considered later.)

The relativist tendencies of democratic ideology do not

seem to trouble the socialist: relativism solves for him a
number of conceptual problems with regard to the
meaning and role of such fundamental democratic concepts as majority rule, tolerance and equality. Yet despite
this advantage, it inevitably must raise doubts not only
about norms in general but the norms one is committed
to – those in whose defence one introduces relativism. In
what way can one be committed to democracy if in
defence of its norms one puts forward the relativist view
that a commitment to a normative position is an indefensible subjective attitude? The relativist view would
require a democrat to submit with good grace to a
majority decision to abandon a democratic form of
government for a totalitarian one. The concept of majority rule would then be regarded as normative only insofar
as it was relativist and as such not a principle of democracy, the principle of last resort (as it is for the conservatives and for some liberals). There is strong evidence
that this is indeed the socialist view. When the principle
of majority rule seems likely to lead to the abandonment
of 'democracy', the socialist views the situation with
equanimity: the demand, for instance, that the government of South Africa instantly introduce majority rule
does not appear to have been modified by the argument
that not only would the 'white tribe' democracy collapse
if it were, but what we call civilization as well. The socialist
retort is that the government should express the will of
the people and that what we call civilization represents an
ethnocentric bias. Both views are relativist rather than
democratic. If one adopts the relativist view and claims
that to speak of cultural superiorities would betray
'ethnocentric prejudices' then what were formerly forces
of order and social harmony – such as law and education
– become forces of social disruption.

One would suppose that, logically, if one assumes that
no valid judgement can be made on the rightness or
wrongness of one cultural trait over another – a position
of cultural relativism – then to insist that a certain trait be
preserved would be anti-relativist. If, for instance, language (as linguists define it) is an arbitrary system of

symbols – and as such functions as a means of communication – then there can be no justification for insisting that the Eskimo language (known as Inupik), spoken in Canada by no more than twenty thousand people, be preserved. Nor can there be any justification for not teaching standard English pronunciation and grammatical usage. If a system is arbitrary, then to allow more than one form will simply make the system unnecessarily complex and difficult to learn; to allow any other 'form' or 'system' tends to defeat the function of communication.

But relativists characteristically ignore questions of function, and focus on the issue of arbitrariness. Since it cannot be proved that 'ain't' is inferior to 'is not' or that the Eskimo way of announcing that the house is on fire is inferior to the English, the relativist is at a loss when it comes to insisting on one or the other. Thus, the American Teachers Association is reputedly opposed to teaching slum children standard English pronunciation and usage although it is hard to understand what language they can be teaching if this is their official position. The Canadian government has been under strong pressure to dub Eskimo dialogue into all TV and radio programmes heard by Eskimos and, unbelievably, to stop teaching English to Eskimos. Only such a position, many say, is truly 'democratic'.

Conservatives emphatically disagree. Their view is that even what is unquestionably arbitrary – if it exists as a social practice – must have a function. Thus it may be true that the traffic rule 'Keep to the right' is arbitrary, but this is not the point; the point is that the arbitrary rule is a functional rule of order necessary to that order. It may also be true that an Eskimo language is as good a medium of communication as English within a certain environment; the point is that language functions as a means of communication and if insistence on 'equality' of the means leads to a breakdown in communication, we must focus on function, not on the arbitrariness or 'equality'.

To the conservative, 'equality' must not be equated with a relativist attitude, if only because it is markedly unfair to those forced to regard as arbitrary that which is in fact functional: slum children allowed to speak substandard English will never be able to enter any but manual occupations; Eskimos forced to communicate in Inupik are forced to remain in a primitive hunting/ gathering culture although such a way of life is now dependent for its very existence on the larger market economy of Western civilization. When some people sincerely assume that such limitations on the opportunities of others are genuinely democratic because they are relativistic, we have every reason for supposing that for them relativism has become an essential and characteristic norm of democracy. Thus a traditional form of equality such as equality before the law, as well as – ironically – even equality of opportunity, have for them lost a good deal of their meaning.

Chapter 14

Socialism and freedom

PROPERTY AND POWER

The concept of property, man's attitude to it, its relation to the 'self', to power and individual freedom are central to a discussion of any brand of socialism. The relation between property and the self – the fact that an enhancement of property enhances the self – is so obvious that frequently even those who regard the concept of property as a legal fiction, use the effect of property as evidence to argue that the State must control the distribution of property if anything that can be called 'freedom' and 'equality' is to exist. (The argument is of course double-edged, for in the minds of non-socialists private ownership stands firmly as a guarantee of freedom against the encroachments of the 'omniowning' State.)

The above argument must be carefully distinguished from the hedonist contention that 'justice' requires property redistribution because poor people cannot enjoy life to the degree that the rich can. The argument is rather that inequalities of influence in the community entail inequalities of freedom. Thus an employer can not only restrict the freedom of his employees whose livelihood depends on his goodwill, but is also – as a man of property and provider of jobs – of more importance to the government; consequently, he has greater influence upon its decisions that his employees could hope to have. The employees, who have more votes, might in a democracy have more effect on who composes the government (at least in theory they do), but the actual decisions of government – no matter who composes it – will be more influenced by the 'important' people who (as employers and producers are rather crucial to the welfare of the nation) often take a close interest in legislation such as only the 'ideal' citizen of democratic theory does. Empirical studies show that influence is correlated with income; consequently – unless one supposes that those who take the ideal citizen's interest in policy-making also show the ideal citizen's altruism – there is a problem of 'freedom' as well as of equality. Some members of the democratic community are able – wittingly or not – to impose their will on others: they have more 'freedom'.

Those who use this argument as the basis for the proposition that the government should control the means of production, sometimes attempt to reinforce it by introducing the issue of the corruption of democratic institutions. They argue that large companies and wealthy individuals contribute to party funds and – by making the parties dependent on their support – gain an additional advantage. Legislators may even be bribed, as seems to happen more frequently in a democratic system which gives greater power to the individual legislators than to the party. This argument, however, appeals more to our moral indignation than to reason. No one has yet produced evidence that one form of democratic government is necessarily composed of more moral members than another. The implicit argument that it would be good if members of the community were so poor that they could not bribe anyone is not particularly appealing from the point of view of freedom. It is, however, significant that anyone to any extent advocating a socialist solution to disparities in influence – and hence in freedom – should introduce it. This question touches on a point neglected (though not entirely overlooked) by Sidney Hook and Max Eastman in their noted debate for and against greater government ownership of the means of production.[4]

Hook argues against the proposition that 'given a collectivist economy, politically only a totalitarian state is compatible with it'.[5] In a rejoinder to Hook, however, Eastman introduces the problem of shifts of power and its consequences for freedom when one pursues the goal of 'efficiency' and 'freedom' in the abstract: 'The whole political future of Europe, and perhaps of mankind, is contained in the question: *What are you going to do with the industries?* If you believe in free competition and the state as a regulative mechanism, then you will turn them over, to the extent compatible with regulation, to private owners. That will create many small powers over against the single power of the state and over against the Communist Party which is boring from within, with its expertly unscrupulous technique to control the state. But if you believe in democratic Socialism, then you have only the power of the state'.[6]

Eastman says a great deal more than this, of course, but because we are focusing our attention on the issues of power and freedom we will limit ourselves to the assertion about 'many small powers against the power of the state'. He does not, however, say anything more about the proposition and consequently it is perhaps not surprising that in his rejoinder Hook concentrates on other issues raised by Eastman. Why has not more been said?

To a democratic socialist, one of the major issues is the existence of different degrees of freedom in a supposedly egalitarian society when there are differences in the amount of property controlled. Eastman, when referring to 'many small powers', is speaking of the power based on property – of what follows when an individual or corporation has control of a means of production. He would not have an argument against a State monopoly of the means of production if this were not so. In effect, he is using a balance of power argument.

One can understand why Hook did not take it up: if the argument is valid, it is a serious objection to even the mixed capitalist-socialist economy that Hook advocates, for every shift of an industry to State control would represent a shift in the present balance of power between citizen and State. A point may well be reached in a democratic economy when we must either alter our

present democratic institutions to take into account the
new power of the State (and the lesser power of the
citizen *vis-à-vis* the State), or we will find our present
system no longer democratic – not because the government has seized power, but because we have unconsciously transferred too much power to it.

The weakness in Eastman's position is that it rests only
on an assertion: he has not related it to the fundamental
proposition that property and self are related. One suspects he did not want to do that because, when he wrote
his rebuttal, deep down he remained a socialist. If you
make the relation between property and self explicit so as
to give a firm theoretical foundation to the empirical
facts about the relation between private property and
power, then you have to admit that the transference of
property to the State will reify it. When this happens a
democratic socialist government becomes not only the
servant of the people but also of the State. No democratic
socialist cares to contemplate such a proposition.

FREEDOM AND EFFICIENCY

The specific problem Hook and Easton debated in the
1940s is now historical: what should be done about State-
owned industries in post-World War II Europe in view of
the desperate need to revive the national economies as
soon as possible while recognizing that the future of
democracy might be jeopardized if a wrong decision was
made. A somewhat similar situation confronts us in the
Third World today: the Third World nations are des-
perately poor and so heavily indebted to the West that if
they default, our own economies may collapse. Will
democratic socialism enable them to attain a higher
national income more quickly than pure 'capitalism' and
at the same time keep them within the democratic camp?
Let us state the position as follows: the issue of the
compatibility of freedom and the assumed efficiency of
planned economies is a matter of our own self-interest
(and can be entirely separated from talk of benevolence
and commitment to freedom and free enterprise).

(Unfortunately, we cannot plunge into a discussion about 'efficiency' and 'freedom' in the way Hook and Eastman did for reasons that will become apparent later – in our discussion of the 'balance of power' argument.)

The concept of 'efficiency' is just as much a normative term as 'freedom' and consequently cannot be measured any more than 'freedom'. If we do not know why some people think it is a good and others do not – why, for instance, factory workers regard 'efficiency experts' with deep suspicion and often reject their advice out of hand – any discussion of efficiency and freedom is idle.

In the first half of this century, 'efficiency' had so high a normative status that it cropped up in the most improbable contexts. I.A. Richards, for instance, spoke of 'more efficient poets' and did not, it seems, mean that such poets wrote more poems. What he did mean is not quite clear, though it appeared to have some relation to the concept 'condensed' (another odd term which seems to imply a poet is more 'efficient' if he packs more meaning into a smaller space). The point is that 'efficiency' has come to be regarded so evidently as a good that it can be used in aesthetics. When this happens, it is clear that efficiency is considered a self-evident truth and can be used to explain some of man's most baffling concepts and problems. To understand this extraordinary development, we have to turn to the changes Marx made in the concept 'work', as well as the need for the concept 'efficiency' to make his concept plausible.

Despite commonly held views of the 'Protestant work ethic', the work ethic derives historically from early Christian ethics. It represents what is necessary if sloth is a sin. Sloth is a sin, of course, because the imperatives of Christian ethics are more than negatives: one cannot be a Christian just by accepting restrictions on one's behaviour – not lying, not stealing, not killing and so forth. Christianity has always denied that the norms important to the individual and necessary to life in a society can be expressed as restrictions. (Hence it denies that 'internalized law' theory, which is derived from Freud – and which focuses on fear – can be called a 'scientific' account of normative behaviour. If some norms require positive action, it is false to suppose that fear of punishment accounts for the observance of norms: there is no conceivable way that fear, 'internalized' or not, could make one, for instance, charitable in a recognizable way.)

Marx completely altered the traditional approach to the work ethic by introducing economic determinism. He predicted the collapse of capitalism as inevitable and used the tool of the labour theory of value (and surplus value) to prove it dialectically. By making labour the basis of value, the object of the 'bourgeois' work ethic was now interpreted as the sin of avarice – not as avoidance of the sin of sloth.

In the Marxian labour theory of value one can detect a hidden assumption of 'efficiency' (or 'productiveness') – a logical way of escaping the possible objection to the theory that a slow worker would theoretically increase the value of the goods he produced just by being inefficient.

Marx's concept of surplus value portrays a capitalist economy as an institutionalized form of cheating in which some people – owners of the means of production – do not make any contribution at all to the value of goods. In consequence, if they are eliminated, an increase in 'efficiency' will result: the same amount of labour will produce a higher return to the workers because they no longer have to support the idle and the non-productive. 'Freedom' is increased, as in the case of a man who no longer has to support an idiot child.

Something strange has happened to the concept of 'work' while it has been used to define 'value': the shift of its normative status is now likely to have very marked consequences on the norm of 'freedom'. According to Christian ethics, work was a good – a behaviour in which the end makes the means (the 'work') good. Under Marxian ethics, 'efficiency' has taken over the normative element; and work itself, though still in principle the unit of value, is something that everyone is supposed to want to reduce by means of the efficiency-norm itself. The Marxian good has now become 'leisure' – which Christian ethics would define as 'idleness'. Christian ethics, of course, makes allowance for rest – holidays – but absolutely denies that man is 'free' when an opportunity for hedonism provided by 'leisure' is represented as 'the good'. The only conceivable social situation in which the latter would be the case would be one in which all 'goods' have been attained and are available to those members of the society who can afford them. No such society exists or is ever likely to exist. The concept of efficiency is being used to distort the concept of freedom. In the debate between those representing democratic, socialist, capitalist and Communist points of view, those who speak of 'relative efficiency' lose sight of what is usually meant by 'freedom'; they are in effect appealing to those who have accepted a Marxian scheme of values. Everyone else thinks the debate is fatuous – perhaps even immoral.

PROPERTY AND FREEDOM

When we speak of 'free enterprise', we are referring to a balance of power between the citizen and the State: property and power are related and hence we cannot possibly be free if the State has a monopoly of economic power. If you give the State this monopoly and even if those in power would like to be benevolent or follow utilitarian principles (there is, of course, no guarantee of this), they are forced to be arbitrary – their decision-making is bound to be irrational. We are faced with the problem of managerial irresponsibility, the bane of State-owned means of production.

Under State ownership, management is placed in an ambiguous position. On the one hand, it must press for favourable legislation (or favourable directives from the centre); on the other hand, it must adopt the planner's point of view and adjust its demands to the benefit of the State as a whole. The problem is that not only are these requirements incompatible – it is impossible to be both an efficient manager and a dutiful public servant – but the means towards the end of a planned economy are never precisely known. One is forced to use the trial and error method when making supposedly rational policy decisions.

Under free enterprise disastrous miscalculations are rare, since economic legislation (equivalent to planning under State capitalism) is controlled by the pressure of public opinion that can be brought to bear upon the legislators. When such pressure cannot be exerted, when management cannot argue that a policy will be detrimental to a particular part of the economy but must instead try to adopt the planner's point of view, the result is submission to an 'authority' which usually lacks expertise (and is not being given the input from special interests that would improve its performance). Authority becomes quite arbitrary, a mere reflection of political power – recognizable as authority solely because it decides policy. What was originally proposed as rational decision-making on the basis of utilitarian principles becomes an irrational expression of arbitrary power.

There is common agreement among the followers of various ideological persuasions that wealth profoundly affects both personal happiness and our conception of freedom. A limitation on the capacity for happiness and the means we choose to pursue it is a very serious limitation on freedom. Consequently, the disposition of income is left in the hands of the individual, who is free to drink it up, accumulate it in the form of property or bank it until he can decide what to do.

Under totalitarian socialism or Communism, access to wealth is effectively removed from individual decision-making by placing the means of production in the hands of the State. The issue between advocates of free-market capitalism and socialist State capitalism is not whether private property and its presumed corollary happiness is allowed, but whether in limiting personal access to property (and happiness) you distribute it more widely and thus justify restrictions on individual freedom. The issue is utilitarian: if an individual is not permitted to become a millionaire, can the money he would have got – but which is instead in the hands of the State – be distributed in such a way that the millionaire's happiness is distributed? If it cannot, then under State capitalism an important element in the concept of freedom has been abolished rather than 'distributed'.

When we speak of distributing happiness by distributing wealth through State capitalism, we lose sight of what we know to be true. To many people it seems logical that if you distribute the money a man could accumulate by free enterprise, you must be distributing the happiness it would have brought him. But if this is not true with regard to an individual's economy, what could possibly make it true socially? The concept of thrift establishes quite clearly that with regard to the utilitarian happiness-freedom equation as a method of distributing justice (by limiting individual access to wealth), State control of the means of production eliminates an exceedingly important aspect of freedom.

Proponents of State capitalism may reply that there is a much more important aspect of freedom involved in the question of private property: if you grant unlimited access to property you grant unlimited access to power; and wherever there are marked discrepancies of power there cannot be freedom in any meaningful sense. Indeed, so certain was Marx about the logic of the relation between property accumulation and power that he predicted an ultimate breakdown in the capitalist social order. This prediction has not been fulfilled, for Marx did not realize that, even before he wrote, capitalism had faced the problem of property and freedom. Instead of limiting access to property as Marx proposed, we set limits to what can be owned: we eliminated slavery instead of capitalism, whereas Communism eliminates capitalism and imposes slavery.[7]

Communism, then, has set out to prevent an imaginary development. Instead of restricting the content of property – human beings cannot be owned – it limits access to it by making everyone an employee of the State. That these employees can themselves own such property as they can accumulate under the circumstances does not alter the fact that they are in a slave-like position. (Slaves in certain circumstances could accumulate some property too, but they could not accumulate very much. This is also the situation of citizens in a Communist State.) Their access to property – and happiness – is limited, while nothing is done to increase the totality of happiness because the State does not distribute what its citizens do not personally have access to. As noted earlier, Communist State capitalism is not geared to such a distribution.

Supporters of socialist and free enterprise ideologies have to a large extent adjusted their views on private property to take into account the objections of their critics. There is a reluctance by the Left to advocate the outright abolition of the concept of property; no one called capitalist argues for absolute freedom to decide about the content of property (what can be owned), its use and disposition. As pointed out earlier, the main difference in viewpoint relates to the question of access to certain types of property (such as ownership of the means of production). What is the typically democratic socialist point of view on this matter?

Communist societies, having limited the access to property, leave it alone once it is in private hands, after reaching its holders under conditions sanctioned by the State. On the one hand, they use drastic measures to syphon off what are considered 'excessive' profits through taxation on 'profiteering'. But, on the other hand, their views resemble that of the freebooter capitalist of yore, who had no sense of social responsibility. (Thus Communists are not concerned with the wide range of benefits accruing to the new privileged classes: the Party, the State bureaucracy and military establishment.)

It is this use of property that the democratic socialist objects to. He wishes to limit legally both the amount and disposition of property – to have the benefits shared, even while retaining the concept of property itself. In effect, he demands that property be employed charitably whether one is charitable or not, and thus converts property from an absolute right to a privilege (which can be exercised only so long as one shows social responsibility).

Even if we agree that some limit on the amount of

property owned must be set (if we are not to fulfil Marx's prediction about the fate of capitalism), enforced redistribution of property in terms of social welfare – as democratic socialists demand – strikes at the very root of the concept of property. If one cannot dispose of property as one sees fit, the very point of it has been legally eliminated (even though nominally the concept remains). To call such welfarism 'social justice' merely distorts the very term about which we have to be clear.

FREEDOM AND HEDONISM: BREAKING WITH THE PAST

When speaking of the 'injustice' of the present distribution of property, C.A.R. Crosland makes a rather odd statement: 'the present distribution of wealth. . . is flagrantly unjust and this is wholly irrespective of . . . the presence or absence of resentment against the injustice'.[8] The statement is odd because it implies that some absolute principle is being violated and that awareness of this fact is irrelevant. Such a view is bound to lead to despotism. Its authoritarian nature implies that those who believe in it will impose it on the public. On the other hand, a principle of justice that cannot be debated does not stand much chance of gaining widespread support among voters. No matter how uninformed, irrational and self-interested the public is, non-debatable ideas simply do not get publicized and consequently do not become issues or win support for the party upholding them. Being authoritarian in nature, they are more likely – if the opposition learns of such non-rational principles – to become a source of weakness. Hence, even if socialists do indeed think of the distribution of property as subject to some kind of 'natural law' which we have to observe whether we like it or not (and at no matter what cost to society), they have to bring their principles down from the empyrean and make them seem rational and desirable. Instead of speculating about the source of the socialist principle of justice (whether it derives from Marx or some particular interpretation of equality), let us look at its rationalizations – the attempts to make it seem 'just'.

Socialism, as was said earlier, has long been viewed as a secularized version of Christian charity (the view expressed by G.B. Shaw in *Androcles and the Lion* with reference to Fabian socialism). To both the Christian and the socialist, poverty is a social evil having widespread ramifications that must be remedied or at least mitigated. To the Christian, the solution lies with the individual through a combination of the work ethic and Christian charity. To the socialist, the solution requires State intervention; by the time socialism evolved, it had become clear that a market economy is an exceedingly complex phenomenon, in which willingness to work cannot remedy a lack of work, and in which individual compassion for the hardship of others cannot always solve the problem of poverty (nor can it be expected to). Therefore, though a government may have no better idea of how to deal with the problems of poverty and unemployment than charitable and hard-working members of the society, it should at least, having full State resources behind it, be able to do more than individuals. Those who think that government does know better – that it can solve problems of poverty through a planned economy – shift over from democratic socialism to Marxism, as many Fabian socialists in fact did. They were thereby opting for an argument for a revolutionary change based on the view that government action is 'somewhat more efficient' than individual charity. One needs, according to this view, to be ready to promise the millennium – which is what Marxism does.

Not everyone can shift from humanitarian concerns to Marxism: the promised millennium entails an indefinite period of ruthlessness that a genuine humanitarian cannot contemplate with equanimity. Now that humanity has had time enough (it seems) to consider the implications of Marxism, humanitarians have detached themselves from the anarchists and Marxists. The latter appear today to appeal to those who are egoistic and prone to violence – who doubtless feel a need for some rationalization or excuse for their inclinations, and do not care what happens to their fellow human beings.

Democratic socialists do care. The problem is that the primary focus on poverty as an issue and the assumption that it can be remedied by altering the distribution of property has led to awkward questions of definition. 'Poor', like 'rich', is a comparative term, and though any decent person is likely to share Dickens's outrage that a child can starve to death when food (though available) is beyond its parents' means, not many feel outraged that some people in North America are so 'poor' that they cannot go to Reno to gamble. Only a person who is convinced that inequality of income violates some natural law will mount the barricades to remedy such an 'injustice'. Capitalist productivity, in fact, has deprived socialists in the Western World of their main argument and left them in the embarrassing position of being unable to establish poverty as 'bad' except as a statement about an inequality.

In view of this situation, one might think that democratic socialism would simply disappear. Yet it has been able to retain enough support to form a major party in most democratic countries except the USA. How can it retain an appeal when it has no clearer programme than any other democratic party and at the same time professes to promote 'justice'.

The answer appears to lie in our shift to hedonism. If everyone believes that 'pleasure' constitutes 'happiness' and if pleasures are purchasable, it follows that a society is markedly unjust if some people cannot afford the happiness that others can. According to this view, working people who object to the fact that many persons on welfare can indulge in pleasures not open to them as workers – e.g. leisure – are merely blinded by 'archaic' views about the good – views deriving in large part from such normative systems as Christianity. Briefly, the modern democratic socialist has broken with earlier socialism; Fabian arguments about socialism as secularized Christianity are rejected: modern socialism is a hedonist philosophy which justifies the redistribution of wealth in hedonist terms, not in those of need and humanitarianism.

To label modern democratic socialism and its concepts of justice and freedom as permeated by hedonism may be considered tendential. However, before assessing the accuracy of the analysis the following point should be considered: Orwell in his *1984* argued in effect that the millennial vision of socialism will not be achieved because of other factors in its philosophy. He used the squalor of life prevalent in *1984* to argue against tyranny and totalitarianism; he struck at the roots of modern totalitarianism by demonstrating that its conditions were essentially antagonistic to hedonistic goals (which he knew to be the 'modern' view of the 'good life').

If we think that Orwell misinterpreted what the modern socialist envisions as the 'good society', we could consider Crosland's views about 'freedom': 'Society's decisions impinge heavily on people's private lives as well as on their social or economic welfare; and they now impinge, in my view, in too restrictive and puritanical a manner. I should like to see action taken both to widen opportunities for enjoyment and relaxation, and to diminish existing restrictions on personal freedom'.[9] Here 'freedom' quite clearly means the opportunity for hedonism. This is what modern socialism is about and if you do not agree that acting in accord with hedonistic views represents 'freedom', you are not a socialist. Orwell broke with the Marxian vision of the 'good society' when he recognized it was anti-hedonistic and – as he saw plainly – surprisingly puritanical.

A democratic socialist has a problem no Communist has: he has to define his concept of freedom in such a way that he can both acknowledge the validity of the concepts held by other democratic parties and represent his own concept as 'better'. Furthermore, whatever construction he places on the concept must be consistent with his party's tradition. The current commitment must seem to be the same as it has always been, although the 'construction' placed on the commitment has changed. Most democratic socialists have abandoned the labour theory of value and Marx's special contribution – the theory of surplus value – but they can hardly admit that early socialist ideology was wrong and that they themselves have changed their minds. Their present stance is to represent the party as advocating a 'just' distribution of the good, not on the ground that the labourer produced the good in the first place (which would have been too close to Marxism) but on the ground of 'fairness'.

Traditional ethics began with the plain fact that in this world the good is not equally distributed. It coped with the issue of a man's satisfaction with his superior possessions by presenting it as the sin of pride; it coped with its opposite – dissatisfaction with the goods of others – by calling it the sin of envy. Traditional ethics did not try to change the situation – to equalize distribution – because it recognized that most goods worth having are not distributable. You cannot take youth or beauty or intelligence or honour from someone who has 'too much' and give it to those who lack them. Long before anyone heard of bell-shaped curves, it was recognized that the concept of value entails inequality of distribution (e.g. there cannot be a concept of intelligence unless it is *unequally* distributed). Once, however, it was decided that the concept of 'equality' was essential to 'justice', the actual distribution of goods poses some awkward problems.

Stripped down to essentials, there are two interrelated possibilities: either one can say that undistributable goods are nothing more than 'prejudices' – the relativist solution – or one can assert that the only goods worth having are distributable – the type of property available in the market-place. If, further, one insists that only what is distributable can be a good, one is committed to a particular sense of 'equality' which is not realized until the good is equally available.

The above argument leads us to the socialist meaning of 'equal opportunity'. This meaning – that the good is there, or 'should be' if you want it – is opposed to another, older sense of 'opportunity' which laid a condition on the availability of the good: you had to work for it and a democratic society provided the necessary conditions.

The older sense of 'equal opportunity' was consistent

with – and probably derived from – Christian ethics. The latter represented the good as entailing effort, and sloth as a deadly sin (as leading to the anti-Christian view that one could be 'good' just by observing restrictions on one's behaviour). The newer, socialist sense of 'equal opportunity' is consistent only with hedonism, which considers effort – work – a source of frustration. A socialist can increase 'freedom' by reducing the working week; hence for him the problem of the good society is to achieve a balance between the productivity that produces the good and the leisure that represents 'freedom' within the framework of an equality of distribution.

At one time the views of the democratic socialist and the Marxist were very close. They both believed firmly in the so-called Protestant work ethic and a certain 'puritanism'. Thus Beatrice Webb, on a visit to Stalin's Russia, as Crosland puts it, 'could write with approval of the serious, youthful Komsomols with their passion for self-discipline and self-improvement: and of the emphasis on personal hygiene and self-control – "there is no spooning in the Parks of Recreation and Rest"'.[10] Crosland, however, who records her observations in a section of his book subtitled 'Liberty and Gaiety in Private Life; the Need for a Reaction against the Fabian Tradition' does not write with approval. In this he is probably quite typical. While the Communists are bent on promoting their orthodox principle of the 'socialist discipline of labour' and pay scanty attention to such matters as leisure or consumer goods, democratic socialists are firmly set on pursuing hedonistic goals both in theory and practice.

WELFARE, HEDONISM AND HUMAN NATURE

It is possible to argue that the concept of the welfare State is an acknowledgement that State welfare schemes are more efficient than private charity; they are less dependent on the coincidence of a need for and an impulse towards charity. In our mobile, heterogeneous modern societies only the State has the organization necessary to administer charity equitably: the parishes of old are now almost a pious fiction. The concept of welfare has also a stronger appeal. It implies an impersonal type of administration and, in contradistinction to charity, it is based on the right to receive rather than the duty to give. Nowadays, however, rights and duties are so 'interrelated' in most people's minds that they are inclined to suppose that no conceptual change has occurred – that charity has merely been made more efficient. What has in fact been done is that the 'sturdy beggar' problem has been made insoluble. When the Fabians argued that no one would so pauperize himself as to qualify for welfare, the argument seemed to appeal to human rationality. But it was not noticed that the argument for State welfare eliminates the key term in Shaw's argument – the concept of 'pauper'. Before the rise of the welfare State, 'pauper' referred to those permanently dependent on charity. The condition was considered shameful. Today it is no longer true that no one will pauperize himself in order to receive welfare or will feel ashamed to 'be on welfare', for indigence and shame do not come into the picture when one speaks about a 'right'. Indeed, once a 'right' to welfare is asserted, for many it is folly not to seek it. Thus the author of a recent study on poverty in the Appalachians recorded that it is an ambition of local youth to qualify for some social assistance, by deception if necessary. In Canada, Caucasians who have married Indians are currently asserting the right to be legally considered Indians, since that status entails a number of privileges including a practically absolute right to welfare.

Those who deny that any normal human being is willing to live off welfare, explain it by saying that the purchasing power of welfare recipients is usually lower than that of the employed. In saying this, they ignore the evidence that one of the main problems of social workers is to get people off welfare who are capable of earning a living; they also overlook the fact that one of the major goods money can buy is 'leisure' – which is free for those on welfare.

Indeed, leisure is now a central good for many, for it is reputed to be the condition necessary to creativity: a great number of the 'arty' people are 'on welfare' by choice. It is often referred to as 'freedom' – the condition that allows one to do as one desires. If one assumes that hedonism reflects man's natural inclinations, then welfare or support from the State represents an 'ideal'. To follow this line of thought, the present system is said to be defective only in that the payments are so low that many people are faced with the hedonist dilemma of trying to decide whether they would be happier if they had more money to spend or more leisure time (to spend their money). Socialists argue that insofar as it is possible, no one should have to confront the problem; the payments should be higher and the qualifications less stringent.

In our society, a modern evolutionist is not likely to believe that hedonism could be part of human nature, for it is inappropriate to man's condition: the universe is not organized to cater to man's hedonist impulses. (One really has to *work* at the satisfaction of hedonist impulses, or, in other words, go against the fundamental hedonist principle that work by definition is not hedonist.) An evolutionist is not thinking clearly if he supposes that hedonism can be integrated with the theory of evolution and thus made 'modern'.

Historically, hedonism arose in ancient class societies where servants and others could be paid to cater to one's desires. It was specifically repudiated by Christianity, which saw it as not only imprudent (a denial of the real self or soul) but as unjust (an exploitation of fellow-men). Those who now reject the logic of Christianity suppose that the objections to hedonism have also been removed – that they can accept hedonism as part of man's nature.

But hedonism conflicts with the sense of self as having extension in time, and with our recognition of man's position in the universe. Of the many factors in our society keeping us from introducing some commonsense into hedonist assumptions, the right to welfare is certainly one. It is the demand that society acknowledge un-enlightened hedonism as the primary assumption about the good – that we 'ought' to be able to cater to our desires without any questions being raised in our minds about what we are doing. Philosophically, ethically and socially this is madness. The 'right' to welfare in the form of 'native rights' has demoralized the native population in North America as surely as wealth has demoralized the rich who have no tradition of responsibility. The amount of money available for hedonism has of course little to do with the degree of dissipation, as anyone who has walked 'skid row' knows. What matters is the assumption about the nature of the good and the opportunity to indulge in it. The 'right' to welfare not only supplies the opportunity but also asserts that unenlightened hedonism is the good.

Chapter 15

Socialism and the modern welfare state

The concept of the welfare State can be understood as a response to the recognition that an actual equalization of property would not achieve an equality of condition unless property were continuously redistributed, or only if property were abolished. If today all assets, public and private, were appraised and titles of ownership were equally distributed in the form of shares, tomorrow some people would be broke – e.g. gamblers and alcoholics – and some – e.g. pawnbrokers and misers – would be well on the way to making a fortune. Within a short time the division between rich and poor would be similar to what it is now: it would not be possible to relate the possession of property to the social contribution.

If one were absolutely determined to make the distribution of property in society reflect the so-called Protestant work ethic, one could pass legislation enforcing the attributes of fundamentalist Protestantism, make gambling, drinking and drug addiction serious social offences and – like G.B. Shaw, who as a socialist professed to be a humanitarian – argue that in the socialist utopia idleness would be a capital offence. But unless one actually abolished property (and thereby pretended that it would be possible for people to regard what they value and what is in limited supply – such as Picasso paintings and well-cooked dinners – as being the same as what they do not value and what is unlimited in supply – such as seawater and air) the interaction between the work ethic – founded on the compensation for effort expended – and property – the object of the work ethic – would quickly result in an unequal distribution of property.

Abolish property and you abolish the incentive to work – the old 'capitalist' dictum used to say. What was formerly an abstract argument is now seen within the context of social change. Modern democratic socialists have virtually adopted the basic argument of old-time capitalists; no matter how much socialists would like to simplify the problem of equality, the evidence is that the abstract formulation against property redistribution is correct. As a result, the basic position about the 'injustice' of property relations and the remedy for it must now be referred to – and modified by – the concept of the welfare State.

In his argument about 'capitalist rationalization', Freud speaks of businessmen's hostility to the principle that every citizen must have a minimum material security and to the 'widening application' of that principle. He speaks of their contempt for the welfare State as killing private initiative and avers that in opposing social security measures they pretend to fight for the freedom and initiative of the worker. He calls their arguments 'sheer rationalizations'.

To argue that objections to the welfare State are rationalizations because both the welfare State and the businessmen aim at economic security, is the same as saying that objections to theft are rationalizations because both the thief and those who object to theft value property. The fact that the ends are the same does not legitimize the means. The businessman's objection is to the means. The businessman – as well as the non-businessman conservative – argues that work by definition is a means to an end – economic security; when the same activity is performed for its own sake it is 'play', no matter how much effort is involved. (One is reminded of the old joke about the mandarin watching two 'foreign devils' playing a strenuous game of tennis: 'Would it not be better', he enquired, 'to hire two coolies to do that for you?') Remove the incentive of economic security by supplying everyone with it gratis and the bulk of the work necessary to civilization will not be undertaken.

Encouraged by various deterministic schools of thought – including psychoanalysis – to reject all reasoning as 'rationalization', the socialist could well believe that some kind of self-interest lay behind criticisms of the egalitarian argument and that the solution to inequality lay in the equalization of property. Fortunately for democratic ideology, actual historical changes have resulted in situations which allow observable facts to reinforce the abstract objections to the redistribution of property. Although Lenin explained to his own satisfaction the failure of Marx's prediction about the development of class consciousness and class conflict by arguing that 'imperialism' resulted in the proletariat's forming a temporary class together with the capitalists to exploit colonial peoples – which then occupied the position that according to the tenets of historical determinism should have been that of the proletariat – the argument was convincing only to a European socialist. Both in the USA and 'colonial' Canada, democratic egalitarianism resulted rather in a blindness to actual facts about non-egalitarian conditions: there was no traditional gentry whose style of life set them apart from the 'workers' and no way of supposing that a class united 'workers' and 'rentiers' as one. Rather, the clear evidence that the rich had personally acquired their riches, that most who were rich were 'self-made' men induced everyone to face the fact that equality of opportunity resulted in inequality. The myth that everyone was bound by the fact of class was replaced by the Horatio Alger myth. North Americans are much more 'conservative' than Europeans because they are convinced (now mostly by tradition) that inequalities of property reflect personal choices about values; also that the surest way to destroy 'civilization' is to socialize property. Private initiative and enterprise rewarded by increased wealth is seen as essential to the industrial economy that supplies a great variety of goods – a variety not possible in any other type of economy.

Acceptance of the relation between having property and striving to acquire it poses a problem, however, if in addition to valuing property one values equality as the ideal condition or if one values democracy as the ideal form of government. Without democratic government as a value no particular difficulty arises about social inequality. But, if democratic government, understood as resting on *equality of power* among the members of society, is an essential norm, the fact of inequality in property cannot be viewed complacently. Great inequalities in property entail inequalities of power – hence, they pose a threat to democratic government. As a consequence, despite the argument about the 'natural' relation between wealth and 'enterprise', much greater effort becomes necessary to equalize wealth in order to equalize power and/or so to organize the attainment and exercise of power as to mitigate or eliminate the economic factor. Socialists keep emphasising the relation between political power and private property but, because they accept the argument about the relation between accumulating wealth and 'enterprise', they no longer advocate the 'radical' solution of equalizing property. Such a solution and the measures designed to attain it are now felt by many socialists to be undemocratic.

Despite a certain degree of agreement about inequality in property, there remains today a marked disagreement between the conservative and socialist about the proper democratic response to the wider consequences of this inequality (apart from the effect on power relations). In accepting the view that a good many people will never be rich no matter what kind of social order exists, the socialist argues that simple acceptance of this fact leads to a denial of 'fraternity'. To him, all members of a State, like all members of a family, ought to share the benefits of the available wealth, even though differences in the matter of personal expenditures remain, just as they do in a family. Curiously, this view of the State as an extended family is now widely accepted. Even staunch conservatives seem to agree that no members of a State should ever go hungry, have inadequate shelter or lack medical treatment. Although the norm itself is seldom discussed, an awareness of 'fraternity' has been evolving. However, since good analyses of this process have been lacking, the concept of the 'welfare State' – which means introduction into the democratic ideology of the concept of 'fraternity' – has given rise to decidedly unfraternal charges and countercharges.

If we regard adherents of current ideological positions as if they themselves had begun with an antecedent ideological position and followed its historical development in their minds, we are likely to be puzzled by the current socialist views on welfare. Historically, socialists were strictly egalitarian with views similar to, if not identical with, the naïve anarchism, Communism and various brands of communalism often found today among young people of an idealistic bent. The egalitarian position has in time been modified so as to keep it within the democratic framework which requires acceptance of 'individualism' as an equally valid norm alongside egalitarianism.

Now, if we suppose that a socialist today follows in his own mind the historical sequence of changes, we will expect him to view welfare legislation as basically an expedient for overcoming unfortunate difficulties that one may find oneself in – for this is how a strict egalitarian would see the situation. We would expect such a man to be deeply suspicious of the argument that certain people require someone else to manage their affairs and that a democratic government is best suited to perform the task. No one who begins with the view that all men are equal can see 'government' as anything other than a servant of the people: logically, it cannot or 'should not' be paternal.

The socialist today focuses on the fact of inequality and uses the concept of 'equality' as a device for criticizing the shortcomings of the social order. Consequently, for him a paternalistic State is a requirement of 'justice' and has no more potential for undemocratic developments than a well-run family (in which the parents promote a fraternal spirit by emphasizing the fact that it is unjust to treat everyone equally if they are not in fact equal). In the socialist's view, the fact of inequality demands the adoption of 'fraternity' as a democratic norm necessary to justice; welfare legislation is the State's way of expressing the fraternal attitude.

The conservative disagrees. To him 'fraternity' is an attitude possible only in the individual; if one believes the State capable of having such an attitude it is because one has personified it and made it an entity apart from, and superior to, the members of society. The conservative will allow this only inasmuch as objectivity is achieved by the government with regard to the application of norms within the society – to achieve the objectivity or 'blindness' of justice necessary to the administration of law. Under no circumstances can the conservative ask from the State anything so closely identified with actual human feelings as the 'charity' which used to be the basis of social welfare. The potential for the destruction of what we call democracy and of 'loving kindness' is too great.

THE PERILS OF FRATERNITY

Under relativism, 'fraternity' or the vague feeling that all men are 'brothers' acquires a normative position that was not possible as long as a more definite statement about human relations seemed realizable. As long as it seemed possible to give some content to 'equality' – as by asserting that men would be 'equal' under 'just' social conditions – the assertions of the behaviourists like Watson and Skinner were thought to be realizable. Everything that 'fraternity' could be made to mean could then be better expressed by 'equality' and the existence of both 'fraternity' and 'equality' in the same ideological scheme was confusing. For centuries, 'fraternity' – by echoing the Christian slogan of 'the brotherhood of man' – served to reassure sceptics that a democratic political order would not undermine society's fundamental religious conceptions. But when norms are represented as mere attitudes and feelings (and, as under relativism, deprived of any conceptual basis) 'fraternity' acquires a renewed vitality as the 'truest' (philosophically most defensible) democratic norm. To be 'democratic' becomes the same as being concerned with the welfare of one's fellow-man –

not just one's neighbour in the community in which one happens to be living.

The non-relativists (who include the conservatives) will ask first, 'Concerned in what way?' and then, 'By what criteria will you judge "welfare" if you do not have a clear conception of good and bad?' Why, with regard to situations in foreign countries, do socialists often ignore the facts which are central to their criticism of what is happening in their own State? If 'fraternity' is indeed now a central 'norm' (as norms are defined by relativists) why should not this fellow-feeling tend more to the conservative view that, if one paid attention to the evidence, Communism is what democracies should resist everywhere?

Relativism induces political naïveté. Whereas the normativist theorist is convinced that man's beliefs determine human behaviour, the relativist believes that this is an illusion, that the real factors are something else and that they are hardly analysable (except by psychiatrists). Consequently, to the relativist, the analyses of normativist political theorists or publicists are at best expressions of their self-interest and consequently much less trustworthy than the fraternal goodwill of the socialist. As long as most people are relativists there is no hope for countering this argument.

It is sometimes argued that the strong tendency of socialists to be uncritical about Communist régimes in other countries reflects an anti-democratic sympathy (the 'totalitarian temptation'). What seems to be the case is that when norms are regarded as attitudes, the profession of a belief in equality and fraternity by Communists is taken as expressing a desire to direct society towards the kind of political order characteristic of modern Western democracies. The facts about flagrantly undemocratic conditions and policies are dismissed as expedients forced on men of goodwill by circumstances. What is ignored is that Communist ideology incorporates concepts such as the dictatorship of the proletariat or the cult of personality which both in theory and practice make anything resembling democratic practice impossible. The history of democracy shows such a steady progression towards the meaningful expression in both politics and social conditions of democratic norms that we can truly say our societies are more 'democratic' than they were in the last century. A comparison of current facts with the logical requirements of norms and our awareness of historical change supplies unequivocal evidence that whether norms are relativist or not, they certainly determine human behaviour. Such being the case, it does not matter in the least whether Communists are 'men of goodwill' or not. What matters is the norms they accept and the ideology in which they are enmeshed. Since the latter differs from the democratic ideology, we cannot possibly expect a Communist régime to 'evolve' into a democratic one. The 'fraternity' and relativism engendered by social-ism induce a strong interest in what happens abroad, but under current circumstances this is equivalent to a dangerous tolerance of totalitarianism.

A further consequence of socialist relativism and of its promotion of 'fraternity' as the essential democratic atti-tude is pacifism with regard to international relations coupled with militancy in support of demands for minor-ity rights within the State. The good socialist sees nothing odd about his readiness to take up arms against his own government but not to counter threats from other States. If he were a strict pacifist, advocating a Gandhi-like passive resistance to what he regarded as unacceptable domestic policy, we might trace socialist pacifism to Christian principles in the way that Fabian socialists traced their views to Christianity. But since the socialist is not a strict pacifist, such an interpretation must be excluded. If, however, one applies the concept of 'fratern-ity', the apparent inconsistency can be reconciled. All that need be done is to interpret 'war' as a quarrel between States – not peoples – and to see the occurrence of such conflicts as not having important consequences for the citizens, should the war be lost.

Such a view might have been plausible before the development of ideologically-based States when the ability of one State to conquer another generally represented technological and cultural superiority – as it did during the days of the imperialist expansion of Britain. But it would be grossly naïve, to say the least, to argue that Communist domination of the West would not mean the imposition of a political order unacceptable to most people. It is much easier for a socialist to overlook such considerations because he feels that the Russian and Chinese peoples – as opposed to the ruling parties – are not interested in spreading Communism. To the socialist, 'fraternity' is a genuine factor in human affairs, for it is a feeling and therefore 'scientifically' true, even though, as a norm, it is not given any conceptual content. This is an appallingly naïve way of looking at human affairs.

PATERNALISM AND IDEOLOGY

Although democratic socialists no longer regard public ownership of the means of production as their primary or even a feasible goal, their traditional view of property as the source of social inequality leads them to approve of public property under certain circumstances. They are prone, for instance, to resist the sale of Crown Land and advocate public ownership of those industries that are by necessity monopolies (e.g. the hydroelectric power and telephone industries) and of the extractive industries, which they view as exploiting public resources for private gain. In this they are opposed by both liberals and conservatives who, because they do so, define themselves in socialist eyes as varieties of a single party representing the same ideology. This dichotomy is reinforced by the socialist emphasis on welfare schemes, which the other two parties view as 'paternalistic' – a threat to the individual and his ability to make his own choices. Conservatives are especially troubled by the realization that the socialist position on public ownership and welfare is bound unduly to enlarge the civil service. For them 'big government' is bad government, whereas for socialists exactly the opposite is true.

The socialist, when advocating State welfare, advocates 'paternalism' of a peculiarly old-fashioned kind: if socialist views were accepted, the State would have the characteristics and power of a Victorian paterfamilias. This would be odd indeed since hitherto democratic ideology has been undermining the authority of the real-life biological family: 'obedience' is not normatively good if 'egalitarianism' and 'independence' are the accepted ideals. 'Responsibility' for the welfare of its members is no longer the duty of the head of the family; in consequence 'obligation' no longer has any meaning. The democratic family does not provide the socialist with a model of the relations between the State and its citizens.

The paternalistic image is also confusing to the conservative who is inclined to see socialist demands upon the State as resembling those of a spoilt child who, while insisting on the right to resist the authority of his parents, also insists that they provide him with what he wants. Such traditional concepts as authority, obligation, law and responsibility are not central to socialist thinking: the State is seen as responsible for the citizens' welfare but there is no reciprocal obligation on the part of the citizens, nor any awareness that there must be a connection between the limits of responsibility and those of authority. Ideology in the sense of a logical relationship between fundamental concepts has almost fallen into abeyance as a result of the socialist attitude towards 'welfare.'

MORAL RESPONSIBILITY, FREEDOM AND CONSERVATISM

Modern democratic theory, in opposing tyranny, does not object merely to the explicit exercise of power (and authority) in the interest of those wielding it: benevolent dictators are also treated as tyrants and as such are regarded as morally reprehensible. Paternalism is considered morally wrong because it undermines moral responsibility – it runs counter to the view that human beings must be trained to act responsibly by being forced to accept the consequences of their own actions.

As children, we do not have enough experience and

foresight to be granted complete independence: responsible parents supervise their children, gradually allowing
them more independence as they gain experience. Irresponsible parents either neglect their children – do not
supervise them – or spoil them by indulging them and
protecting them against the consequences of their behaviour so that the child grows up to be an irresponsible
adult, incapable of controlling impulses and acknowledging personal responsibility.

The argument against paternalism – the view that it is
morally wrong – is based on the idea that it converts
adults into the equivalent of overindulged and over-
protected children. From the viewpoint of political
science, paternalism creates the problem of educating a
special class of people capable of being benevolent in a
society where everyone else is taught to be egoistic, and of
ensuring that the élite will remain benevolent.

Paternalism has now assumed the guise of the welfare
State, which, if its government is arrived at democratically,
is considered democratic rather than tyrannical. Both
conservatives and socialists can agree that the communal
sense requires the community to intervene through the
agency of government when misfortune – disease, the
inability to earn a living and so forth – strikes a member
of the community. But conservatives differ from both
socialists and liberals when it comes to the predictable
consequences of behaviour: the issues of moral responsibility. The conservative remains opposed to any intervention by the State which is likely to diminish the moral
responsibility of the public and to create a special class
exercising this responsibility on behalf of the public. The
socialist and liberal, however, treat welfare as the logical
extension of charity: if we agree that there is a need for
hospitals and homes for the aged, we must agree that
spendthrifts should be supported by the State and
criminals treated as mentally ill. Many people suppose
that this is a scientific view. Determinism rather than
empiricism is now the basis of the social sciences; the
cause of human behaviour is felt to be the same as the
cause of animal behaviour. (A similar belief is the

thoroughly unscientific view that human beings did not evolve and consequently – like animals – act on the basis of biological impulse modified by personal experience, of which normative experience is not a part because norms are not known to affect animals.) Conservatives do not agree, either because they insist on the empirical evidence that evolution took place or (when they ignore evolution) because they focus on the empirical evidence that man is capable of acting normatively – of being and feeling responsible in a way no animal can.

The conservative, then, is distinguished by a rejection of determinism, an acceptance of moral responsibility and therefore opposition to the welfare State which to him is a return to paternalism. Further, the 'security' which the welfare State is supposed to provide is to him like the moral irresponsibility of a spoilt child – an irresponsibility transferred to adults.

The paternalistic mood is now affecting even private enterprise. Thus even banks, traditionally the most conservative of all institutions, are now lending billions of dollars to other countries because the loans are guaranteed by their own government. They are acting irresponsibly, as responsibility has been taken over by a paternalistic government. If liberal democracies continue in this fashion, one can foresee a time when it will be necessary to start educating an élite class of guardians: from the community in general, one expects less and less responsibility. Strictly speaking, we can no longer be called 'free' because the purpose of freedom and the training in freedom through responsibility have been taken from us.

To the conservative, the danger in such a situation is that the State no longer provides the conditions under which man can be free – through restrictions on the operation of egoism, as under the Hobbesian conception of sovereignty – but is now the promoter of egoism because it encourages irresponsibility among its members. Hitherto, we have not defined egoism as a norm, a sort of ideal freedom, but as a pathological condition whose most extreme expression is found in the psychopath who tends to regard his fellow-men as mere objects. Freedom has served to define egoism as pathological by asserting that normal human beings have a sense of self which relates them to others of their kind. It has asserted that if you do not have a sense of responsibility, you are mentally ill or on the way to becoming so. Drifters, recluses and the utterly imprudent, far from representing some kind of ideal exercise of freedom, have been labelled as sick. If the State, under the guise of welfare, asserts that it provides the responsibility formerly expected of the individual, then what was formerly pathological becomes 'normal' (not, of course, in the sense that everyone behaves this way, but in the sense that no one sees anything wrong with it). The conservative thus finds himself in a difficult position. When he points out that irresponsibility always requires someone's intervention, he is told that he is arguing for the welfare State. When he says that he is arguing for moral responsibility in the individual, he is told that history shows he is being unrealistic, because no society has ever been able to induce responsibility in everyone. If this were possible, his opponents say, we would not need laws of any kind.

When stressing the need for the rule of law, the conservative is not speaking about the replacement of ethics by law but of the use of law – coercive power – to reinforce authority, which presupposes a rational and ethical sense of moral responsibility on the part of both the authority and those subject to it. Tyranny can be defined as the absence of such authority and as a reliance on coercive power. The conservative presupposition is the acceptance of moral responsibility, called authority (with reference to society) and mythicized into the theory of the social contract. When speaking of freedom outside contractual theory, says the conservative, one is discussing the merits of anarchy as opposed to tyranny (or of social anarchy operating within the confines of totalitarianism, or what will end as totalitarianism). To the conservative, the welfare State, by denying that 'responsibility' has normative connotations (as part of normative concepts), and acting as if responsibility were something the State exercised in order to enable the members of society to be irresponsible, demonstrates that its leaders have no real conception of 'freedom'. Indeed, this is the fallacy of regarding the welfare State as a condition for 'freedom'. For what kind of 'freedom' can such a State offer? It makes the citizens part of an impersonal system running their lives; the State itself becomes a reflection of a mechanistic universe. Mankind, of course, has always tried to make the State a reflection of the way the universe is thought to be organized – a sort of mini-universe designed exclusively for man, by man – but such a mechanistic model is in conflict with men's sense of free will and their sense of self. It is no consolation to be told by the State that the only kind of freedom one can expect is the freedom to behave as if men lacked free will.

Chapter 16

Freedom in democracy

ANTINOMIAN LIBERALISM AND 'COMPULSORY RATIONAL FREEDOM'

It is not easy to specify what 'freedom' means to socialists. For many years, theoreticians of democratic socialism felt little need to discuss their ideology in terms of the fundamental democratic norm of freedom. Although their ideology's attitude to property set it apart from both liberalism and conservatism, its acceptance of democratic procedures seemed sufficient to guarantee that its basic position was indeed democratic. The fact that many objections had been raised to the socialist stance on 'property' made the socialists – vying for voters' support while facing repeated failures of socialist régimes throughout the world – reluctant to engage in discussing their historical attitude to property and the concomitant issue of freedom. Instead, they became united to oppose those liberal views which can be classified under the heading of 'antinomian liberalism'.

What I shall call 'antinomian liberalism' equates freedom with the absence of coercion (i.e. regards it as a good) – an approach which makes it difficult to answer such questions as: should the State legislate on abortion, euthanasia and other ethical matters? or, does such legislation limit 'freedom'?

Liberals are quite certain that it does; judging from J.S. Mill's *On Liberty*, they have always thought so. Mill's mentor, Bentham, went even further: he raised the question whether laws against murder and theft are restrictions on 'freedom' which can only be justified on the utilitarian ground of the greatest good of the greatest number.

Outside the utilitarian tradition, the liberals' reasoning is based on quite different premises. It can be summarized as follows: inasmuch as 'freedom' is regarded as a good, or necessary to the good, no part of its content can be an evil; if murder or theft is considered wrongful behaviour, restrictions on the latter cannot be limitations on 'freedom'. If they are, the freedom in question is 'antinomian freedom' or what, before linguistic philosophers said the distinction was merely one of 'attitude' to the behaviour referred to, used to be called 'licence'.

(The disappearance of the concept of 'licence' under the influence of linguistic philosophy – which disposes of problems by pretending they are purely verbal – has not advanced 'freedom' in any intelligible sense, but, under the guise of relativism, has advanced antinomianism. The main support for relativism today is not derived from philosophic argument relating our concepts of 'truth' and 'good', but from political reasoning, referring to such questions as 'freedom' and 'tolerance' of the kind raised by J.S. Mill.)

The arguments of people who regard themselves as 'liberals' are based on the assumption that when speaking about 'freedom' we think of restrictions on our behaviour, and that we do not need to ask why such restrictions exist. While the liberal argument for freedom is thus definitely antinomian, the socialist argument is not. All socialists define 'freedom' in such a way that goods such as education and distributive justice are normative absolutes: they are *not* relative to anything. Whether they know it or not, socialists reject the liberals' antinomian position which assumes 'liberty' to be a negation of coercion.

There can be little doubt that conservatives also reject the antinomian view of freedom. They might not know how to reject the argument that laws against murder limit freedom, but they would certainly feel that there is something wrong with such an argument, whereas a liberal would not. He, of course, supports laws against murder just as much as a conservative or socialist, but his arguments are not based on the wrongness of murder but on weighing the value of freedom against the non-value of murder, a position that both the socialist and the conservative find incomprehensible.

The socialist views on freedom, however, are far from being indistinguishable from those of the conservatives. One way of showing the difference is to take Professor Berlin's discussion of freedom[11] as a basis for analysis and demonstrate the affinities between the distinction he makes with regard to 'freedom to' and 'freedom from' and the ideological position of socialists and conservatives in this matter.

Berlin's dichotomous view of freedom embraces two notions: the positive 'freedom to' (freedom to make choices and be guided by reason) and the negative 'freedom from' (absence of obstacles to freedom of choice, absence of interference); the result is an expression of human values and is not an antinomian concept of freedom. Yet the difficulty most people have in thinking of 'freedom to' and 'freedom from' as aspects of a single concept, rather than as evidence of how remarkably flexible the English language is, suggests that people are generally convinced that 'freedom' as a value entails the view that its content is necessarily about the desirable good. Consequently 'freedom from' does not make sense as 'freedom', although it makes very good sense by implying that we have more than one value in freedom. Requiring us to keep this in mind, Berlin's distinction remains valuable; the same point, however, could be less confusingly made by rejecting the utilitarian tradition that freedom itself is adiaphorous until put into a utilitarian framework. No one except adherents of a particular liberal tradition accepts such a view.

Now with regard to the main argument (on the treatment of freedom by conservatives and socialists), 'freedom from' can be assumed to imply that the State performs a function (the Hobbesian social contract). We can express the idea categorically and speak of security, which we then define as freedom from something or other (want, fear, etc.). Since both the conservative and socialist notions of the desirability of 'freedom from' can be covered by the concept of security (or the lack of it), in the abstract, the 'freedom from' of conservatism does not differ from that of the socialists. But when the 'freedom from' of conservatism is linked with the 'freedom to' of conservatism, the 'content' of security and insecurity becomes markedly different from that of socialism. The conservative concept of 'freedom to' reflects the fact that to the conservative the family rather than the State is the fundamental social unit, which completely alters the meaning of 'freedom from' interpreted in terms of 'security'. Since the conservative regards the family as the fundamental social unit – which to him is also an economic unit – he does not see State welfare schemes as increasing 'security' but as decreasing freedom.

The distinction between 'freedom from' and 'freedom to' permits an analysis of the differences between being 'conservative' and 'socialist' without pretending it is merely a matter of self-interest (materialist determinism in the grossest sense): that it is beyond the realm of political theory. No theorist can of course tolerate such a narrow approach to his field.

What makes the socialist conception of 'freedom' distinctive is an attempt to incorporate some other values under the rubric of 'equality'. In his book *Choose Freedom*, Hattersley begins a chapter entitled 'Choose Equality' as follows: 'That in the past the pursuit of liberty through equality has sometimes failed is not in dispute. But the pursuit of liberty through the unregulated economy and the promotion of freedom by the state simply abandoning restraint over weak and powerful alike have failed continually and conspicuously'.[12] A point worth noting here is the assumption that democratic values must be integrated (are not just separate rules, as relativist liberalism implies) and the rejection of the 'freedom from' concept as a type of freedom. According to Hattersley, who italicizes the following sentence, presumably because he considers it his main point, 'Socialism requires the use of collective power to increase individual rights and to extend individual freedom'.[13]

No liberal (or for that matter, conservative) could subscribe to the view that collective power should be used to 'extend freedom'. By liberal definition, power (meaning coercive measures here) would limit freedom, for by defining freedom only in terms of coercion, the liberal cannot incorporate any other values unless he holds to Utilitarianism: the dilemma Mill seems to have faced. (He evidently did not subscribe to pure Utilitarianism, but having defined liberty in terms of coercion, he could retain specific values only by holding a Utilitarianism that he knew was not compatible with the values in which he believed.)

Curiously, although the socialist does not define freedom with reference to coercion, he incorporates the coercive element as a means of attaining freedom. Since, according to him, the individual who lacks freedom lacks power, the logical response to this situation is solidarity or collective coercive action by those who, as individuals, lack freedom because the State fosters inequality.

Collective action has of course often been the outcome of tense social situations since Spartacus's uprising, but when analysing 'solidarity' as a response to supposed inequality and lack of freedom, we are looking not at a mere consequence of a social situation but at a *norm*, something based on choice, not determinism. We also have a new way of distinguishing democratic socialism from Communism: while Marxian socialists believe that capitalism entails a type of unfreedom for the proletariat that can only lead to class war, the modern democratic socialist has arrived at a norm which requires collective action as a normative response to a perceived lack of equality and freedom. Even in a democracy the 'good' man now supports collective action against government policy. This view reflects a major normative change in democratic thinking. The idea is especially important because it is no longer confined to socialist circles.

But to recapitulate: socialist thought deals with 'freedom' in terms of goods other than the absence of coercion; it sees the absence of these goods as reducing individual power, and hence requiring solidarity as a type of democratic action if the goods are to be incorporated into a society based on majority rule, which is in effect coercive power.

Keith Dixon, aware of this type of coerciveness, makes the following point: 'Political systems which aim at implementing the "summum bonum" through which all moral and political conflict and debate is magically resolved usually tend to the imposition upon their citizens of what Professor Maurice Cranston has dubbed "compulsive rational freedom". That is, "freedom" comes to be defined as "justified coercion" in the interest of historical necessity or the future realisation of some mythical utopian society'.[14] The point is well taken although Dixon has misquoted Cranston whose phrase reads: 'compulsory rational freedom'.[15]

What transpires from this statement is that socialists today are using the distinction between democratic and Marxian socialism to get rid of the objections to the concept of compulsory rational freedom. It is clear from Dixon's formulation that he does not see attempts to unite human values under the concept of freedom and then enforce them by political means, as an objection to socialism but to 'some mythical utopian society', or (presumably) Communism. He goes on to say that 'inequalities themselves are a form of constraint' and argues that his analyses of freedom and equality are not necessarily socialist.

Cranston's expression is felicitous: the word 'compulsory' indicates a politico-legal concept; when united with 'rational' and used to modify 'freedom', it forms a memorable phrase. We must insist that the argument is not that socialists, whether democratic or Communist, are wicked or foolish for being ready to accept 'compulsory rational freedom', but that *any* attempt by anyone to define 'freedom' so that it is both a good the State enforces and a good which incorporates other goods will result in the intellectual aberration described as 'compulsory rational freedom'.

This concept is very different from 'antinomian freedom' and so are the objections that can be advanced against it. There is a general feeling that a concept of 'freedom' which represents *inter alia* laws against murder as restrictions on freedom must be false. However, in the absence of analytical assistance from philosophers or theologians (after all, antinomianism is theological in its implications), most people probably assume that human values must therefore be incorporated into the very same concept (of freedom) and that 'freedom' should be enforced by the State along with all other laws. It is hard not to conclude that in consequence, although they do not know it, many people are crypto-totalitarians. They will not believe it even when so charged, for they are unaware of their true position as implied by their advocacy of various forms of coercive action – which they view as democratic processes – under the rubric of freedom.

THE SWORD OF THE STATE AS AN INSTRUMENT OF IDEOLOGICAL JUSTICE

There is an evident ambiguity in the democratic socialists' attitude to the use of force. Although they may not be openly advocating revolution, they consider its prospect with equanimity. They are also prepared to countenance the use of force to induce 'justice' while, rather oddly, being only mild advocates of the coercive element, which has always been considered necessary to a legal order. To understand this, one must look more closely at the argument that attempts to integrate the concepts of freedom and equality necessarily entail the use of force and the loss of freedom.

Some inequalities are clearly the product of society: the caste system in India and the class divisions in Britain are of this nature. Though the law has been used, as in India, to break down the system, it is only by reference to the antinomian view – that coercion through legal measures entails a loss of freedom – that one could argue that

under such circumstances attempts to promote equality
lead to a loss of freedom. But what of other inequalities
reflected in the underrepresentation of women and native
Indians in North American professions and in a dispro-
portionately high crime rate among blacks, Indians and
Latin Americans in the USA? Suppose one sets out to
remedy such inequalities by coercive legal means applied
to the entire social groups. Are we still promoting 'justice'
and 'freedom' because we talk about inequalities that we
disapprove of? Is the coercion involved a justifiable means
to an end rather than an interference with 'liberty'?
Questions of this kind lend importance to the kind of
'inequalities' one has in mind when talking of a 'just
society', and to the relationship between the liberal,
conservative and socialist positions. These three political
persuasions of course all agree that liberty and equality
are goods a democratic society must promote, but it
nonetheless matters how a particular type of inequality is
interpreted by the holder of a given ideology: his ideas of
freedom and justice depend on it.

Liberals greatly simplified the issues by introducing the
slogan 'cultural equality' and speaking of a 'multi-cultural
society'. Instead of viewing all differences between human
beings as 'inequalities', which the just society needed to
remedy, they asserted that only certain differences definable under a normative order as 'undesirable' (such as
illiteracy) are true 'inequalities'.

Since socialists do not explain what differences between
human beings constitute for them 'inequalities', we have
to assume: first, that for the socialist potentially *any*
difference can constitute an inequality which a democratic State ought to remedy; second, that whether it
does so depends on other factors.

This would not be of great political significance if all
'inequalities' could be defined sociologically; if 'equality'
were like the epistemological concept of 'essence' and
'inequalities' were like 'accidents'; or if it could be
plausibly argued that human beings would be equal if
they all had equal opportunity. The democratic norm
'equality of opportunity' can thus be seen as a political

way of speaking of Watsonian behaviourism, or perhaps behaviourism can be a psychologist's way of discussing the norm 'equality of opportunity'. Whichever it is, 'equality of opportunity' would be a proper way of discussing 'equality' only if the type of behaviourism promulgated by Watson at the beginning of the twentieth century were plausible.

In fact, it is not. No possible type of 'conditioning' can, for instance, enable a mentally defective child to become a modern physician any more than training could enable an earwig to do so. If there is not a genetic element related to cultural differences, there is no explanation of why 'culture' is peculiar to the human species.

Although considerations of this kind may seem remote from the question of freedom, equality and State coerciveness, they are in fact crucial. It must be remembered that attempts to link equality and freedom entail a degree of coercion that destroys freedom without increasing equality. Insofar as differences between people are not sociological and therefore not changeable by behaviourist methods, attempts to do so are simply arbitrary acts of coercion.

To supply specific examples of differences between human beings that are not sociological is a delicate matter (Eysenck got into serious trouble simply for trying) since such examples imply a knowledge of human potential and motivations which are not self-evident truths. What should be noted, however, is that having firm opinions on such matters does distinguish conservative, liberal and socialist views: the conservative is the most reluctant to see differences between men as sociological only, the socialist the most eager. The concept of 'class' (sociological difference in opportunity) is more important to socialists than to other parties; hence to them 'remedying' the differences by coercive methods seems thoroughly democratic.

We are not here discussing some remote possibilities or abstract processes of thought that may or may not occur to subtle thinkers; rather, we are facing one of the obvious features of modern democratic thought: the issue of equality of opportunity as linked to statistical findings and the need of a 'just' society to remedy matters where necessary. Are native Indians underrepresented in the professions? If so, then clearly they have not had the 'opportunities' open to others; so the law must step in. Do the poor have a higher crime rate than the middle class? If this is the case, then the difference has been 'caused' by poverty and the law must abandon the principle of equality of treatment in order to redress the 'wrong'.

Many people are convinced that such views are based on 'science'; also that the trouble with 'conservatives' is that they refuse to change their outmoded interpretations based on values held by the individual. Even more disquieting, the coerciveness advocated as a means to 'remedy' such inequalities is perceived as not different in kind from the coerciveness we normally accept in regard to the law.

FREEDOM AND THE RULE OF LAW

Attempts to make democratic ideology unitary – when arguing that it is about freedom – face two related problems: Rousseau's 'enforced freedom' and the concept of the rule of law. Democratic societies reject in principle the idea of enforced freedom; in so doing they deny that laws which promote norms, even such as equality or distributive justice, are of the same kind as laws against murder or theft. Thus, when we want to talk about ethics and about our relation to an authority which may not agree with our conception of ethics, we are back to Berlin's distinction between 'freedom from' and 'freedom to' as essential to the understanding of freedom.

No attempt will be made here to argue the case for or against the norms themselves; the question to be examined is whether promoting an acknowledged democratic norm – such as equality – by means of democratically instituted laws exceeds the authority of a democratic State. Is there a material difference between a democratic State's enforcement of laws against murder and its enforcement of laws in support of equality? (Berlin's distinction again?) A democratic State certainly has the power to act in this way, but does it really have the authority?

The answer is obviously 'Yes' if by authority we mean support from the public – a relativist conception of authority. In political theory – as reflected in a tradition that goes back to Hobbes – the authority of a State derives from its function, which is not a matter of acting in accordance with majority rule. If it were, we could do without a State; everything political would be much clearer.

Democratic societies gave up attempts to legislate morality and force people to be 'free' as far back as the age that followed the Wars of Religion. Attempts to revive former practices (of legislating morality), as during Prohibition in the USA, have only resulted in wholesale violations of the law.

The so-called coercive element in law – the 'power of the sword' – is more a statement about power (pragmatic capacity) than coerciveness. The power of the sword is what enables society to do something about normative violations, yet be just. Thus laws against murder and theft are not primarily designed to frighten citizens into being law-abiding. Rather, State power is the pragmatic expression of its authority, enabling the State to deal with deviants without being arbitrary or restricting freedom in any meaningful sense. The assumption is that in a democratic society moral attitudes have been inculcated by a separate body: traditionally the Church. The problem faced by the State is the threat posed to communal life by imperfections in normative education. No one supposes the defects are correctible by coercive measures, but we do suppose that the State's coerciveness protects the citizens so long as the coercion is not an attempt to create a moral attitude – so long as we are not attempting to legislate morality.

The system was reasonably clear when capital punishment was an allowable aspect of State power, while torture was not. By long odds, while torture is the most effective form of coercion, capital punishment is not:

having been subjected to the supposed coercive progress, those supposedly coerced cease to be coercible. Instead of drawing the obvious conclusion that the State's power is not designed to give it moral authority but to enable it to discharge its function (which in a democracy is not coerciveness), critics of capital punishment use the concept of coerciveness to exemplify their hostility to the power of the State. By doing so, they reveal their tendency to define 'freedom' by the individual's willingness to frustrate the power and authority of the State.

It is non-socialists primarily of conservative bent, who – while being rather unlikely to see law as the source of morality – consider deliberate frustrating of the law to be immoral. Saying 'no' to the State, the socialists (and some liberals), who have adopted this essentially existentialist idea of freedom, entrench egoism in their political philosophy.

The previous major attempt to obtain social and political kudos out of egoism was Bentham's Utilitarianism, which has the defect of becoming impossibly complicated when one tries to apply it. The existentialist solution of saying 'No' does, of course, work (especially now that we have abolished capital punishment), but it has the unfortunate effect of making law and order impracticable. At present this is a serious defect in the left-of-centre concept of freedom.

ENDS AND MEANS: SOCIALIST EQUALITY AND DEMOCRATIC FREEDOM

'Freedom' is the term we apply when thinking about the optimal working of a political system as judged by those subject to that system. It is a combination of 'justice' – as perceived by the ancient Greeks – and 'democracy', which we now consider a necessary aspect of justice. Today, everyone in a democracy, whether liberal, conservative or socialist, is agreed about the value of 'freedom' – a point which might seem irrelevant when analysing the particular notions of freedom held by the three ideologies. But not to be aware of this tendency when substituting some other concept, such as equality, as the central term is bound to lead to self-deception.

Such is the case with Roy Hattersley. 'Liberty is our aim. Equality is the way in which it can be truly achieved', he says; and quoting Crosland with approval, he asserts: 'Until we are equal we cannot be free.'[16]

What is especially interesting about this socialist view is that liberty or freedom is seemingly retained as the central concept – 'Liberty is our aim' – and equality related to it as the means to the end. What can be wrong about that? (After all, traditionally philosophers have been trying to distinguish means from ends so that we could have a clearer idea of what we believe in and how we propose to achieve it.)

What is wrong can be stated as an aphorism: 'sequential' goods may turn out to be pragmatic evils. Its meaning can be made clear by pointing to conditions in the USSR. According to the traditional Communist argument, present conditions – which are a way-station on the road to 'freedom' – are perhaps objectionable now, but nevertheless necessary.

Is there any difference between this rationalization of tyranny and the democratic socialist argument that 'equality' is the means to 'freedom'? Democratic socialists would say 'Yes'. They would not dream of trying to attain their goal by the methods used in the USSR. Indeed, one may argue that even if they wanted to, they could not, for the democratic political system would lead to their losing office – and hence their coercive power – the moment the opposition effectively objected to what they were doing. However, this argument misses the point for there is nothing in the democratic ideology which says that citizens 'ought' to throw out of office anyone who advocates a disagreeable policy. The strength of democracy is that it is not based on a hedonist ideology.

Yet there is a lurking danger. A democratic political system can be converted into a tyranny without a revolution or change of basic institutions, simply by an appeal to the means-end dichotomy: make a sacrifice of 'freedom' in the sense 'desired' so as to attain the desirable, 'true' freedom later on. The serious danger of this appeal lies in its seeming ethical element: the abandonment of personal hedonist standards (one's present feelings) for those of genuine ethics – 'freedom' as agreed on by everybody, whether liberal, conservative or socialist (or, for that matter, Communist, Fascist, etc.).

It is precisely this situation that the tag 'A sequential good is a pragmatic evil' is meant to epitomize. Political theory and ethics have become independent disciplines: the tag expresses an 'ideological' point of view. With this in mind, we can now look at the political message it contains.

'Means to ends' arguments, in which the criterion of the good is hedonist – do I like what I experience? – naturally raise the question of just how long one has to put up with the undesired to attain the (theoretically) desirable. Thus in Marxist terms, just how long does the 'withering' take when the State is withering away; in democratic socialist terms, how long does the noxious imposed 'equality' (with its forced measures such as redistribution of property) take before we are all 'free'?

Liberals who keep to 'orthodoxy' are not faced with this problem. Postponed goods are dealt with by the criterion of 'immediacy' in the hedonist calculus of Bentham: if you cannot say exactly how long it will take to obtain the good – freedom, in political terms – you cannot call the rule you apply 'good'.

Conservatives also do not have the problem. Since they do not define the good hedonistically, the question of how long they will be oppressed before they feel 'free' strikes them as not only bizarre but immoral. The utter indifference of Communists to the need for answering the question of just how long is the interval between means and ends (or their inability to find an answer) accounts for the conservatives' conviction that Communism is wrong and that socialism in this respect is not much different.

Socialists have undoubtedly received considerable support from sociologists and social psychologists: human beings can be conditioned to accept as 'true' anything at all. The length of time between the feeling of 'rightness', 'good' or 'truth' and the actual experience is determined solely by the 'expertise' of the conditioner and his control over the circumstances. The more control he has, the sooner the 'freedom'. Such is the present situation: behaviourists argue that the more control they are given, the greater the ensuing 'freedom'. Socialists agree. But despite the fact that one set appears to argue about psychology and the other about politics, the result is a basic situation condemned by traditional ethics on the ground that the end does not justify the means. Political theory, as a discipline independent from ethics, could express this idea by saying 'Sequential goods are pragmatic evils' – which is an abstract way of asserting that socialism is wrong when it claims that equality is the means towards 'freedom'.

Chapter 17

Marxist impact on socialism

MARXISM AND DEMOCRATIC SOCIALISM

When it comes to instituting and maintaining socialism, if one believes in it, democratic political institutions are a great inconvenience. The threat posed by socialism to private property, to the means of earning a living and to maintaining a high standard of living ensures that the ablest and most enterprising citizens will resist socialist ideology. Willingness to pay for expropriated private property is irrelevant. The threat is not to what one owns but to one's livelihood and capacity to 'better' oneself. Under liberal democracy, the arguments advanced in favour of this position will not be dismissed, but socialism – both democratic and Marxian – regards them as 'rationalizations' by the propertied class. Yet it is not only the property owners who put them forward but also those who feel confident they can 'build a better mousetrap' or run their own business or support themselves without 'public assistance'. Socialism dismisses them all as misguided. Everyone who does not adhere to the socialist view is regarded by socialists as in some way 'corrupt' and 'undemocratic' and therefore to be excluded from decision-making. A socialist may consciously reject Marxist theorizing about the 'dictatorship of the proletariat' but in curtailing what he perceives as an undemocratically inclined class, he unconsciously moves towards a Communist view and the institutional forms consonant with it. This happened to Castro and to many well-educated

African leaders: the normative assumptions made under 'socialism' are such that in the end only a State run along Communist lines can institute and maintain their normative system.

The reason for this is that the norms of both ideologies (socialist and Communist) rest on assumptions which are in serious conflict with individualism – a norm fundamental to democracy. Both persuasions believe that the concept of property is a legal fiction. The case they make is based on the fact that the concept's content – what can be legally owned – does rest on law. To look back in time: the laws against slavery excluded human beings from the concept itself; the copyright laws incorporated words and music – items which had formerly been thought of as public property. So it is inferred that the concept of property itself must be a legal fiction. Consequently, one may well argue that the smaller the number of things that can be owned privately, the greater are the public good and the sense of community: the less there is that is ownable, the more there is that must be shared.

Clearly, the sense of community is not increased under either of the two systems. Once something is placed outside the sphere of private property, it tends to be treated with indifference. Members of both persuasions offer various explanations for what amounts to a failure in prediction in the matter of attitudes to public property, yet it never occurs to them that a failure in prediction reflects an inadequate explanation of the nature of the problem. (An 'explanation' is a statement about preceding, constituent factors that make a prediction possible. A failure in prediction is a failure in explanation.)

The assumption that the concept of property is a legal fiction is quite false. Both babies and animals have a property concept. Being related to the concept of self, it is linked with individualism. Those who assert that property is a legal fiction also make the right of the individual a legal fiction instead of, as in democracy, a constitutional principle which helps define 'justice'. As a consequence, a democratic socialist is committed to norms of his system only so far as the law forces him to be

– and insofar as the conception of 'internalized law' affects his behaviour. But we have nothing to fear from a democratic socialist holding office in an established democracy. Both the laws under which he operates and the way he was reared ensure that he will respect the rights of the individual.

This, however, does not hold true of Third World countries. What the law will be there depends on the normative commitments of men in power. First, since socialism makes individual rights as much a fiction as property and, second, since it is the belief that property must be 'equitably' distributed that makes one a socialist, even those who are convinced they are democratic socialists – not Communists – will soon drop the democratic trappings for the sake of their fundamental beliefs.

Although some people speak of 'creeping socialism' as an internal threat and think of it as a movement towards Communism, there is a point within democracies beyond which socialism cannot grow. This is because of its conflict with the norm of individualism: the distributive justice of which socialism speaks does not seem just enough. But in the Third World countries, socialism of the democratic variety has turned into something indistinguishable from Communism. As a result, democracies today are faced with the kind of 'encirclement' that the former Soviet Union's orthodox ideology has ascribed to its own situation and which Mao Tse-Tung once applied to internal Chinese conditions by using the phrase 'encirclement of cities'. ('The revolutionary village', as he put it, 'can encircle the cities'.) Mao's ideas fell in abeyance, but ironically what Jean-François Revel – referring to the Communist slogan of 'capitalist encirclement' – has called 'the greatest strategic farce of modern times', had for a time ceased to be a farce.

RADICALIZATION OF THE DEMOCRATIC LEFT

Democratic socialists are no longer characterized by an all-out advocacy of the central tenet of Marxian socialism – State ownership of the means of production; yet as late as the 1950s what was considered the main obstacle to increased nationalization was the problem of compensation. The most likely reason for this change is 'efficiency', the very concept which at one time served as an argument in favour of State ownership. Economic enterprises do poorly when profitability – the means of appraising efficiency – is removed; not many socialists are such doctrinaire Marxists as to endanger the economic basis of a free market society by demanding State capitalism at any cost. Inasmuch as there is still support for State-owned enterprises, it seems based on the fact that they can afford 'featherbedding' that is not possible in private industry. Thus under State ownership, uneconomic coalmines can be kept open; furthermore, the workers can go on strike and close most of the mines when the government announces closure. It appears that the main attraction of State capitalism is the removal of certain parts of the economy from economic considerations. Old programmes of State ownership are self-limiting in the sense that some socialists (and liberals) still advocate nationalization but only insofar as the economy can afford it.

But the differences between the various shades of the left (from the Marxists to the left-wing liberals) with regard to property in general are less pronounced than before: the process of radicalization has affected both the socialists and liberals. While it is now recognized (as was said before) that in order to have an efficient economy, the means of production must remain in private hands, the matter of distributive justice has become central to socialist-liberal thinking. It is the present motivation of both socialist and liberal persuasions that is crucial. (Here I take issue with John Dunn, according to whom 'the main residual distinction between the views of Rawls and Nozick and a socialist conception of the good arises over their. . . assumption that substantial material incentives are likely to remain a precondition for energetic and effective productive activity'.[17] In other words, ensuring that there is property to distribute is as important to a liberal as distributing property; but this implies a distinction between liberals and socialists that does not strike me as fundamental. Indeed, as regards de-emphasizing State ownership of the means of production, socialists today seem to agree with liberals.) The real issue is that treating property not as property, but as a good to be distributed, is a very radical view shared by many socialist-liberals.

The principal characteristic of this view is its supposed self-evidence. It is not advanced by its adherents as necessary to 'equality' or 'self-realization' – traditionally linked with democratic values – but as an intrinsic good and a part of fundamental social justice. When such a value judgement is made at a time when few people believe in the 'natural law' principles, one has to look elsewhere for the relevant ideological premises. Since neither liberals nor democratic socialists argue that distributive justice is either democratic or a means to increase the production of goods, one is bound to look to the Marxian theory and to an ideologically-based attitude to property as the sources of influence.

Just how this can be done without self-awareness of what one is doing can be seen in Dunn's discussion of the shortcomings of Nozick and Rawls as thinkers – as being philosophers who have failed to become doctrinaire Marxian socialists. How does Dunn refer to the concept of 'property'? To him, it is another term for 'legitimate appropriation'; he also speaks of Rawls as having 'prudently' avoided giving an account of such a matter. Now if 'legitimate appropriation' does express the nature of property, it would indeed be prudent for anyone to avoid trying to give an account of a just society as one recognizing the concept of property, for 'appropriation' when it is not used as a technical legal term, implies a socially dubious kind of act (somewhat akin to stealing) and consequently as expressing self-contradiction when attached to the term 'legitimate'. Dunn's position shows at the outset that there is something seriously wrong with his conceptualization of 'property'; there is also something deceitful about the intellectual processes of all those who would defend such a stance. It would not be difficult to establish that Dunn's conception of the nature

of property does not fit known anthropological and sociological facts about the concept; but it may well be impossible to convince the socialists (and liberals) holding the
view that they would not 'normally' have such a concept:
it cannot be derived either from our traditional democratic values or from known facts about property.

Radicalization of Socialism: Pervasiveness of Coercion

In the late nineteenth century, both Fabian and Marxian
socialists could hold similar views on the nature of the
good society yet differ in their action programmes. Each
group was certain that its vision of the good was inevitable
– any kind of evolution was thought of as progressing
'naturally' from the lower to the higher – but they
differed in their conceptions of the process involved and
the question of how individuals could assist it by conscious
participation. The view reflected an optimism the Victorians had but which has since been lost (although the
nineteenth-century belief in a Heraclitean 'flux' which
lies at the root of progress has been retained). The very
marked difference in policy between those socialists who
believe in slow peaceful evolution and those who believe
in rapid revolutionary change is no longer as clear as it
once was. It is no longer customary to believe that an
evolutionary process will improve man's lot. Present
beliefs about the nature of change are such that anyone
who desires change in general – who has a conception of
the good as something other than what in fact exists – is a
potential 'radical'. Thus socialist radicalism is enhanced
by its very conception of the good as something other
than present fundamental relations.

Democratic socialists may not believe in the seizure of
political power as Communists do, nor do they believe, as
the Fabians did, that democracy is a kind of political
order that entails progress. To the conservatives, if something called 'progress' is not a natural process, it must be
a defence of coercion by someone who has no right (no
authority) to coerce. Social good (as opposed to one's

personal good) is conceived of by socialists as entailing coercion because man is seen as hedonist and egoist – as indifferent to social good unless he happens to be a socialist. The socialist is thus justified in instituting coercive measures to achieve his vision of the good: first, because in doing this he is supposedly not acting simply in self-interest; second, because if he does not coerce, the necessary reforms or consideration of the rights of others will not occur. Consequently, we have to have a charter of rights such that some people are coerced into respecting them. Presumably no one would voluntarily recognize them.

Politically this means that the liberal-socialist defines himself as the champion of the 'underprivileged', who in turn are defined as those lacking, or not having enough, political power to have their needs recognized by society. Under this conception of the good, the best plan would be so to distribute political power that the attention of the liberal-socialist would be unnecessary. A participatory democracy in which the needs of all imaginable 'classes' or groups would receive equal recognition would of course be best but, since no one has been able to suggest a political system to accomplish this, liberal-socialists are increasingly defining themselves as champions of the underdog – advocates of prisoners' rights, native rights, women's rights, 'gay' rights, children's rights and the rights of any other imaginable class. Under this conception of society – permanently fragmented yet dependent on coercion – it is no longer just the criminal class which is coerced into a *modus vivendi*, but everybody.

This conception of pervasive coercion is much more pervasive than anything conceived by Hobbes. His initial assumption, which allowed for a measure of co-operativeness, is now unimaginable. Modern liberal-socialism appears in one way at least more radical than Marxism, for orthodox Communism sees class conflict as limited to the relations between three (and eventually two) classes and envisions an end to the process, whereas liberal-socialism sees class conflict as infinitely divisible and never-ending. The need for such a conflict is implied and so is coerciveness. There will not be a millenium. Violence must be institutionalized.

The postulate that society is coercive because of man's nature was advanced by Hobbes and others who begin with the assumption that either individuality is the same as egoism or that it necessarily entails it. Yet the degree of coerciveness imagined as necessary was in reality quite small. The Hobbesian argument for the rational accept-ance of an authority that leads to coercive powers is so conceived that actual coercion with regard to those who acknowledge the cogency of the argument is seldom necessary. Normal people do not obey the law because of policemen but because of the argument for policemen. It is the irrationalists who need to be literally coerced. The present post-participatory democratic view, however, is that society is even more coercive than Hobbes imagined: we are no longer coerced by society – as Hobbes would say – into being consistently prudent, but into being con-sistently altruistic.

CLASS RESPONSIBILITY AND NATIVISM

Deriving directly from Marx and undermining the entire democratic ethical system is the Marxist concept of classes. Many people in our society assume that if they reject the Marxian view of class conflict, they have re-jected Marx and are thinking in democratic terms. This, however, does not follow at all. Our normative system cannot work in the absence of a concept of individual responsibility and its concomitant 'innocence' (the latter in the sense of not being responsible when the behaviour can be shown as determined by circumstances, rather than 'self'). To shift to notions of class responsibility and individual irresponsibility is to abandon the democratic ethical system. That one happens not to believe that capital and labour are in irreconcilable conflict does not change matters. Establishing this implies only that the person in question is not an orthodox Marxist. The point is that to think in class terms when thinking norma-tively means that one's views will either coincide with

Communist policy or be receptive to views consistent with that policy (and inconsistent with democratic ideas).

Western societies have for some time been marked by 'relativism' – at this point used in the broad sense of the abandonment of norms as 'explanatory' (as determinants of human behaviour in the sense that the teaching of norms is held to matter with regard to one's behaviour). The tendency in the present century has been to shift to various forms of determinist explanation which exclude the possibility of choice. Animalism, experientialism and environmentalism cover the current theories: the first representing Freud's early views about the importance of biological drives; the second being the view that these drives, interacting with early experience, account for all future behaviour; the third being the much more general approach that behaviour is to be explained in terms of one's biological inheritance interacting throughout life with various environmental influences (including, in some accounts, norms). What these theories have in common is that they are all deterministic views which portray 'choice' – and hence 'responsibility' – as illusions. Marx himself cannot be held directly responsible for the general acceptance of this determinism in the West, since its proponents, with the exception of outright Marxists, pay little attention to economic factors. Determinism came in with Darwin; but if it is he, rather than Marx, who is responsible for our adoption of determinism as the 'scientific' explanation of the human condition, Marx has nonetheless been chiefly responsible for the direction that determinist thinking has taken in Western society.

It is not logically necessary for a determinist to think in terms of classes; whenever we find an emphasis on 'classes' in the social sciences, we must look to the influence of an ideology which represents classes as fundamental units in social analysis.

When one considers the status of biological classes – the race element – in current discussions of social relations, the suspicion that Marxian views are operating can be confirmed. In Marxian analysis, the concept of biological classes is dismissed as ideologically irrelevant.

Although such psychologists as Carleton Coon and H.J. Eysenck have brought forward rather clear evidence that the racial factor is important and should consequently play some part in arriving at decisions on social policy, our society – acting on the normative plea of egalitarianism – insists that biological classes be disregarded. At the same time it is argued that similar kinds of differences, presumably also socially irrelevant, like the IQ, be taken into account in the treatment of individuals, when before the courts. It is difficult to justify such a distinction in terms of what 'science' requires.

Stranger still, a racist concept – nativism – has been introduced in North America in the guise of a social class having special privileges. If an individual can establish, or even simply assert, that somewhere in his ancestry there was a member of a certain biological class, such as native Indian, he is allowed to claim compensation for the historical ill-treatment of his claimed biological class by another biological class. As a result, an American (or Canadian) citizen – even though his ancestors happened to be Europeans who did not arrive on the North American continent until the present century – may be required as a member of one biological class to 'compensate' another biological class for something that happened in history to people whom the 'victimized' class claims as ancestors. If he resists the argument on the grounds that it is clearly racist and violates democratic principles, such resistance is branded as 'racist'.

A nativist argument does not follow from the democratic ideology, which is opposed to the notion that any class should have exclusive privileges. But class thinking is central to Marxism-Leninism: the concept of the 'dictatorship of the proletariat' assigns important privileges to a single class and justifies these privileges in terms of historical class relations. This is clear evidence of norms derived from an alien ideology being represented as democratic and a matter of elementary justice.

The widespread acceptance of such alien normative thinking undoubtedly derives from anti-rationalistic thinking. Under relativism, it is thought useless to analyse the logic of norms. Consequently, the fact that nativism is pure and simple racism is obscured by relativists; the relationship between Marxism and nativism is dismissed by them as an illusion.

Such self-assurance in the face of evidence to the contrary reflects a social determinism which is traceable to the Marxian view of norms. Many people in Western societies have abandoned the belief that democratic norms are not mere reflections of what is happening in their own society but transcend the circumstances and determine what is occurring. They do not see that from the standpoint of democratic ideology, nativism is a form of racism, which is not made 'democratic' by pretending it is 'justice'. It can be so labelled only if one thinks in terms of classes – which is the Marxian way of thinking.

According to democratic justice it has never been enough to establish that someone is 'guilty' in the sense that he or she 'actually did what is considered wrong'. It has also been necessary to establish 'responsibility' – that choice was possible. But of course, under determinism no choice is possible; the courts become increasingly devices for allowing 'behavioural mod' on the part of society. Since both capital punishment and the penalty of imprisonment are incompatible with this new view of 'justice', capital punishment has been abandoned by all 'right-thinking' people and imprisonment without 're-habilitation' is seen as 'unjust'. The best modern prisons in the West are now rather attractive recreational centres where criminals can relax from the effort of supporting themselves. They have special privileges which compensate them for the 'injustice' of being deprived of liberty. The pleas used in extenuation of such treatment refer to 'humanitarianism', as if opponents were advocating the alternative of dungeons and racks. Opponents of the new conception of justice argue that, first, it is inconsistent with the democratic concept of individual responsibility; second, it is the logical development not of democratic norms but of Marxian determinism.[18] To abandon the concept of individual responsibility and to think of behaviour in deterministic terms is to cease being democratic.

DOES THE 'TOTALITARIAN TEMPTATION' LEAD TO SUICIDE?

In keeping with the strong tendency in twentieth century thought to approach questions about human behaviour as if it were irrational, Revel begins his discussion of the 'totalitarian urge' with the question 'Does there lurk in us a wish for totalitarian rule?'[19] This is the kind of question psychoanalysts may say needs to be asked but which is alien to political philosophers. Unless the factors in question are external to the individual – matters for behaviouralists and determinists but not for political philosophers – it is not possible to make explicit what is not even conscious.

However, Revel's answer to his own question is in keeping with the views about motivation that political theorists can accept. Indeed, they may do well to give it even more attention than Revel himself. He asserts that there is a totalitarian urge of which there are two components: 'The first component is not really a desire for totalitarianism, since it is based on the people's ignorance of Communist regimes. . . It is a political expression of the class struggle. . . without a clear picture of the future form of government. . . The Communist alternative is simply seen as the opposite of the faults of the society in which they are living. . . the other component of the desire for totalitarianism among élites, is based on a clear knowledge of the kind of society they are choosing'.[20]

As Revel observes about the second component: 'This calls for a more complex psychosocial interpretation'. In fact, he needs an entire book to set it forth, so that one is likely to miss the importance of his first point.

The first point is probably more important to members of democratic societies because it refers to the curious readiness of relatively large numbers of people in the West, in defiance of their established institutions and traditions, to accept the establishment of Communist régimes elsewhere and even to lend active support to Communist movements abroad. If enough of the latter succeed in setting up new Communist régimes, the chances of survival of liberal democracies will be very much reduced.[21]

Yet many jump to the conclusion that socialism (including the Marxist variety) poses no threat to democratic society because there seems to be little chance of many people in the English-speaking world choosing Marxian socialism as their ideology. This assumption is based on general indifference to Communism as ideology, an indifference manifested first, in the rejection of the socialist concepts of property and second, in the belief that free enterprise supplies the only desirable kind of 'freedom'. Most people are tempted neither by democratic socialism nor Communism.

Such a view, however, does not reflect voting behaviour. Yet, although the English-speaking world is generally indifferent to the appeal of Communist parties, it is not opposed to the various brands of 'socialism'. As we know from reactions to unilateral disarmament proposals and talk about 'imperialism',[22] 'racism' and so forth, many 'anti-Communists' will accept Communist propositions if they are detached from the ideology. It seems that what troubles most people is the intellectuality of ideology. The Anglo-Saxon civilization is committed to an empiricism that represents intellectualism as both a bore and a chore that is unnecessary, if not misleading. So most people are not concerned with it and unwittingly become party liners: they are convinced that they do not need to reflect about their behaviour. They all 'know' they are not believers in 'Communism' and wrongly deduce that therefore they are not party liners. Lenin called such people 'useful idiots'.

A Digression on 'Plunging into the Unknown' and the Issue of Freedom

When one speaks of the readiness of socialists to plunge into the unknown it is not inadvertent socialism that matters, but the nebulous concept of 'freedom' adhered to by a society committed to empiricism. When the members of such a society speak of 'freedom' they hold very confusing notions; in pursuit of 'freedom' they are capable of anything: the concept obviously creates an intellectual abyss into which everyone tumbles. At this point conservatives are hard put to explain the dangers of liberal-socialism.

Once upon a time, freedom was not so much a value as a fact or supposed fact. Man seemed not to have a 'nature' that committed him to limited courses of action but was 'free' – seemed to have no such limitations as animals and inanimate things. (This situation can be thought of as a value [free will] or as a moral defect [wilfulness] or, of course, as an illusion [if one adopts a determinist view]. The adopted stance can become a source of serious disagreement to the point of insisting that we have not the faintest idea what our opponents are talking about.)

Democratic societies consider 'freedom' a good; because the concept originated an apparent 'fact' (in the above-mentioned sense), the temptation is to argue that the real or pure meaning refers to the absence of restrictions on human behaviour. Social conditions require that freedom always be a compromise between the wants and needs of individuals and the consequences of their being members of society. Respect for 'freedom' requires us eventually to explore those social restrictions – *modus vivendi* rules – that can be abandoned, while there is a good chance to continue living as well as before. It implies getting rid of 'taboos' and outmoded restrictions and being ready to take a chance on the unknown (such action being considered 'liberal' or 'scientific' or 'moral').

By contrast, the conservative viewpoint is that 'freedom' is a good only because it enables one to exercise choice with regard to the imposed restrictions. Animals do not have a choice in respect to what they think is the good: the matter is determined for them either by their biology or by an interaction between their biology and their personal experience. Human conceptions of the good are conceptual (mental) rather than biological. Human beings can profit from a 'revelation' on such matters in a way which is unique to them. They also have reason to believe that the conception of freedom is valid (for them) and that therefore there is something special about their species. It is hard to believe that it follows from the conception of 'freedom' that 'plunging into the unknown' is a good, or that it is 'scientific' or 'moral'.

Freedom of Self-destruction

The concept of 'freedom' which sets the individual and society in opposition rests on the assumption that man is like other animal species; that as individuals we do not need ethical prescriptions or a formal education; that we can rely on our instincts; and that the good and the desired are the same thing. This is a naturist view; first taught by the Romantics it is still generally accepted – and not just by the young. While most people agree that freedom has to be restricted to enable human beings to live together, they have not abandoned the Romantic idea that apart from *modus vivendi* considerations men do not need ethics, education and authority and that they can operate on the basis of desire. (If this were not so, it would hardly be possible to understand how anyone could advocate ethical relativism.) Indeed, this assumption became so common in the 1960s and 1970s that most people attempted to define the good in terms of anarchistic desire and invariably set it in opposition to 'freedom'. During that period a booming economy enabled Western society to support those who chose to 'drop out and turn on' (a conception of 'freedom' within the liberal-socialist tradition). Nowadays fewer young people are attracted by such a notion of liberty because they know that the consequences for them personally will not be anything that can be defined as 'freedom'. The time for anarchistic nonsense is past; but do socialists realize it? Anything that any culture has called civilization has always rested on convention and authority, not on anarchistic ideas of freedom or on ethical conceptions about relativism as a good. Failing to reconsider its conception of freedom, socialism is taking the road to self-destruction.

The Irrational Logic of Ideology

Theoretically, the spectacular failure of Marxian predictions about the future course of capitalist societies should be evidence that Marx's analysis was wrong. Logically, a genuine scientific explanation differs from a prediction only with regard to the point in time referred to: an explanation refers to the present or past and a prediction to the future – the 'prediction' serving as evidence that the explanation is correct by making the course of history an 'experiment' testing the hypothesis. The implication is that for those who truly understand it, history is an experimental science.

Unfortunately, one can also employ 'explanation' as a correlative of 'understanding'. If I can say 'I understand' as a result of something you say, then what you said is an 'explanation' although it allows no prediction whatsoever. Thus a great many people do not understand the significance of the failure of Marx's predictions but are convinced of the 'truth' of his views by the fact that they can say 'I now understand the working of capitalism'. The reason for Marx's appeal is similar to that of Freud: his views provide his followers with a way of 'understanding' (in the sense of 'talking about'): henceforth, because of the nature of language, they will assume that his explanation is the same as a scientific explanation (whose correlative is prediction). Many socialists suppose that the day will come when Marxian predictions will be fulfilled. After all, no actual timetable was drawn up. Hence, those who do not understand the difference between the two types of explanation suppose that Marx has the entire course of history to prove his theory.

One of the problems about this situation, discussed by Revel, is that by defending free enterprise one defends, at least in part, anarchy (although probably no one today who defends free enterprise would pretend to argue for political anarchy); whereas socialists are much more consistent as regards what is necessary to social order. They agree on the need for political authority but are not convinced that it should be excluded from the marketplace. Why should not the argument for sovereignty be an argument for 'totalitarianism' (as critics of sovereignty have suggested is the case)?

Now the Hobbesian argument was that authority exists because it serves a function and continues to exist only because it serves its function; the implication is that the sovereign is free to do anything whatsoever, so long as the function is served. There are no limits apart from those set by functionality. The sovereign cannot be a 'tyrant' – someone in a position of power who acts on impulse: his position is determined by serving a function rather than by the fact that he holds power (the power deriving from the function rather than vice versa, as in legalistic theories). This being the case, an argument for sovereignty would only appear to be an argument for something approaching 'totalitarian' rule. Hence anyone acknowledging the need for political authority would look on economic anarchy (free enterprise) as no different from arguments for political anarchy. Certainly such is the frame of mind of non-Marxian socialists: if we need political authority, we have to extend it to cover economic matters.

Thus J.S. Mill's arguments for liberty (including free enterprise) are hard to distinguish from arguments for anarchy because Mill did not make clear the cases in which the arguments for liberty were not arguments for anarchy. Hobbes and Mill are at opposite poles: it is not clear when Hobbes is not arguing for a sort of 'totalitarianism', nor is it clear when Mill is not arguing for anarchy. Unfortunately, we cannot combine the two and hope to arrive at a golden mean because they both argue as if the other possibility did not deserve much attention.

Mill, like Marx, was a meliorist, whereas Hobbes was definitely not. Hobbes conceived of man as impulsive by nature and quite unable to live in harmony with other men unless a sovereign power forced him to think in

terms of long-range interests. Hobbes conceded, however, that without compulsion men can recognize their
long-range interests – that they think 'egoistically' or as
we usually say 'rationally' or 'prudently'. Both Mill and
Marx thought of the anarchistic elements in man (our
hedonism or impulsive desires) as peculiar to our situation rather than to our 'nature', so that improvement in
our condition ('meliorism', to use the Victorian term)
was possible. The problem was to produce social conditions that would bring out the best in man. It is hard
not to conclude that from the very beginning, Marx and
Mill (socialism and liberalism) worked together and that
this was not an historical accident.

One tends to forget that Mill argued that 'imperialism'
is a good because it is 'educational': men in the 'infancy'
of civilization need to learn what the really civilized have
discovered. 'Culture' to Mill (as well as Marx) did not
have the relativistic meaning it has acquired in modern
anthropology – the composite views of the composite
called 'society' – but referred to the kind of knowledge
which has been discovered by experience to be good and
true.

Mill and Marx (democratic socialism and Communism)
are also in agreement because of their expectations of
what will happen to human character if conditions are
'right'. Both assume what Hobbes does: anarchy is not
what we want; to be sure, it may be the situation in which
we find ourselves. We want something 'better' because we
can imagine it. What is difficult to imagine is how to get
what we want; the means – not the end – is the problem.

Both Marx and Mill assume that a temporary 'totalitarianism' will solve the problem; if the appropriate social
conditions exist, mankind will have the personal qualities
that will make sovereignty unnecessary; if an argument
for economic anarchy (free enterprise) is possible, then
an argument for political anarchy (the withering away of
the State) also is. The two go together. Under present
conditions neither is possible, but ideologists do not
speak of short-sighted views. As far as they are concerned,
the question is what the future holds.

According to Revel, the socialists are wrong in their estimation. Are they 'committing suicide' because Marx's prediction about the future of capitalism was wrong?

Revel is convinced that socialist and Communist thinking will be brought into disrepute by the discrepancies between predictions about the future fate of capitalism and its historical course. It is suicidal to ignore facts. Indeed, 'insanity' has always been defined in terms of marked discrepancies between beliefs and facts. Where 'faith' takes us beyond facts (in the sense of sensory evidence), insanity makes one ignore them. Adherence to ideology, which in Marx's day was an act of faith, is now insanity or hypocrisy, depending on the degree of belief one can plausibly assign to the advocates.

Very serious doubts must now arise not only about the ideology of Communism but about the mentality of its advocates: are they hypocrites, madmen or power-hungry psychopaths? The emphasis is shifting to psychological questions.

When speaking about the capacity of socialist ideologues to cope with discrepancies between what they say they believe and what the facts are, Revel uses the phrase the 'irrational logic of the emotions'.[23] 'Irrational logic' is certainly an expression to conjure with: it is neither nonsense nor unintelligible. Hume himself said that what is illogical when dealing with facts is the assumption that facts have a logic: facts are not predictable. Since Hume's day, science has followed this dictum; it no longer attempts to make sense of its views. Thus the wave theory and the corpuscular theory of light – which are incompatible – are combined in the quantum theory which, although rationally unintelligible, has proved to be pragmatically useful. The reasoning of a scientific mind being such – 'illogic' is now accepted by science – why insist that a political mind should follow a different course – a pre-Humean conception of reason? There is also a 'pragmatic' point to being a Communist. A growing number of writers who have lived under a Communist régime will testify accordingly. This alone is perhaps more important than discrepancies between Communist theory and the realm of facts. To put too much stress on these discrepancies is to underestimate the recuperative powers of Communist ideology. As courses in the physical sciences tell students today not to pay much attention to logical discrepancies, why should we be surprised when a physicist – a Pontecorvo or a Fuchs – becomes a devout Communist and remains unmoved by arguments based on divergences between facts and theory? Science tells him that logic of this kind is irrational.

Chapter 18

Return to utopianism

SCEPTICAL GRADUALISM: HARRINGTON'S PROGNOSIS

In an age of perestroika, Michael Harrington may have been the most significant socialist commentator in North America, for, unlike most socialists, he was not a polemicist out to expose wicked capitalists – and thus imply that socialism is better, no matter what – but rather to admit, as part of his argument, that 'capitalism was a radical new innovation, the greatest achievement of humankind in history'.[24] In other words, he did not see capitalism as a mistake to be corrected by socialism. It was unusual for an unrepentant socialist to begin with such a premise. His was not a concession to the realities of current events (such as the demise of Marxian-based economic and political régimes and structures) but a genuine belief supported by social analysis; as such it marks off Harrington's views from run-of-the-mill socialist apologetics.

Harrington's significance, however, does not lie in a sort of negative virtue – in not basing his defence of socialism on some supposed moral, social and economic retrogression introduced by capitalism – but rather on the fact that socialism for him is a promise, a secular parallel to the salvation offered by religion. 'Socialism, I want to propose', he says in his opening statement, 'is the hope for human freedom and justice under the unprecedented conditions of life that humanity will face in the twenty-first century'.[25]

Now the interesting part is that this secular promise is 'spiritual' and not materialistic, in the way the religions (as distinct from sects) offer salvation rather than material betterment and expect to gain converts precisely because of this appeal to man's sense of being part of creation (rather than in opposition to and isolated from it). Reinforcing this 'spiritual' element is Harrington's rejection of materialist determinism: 'There is no guarantee', he says, 'that socialism will triumph – or that freedom and justice, even to the limited degree that they have been achieved until now, will survive the next century'.[26]

The view that a human ideal, like salvation, requires personal effort represents a major break with Marxism, which lost a good deal of missionizing force by talking of the inevitability of what it projected as truth. Just as most people today are practically illiterate about 'science' and indifferent to what science says is happening – a sphere entirely apart from everyday life – so the people supposedly to be benefited by Communism, the proletariat, never took much interest in it, for the theory itself implied that it really did not matter whether they did or not.

To represent any system of values as inevitable is a bad mistake psychologically, for the argument creates apathy among those who should support it and organized resistance from the opposition. For this reason, Harrington's rather casual detachment of democratic socialism from the Marxist version deserves more emphasis than given by him; if 'socialism' (in any form) is to survive the difficulties faced by Communism, only 'idealism' in the psychological sense will enable it to do so.

Harrington may have played down the need for democratic socialists to be idealists because of the danger of the clash between such an idea and that contained in his second hypothesis: 'the fate of human freedom and justice depends upon social and economic structures'.[27] But it would be wrong to infer that Harrington's views were dependent on materialist determinism. It is important to understand what he is here saying: his very praise of capitalism is contingent on it.

Basically, Harrington sees capitalism as a sort of transition between the order imposed on man by sovereignty and the freedom and justice possible under socialism: 'Prior to capitalism, one or another kind of authoritarianism was pervasive. Then capitalism created, not the full reality of freedom – and certainly not of justice – but a space in which men and women could fight for and win democratic rights and even make advances toward justice'.[28]

The basic defence of Hobbesian sovereignty, let us remember, has been that it provided the condition for 'freedom' and 'justice' in some undefined and frankly unimaginable sense, for at best it merely got rid of the intolerable state of nature. It is this view of hypothetical prehistory that seems to be the one Harrington reasons from rather than from Rousseau's version that Marx probably used. In effect, in Harrington's mind capitalism removed the potential for tyranny in Hobbesian sovereignty by depersonalizing the forces for order: 'Discipline was now economic, not political. One worked at the prevailing wage in obedience to an impersonal market'.[29]

Linking ideals like 'freedom' and 'justice' with economic and social structures well suited Marxian socialism; as a result, it failed as a practicable ideology. A critic of socialism, like Hayek, would say that this happened because the normal sequence of cause-effect relations was inverted by ideological expectations. Ideological notions behind the concepts of 'freedom' and 'justice' were allowed to determine the operations of the market-place. The market ceased to function as a reflection of human interests.

In the abstract, it is not possible to deny a relation between economic and social structure and any valid sense of such ideals as freedom and justice. (On this point, the left and right do not necessarily disagree.) But we now know what Harrington did not know for certain when he was writing: it is not possible to force the market-place to conform to one's ideological position about the meaning of the two ideals ('freedom' and 'justice'); this is because the market-place is based on 'desire' rather than an ideology-ruled principle.

Harrington's prognosis on socialism is careful and tentative, his argument (third hypothesis) is qualified: 'The revolution we are now living through is creating a social and political environment that, if it is not subjected to democratic control from below, will subvert the possibilities of freedom and justice'.[30] His reasoning – anchored as it is on past thought and intellectual tradition – points at an unknown future: Hobbes – capitalism – (socialism?). There is no hint of historical determinism. To him, the question is 'idealism' and its concomitant psychological idealism: what do we want to happen?

At a time when command-economies are debating how to shift to market-based ones without causing the collapse of society, it may seem odd to take seriously an opposing view, socialist gradualism or the slow movement towards socialism. Has nothing at all been learned about the utter impracticality of socialism? Is the concept of gradualism not just a return to that typically English version of socialism, Fabian socialism, which could perhaps be defined as 'conservative socialism'? Harrington's ideas have affinities with Fabianism as in his emphasis on socialism as primarily ethical rather than economic or political. Socialism, according to him, 'had to seek nothing less than a "moral and intellectual reform" of the society. Like the Protestant Reformation, it was the carrier of a new morality'. Harrington links up this moral view with 'gradualism', which he sets in opposition to Marxism: 'This meant that the transition to socialism would be much more protracted and profound than most socialists, including Marx, had thought'.[31] One should note, however, that Harrington's emphasis on gradualism derives from the profundity and pervasiveness of change rather than from the need to adapt the end (socialism) to democratic (slow) means, as seems to have been the case with Fabian Socialism.

So what is the 'end' for Harrington? What is his definition of socialism which sustains his faith that even though socialist belief in socialism as an economic system and historical necessity has not proved viable, it nonetheless deserves the support of men of good will? Why does he say that if the 'new socialism' is '*primarily* economistic [his emphasis] it will fail utterly'? Thus Harrington:

> If socialization is no longer thought of as the automatic consequence of the economic development of capitalist society, as a transition from capitalist monopoly to socialist monopoly; if, on the contrary, socialization is understood as the conscious control of their destiny by the people; then it is clearly a goal that extends to all of society, not just to the economy.[32]

The definition of socialism as 'the conscious control of their destiny by the people' is an inversion of the Communist argument based on the materialist determination of history. Harrington is also arguing for socialism as a force counteracting the market-place ('capitalism') as the determinant of the quality of life. Reinforcing this individualist, and pragmatic, resistance to market-place, determinism is a revival of 'fraternity' – that eighteenth-century, ethico-political slogan which owing to the impact of the Marxian conception of class warfare has been practically   eliminated   from   the   democratic political vocabulary. Thus Harrington contemplates the revival of new socialism under the norm of 'solidarity':

> First and foremost, there is the need for a global solidarity, a sense of world citizenship. I am under no illusion that such a consciousness is the work of a year, or even a decade. . . . The politics of international economic and social solidarity must be presented as a practical solution to immediate problems as well as a recognition of . . . oneness of humankind.[33]

The following points have to be made: First, as a 'first and foremost' appeal to partisanship on the ground that it is not partisanship but an ethical commitment (it appeals to something universal), it conveys either a touch of cynicism or a curious naïveté. Socialism has not somehow gained a monopoly of the norm 'brotherhood' which remains, for instance, fundamental to Christianity despite all its sectarian versions. There is no evidence after all that socialism is the political version of Christianity. Second, as a psychological appeal to members of a necessarily competitive society – in which everyone has to achieve his own status – 'fraternity' offers respite or peace of mind; in effect, respect and security even if one achieves nothing. Third, it counters directly the anomie which Communism was supposed to but did not counter, because it was not genuinely 'fraternal' but merely partisan. The 'existentialist' problem of individual significance is answered by the new socialism by assuring the faithful that if they have faith they will have significance as members of an enduring world community – the individual may die but mankind lives on. In other words, the appeal is a secular version of the Christian promise.

There is, of course, a danger in such Utopian views and Harrington speaks as if he (almost) recognized it: 'We must not forget that the Promethean Marxist dream of a "new socialist man," of people who naturally and easily co-operated with one another, became the rationale for the totalitarian conformity of Joseph Stalin'. He even notices a 'surprising convergence between the most avantgarde, anarchistic Left opponents of the bureaucratic state and the revived religious fundamentalism in the United States and the various antitax movements throughout the West'.[34]

So, then, what does he propose so as to take into account the fact that (a) the ideal of an ultimate secular 'fraternity' accounts for totalitarianism and that (b) such fraternity without totalitarianism is already promised by fundamentalism? It is the 'ancient republican ideal',[35] or the 'heavenly city' of the eighteenth-century philosophers, or 'the Greek polis without slaves' (Max Horkheimer's expression). 'Is such a socialist republicanism possible?' Harrington asks. 'Can we really create a space for personal and community freedom in a modern society? No one can be sure. All we can say with confidence is that if such freedom is to come into existence, it will be the result of new global structures of solidarity and justice. Which is to say, of socialism'.[36] This, of course, is a bit vague, considering that the residues of Marxism, Leninism and Stalinism are still with us.

SOCIALISM AS RUTHLESSNESS IN THE EXERCISE OF POWER

A good many who may not subscribe to Harrington's faith in socialism as a good can nonetheless have some sympathy for his position, for it lies well within the democratic tradition. It is true that formerly it only doubtfully did, for he initially held to a determinism – the inevitability of socialism – which does not easily fit a system of government that emphasizes choice as significant both politically and ethically. Since now, in his last book, he has definitely abandoned the notion of inevitability, his socialism has achieved the quality of 'oughtness' (opposed to determinism) by which it is linked to the choice characterizing the democratic process. (This, incidentally, is something that Marxist/Communists now calling themselves 'democratic socialists' still do not seem to understand: what is genuinely ethical has to be genuinely chosen, which means with regard to an ideology the use of a democratic methodology in achieving and retaining office).

But if Harrington understands this, or at least senses it, the author of *Rethinking Socialism*, Kitching, does not. His book is subtitled 'A Theory for a Better Practice', so that it is not 'an ideology' he is concerned with but a 'methodology'. It is a methodology of the kind that brought Communism into disrepute: how does one get and retain political power by using ideology as bait?

Kitching's very definition of 'socialism' is based on 'power' not ideology: 'Socialism is the greatest possible degree of conscious human control over the personal, social and natural environment exercised democratically'.[37] In this definition, 'democracy' has been reduced to an adverbial modification of the exercise of power, even though a good century and a half ago it was recognized that such a view is decidedly ambiguous. Lincoln's 'of', 'by' and 'for' is the minimum clarification of the word 'democratically', for when it is not so analysed, 'exercised democratically' can mean 'for the people' in the way the Communist Party acted 'for' the people in the Soviet Union. A hypothetic objection only? Hardly. A mere twenty-five pages later, Kitching boldly refers to 'my conviction that some socialist form of dictatorship presents the best prospect'.[38] Such a view should not come as a surprise, for Kitching has the arrogance to assign himself a prominent place in the history of human thought. He refers to his fatuous definition of socialism as the 'Mikhailovsky/Kitching criterion' and is good enough to supply us with a handy colloquial reference to it, 'the M/K criterion'. The criterion has a ruthlessness that should give pause to anyone who supposes that democratic socialism cannot by definition be undemocratic: 'Everything that impedes advance towards such control is immoral, unjust, pernicious and unreasonable and a retrogression from socialism'.[39] From a genuinely moral and a genuinely democratic view, socialism (whether calling itself democratic or Marxist) is ruthless if it denies the ethical premise that the good has to be a matter of choice – it cannot be coerced. Historically, of course, coerciveness has been associated with despotism to such a degree that some people identify the two terms. By contrasting 'despotism' and 'democracy' they conclude that a democratically elected government 'cannot' or 'should not' be coercive. Why, then, specifically link socialism in all its forms with a strong tendency to coerciveness? The answer lies in the choice Kitching, the sociologist, has made. His earlier written work[40] shows that he strongly believes in materialist determinism, as did Marx, but does not presume to have such an understanding of the process that he can make predictions about the future. To a sociologist who believes in materialist determinism, 'the good' becomes control over the process. Hence dealing with socialism as 'the good' – something Kitching and other socialists believe in and accordingly want instituted in their society – Kitching defines it as 'the greatest possible degree of conscious human control over the personal, social and natural environment'. It is the corollary, however, that makes for the ruthlessness: 'Everything that impedes . . . is immoral'.

In the former USSR 'immoral' impediments had notoriously included criticism of Party policy. If Kitching's view can be called 'socialism', is there anything he says that would lead him and others who gained political power to hold any other view? There is no reason whatsoever to say that there is, for, unlike Harrington, he derives his ethical views from the premise of materialist determinism. Given that, he can justify ruthlessness in the exercise of political power and even – by the ambiguity of 'democracy' used as an adverb – pretend that ruthlessness is democratic. Stalin did the same.

HAYEK'S TESTAMENT

The late F.A. Hayek – a life-long critic of socialist theory and practice – recently came up with a political testament in which he exposes what he calls the 'fatal conceit' of socialism.

Whatever the fatal conceit of socialists may be, the fatal conceit of conservatives has been their negativism – a propensity to expose the errors of others without demonstrating what the good is; as a result they have acquired the reputation of being defenders of the *status quo* although there is no one properly called 'conservative' who is satisfied with things as they are or have been. Hayek escapes the conservative conceit by resting his case against socialism on its failure to understand the nature of the good, which for him entails the recognition that civilization and its rules are the product of age-old experience or (dare one say it?) Utilitarianism as an unconscious historical process.

To understand his position about the fatal conceit of socialism, we must be clear about his premise – the position he argues from. Hayek holds to a stance, which virtually vanished from the intellectual scene with the Victorians, that if we are prepared to speak of biological evolution, we must also be willing to talk of cultural evolution – progress – and its corollary 'civilization'.

Hayek's case against socialism and in favour of capitalism rests on our being open to that view.

To Hayek, 'capitalism' is not the supposed late historical development Marx spoke of; it refers specifically to the market-place when recognized as the force behind and an agency necessary to, civilization. 'Socialism', to him, is the denial of rejection of this view: it is a kind of ignorance of, or nescience about, 'civilization' and its significance.

Uniting Human Motivation and Concepts of the Good

If we are to understand Hayek's views of the fatal conceit of socialism, we need to be quite clear about what he regards as the truth – his premise about the nature of truth and the good. His view informs the entire book, of course, but is perhaps best expressed in chapter eight:

> So far as we know, the extended order is probably the most complex structure in the universe – a structure in which biological organisms that are already highly complex have acquired the capacity to learn, to assimilate, parts of suprapersonal traditions enabling them to adapt themselves from moment to moment into an ever-changing structure possessing an order of a still higher level of complexity. Step by step, momentary impediments to further population increase are penetrated, increases in population provide a foundation for further ones, and so on, leading to a progressive and cumulative process that does not end.[41]

Although at first glance the above paragraph may not seem particularly significant, it is of crucial importance because it is a theory of progress, something we have needed ever since we lost faith in the seventeenth-century conception of the 'fortunate fall', which represented 'knowledge' as the basis of progress and, therefore – like Milton himself – accepted 'original sin' as a good. ('The paradox of the fortunate fall', Lovejoy called it.)

Using this conception, eighteenth and nineteenth-century Europe performed prodigies. What the world now calls 'civilization' is largely Western European culture, right down to the way people cut their hair. Its weakness, however, was recognized by Hume almost before the system was established: the concept of the 'good' is detached from 'motivation', whereas to give any direction to what one is doing – make any genuine progress – one's motivation and the good have to be the same.

There can be no question that conflicts between motivation and concepts of the good, which in theory should not exist, do in fact exist and are the cause of major social discords; they are also the cause of the deeply worrying lack of direction characteristic of our society. Our theory of the good has its basis in a decidedly non-materialist conception of the good, whereas our social order, as Hayek repeatedly observes, has its basis in decidedly materialist preoccupations – the market-place. The problem is to unify the two in such a way that we can again speak of 'progress' – have a sense of direction and give meaning to life. Without it, some people are bound to feel exploited simply because they do not have as much as others.

Hayek does not himself say so, but his insistence on 'progress' and his rejection of 'equality' as the good implies that in the absence of a concept of progress, society must embrace that of 'equality' as the good. Furthermore – this he does say – the latter (equality) is incompatible with 'civilization', which, Hayek maintains, depends on acknowledging the market-place as the source of civilization and the good:

> It is no exaggeration to say that this notion [choice as the product of the market-place] marks the emancipation of the individual. To the development of the individualist spirit are due ... the division of skills, knowledge and labour on which advanced civilization rests.[42]

The conflict between motivation and concepts of the good – which Hayek is trying to resolve by means of a theory of progress was already recognized in the late nineteenth century by both capitalists and socialists. Thus

Andrew Carnegie (1835–1918), as typical a nineteenth-century 'capitalist' as any (who said 'a man who dies rich, dies disgraced'), was, like most of his wealthy contemporaries, a 'philanthropist' – a concept which apparently reflected an attempt to integrate capitalist motivation with Christian concepts of the good. It also explains the otherwise odd phenomenon of capitalists, such as Robert Owen, who were also Utopian socialists. They attempted to unite both motivations (capitalistic and philanthropic) without modifying either of them. Capitalism was a good because it enabled one to be philanthropic; so was philanthropy because it enabled one to defend capitalism. Now so long as such views seemed sound, socialism appeared a good, even if it was despotic. If philanthropy is a good, then when made compulsory – as in the welfare State – it is better, because one no longer has to rely on human nature and the sense of charity.

No one attacking socialism can disregard the above normative framework: future debates will have to consider this. In this sense, the current failure of Communism has not altered the situation. This very point makes Hayek important. Economists have long recognized that Marx was in no way an economist: his social and political views, founded on ignorance of economics, were bound to fail in practice. Indeed they have.

The question is: what views can be offered in the future? The only theory available to us which relates market-place to society is philanthropy, either voluntary – as under capitalism – or compulsory – as under socialism. Such was Hayek's task: to relate human motivation – what leads to the market-place – with an intelligible concept of the good – what leads to society. This he did, though, let it be said, rather vaguely. However, he knew what had to be done, which is much more than anyone else has understood during the last hundred or so years.

Hayek's pragmatism

Hayek's readiness to speak of (a) 'civilization' as a higher stage of the general social science concept of 'culture' and (b) 'progress' in respect to cultural evolution, is both conservative and revolutionary. It is conservative in harking back to a time when it was a 'self-evident' truth (an ethnocentric one we would say nowadays) that European civilization is superior to, say, that of the Yaghans of South America (now extinct) but revolutionary as it denies the validity of cultural equality (that lies for instance behind the political policy called 'multiculturalism').

Hayek's views, like those of Burke, are 'conservative', for their 'normative logic' (if the term is permissible) rests on the importance of English law – and hence on Anglo-Saxon normative conceptions – of 'precedent' as a bedrock of the concept of justice. This is point one of Hayek's argument about the fatal conceit of acting on 'pure principle'. Such action is alien to the spirit of justice.

Hayek's views are also 'revolutionary', for to him cultural equality has no general viability: it is not that just any tradition is good (the argument from 'precedent' is not an argument from custom) but only that of a certain level of civilization. This view, one should remember, is essentially 'liberal', for it is J.S. Mill's view that 'liberty' as a good presupposed a certain cultural level. There is nothing 'wrong' in the sense 'illiberal' in warning someone that a bridge is unsafe (and preventing him from crossing it) and hence nothing wrong by definition in 'imperialism' or 'élitism' (defined in terms of some sort of cultural ranking or 'knowing').

Basically Hayek's argument is a rejection of the 'end of ideology' debate. Ideology is about cultural relativism: if one is to argue in favour of an ideology (a statement about the nature of a society in terms of 'good'), one has to believe it matters a good deal whether a society is socialist, capitalist or hunter–gathering. Within limits, even an extreme individual relativism – an assumption that norms are a matter of personal taste – is a possible 'private' position for a member of a society. On the other hand, it is not a feasible position for anyone interested in the survival of society, let alone civilization. Once we deal

with human beings in interaction, it is not possible to be
relativistic: pragmatism, or the question of why we behave
as we do, comes to the fore as a question the individual
asks himself. This is point two in understanding Hayek's
argument.

Point three is the crucial issue with regard to conservative-liberal views: what is the 'aim' or 'end' of distributive justice? Is it 'equality'?

Now we know it cannot be for Hayek. He argues for
civilization on non-egalitarian grounds: it matters whether
one is a Yaghan or not. His argument is 'pragmatic', or is
a limited form of Utilitarianism – an argument not for the
greatest good to the greatest number but the greatest
good to 'me' as a member of a society.

If all societies were 'equal', this would be an argument
for customary law and practice. But for Hayek – or Mill –
societies are not all equal. Hayek has argued that the
goods we recognize – including those recognized by the
socialists – are the product of a market-place (capitalism)
which will be destroyed if we assume that distributive
justice is incompatible with what the market-place produces. This is not an argument for *laissez-faire*, as it was
taken to be in the nineteenth century, but an argument
against the socialist ideology. The fatal conceit of the
latter is that we human beings are so 'rational' that we
have reached the present situation not through reliance
on precedent but on the basis of sheer conceit; we know
what we are doing and we order our lives accordingly.
The underlying assumption is that distributive justice
means equality in the distribution of goods.

The best answer to this is Hayek's pragmatic proposition: the view will not work. History has shown that he is
right – that his proposition is normatively 'good', even if
it falls into the category of instrumentalism.

In conclusion, the following three points can be made
about Hayek's pragmatism:
(a)   'I do not claim that the results of group selection of
traditions are necessarily "good"', he says, [but] 'I do
claim that . . . without the particular traditions I have mentioned [such as the concepts of "property", "contract",

"truth" as good, etc., which he relates to the market-place] the extended order of civilization could not continue to exist'.[43] This surely seems to be begging the question. But it is not. Rather, Hayek is reviving a point that pragmatists originated but did not exploit. (They thought they were focusing on epistemology when they were talking about axiology: does 'good' mean anything when one cannot derive it from 'objective' reality?). As Hayek expresses it (obscurely, I admit): 'We need not only an evolutionary epistemology but also an evolutionary account of moral traditions'.[44] What he is trying to supply is a theory of progress, or a revival of pragmatism as a significant axiological vision. When doing this he produces a defence of 'capitalism' and exposes the 'fatal conceit' of socialism.

(b)   To illustrate the fundamentally pragmatic nature of Hayek's argument one can reduce it to the statement: if we want X (civilization) then what we must value is Y ('capitalism': as respect of the consequences of the market-place).

This thought has been long derided by socialists as a 'vested interest' argument: those who benefit most from market-place economy support it because they are 'selfish' whereas socialists are highly moral folk devoted to mankind in general. Hayek's point is that the 'goods' which the socialists want to distribute more 'equitably' depend on the 'inequities' of the market-place so that insofar as you undermine one, you undermine the other.

(c)   As an epistemological system, one about the nature of truth and knowledge, pragmatism did not make much sense: it is not true that we suppose something is 'true' because it 'works', but rather that we value a truth, practice or piece of information in terms of what it means to us. It is not only that pragmatism has been a major influence in education: that influence has probably been much greater than most of us imagine. We have now accepted completely the shift from 'classical' education (what does a member of the upper class need to know so as to be recognized as a member of that class?) to a 'liberal' education and even 'free-schools' (what do I need to know to get what I want?). But because the pragmatists did not explain what they were arguing for, this essential point about our conception of values -- they must relate to us – has been blocked out of most people's consciousness.

While the pragmatists were arguing for a functional approach (as opposed to a natural law) to values, Hayek has adapted the argument to a larger social question of economics: what conditions are necessary if I am ever to have goods to distribute 'equitably'?

Hayek's answer is – capitalism. He argues, as did Burke about 'society', that it was arrived at without any cause–effect analysis or conscious choice making. Consequently, Hayek argues, we cannot pretend that a 'rational' re-ordering will be superior, since we do not really have the kind of knowledge of the working of our society or the economic system to 'rationally' reorder it. Judging from the events in East Central and Eastern Europe consequent on the failure of a 'rational' system, Hayek would appear to be right and amply justified in calling the supposed 'rational' elements, or arguments for socialism, a 'fatal conceit'.

Part IV

The tyranny of ideology

Chapter 19

The illusion of the 'end of ideology'

THE 'END OF IDEOLOGY' DEBATE: AFTERTHOUGHTS

The response of a reviewer in *The Economist* (8 August 1964) to *Political Thought Since World War II*[1] is relevant to the debate. He wrote: 'What has happened since the thirties, if these writers are any indication, is not a repudiation of the Marxist universe, but a willingness to accept the influence of illusion on human behaviour'. As William Delany, who quotes the review, remarks: 'This review supports Professor Christoph's observation that the word ideology continues to have low status in Britain'.[2] It also has a low status in the USA according to the testimony of the editor of *The End of Ideology Debate*: 'The interesting point here . . . is not that we have reached the end of the ideological age, but rather that there almost never was an ideological age in America. The United States in the 1950s and 1960s is the outgrowth of what Michael Harrington has termed "the *accidental* century"; our contemporary crises are the result of unplanning technologically, economically and politically'.[3] The implication is that there is a body of political theorists who are convinced that political theorizing and thinking about human behaviour have very little to do with what actually happens. The end of ideology is for them the beginning of 'realism'.

If this is true, there is little point in defining ideology: the issue is not whether some systematized set of norms and beliefs is influential but whether thinking about human behaviour has any effect on behaviour. The assertion quoted above referred to the 'willingness to accept the influence of *illusion* on human behaviour'. Until one comes to some decision about the influence of 'illusion', it would be a waste of time to speak about a particular kind of illusion. Do only actual 'facts' – conditions in the objective reality in which men live – affect them or does it matter how one interprets 'experience'?

One would suppose that Franz Mesmer's discovery of hypnotism in the eighteenth century provided empirical evidence that what really matters is man's conceptualization of reality. If one shows a bowl of bananas to a man under hypnosis and tells him they are éclairs or handguns, he will respond to the conceptualization offered rather than to what is actually present to his senses. People nowadays are subjected to a hypothesis (also a conceptualization) that human beings respond the way lower animals do; and because the latter have evolved from the inanimate, men are driven by the same system of causation as that operating in the inanimate world. Such a view makes the theory of evolution meaningless. It is also the basis of modern fatalist determinism. Fatalism turns behaviouralism into self-evident truth, rendering the influence of thought on behaviour an illusion.

Following this line of thought, one could argue, for instance, that as socialism has no effect on sand and rocks, it cannot have any on human beings. Should empirical evidence show this to be untrue, one is led to the conclusion that the evidence is illusory; and that the 'explanation' of the 'illusion' is that evolution somehow made men subject to more complex cause-effect relations (while not removing them from the determinist scheme). The question whether the evolution of life constituted the development of a system of cause–effect independent of the inanimate world is not raised.

The determinist scheme is necessarily anti-rational. In order to implement it, evidence for the influence of reason on behaviour has to be discounted and biological needs, as in lower animals, represented as crucial. Hence the various schools of psycho-analysis, though known to violate the methodological procedure of science, are widely accepted as 'scientific'. In essence, they claim that the evolution of the human brain has had no real effect on men's behaviour, except to make them more poorly 'adjusted' than animals. (The fact that such a view presents the evolution of the human brain as a biological mistake – and thus violates the theory of evolution, which sees biological change as biologically advantageous – is ignored.) If the human brain is functional, it is no longer possible to hold that the 'unconscious' (our animal drives) is the determining factor in behaviour and that the latter is to be understood as a highly complex interaction between our biological drives and circumstances in the environment. 'Illusions', such as ideologies, then become very real factors in human behaviour. (It is the behaviouralist perspectives of the social sciences that become an 'illusion'.)

The extent to which reason and ideology affect behaviour is obscured in democratic societies by the longstanding tradition which claims that democracies are not ideologically based; that, unlike totalitarian societies, they 'muddle through', responding to circumstances, rather than planning. There has been no Western equivalent of Lysenko who would determine agricultural policy on the basis of what 'democratic theory' requires.

But to argue that democratic ideology is an absence of ideology would make it difficult to understand the history of democratic societies. Despite the apparent absence of any set of 'directors', there has been a direction to historical change. Although the past is often seen in terms of the 'good old days' of greater contentment and less crime, few of those who criticize democracies would contend that modern democracies are less democratic. If democracies had simply been 'muddling through' and responding to circumstances, one would expect various social factors to have moved them now towards, now away from, the concept of democracy. Yet, despite the seeming absence of ideological factors in their citizens' behaviour, democratic societies are somehow directing themselves.

All the talk about the end of ideology and denying that ideals influence men does not change the fact that democratic ideals are operating in society. This being the case, it is difficult to understand how reputable students of political behaviour can speak of the 'end of ideology'.

FRAGMENTIZATION OF IDEOLOGIES

Writing at the time of 'end of ideology' debate, Michael Harrington quoted Orwell's comment about the condition of the 'proles' in *1984*: 'And even when they became discontented, as they sometimes did, their discontent led nowhere, because, being without general ideas, they could only focus on their specific grievances'. Harrington's comment on this passage is that 'Orwell pictured this retrogression as the outcome of totalitarianism and permanent war'.[4] At first glance, the comment may seem illogical. (A full quotation from Orwell – not given here – includes a description of the proles' condition.) The point to be made is that Orwell's technique as a novelist was to illustrate a general idea by supplying an example. Harrington, who would seem not to have read I.A. Richards treats the imaginary situation described in *1984* as if it were a *fact* upon which he can place his own construction. It seems that to him *1984* is primarily a discussion of the horrors of totalitarianism and a state of war rather than of the factors leading to such horrors. One such factor, Orwell says, is the absence of 'general ideas'.

To replace the term 'general ideas' with 'ideology' is not tantamount to twisting Orwell's meaning. There is evidence throughout *1984* and his other writings that Orwell regarded ideologies as necessary though dangerous. In the quoted passage, he makes one point about the 'necessity': in the absence of an ideology, one focuses on specific grievances to no avail. (Such a thought deserves the attention of those who speak – or spoke – of the end of ideology, or are so indifferent to 'general ideas' that even a discussion of the end of ideology is for them pointless.)

To understand Orwell's point, the first thing one needs to do is to define 'grievance' in such a way that one can think of grievances in the absence of general ideas. This means one has to think of grievances in the absence of 'justice', which is, of course, a 'general idea'. Then a 'grievance' becomes a personal dissatisfaction for which one holds someone else responsible, whether he (or she) is or is not. If I am poor or unemployed, I am merely discontented if I dislike my condition; but if I hold someone else responsible, I have a grievance.

Grievances are very widespread in democratic societies, even though they are characterized by conditions which should make for less discontent than in the case of other systems. This situation baffles democratic régimes, which try to cope with the problem by describing how superior conditions under democracy are, and by making obviously unjust concessions to minorities with 'grievances'. If Orwell is correct, such approaches are unnecessary and solve nothing. There is no welfare payment high enough to convince the recipients that they do not have a grievance and none so low that revolution would inevitably follow. In the absence of a concept of justice, 'grievances' are politically irrelevant; they reflect an egoism which makes organized opposition to the State impossible.

Matters are very different when the validity of 'general ideas' is recognized. Ideologies make personal grievances of the kind referred to irrelevant. This is why totalitarian régimes can exist without serious opposition even when the standard of living is deplorable. They define current conditions as irrelevant or temporary; something else is much more important. This is why Orwell saw ideologies as dangerous.

By some, who in the 1960s assumed the end of ideology to be a truism, the situation was seen as the end of a threat of intolerable conditions formerly presented by the ideology as tolerable – as mere sacrifices for a better future – through the medium of false promises. The danger here lies in extending the same criteria to all ideological systems, totalitarian or democratic. If all ideologies are seen as a sort of lying, there is no way to define 'justice' in such systems. Without a concept of justice, citizens are left with nothing but an unreasonable grievance: they assign responsibility in the absence of any rational concept of responsibility. Conversely, the fact that 'unreasonable' grievances are widespread in Western society can be interpreted as evidence that some sort of 'end of ideology' has come and that any rational conception of justice has been lost.

All this, of course, does not mark the real end of ideology but only the end of the 'end of ideology' debate that took place in the USA in the 1960's. To stop thinking about ideologies does not imply their disappearance. All that has happened is that they have become fragmented.

What does this 'fragmentation' imply? Ideas that were originally part of a more or less coherent system remain as specific beliefs which are mistaken for 'facts'. Consider for instance Lenin's attempt to explain the failure of Marx's prediction about capitalism. He introduced the notion of 'imperialism' seen as the exploitation of one society by another in such a way that the exploiting society operates as 'capitalists' in relation to the 'proletarians' of the exploited external society. Being ideologically-focused, such a theory gives rise to doubts; it needs solid substantiation through historical analysis of actual facts about international relations. Arguing that one is indifferent to mere theories does not get rid of the assertion about 'imperialism' but only puts it into the class 'facts about colonial relations asserted by those who have studied the issue'. Consequently many non-Communists take Lenin's assertion about imperialism on trust. In a similar way, they accept the assertion that the earth goes round the sun or that arsenic is poisonous. Hardly any of us have any idea what line of thought or evidence lies behind the latter assertions. We take them on trust because we have no reason to believe they are lies. To what extent the proponents of Lenin's theory of imperialism are lying is another matter; what is evident is that the theory does not have the same basis as assertions in physics or chemistry. But instead of drawing the obvious conclusion that in this case one should remain particularly conscious of just what the basis is, the tendency is to discard analysis and ignore the importance of being aware of the ideological element in current beliefs. In the days of the end of ideology debate one detected a feeling almost of relief that there is no need to concern oneself with ideologies. Consequently, although the debate has not been resumed in the same form, the result is not a matter for self-congratulation. The emergent spirit of self-deception has opened Western society to bits and pieces of alien ideologies which, although operating as fragments, have polluted the language and distorted the outlook of the public.

IS CONVERGENCE OF IDEOLOGICALLY DISPARATE SYSTEMS POSSIBLE?

When people begin to speculate about the convergence of ideologically disparate systems – as was the case in the 1960s – by arguing that similarities in economic structures and the need to solve common problems 'scientifically' will make the Communist countries and Western democracies almost indistinguishable, it is apparent that ideological considerations are being dismissed as of no great significance in human affairs.

Part of the argument for such 'convergence' rests on an attack on the view that norms and beliefs have an effect on human behaviour. Another, more insidious, argument is that when one considers the norms and beliefs of West and East, no great difference can be detected. More specifically, according to these views, when the political norms of equality, freedom and individualism are discussed singly (as individual concepts) in both parts of the world they do not appear all that different. It is only when such concepts become part of an ideological structure that marked differences arise. 'Therefore', say those who are moved by visions of a peaceable kingdom, 'let us get rid of the ideological structures or at least let the march of history relegate them to the murky past'.

In a world faced with the threat of nuclear destruction,

this argument appears particularly appealing: all one has to do is to stop formulating concepts into antagonistic systems. One is not even being asked to give up the concepts, only to stop systematizing and articulating them.

This argument is not new: it was advanced long ago, during the French Wars of Religion. The norms and beliefs of Catholics and Huguenots did not then, nor do they now, differ markedly; but their systematizations did. Today these systematizations are of no great moment: only theologians can give a clear account of them. Consequently, the argument runs, in most societies Catholics and Protestants can live in harmony, scarcely aware, as individuals, of who is what. The same is supposed to apply to other religions. There are exceptions to such religious harmony, to be sure, but the view of the 'anti-systematizers' is that, for some obscure reason, the people in such countries (e.g. Ireland, Iran or India) suffer from 'aggression' in the psycho-analytical sense. Transferring the argument to the sphere of politics, presumably all those who stressed the ideological differences between the USA and the USSR were similarly affected.

The odd part of the view that systematized belief is not good for our society is that at one and the same time it is widely accepted that systematized belief about the physical world is essential. We call it 'science' and have come to regard it as a normative good which we use to attack other attempts at systematization. The issue, scientism, will not be discussed here. The immediate issue is whether our norms can be left unsystematized, not whether they can or must be incorporated into 'science'.

No matter how one interprets the nature of norms, they keep coming into conflict. Whether one sees them as coming from within and reflecting desires or coming from without and representing duties, they most certainly are not already systematized for us any more than our perceptions of reality are. We do not know 'science' simply because we automatically base our interpretations of reality on the same perceptions as science does; nor do we have compatible desires even if norms are regarded as 'desires'. The problem with regard to both perceptions and desires has always been that of systematizing them so that they become reliable guides to behaviour. Nothing is solved in relation to the personal behaviour of two persons by pointing out what each of them believes: that both murder and suffering are 'wrong'. What if the issue is euthanasia?

Matters become much more complicated in the case of political norms, all of which are already systematizations and not, like social norms, just attitudes to specific situations. It is fairly easy to define 'theft', for instance, in a way acceptable to most people, but trying to define 'freedom' is another matter. To some people, property is a legal concept; to others it is related to the 'self'. If 'property' is viewed as a legal fiction, the conception of 'theft' does not change much as compared with the other alternative. But the concept of 'freedom' is markedly altered when one person thinks of the State as capable of making any decision whatsoever about the disposition of property, while the other person insists that granting the State such a right is an attack on individualism (because of the assumed relation between property and self) – and hence on 'freedom'. Under such circumstances, it is absurd to ask a Communist and a democrat whether they believe in 'freedom' or 'equality': they will both say 'Yes'. It would be disastrous to assume that there is therefore no real difference between their views; that one day the two ideological systems will come into accord because there 'already is agreement on basic norms'. In reality, no such agreement exists. The norms that both systems are supposed to agree on are integral parts of ideological systems. To take them out of these systems and pretend they resemble social norms – which can be so treated – is to make the political norms appear vague and unimportant generalities that one can dispense with: already a false perception.

To recapitulate: nothing has changed regarding the importance of recognizing the need to systematize norms. Conflicts between systems have become secularized. To argue that they 'should not' be, that Communists and

democrats should come to live together in the way
Protestants and Catholics mostly do, is tantamount to
arguing that we should stop systematizing our norms and
beliefs. But this is impossible. That would not be an
expression of 'tolerance' but of mindlessness.

'CONVERGENCE' AND FREEDOM TO INDUSTRIALIZE

Consider the following hypothetical statement: 'The
issue of whether one's society should be capitalist or
Communist does not concern any society except those
which are neither. It is an issue for the Third World. The
decision must be made in terms of the immediate effects
as well as the potential of one or the other system to bring
about rapid industrialization (if feasible) and break down
traditional relations that hinder such a process. The very
ruthlessness of Communism, its readiness to treat people
as members of classes rather than individuals, makes it
most suited to bring all societies into the mainstream and
produce the millennium in which people everywhere will
be living in abundance'.

The views contained in the above statement are quite
common in the Third World. Accordingly, the resistance
of Western democratic societies to the development of
Communism in the Third World is regarded as a form of
oppression, while assistance from Communist powers is
seen as fraternal altruism. Moreover, a great many people
among the intelligentsia in the West – not necessarily
Communists or fellow-travellers – are convinced that the
present situation in South America and Africa represents
an attempt by 'capitalist' societies to maintain an exploit-
able market and a source of cheap raw materials in the
face of resistance from those who desire the freedom to
develop in the quickest possible way. To their mind,
Communism offers the right tool: freedom to industrialize.

The view that Communism offers such a new 'freedom'
rests, of course, on a materialist conception of history
derived from Marx. It is often reinforced by the social

sciences. If, on the one hand, industrialization is shown as causing a great many problems such as slums (with their crime-breeding potential), it is supposed, on the other hand, to solve the more pressing problems of over-population and subsistence living which are plaguing the Third World. Thus, to factory workers large families are a burden rather than an advantage, as they are in agricultural communities; once the birth-rate is prudentially controlled, people can rise above the subsistence level. Consequently, what allows individual choice in such a personal matter as the family, while permitting control over breeding, and hence over poverty, is freedom to industrialize. Communism – so the argument goes – offers such a freedom; furthermore, to speak of current differences with regard to freedom as enjoyed by democracies in contrast to Communist countries, is short-sighted if not irrelevant, for Communism is supposed to provide ultimately the conditions of liberty enjoyed under democracy.

The fallacy of this peculiar idea of 'freedom' used in support of the theory of future 'convergence' of the two systems stemmed from a fundamental ignorance of the factors which are part of democratic ideology. Democratic values are premised on the individual, on the awareness of what is necessary to individualism and of the dangers inherent in the exercise of power and authority.

Although acceptance of democratic ideology does not commit one to the view that man is egoistic – egoism does not equal individualism – it cannot be denied that positions of power do attract egoists. Hence the exercise of power by those holding public office must be carefully circumscribed, as by limiting the period of tenure and ensuring that office-holders have no say in the selection of their successors. This is done through the device of democratic elections.

What democracy usually does, but the Communist system cannot do, is to prevent the rise of tyrants – those so utterly egoistic and powerful that only their particular views of right and wrong, good and bad, prevail. A remarkable feature of the democratic system is that constitutional law operates quite effectively: indeed, more efficiently than criminal law. Somehow, democracies have made the rule of law prevail with regard to their constitutions. Democratic society – apart from providing a definition of tyranny, which Communism does not – successfully prevents tyrants from arising. To speak of the convergence of such systems, or the potential from 'freedom' under the industrial productivity of Communism, is nonsense.

PERCEPTIONS OF IDEOLOGY

Unprofessed Ideology

Although it is common in democracies to refer to Communism as an alien ideology when making a distinction between the views of East and West, historically Communism is not alien in the way that Eastern religions are. While the latter developed independently of the assumptions of Christian thought, this was not true of Communism. It evolved from the same assumptions and circumstances that gave rise to modern democratic thinking. It is alien as a system of thought or ideology rather than as a set of premises: the common origin that Communism shares with democracy should not obscure this fact. What sets it apart is its particular form of systematization. And what makes it insidious is that Communists, increasingly suspicious of 'ideology', are convinced that systematization is not an ideology but a set of truths. (The distrust of 'ideology' by the Communists has orthodox Marxian roots: an ideology is an attitude which distorts reality.) Ironically, both Communists and democrats believe that 'ideology' refers to something other than what they themselves believe in and that it is the ideologues who are doomed.

In democratic thinking, this view has produced a curious kind of complacency in the face of obvious threats from the Communist world: the assumption is that if a belief can be shown to be false, it must be innocuous. The basis of this complacency goes back to empirical assumptions about the source of beliefs and to determinist assumptions about human motivation and causation. Thus 'true' beliefs in some way 'correspond' to the reality which is the actual determinant of events, so that those wise enough to realize the truth have a capacity to manipulate circumstances to their advantage. (This is not the case with the deceived. They will always be the victims of circumstances that are beyond their control; in any confrontation they must either come to realize the truth or be defeated.) According to this view, if we establish that Communism is false, we have proved that it must eventually operate on our principles or vanish; also, that those who speak of the need for defence against Communist aggression are clearly 'warmongers'.

Having evolved under the same empirical assumptions, Communism holds similar views as to what will happen to false systems of belief, or ideologies, but it links these beliefs with social classes. Thus in Communist thought, ideologies assume the role of class systems: they will not simply fade away but will inevitably fight for survival and privilege. It is then only commonsense for the Communist society to be prepared for the inevitable clash and, if possible, to forestall the latter by pre-emptive action.

The common assumption about ideology puts the democratic world at a great disadvantage *vis-à-vis* Communism. Convinced that Communism must become more 'realistic' – less ideological – the West plays for time: whatever the present stance of Communism, most people believe it will eventually change to accord with realities. This assumption endangered Western society by leading to an imprudent policy of ignoring the fact of Soviet military power. But there are also some wider if less obvious implications. Our anti-ideological views are anti-normative and anti-intellectual. The 'liberal' thinker is not only opposed to any kind of 'ism' but to any kind of belief, systematized or not, which is not directly traceable to empirical observation. 'Freedom' means to him a resistance to the inculcation of any non-empirical views, including democratic norms; 'education' is tantamount to instruction in beliefs supportable by scientific methodology. Everything else is 'propaganda' and as such has no place in a free society. In the eyes of some liberals, a bulwark against Communism such as the normative system of Christianity is hardly better than Communism itself and should be no part of an institutionalized democratic social system: neither of the two systems of ideas should be suppressed, nor should they be propagated. This *laissez-faire* approach to the market-place of ideas puts democracy at a disadvantage compared with a society which operates on the assumption that Communism is true because it is not an ideology but a science and as such should be disseminated. It also prevents democratic societies from evolving a system that can counter the appeal of Communism as an ideology. An ideology, whether true or false, gives a direction to life, a purposiveness that is necessary to a species capable of perceiving the self as extending in time. Under an ideology, there is not much point in adapting to the circumstances of the moment when they are recognized as but an incident in one's life, or in speaking about norms in terms of desires when – because of our capacity to think beyond the immediate – what we are really interested in is the desirable. The liberal conception of democracy fails to function with regard to the needs of the self.

Cynicism: The Ideology That Ends Ideology

Considering the role of faith in general, while assuming a parallel between religion and ideology, it is worth reflecting on Professor Joseph M. Bochenski's statement that 'Many people seem incapable of realizing that such things as believers can exist in the contemporary world. They themselves are often quite sceptical about everything except the practical efficiency of the means used; they sometimes become quite incapable of attaching any importance to aims and, therefore, think that Communists are behaving as they do'.[5] The people to whom Bochenski refers as 'sceptical' could be called 'cynics'; one could then argue that cynicism is a pervasive modern ideology which denies that other ideologies are functional; that it is an aspect of modern anti-intellectualism. For if cynicism is valid, no other creed or ideology is: one need not bother to analyse their component values and beliefs or consider their influence.

The cynics' views derive from one of the factors in our society which promote egoism – the view that self-interest is the sole factor in human behaviour. The egoist rests his case for egoism on the assumption that everyone is an egoist. He is a cynic who dismisses as illusions the evidence for the operation of altruistic faiths or any kind of non-egoist beliefs. In particular, he is certain that Communism is not only false but, as an ideology, inoperative: Marxist views on property totally disregard the relation between the ego and property.

The recognition that Marxism is a false ideology is a different thing from the cynical view that Communists cannot be such because everyone is necessarily an egoist. The latter belief leads to the complacent conclusion that at a given moment leaders of the Communist Party are not Communists; that the members of Communist nations are Communists only in the sense that their thinking about life has been distorted by 'propaganda'; that avowed Communists in Western societies are not acting on the basis of Communist beliefs; that one day everyone on earth will be an egoist, and consequently all other ideologies will wither away. The cynic's faith differs from that of the Communist in that the cynic does not expect the State to wither away but expects the ideology teaching this view to do so. To him, Communism is of no import.

An issue worth looking into is Marxist revisionism of the pre-Gorbachev era. Granted that revisionism was occurring, one can argue that the ideology was therefore still operating: it was worth amending and it must have had some adherents. The cynic, however, regarded revisionism as an academic exercise, a form of Orwellian 'newspeak' which is not believed in by those who are responsible for creating it (but may be by those subjected to it). He adopted the liberal view of believing that all ideological problems can be solved by promoting complete 'freedom of speech' and a system of 'free' educational establishments in which decisions about the scope and content of studies would be made by the students themselves (to prevent 'propaganda' from operating under the guise of 'education'). Applying a cynical view of human motivation to international affairs in particular to an issue such as nuclear armament, the cynic used to say that the public need only demonstrate that we are not ideologues opposed to Communism, but simple folk with the same motivations and goals as the Kremlin rulers; that having proved this by unilateral disarmament one can expect that the folk in the Kremlin will at once address themselves to the same egoist problem of making as much money as they possibly can.

Thus, under cynicism, there is no norm for ideology as a factor in human behaviour. To be sure, it is unwise to speak of Communism as a cynical ideology, for its appeal rests on a rejection of the cynical view of man. Like the major religions, it rejects the cynic's emphasis on the 'ego' and appeals to all those who recognize the essential meaninglessness of philosophies based on the ego's supremacy in a universe in which the 'death' of the individual is an absolute certainty.

SOVIET IDEOLOGY AND THE 'END OF IDEOLOGY'

In a symposium on Marxist ideology organized at the time of the 'end of ideology' debate, Professor Daniel Bell raised the following question: to what extent can one expect a sufficient change in the USSR's ideological position to allow it to abandon its 'historic mission' to realize Communism and enable democratic societies to look forward to peaceful coexistence?

Bell makes much of 'signs' of accommodation but neglects a striking incident that occurred in 1940. Considering Bell's view about the value of 'signs', this incident is worth recalling. When Trotsky, the orthodox Marxian advocate of world-wide revolution, had an icepick driven into his brain on orders from Moscow, to what extent did this 'liquidation' signalize a change in Soviet ideology? Were it not for the fact that the Soviet Union at that time had already moved into Poland and the Baltic countries, the assassination could have been taken to symbolize rejection of the idea of Communism's 'historic mission'. In view of the subsequent expansion of the Soviet empire, the act was like a psychopathic bridge-player's shooting a partner for failing to play his cards close enough to his chest.

Writing in the 1960s, however, Bell believed that 'the Soviet régime, if one reads the signs correctly, has "opted out" of the revolutionary game'. He argued that 'It does not particularly matter whether this is due to its vast internal problems . . . or because in the thermonuclear age Russia has learned that the risks of promoting revolution . . . are too great'.[6] If the issue is 'to read the signs correctly', it hardly matters why the signs are what they are. To make 'signs' the central issue in political analysis is to replace political theorizing with literary analysis applied to politics. In view of our imperfect understanding of symbols, this is a most unwise procedure. It is Bell's faith in symbols that convinced him that Communism is becoming democratic.

In adopting the view that 'the Soviet régime has opted out of the revolutionary game' Bell draws upon a sociological parallel between Communism and Catholicism: 'The vicissitudes of ideology . . . of the Soviet régime have been no different, in sociological principle, from the vicissitudes of dogma in the history of the Catholic Church'.[7] What he has in mind is that the Catholic Church, while still defining itself as 'universal', does not attempt to enforce this claim on those who do not accept it. Bell's implicit argument is that since the Catholic Church is no longer a revolutionary force, neither is Communism.

A Catholic theologian would certainly want to know what 'vicissitudes' of dogma Bell has in mind. Certain terms, not matters of dogma, have indeed changed in the course of centuries. R.H. Tawney for instance wrote a study about the changes in the meaning of 'usury'. But even the most virulent critics of the Church have not spoken of the 'vicissitudes' of dogma. The usual criticism is that there have not been any, that the Church remains adamant on all matters of dogma and refuses to 'adjust' to modern views.

That there no longer are any wars of religion of the sixteenth or seventeenth-century type is not due to some 'adjustment' of dogma. The absence of such wars in modern times may in the minds of some people reflect 'changes' in dogma –'vicissitudes', as it were. The issue in seventeenth-century France, however, was mainly 'sovereignty', not 'dogma'. It was ultimately settled by clarifying the concept of sovereignty; by defining the sovereign power as 'above' disputes about dogma; and, to put it normatively, by making 'tolerance' an attribute of sovereignty. (This, by the way, means that under Islam, the civil power is not fully sovereign – a matter that Western powers need to take into account in their foreign policy.) In the present context, however, this raises questions about Bell's conception of history: is there for him some sociological principle which requires credential systems – creeds and ideologies – to undergo a process of accommodation to each other? Specifically, one may ask, is 'tolerance' a fundamental principle of political and social theory. It is utterly far-fetched to assume that the claims made by Communist ideology to be a universal creed are somehow disallowed and made ineffectual by the history of the Church.

Why should Bell suppose that Communism will become democratic, while he stresses that its 'basic demand' is 'for belief in the Party itself'.[8] Are we to suppose that 'democracy' is a universal creed that *must* prevail? What is to be made of such inevitability in the face of the 'historic mission' of Communism? Can perhaps the history of the relations between Catholicism and Protestantism give a clue?

The question centres on the role that the claim to universality plays in each ideology and creed. In democratic thinking and that of the two religious creeds, such a claim depends on the belief of being 'true'. Religions will prevail inasmuch as truth will. It is not necessary to make them prevail. As an act of charity we may wish to propagate our sets of beliefs for the benefit of others but there is no need to insist on such benevolence. Tolerance is never excluded as a possibility. But matters are quite different with the claims made by Communism. Marxist ideology proclaims democratic, 'capitalist' societies to be by nature in conflict with 'socialist' societies: it makes a statement about international relations that democracy does not. Is 'peaceful coexistence' in such circumstance plausible?

Clearly, one cannot use the facts of religious accommodation and the emergence of tolerance to argue that one day Communism and democracy will be able to coexist peacefully. (There is no evidence that either Protestants or Catholics have altered their credential systems in order to live in peace.) Now the issue is whether a system like Communism, which asserts that conflict is inevitable, can reform itself and abandon this view.

Even if one accepted that a credential system – creed or ideology – could have the function ascribed by Bell, it was difficult to see how this could happen. The belief in conflict is here the ideology's structural part; hence an argument for accommodation implies that what is a structural part (of what is necessary to human thought) will imperceptibly alter as conditions change. People who do not believe that ideologies or creeds are necessary can accept this: if an ideology is simply a superstructure, it will change. But even Marx, who took such a position, excepted his own views from the process. Bell was asking us to believe that Marxians will be able to abandon one position in order to hold another. They might do it as individuals, but in view of Bell's own emphasis on the importance of belief in the Party, envisaging such a change was like expecting the Vatican to announce that, after due consideration, it has decided that Luther was right after all.

THE 'END OF HISTORY' AS AN 'END OF IDEOLOGY'

The 'end of ideology' debate of the 1960s never really ended because the participants did not state what their premises were; hence these premises were not discussed in a way that would allow anyone to come to a conclusion about their validity. This has been made clear by a revival of the issues in a new format – the 'end of history' debate prompted by an essay of this title (though with an interrogation mark) by Francis Fukuyama in *The National Interest* (Summer 1989).

What primarily strikes one about its author is his ingenuousness. Fukuyama is a naïve pragmatist. According to him, Marxism-Leninism failed because it did not work; what destroyed Fascism 'was not universal moral revulsion against it . . . but its lack of success'; what ensures the 'end of history' – defined as the end of ideological debates – is general acceptance of liberal democracy as the 'final form of government'.

From the vantage point of our ability to understand the 'end of ideology' debate, Fukuyama's naïveté is our gain. Proponents of the 'end of ideology' debate in the 1960s were pragmatists and argued from the premises of pragmatism; their opponents necessarily have to reject the purely pragmatist argument. Let us use this idea in examining the views attributed to Fukuyama that history can be seen as the narrative of competing ideologies and that now, with the 'victory of Western economic and political liberalism', as one reviewer put it, 'the story is complete and the world has reached the end of history'.

It is, of course, *not* true that 'history has largely been the narrative of competing ideologies'. The word ideology was not even in use before the nineteenth century. It is true, however, that since the rise of the ideological State – which includes the emergence of democracy – European history can best be understood in terms of ideological conflict. (Note, for instance, Metternich's outburst: 'I will burn democracy out of Europe with a red-hot iron'.) However, just how important ideology itself has been is an open question. Do we regard 'nationalism' as part of ideology? Is, for example, the issue of 'slavery' in the American Civil War an ideological issue or an aspect of materialist determinism, as in Beard's discussion of northern industrialism versus southern agriculturalism?

The issues were not adequately discussed during the 'end of ideology' debate because no one challenged the arguments offered by some participants that human beings are pragmatists whose pronouncements on 'ideals' and 'ideology' are rationalizations. An excellent case could have been made for the view that it is totally insufficient to contend that pragmatic concepts of 'truth' guide behaviour. Ideology does not end when pragmatism is accepted as 'truth'; nor does history.

A Digression on Pragmatism

Pragmatism performed an essential function as advice about policy in respect to learning. It set limits to the knowledge an individual should strive to acquire, thus putting an end to the sciolism and dilettantism that characterize the educated class when 'knowledge' is represented as a good without any limit being applied to it. The whole body of knowledge is far, far greater than any individual can hope to acquire. Some limit must be imposed on knowledge as a good; Dewey did so in his bold proposal for a criterion: 'What is the cash value?'

Dewey's point revolutionized education in America – the notion of the importance of classical education has disappeared. It also shifted the focus of American science away from theoretical questions (which sometimes are called 'ideological' questions) to immediate practical issues – to 'social problems', as the behavioural sciences called them. Worse still, however, the pragmatist view obscured the essential wrong-headedness and expediency in such an approach to knowledge, for it defined 'truth' – and hence 'genuine' knowledge – in such a way as to justify the directive as to what one should learn. The 'cash value' advice was represented by the pragmatists themselves as the source of 'truth'; consequently, those influenced by the pragmatic definition not only conceived themselves as practical men capable of solving practical problems but came to think of any other approach to 'truth' and 'knowledge' as woolly-minded.

Their utter incomprehension of any other viewpoint

was apparent in the 'end of ideology' debate of the 1960s. Now it is Fukuyama's 'end of history' view that most clearly establishes that the underlying issue has always been the validity (or lack of validity) of pragmatism as a means of defining truth instead of being simply advice about selecting a field of study and adhering to one's choice.

Our main objection to talking about the end of ideology – or history – is that proponents of the view reveal no sense of history; they are preoccupied with immediate circumstance. This is obvious, for instance, when they derive Gorbachev's policy from the 'failure' of Communism and subsequently jump to a conclusion about the 'end of history'. The argument runs like this: if Communism is not pragmatically 'true' then it does not exist; therefore it no longer conflicts with democracy; consequently, there is no more cold war and no more 'history' (because 'history' has been defined in terms of conflict). To this, one must object that (a) there was a large body of opposition to Gorbachev which seemed to have been uninfluenced by the 'failure' of Communism; and (b) for many years it has been argued in the West that most Communists are 'hypocrites' for it does not matter to them whether Communism is a pragmatic good or not: what matters is whether they hold positions of power.

Fukuyama's argument that the triumph of liberal democracy will end history by ending those details of history regarded as significant must come as a surprise to those whose thoughts on liberal democracy are similar to those of J.S. Mill. For Mill, the 'good' of liberal democracy derived from scepticism – from the view that we do not know the 'truth' and have much to learn from the continuance of history (and always will because of our epistemological limitations). Under the liberal democratic ideology – as put forward by Mill – there cannot be a political millennium of the kind postulated by Hegel or Marx. If you pretend that there can be, you are not reasoning from the postulates of liberal democracy.

Fukuyama indeed begins with Alexander Kojève, 'a brilliant Russian émigré', he gushes, 'who taught a highly influential series of seminars in the 1930s' and who 'sought to resurrect the Hegel of the *Phenomenology of Mind* . . . who proclaimed history to be at an end in 1806' (p.4).

Most of us are likely to feel that there can be no possible way of basing a prediction about the failure of liberal democracy on such historical facts, especially when Fukuyama boldly goes on to say that 'Kojève, far from rejecting Hegel in light of the turbulent events of the next century and a half, insisted that the latter [*sic!*] had been essentially correct' (p.5). One suspects that anyone who can regard as 'brilliant' someone who can hold such a view about historical developments, is himself likely to show equal brilliance in dazzling us with 'truths' that have no relation to historical facts.

What Fukuyama has to say in a supplement to the end of ideology debate, however, deserves notice because it is based on a common but non-technical interpretation of 'ideology' – the very one that has thoroughly confused the debate following the publication of his article. 'Ideology in this sense' Fukuyama says with reference to Hegel's views [includes] 'religion, culture, and the complex of moral values underlying any society' (pp. 5–6). But such a broad conception of ideology cannot serve the function which the terms needs to fulfil in political theory.

Ever since the rise of the ideological State – in which legitimacy is determined by the kind of legislation passed rather than by the means of attaining office – political theory has needed a means of distinguishing between the principles used in determining legislation and those used in everyday social intercourse (morals) or those promoted by the Church (dealing with the salvation of the soul). In the days of personal rule, the principles followed by a monarch could be called 'policy' and '*raison d'état*' (referring, for instance, to the policy of Queen Elizabeth I with regard to religious disputes). It was when the theory of sovereignty introduced the notion of government as a function served (and essentially impersonal) that it became apparent, that a new designation (such as 'ideology') for the basic principles observed is in order. Indeed, precisely because the term 'ideology' is necessary to analyses of the modern State, it was confusing when in the 1960s a group of (mainly) American sociologists began arguing for the 'end of ideology'.

Fukuyama's inability to recognize ideology as a technical concept necessary to political theory makes him discuss the future of liberal democracy in a way that would bewilder J.S. Mill. For Mill, liberal democracy was not a good that can be introduced everywhere – a sort of faith promoting political salvation – but rather the demand that, when the people are claimed to be sovereign (when democracy actually exists in practice), the attributes of the sovereign power – especially tolerance – must be observed.

If you ignore the fact that 'liberal democracy' is ideological – is about political behaviour, not behaviour in general – then its label becomes a mere synonym for relativist values. What Fukuyama is unwittingly arguing for, is relativism based on pragmatic principles, a return to the old 'reason of State' which, one would think, went out with the Tudors.

Chapter 20

Ideology as power

A NOTE ON POWER

Thesis: Communist theory has no adequate conception of 'power' – hence no clear conception of 'liberty' – because it has detached its theory from contractual theory which is our basic source giving significance to power in human relations.

1   Hobbes argued that 'power' is not something that comes into being with a 'contract'. He saw the latter as 'authority' or the acknowledgement of a special kind of power as 'legitimate' or 'rational'. To him, pre-contractual 'power' implied 'present means to obtain some future end'. As such, of course, it exists whether a State exists or not; hence any political theory which ignores this conception – as both Marxian theory and Mill's theory of liberty do – is likely to take us back to the state of nature (anarchy), the state that Hobbes recognized as psychologically intolerable.

2   The Hobbesian conception of power as both 'natural' to man and 'intolerable', which rests on egoist theory, is also the premise of such psychological theses as Adler's dominance–submission theory of social relations. In its essence, the argument is that the need to satisfy biological needs forces man to be an egoist and to value power: that is, as biological beings we need 'power' in a very general sense ('ability' to satisfy drives or Hobbes's conception of 'means towards end'), but as rational beings we recognize that being able to satisfy drives in a

world of egoists makes 'dominance' – the specific ability ('power') to cow and coerce others – a logical or prudential value for the gregarious.

3 Logically, even before anything that can be called political theory emerged, 'power' had come to be used in two markedly different senses, one descriptive and one normative: power as 'ability' and power as 'dominance'. The fact that the second is normative and not descriptive, as psychoanalysts imagine, can be seen from the fact that those holding a normative system that defines 'dominance' and 'domineeringness' (the desire to be dominant) as a sin ('pride') – as Christianity does – have avoided the situation (sociality) that makes being dominant and domineering prudential goods. Normatively speaking, the genuinely 'meek' are shy. (Non-normatively speaking, the shy are 'meek'.)

4 To the analysis of 'power' (the movement from power as 'ability' to power as 'dominance' and 'domineeringness') Hobbes added a third conception – power as 'authority'. In his view, the latter represented an extension of the rationality behind the second conception and a logical extension of what man was already doing in the state of nature. Man in such a state is rationally 'power - hungry' (seeks to be dominant) because he understands his situation as an egoist among egoists. This being the case, there is no logical difficulty in moving from power-hunger ('I want to be dominant') to authority ('I accept domination'): the two serve the same function. The perception of 'power' as entailing either 'power-hunger' or 'authority' (but not both) is Hobbes's contribution to political and psychological theory.

5 With regard to the exercise of power under contract theory (implying the right to exercise power), there is a basic problem of 'tolerance'. Although in general 'authority' has the right to power, there are circumstances when the right should not be exercised. The problem has existed ever since the massacre of St. Bartholomew's Eve. The Wars of Religion are at the heart of political theory: there has to be a conception of 'ought' held by the sovereign power (assumed to be above 'oughts' when

considered in relation to its subjects) such that the sovereign's supreme power derives from the position assigned to it by those subject to it. We trust that the sovereign power is serving its function and are therefore 'loyal'. If the sovereign power is not non-partisan, we are not going to trust it. (The beneficiaries of the despotism are not 'loyal' but cynical: they will shift to whomsoever that seems most likely to serve their interests.)

6 In the minds of members of democracies, the 'ought-ness' of tolerance has been confused by relativism – in particular the view that the basis of 'ought' is that there is no such basis. Under Communism, the situation is different because no distinction is drawn between *de facto* sovereignty (someone has power) and *de jure* sovereignty (the power which someone has derives from the function served – the contract argument). Marx supposed that one day *de facto* sovereignty (power) would simply disappear: the State would 'wither away'. Non-Marxists cannot help wondering what there is in Communist theory that is supposed to make facts go away.

IDEOLOGY, POWER AND AUTHORITY

When modern States adopted an elective process of setting up government (what we loosely call democracy) there was necessarily a move to an ideologically-based State. We have completely abandoned the Greek classification of various types of government and never speak of the shift in terms of the method of attaining government: we speak in terms of ideology (democracy, Communism) because this is what makes the move meaningful. (We realize now that an electoral system as such is not necessarily superior to an hereditary system; it does not guarantee a better form of government: after all, all modern States, except a few petty authoritarian régimes, use some electoral system.) Thus 'ideology' is conceptually central to the modern State. If we ignore this or argue that it is not important and say, for instance, that those in office (*apparatchiki* of various persuasions) are hypocrites and only pretend that ideology matters, we have in effect decided to speak only about 'power' and either ignore the crucial matter of authority or see it as an aspect and outcome of 'power'.

To do this means to abandon the reasoning behind the theory of sovereignty: political power is possible because it serves a function. Consensus on the function served (general acceptance of 'authority') is what supplies the State with its coercive power.

No one has attempted to make the contrary case: that we human beings are by nature so submissive (obedient) that, once dominated, we forever after submit – and assist the domineering in coercing others into submission. Both psychologically and historically such a view would be absurd. Yet something like it becomes necessary when we eliminate the concept of 'authority' from the analysis of political behaviour and assume that it is enough to suppose that most office-seekers are 'power-hungry'. Assuming they are, attainment of public office will not satisfy the hunger unless most other people respect their authority when they attain office (and are unaware of their motivation). In other words, those who are not motivated by ideology and the nature of authority have to be expert hypocrites; they must never appear to be anything other than devout believers in ideology and devoted public servants. This being the case, what is the evidence that they are such hypocrites? Hardly any, of course. Under Communism, the official line is usually strictly followed and there is little criticism of public officials. This is one way of saying that to deny that ideology plays an all-important role in Communist systems makes no sense.

The question of 'hypocrisy' does not arise under the democratic ideology because of our assumptions about individuality and individualism: we do not normally expect office holders to submerge their personalities because they are exercising the function of authority. There are some naïve people who speak grandly of 'public trust' and perceive evidence of 'corruption' whenever there is evidence of self-interest in the behaviour of an office-holder. Most of us, however, begin with the view that individualism is a central democratic value and that questions of corruption arise only when a 'conflict of interest' arises, not when matters of self-interest alone are at stake.

Thus nothing whatsoever was established against Nixon until it was found that his continuance in office was a threat to the process that put him there. Then he had to go; he himself acknowledged the fact. But he was not really 'corrupt': the democratic ideology has never ceased operating; together with the latter there has been a consensus that 'power' is not the basis of our social order. The lesson of democratic ideology and its importance is that Nixon resigned, whereas Stalin died in office.

If one asks why some ideologies really do limit power, the answer may be that they are closely linked with the concept of sovereignty which derives power from a concept (and a function), not from a factual situation. Both Nixon and Stalin had power but, if one is to draw a lesson for prosperity, it is not the fact of their power alone that really matters. What matters is what gave them power – the ideology; hence if one wants to control 'power' – prevent tyranny – one should look to the ideology, not the mere facts about someone's power. This is something behaviouralists do not understand despite the abundant historical evidence about the operation of democratic and Communist societies. While democratic ideologies limit power, the Communist ideology does the opposite: it entrenches power in the system , which under the tutelage of Lenin and his successors has become an organizational fist.

IDEOLOGY AND THE ENTRENCHMENT OF POWER

The concept of ideology is likely to be referred to in our society as the 'set of personal values'. The reason for this linguistic innovation, no doubt befitting the jargon of the social sciences, is that those subscribing to Hume's view that 'reason is the slave of the passions' needed a term for the beliefs known to be related to behaviour (what others call morals) which were not in any way enforced (as through the processes analysed in the 'internalized law' theory of norms). The concept of ideology was available because in our society beliefs (and belief systems) are neither deliberately inculcated nor enforced: 'faith' means what one chooses to believe, not what is orthodox. Ideology means what it does because a coerced belief in anything is unthinkable: attempting to induce it is called 'brainwashing'.

Matters are very different under Communism. As Djilas, who certainly ought to know, said in an interview: 'Ideology was. . . only a name . . . under which we could summarily deal with our opponents'.[9] Thus, in his view, ideology under Communism is a method for entrenching power rather than a reference to the beliefs and values used to guide one's behaviour. How did this happen?

Djilas's revelations tell us a good deal about the function of an ideology in gaining power: 'No matter what your ideology may be, once you believe that you are in possession of some infallible truth, you become a combatant in a religious war'.[10] Ideology, says Djilas, enables one to be ruthless and override any scruples that might limit the means one employs to gain power. ('There is nothing to prevent [you] from robbing, burning and slaughtering in the name of your truth'.) It also makes the attainment of power one of the means towards propagation of the truth.

When an ideology is the determinant of truth, the system is irrationalist in tendency, even if the ideology can be said to be 'true' in terms of some other criterion of truth. Thus, even if one accepts the idea that Communism is 'scientific' – that it is 'true' as determined by something other than Communism itself – it is adherence to the system, the ideology, not the 'truth' that matters when the ideology is institutionalized. When a belief-system is institutionalized, one can no longer test one's own adherence to the truth by such traditional means as that supplied by the 'correspondence' theory of truth, which is the basis of empiricism. It is authority that now prevails: an ideology-determined truth entails an irrationalism that leads to authoritarianism.[11] Being 'correct' – not being a 'revisionist' (to use an ideological concept) –

replaces being 'right'. The latter term, incidentally, makes sense only if there is some means of deciding on 'truth' which is external to the system that is considered orthodox.

It is very doubtful whether either Lenin or Stalin reasoned these issues out. They did not in fact need to. Once one has power, its exercise and the rationalization of one's actions are sufficient to result in either an insistence on irrationalism – belief in the ideology, not some other basis of truth – or an insistence on authority: 'Believe in me, not yourself'. The result is to entrench power and confirm a belief by those holding power that totalitarianism is good for the people.

The Consequences of Communist Ideology

Our society has so generalized the concept of ideology that the term can cover unsystematized beliefs which have only a very limited range of application. (The norm 'tolerance', for instance, is by some people referred to as an 'ideology'.) This is why we find it difficult to believe that an ideology could be used to entrench political power. 'Ideology', so conceived, seems too trivial to be transformed into anything so formidable as political power, even if it represents the views of the head of State. For most citizens in a democracy, the question is not what the head of State believes in or professes to believe in but what the members of society do; furthermore, most people would say that the mere fact that a political order is not democratic does not change the situation. This is also a reason why many innocents suppose one can 'experiment' with Communism: so long as the populace is uncommitted, they argue, it does not matter what the members of the government believe or profess to believe. They cannot possibly induce a false belief because, as Milton said, 'the mind is its own place'. Therefore, they insist, totalitarianism is impossible and references to a 'totalitarian' ideology are the result of vague thinking.

What is central to Communist ideology – and what essentially distinguishes it from religion – is that it is a system as well as a belief. Its systematic element gives enormous added power to what already depends on the system – political authority. It gives totalitarian power when the nature of the ideological system is determined by those having political authority (which has been true ever since Lenin's argument about the role of the Party with respect to ideology was accepted). So long as the system is maintained, actual 'beliefs' can be drastically changed from what was originally professed; at times, adherents (*apparatchiki*) can indeed sound like hypocrites. The system will, of course, be maintained by those in power, for it is the system itself that promotes political power.

An analysis of the distinction (as well as of certain similarities) between Communist ideology and religion can reveal important political implications. Both religion and ideology entail a credential element which has to be taken on faith. It can be established that all beliefs, including those of science, rest on unprovable assumptions. When deciding on what to believe, one usually tends to consider the desirability of consequences rather than the plausibility of premises. What distinguishes Communist ideology from a religion such as Christianity is not the notion that the premises of the former are somehow 'scientific' while those of the latter are not, but the assumption about 'system'. Like other religions, Christianity has been striving to arrive at a system for its beliefs, whereas Communism begins with the view that it is by nature a system. In consequence, it is utterly impossible for anything called religion to hold, say, that 'God is dead' in order to arrive at a system, whereas Communism can abandon any of its views: its 'validity' is determined by its system, not by its premises. This difference makes it exceptionally difficult for many Westerners to understand Communism. The closer they are to the view that it is 'logically' impossible to change assumptions in order to retain a Communist 'system', the less likely they are to understand what they are facing. If what is 'logical' is the system rather than the premises, it is not 'logically' impossible to abandon premises in order to reach a desired conclusion. One must stop hoping that one can change Communism or its appeal by calling an abandonment of premises 'hypocritical' or 'expedient'. Doing this is tantamount to employing false logic to achieve one thing only – becoming complacent about future relations between Communism and democracy. To follow traditional logic does not guarantee victory.

Another important aspect of the relationship between ideology and power is the coincidence of system – in both ideology and political power – under Communism. This concurrence makes totalitarianism inevitable.

A good deal of the systematic deception inflicted on the West by adherents of the Communist ideology concerns the nature of political power. In terms of Western political theory, the issue can be stated as follows: the jurisdiction of the traditional 'sovereign' power was limited ('sovereign' did not mean 'universal' or omnipotent); it was a 'system' dealing with one particular problem ('security'). This jurisdiction moves towards totalitarianism (from the Hobbesian to Fascism or Communism) when 'system' as a means towards an end ('security') becomes a statement about the nature of truth – an ideology.

Communists argue that one does not get genuine government unless one has Communism: all non-Communist governments are 'tyrannies', whereas Communist régimes, despite evidence of tyranny, are what everyone really wants – genuine governments. It is making 'system' the basis of truth that promotes this strange development.

The power of a democratic government, or even that of traditional despotism is limited by the fact that we never supposed that government was capable of saying anything whatsoever about the 'truth'. Government had a function and its jurisdiction began and ended with that function. It entailed 'system' because it necessarily continued over time, as did the problem it dealt with.[12] If one argues that the government exists to promote 'truth' conceived as a system (thesis-antithesis-synthesis, or anything else for that matter) then limitations on government are removed.

EMPIRICIST PERCEPTIONS OF IDEOLOGICAL INSTRUMENTALISM

Sceptics notwithstanding, there is reason to believe that ideology (or what is known as Marxism-Leninism) provides for the State – in contrast to democratic ideology – a potential instrument of power. Consequently, the Soviet State used to support it and, as Zinoviev testifies, [convert it] 'into a devastating instrument of power'.[13] Democratic States are opposed to the very idea of ideology playing such a role. Numerous sceptics doubt whether this is even possible. What is the basis of this disbelief?

With regard to the actual historical development of ideas (as opposed to what Marxism says is true), both Marxian materialist determinism (what ideology says) and empiricism (what science and philosophy say) have a common origin in Hume's argument about the impotence of belief. As a result, the Soviet State could, without compunction, use Marxian ideology as an instrument of power, while the philosophically and scientifically inclined in Western society could watch this happen and yet deny it is happening. Both Soviet *apparatchiki* and Western philosophers agreed that Zinoviev is 'wrong' because it is 'logically' impossible for him to be right. Evidence, therefore, that he is right is not really there. He who sees such evidence is considered 'prejudiced' or psychologically unbalanced.

The logic of this view, as set forth by Hume, is that the act of belief cannot be related to the truth of what is believed. Thus believing carries no consequences, for it is something other than 'truth' that accounts for belief and other types of behaviour; it is 'emotion' that moves us to act. (Hence – to project Hume's view – when Zinoviev and Western observers say that it is evidence of Soviet tyranny which makes them condemn the Communist régime, all they are showing is 'prejudice' – an emotionally-based objection that science and philosophy must reject.)

In arriving at his view, Hume used the concept of 'empiricism' not in the sense of evidence supplied by his senses, but as a theory of the nature of facts as human beings perceive them, which is a very different thing. We must always keep this in mind when someone tells us what 'science says'. Almost never does it mean: 'The facts are that . . ., etc'. The more usual meaning is: 'Despite facts and logic, science demands that you believe'. If you are an authoritarian, you may obey. If you are not, it is hard to predict what you will do.

If you accept Hume, you do not have to believe in Marx but you may be inclined to assume that Marxian views are in the 'best tradition' of science and philosophy, even though you may not be familiar with exactly what Marx says. This part does not matter: in the Humean empiricist tradition facts are not particularly important. One pretends they are and, whenever possible, one uses them to support one's views. But when one speaks about the 'importance' of an ideology, it is not (and cannot be) the facts that matter because 'facts' do not affect behaviour.

It is this idea that makes Marxist ideology a devastating instrument of power; it also makes it difficult for non-Marxists to see that it is such. Adherence to Humean empiricism prevents one from using facts to correct one's beliefs.

Totalist Conception of the Good

Although Marx spoke of his system of ideas as socialism, and the former USSR disposed of criticism by claiming that society was still in a state of 'socialism', Communism differs from socialism – as the rest of us understand these two terms – with regard to the coercive power which is conferred by Communist ideology on those chosen to uphold it. The reason is that Communism is totalist or hermetic in the sense that implementation of the system is regarded as entailing all other goods. Socialism, at least as understood outside the Communist world, when implemented, yields but one good, or at most the limited set of values related to equality in the distribution of property ('distributive justice' as socialists define it). Hence democratic socialists invariably combine their socialism with some supplementary system of values, such as Christianity or liberalism. Indeed, one can be sure one is listening to a form of democratic socialism rather than Communism when the advocate stresses the need for socialism to be incorporated into some larger normative scheme. Such an idea is incomprehensible to a true Communist.

Once we grasp that the main value claimed by Communism derives from its totalist conception of the good, or – to use a utilitarian term – its 'fecundity' or capacity to beget the good, it is obvious why Communist ideologues are impatient with criticisms that emphasize particular normative details. One can imagine their saying: 'Yes, Communism does advocate State capitalism and yes, people can take exception to the policy on ethical and pragmatic grounds, but the real point is that the work of Communism has never been represented as deriving from its advocacy of socialist norms'. Marx neither invented the socialist conception of the good nor pretended to do so. Rather he claimed that a socialist society that would come into being 'naturally' (as a product of historical forces which he and Engels said were operating), would be fecund of good (to use Bentham's term again for the sake of brevity). Socialist policies are of so little importance in Communist theory that they have sometimes been simply ignored, as in present-day China. This does not mean that Communism has changed. What matters is that Communist ideology, because of the way it envisions values, can see itself as the source of all good, despite the actual conditions in society. In consequence, the practical advantage – eagerly exploited by Communism – is its expectation of being judged by its promises and predictions rather than by its accomplishments.

Given that all genuine values derive from the operation of the ideology within society, it is easy to see that, in a Communist State, power is placed in the hands of those who are responsible for upholding the ideology: the Party and especially the General Secretary. Lenin was the first to grasp this aspect of Communist ideology; Stalin was the first to profit from Lenin's line of thought.

Lenin's position is so alien to the Western mixture of values and beliefs that come under the name of ideology that some people are likely to see him as a man who rationalized the actual fact of his political power. Traditionally, in our society there had been no system of thought which was represented as the source of all good. The change was brought about by modern scientism which introduced the kind of thinking about truth and values that Communism originated. Science was first conceived of as a method of arriving at a certain kind of truth, whereas now it reputedly supplies both the good and the truth. To understand Lenin's legacy and the meaning of Zinoviev's statement about power and ideology one needs to think of scientism rather than the psychological concept of 'rationalization'.

Under Communism, 'rationalization' is never necessary (or possible): Communists can lie about what they do and make excuses in the face of the criticism of others, but the peculiar type of excuse one calls 'rationalization' – justifying one's behaviour to one's conscience – cannot arise when the belief system itself professes to supply a complete normative framework. Communism being accepted as the source of all good, a true Communist cannot have a conscience at odds with his behaviour as a Communist. What is thereby promoted is a ruthlessness by those in power that elsewhere would be regarded as the behaviour of psychopaths, but this does not trouble the Communist conscience.

The psychology of such behaviour is often misunderstood because the meaning of ideology is not grasped. One often thinks of ideology as a very limited set of ideas that allow major parts of our behaviour and intellectual processes to derive from other sources. The tendency is to insist on the latter. We say that everyone 'ought' to have a conscience. As it is recognized that there need be no relation between holding public office and having a conscience, we try to circumscribe political power so as to preserve the normative system which is considered to be much larger than the set of norms related to 'authority' and democratic values.

There has been some change in this view in the West – a steady movement towards the Marxian view that the material environment determines what one calls 'good' and 'bad'. Yet, so long as we retain some semblance of freedom – the Church, for instance, is still allowed in our society to query the views of materialist determinism – we are not likely to institute a political régime in which it is possible to be utterly ruthless and unconscionable in the exercise of power.

The difference between Communism and other normative systems can be seen in the *post-mortem* reputations of Hitler and Stalin, who were psychologically similar but lived in ideologically different societies. Hitler is now viewed by many Germans with stunned disbelief. How could that have happened? they ask themselves. The criticism of Stalin in Russia, on the other hand, has long been muted, to say the least. The general attitude seems to have been mainly one of doubt about the legitimacy of criticism. This attitude, which stems from the fecundity of Communist ideology with regard to concepts of the good, puts into the hands of the Communist Party a power that no other ideology wields.

THE LENINIST LEGACY

If we limit ourselves to the original Marxian conception of Communism, it is by no means clear to us what role Communist theory plays in human behaviour. It required the very pragmatic Lenin to define ideology in terms of political power, so that by definition an ideologist must also be someone deeply involved in political action. By making an actual political party and its interests the supposed source of theoretical truths, Lenin's politicizing of theoretical discussions appears to be the source of the conception of ideologies as political statements that go far beyond mere theorizing. How else can we explain how a word coined to replace the term 'metaphysics' has the meaning it acquired?

Lenin allowed for only two ideologies, one 'socialist' and the other 'bourgeois' – projecting a picture of the world divided into two conflicting ideologies. Why, according to him, is one of them true? Answering this question, Alain Besançon goes to the crux of Leninism: 'Because it is the ideology of the working class, and that class, because of its adherence to Marxism-Leninism, cannot be wrong. But what if the working class were not Leninist? The reason for this would be that it succumbed to the influence of bourgeois ideology'.[14] Clearly, the Leninist conception of ideology must be discussed not only in terms of power but also in terms of conflict, aggression and domination.

As Alfred G. Meyer puts it, 'Lenin thought that he had reunited theory and practice . . . not . . . in the working class . . . but in the party, the active machinery of consciousness'; he had done so because, unlike that of Marx, Lenin's 'faith in history' as a sort of divine force was shaky: 'distrusting spontaneity, he turned consciousness into an organized force'.[15] Although the sequence of ideas here may appear ambiguous, the consequences of politicizing 'consciousness' are very clear: 'The ambiguities of Leninism', Meyer notes, 'led to bitter conflicts within the party, conflicts which both before and after his death were resolved not by exhaustive argument but by political pressure from Lenin or from the party machine that succeeded him'.[16]

The issues are worth discussing not because Meyer in presenting them has made a significant contribution to the analysis of Communist ideology – he has not – but because the Leninist legacy goes far beyond defining the role of the Communist Party with regard to Communist theory. Since Lenin, the question of which States will become Communist has been determined with reference not to Marxism but to Leninism. What matters is: which States have a well-organized Communist Party; and where are conditions such that the 'authority' of the Party – and its power – is most likely to increase? Long ago, the USSR abandoned Marxian theory for Leninism; the old-line Marxian, Trotsky, was assassinated for propagating outmoded views. Trying to expose the shortcomings of Marxian theory is a waste of time; it is the pragmatism of Lenin that confronts us.

Such an assertion should not be taken as emanating from the view that ideas do not matter. They most certainly do. The views of both Marx and Lenin have had a profound effect on history. The answer to the question of which has been more important depends on whether 'importance' refers to sequences of events or present conditions: without Marx, there would be no Lenin, but without Lenin there would not be anything that could be called the 'menace of Communism'. Lenin made Marxian philosophy politically important. Without Lenin, Communist theory would be of interest to the historian of ideas; but it would be an ivory tower discipline, in effect a theory about the unimportance of theory.

Imperialist Coercion – By Whose Definition?

Implicit in Marx is the view that coercion (the use of power) causes change: that there will be a revolution and the side with the most people on it will win. To Marx, it is historical forces unconnected with present distributions of power that are bound to bring about the changes. 'Workers of the world' may well be expected to unite, but the issue is forethought rather than 'necessity' or the assertion of 'rights'. It is the forces of history that do the coercing, not the workers of the world.

Unlike Marx and Engels, Lenin was not faced with the task of convincing anyone (except possibly himself) of the importance of historical forces. Yet to maintain his own position as their instrument, he did what every successful Communist leader has done since. He represented power and the manipulation of power as essential to the implementation of Communism. It would be hard to express it more forcefully than Bertram D. Wolfe did: 'Leninism can be understood as a strategy and tactics for the conquest of power, for the maintenance of expansion of power, for making that power absolute and total'.[17]

Since no democratic leader has ever envisaged 'power'

as essential to democracy, one can reasonably suspect that coercion – in the sense of action against resistance – is much more important to the original Marxian theory than historical necessity. Whoever commits himself to Communism does so out of a predilection for coercion rather than 'reason'. Otherwise it would be difficult to understand the persuasiveness that Leninist theories of coercion, in particular his theory of imperialism, have for many non-Communists.

Lenin's incorporation of coercion into the concept of imperialism has led to rather strange consequences. There are people living in the countries that were once colonial and are now Communist who look back to the 'good old days' of imperialism; whereas the consensus outside such countries is that nothing good whatsoever can be said for those days: by definition, they were 'coercive' and 'exploitative'. Not many people realize that this last is so by Leninist definition, not by the evidence of history.

It is not the cogency of Lenin's attempt to explain why history was not moving in the direction predicted by Marx that tells us why Lenin's claim that Marxian truth was delayed by colonial exploitation is acceptable to all and sundry in Western democracies. Yet the very same people ignore the fact that our modern notion of colonialism as exploitative originated with Lenin; furthermore, that mercantilist principles, which for a time encouraged colonialism – and whose nature was recognized by Marx – bear no relation to Lenin's ideas. Mercantilism was a system of marketing, not of exploitation; it encouraged colonialism in accordance with an economic theory, not as the result of some rampant tendency towards avarice and acquisition in Western society. In our time, Western democracies feel guilty about their 'imperialist' past, partly because Lenin's theory tells them one ought to feel guilty. In his analysis of what 'liberty' requires, J.S. Mill's representation of colonies as exceptions strikes everybody as prejudice. People feel guilty because they deny one of Mill's implicit premises: that authority is a valid concept, not just a deceptive way of speaking about power and coercion. They are convinced that democratic nations ought not to have had colonies in the first place; hence a theory which says that greed overrode democratic inclinations and made Western countries 'imperialistic', strikes them as a self-evident truth. Its realization, they feel, should enable one to correct past errors and try to make amends.

Lenin's theory only seems true because it explains what the West would like to have explained as an aberration of the past. It also provides a basis for regarding those who refuse to accept it – such as people in what was formerly Rhodesia, or in South Africa – as needing to be taught a lesson: needing to be coerced by the 'enlightened' citizens of the countries which themselves were once just as 'imperialistic'. The difference is that now, trying to coerce others into an acceptance of Leninist theory, Westerners are motivated by 'freedom' rather than avarice and a lust for power, as is the case of 'imperialists'. Hence, they assure themselves that the coercion for which they are pressing is not really wrong. Can they possibly be unaware that they are using a Communist theory? Few individuals (if any) really recognize the source of their views. Lenin incorporated coercive power into Marxian theory and nowadays people who are non-Marxians act in accordance with this theory.

THE STALINIST LEGACY: THE VILLAINY OF SYSTEMATIC DECEPTION

In an interview (with G.R. Urban) which became part of a comprehensive symposium on Stalinism, Kolakowski made an admirably succinct appraisal: 'Stalinism is not an incidental evil which somehow superimposed itself on an otherwise benign vision. On the contrary: the tyranny of one man, the worship of a personalized ideology and the power-structure derived from it, is *the* perfect embodiment of the spirit of Communism. . . . All other variants of Communism-in-power are half-baked, diluted, timorous, immature or senile by comparison. Since the death of Stalin, Soviet Communism has not been able to regain its health, though as far as the institutional framework is concerned, the legacy of Stalinism survives intact.'[18] A question by the interviewer followed: 'If the institutional incarnation is intact, why could Stalinism not survive Stalin?' Kolakowski explained that 'Under Stalin, the police-terror, the purges and massacres affected too many members of the *apparat*. That they affected the people at large would not have mattered, because the population as such is of no importance in the Soviet system, but the continuing insecurity of the *apparat* was intolerable'.[19]

The point made is important to a student of political philosophy. It miniaturizes Hobbes's contract theory, relating it to Lenin's view of the Party as the vanguard of the proletariat. The members of the *apparat*, like Hobbes's subscribers to the contract, must achieve security or they will not submit to the sovereign power. The idea deserves careful consideration: it shows contract theory to be a part of normal thinking. Within the given context, however, it is only a small part of Kolakowski's overall position that the promise of 'security' in Communism is Utopian – a deception – which makes Communism immoral and in part accounts for its totalitarianism. Furthermore, the inability of most people to understand the deceptive nature of the system may explain the grotesque misinterpretation in the West of Communism in the USSR.

The difficulty of grasping the problem can be explained by reference to 'security' as a norm. Kolakowski makes the important point that democracies lose the battle with Communism in the Third World because their system does not promise security. Starving people are easy prey for those who promise that under Communism their material conditions will be radically improved, as all available goods will be redistributed. While democratic ideology makes no such Utopian promises, Communism professes to offer more than any other system, in particular to offer what has always been considered fundamental – 'security'.

However, the kind of 'security' promised by the Communists is different from that offered by the social contract. It is in fact the kind that the contract theory offers security against. Under the social contract, your fellow-man is not allowed to murder you for your property or steal what you own. Indeed, you can count on this. This is your 'security'. No other kind of security is promised because our universe is such that any other type of promise by one's fellow-man would be false. God can promise more but not man. To pose the question 'What can human beings honestly promise one another and be able to live up to their promises?' is to look at a fundamental difference between democracy and Communism. Kolakowski's crucial testimony is that Communists are liars because they know that their promises will not be fulfilled.

Kolakowski's point (which, of course, is an ethical one) is not likely to be immediately clear in a relativist society. One needs some insight into non-relativist ethical thought. An excursion into the status of both 'security' and 'promise-keeping' in rationalist ethical schemes is therefore appropriate.

As a norm, 'security' is not generally understood because its rational basis was abandoned when it was accepted that Hume was right. Thus any 'norm' or belief affecting behaviour is capable of doing so because it has a basis in 'emotion' rather than 'reason'. 'Timid' people, for instance, value 'security' because they are 'timid' – which is what having this norm means psychologically. Consequently, anyone who makes 'security' the basis for his analysis of behaviour, has to be understood in terms of 'timidity' (which, politically speaking, may be called conservatism). Hobbes admitted to having been born prematurely because of his mother's apprehension about the Armada; he never recovered from this experience. Hence the *Leviathan* is really about *angst*. QED.

The norm 'security' is related to man's capacity to think of himself as extending in time. Animals can be timid and apprehensive but only human beings can suffer from *angst*. We can worry about the future because first, we can conceive of it and ourselves as existing together; and second, we know we do not have all the factors relevant to future conditions under our control. 'Security' as a good has nothing to do with being 'nervous'; hence, of course, political theory and psychological theory are unrelated.

As a norm, promise-keeping is usually linked with truth-telling, just as truth-telling is often confused with 'truth' as a good. (Similarly, 'truth' is confused with 'knowledge'; 'knowledge' is confused with 'experience'; 'experience' with 'empiricism' and so on.) Promise-keeping, however, is usually thought to be more important than truth-telling, which is subject to exceptions. (Thus non-Kantians do not feel guilty about colouring an anecdote or flattering a woman and would not hesitate to save the life of an innocent man by telling a lie. However, most such people – whom Kant would consider depraved – would disapprove of promise-breaking.)

Promise-keeping holds a special normative place because the keeping of promises is effective proof that human behaviour is not part of a mechanistic scheme. We have no idea what circumstances will exist in the future, but if we believe in free will we also believe that we are separate from any mechanistic system and superior to it. Furthermore, we can make a prediction about our behaviour – this is what a promise is. By keeping the promise we can prove we are right in our conjecture about free will and mechanism. For this reason, promise-keeping is normatively much more important than truth-telling and Communism as a system can be properly represented as fundamentally dishonest by making promises it cannot possibly keep; only chance factors may at times fulfil them. The Communist system enables the ideology of deception to survive by institutionalizing it. But why is the West always so prone to deny this perverse manifestation of the Marxist principle of the 'unity of theory and practice'?

POWER, ACTIVE MEASURES AND INSTRUMENTALISM

Combined, the Leninist and Stalinist legacies resulted in the state of political warfare manifested in an array of 'active measures'. How can these measures be accounted for in terms of political theory and ethics?

Active Measures and the 'Good'

The view that Communism is 'scientific' is not meant to appeal to scientists who want to know the truth about politics, but to the common man who wants to get a concept of the 'good' out of the fact that the State has power over him. As a political ideology, Communism, especially as shaped by Lenin and Stalin, says why this is so in a way which is alien to democracy. It justifies the various forms of deceit and terrorism – the core of 'active measures' – which democracy cannot possibly justify.[20]

Under democracy, the citizen wants to think of the State's power as a good *only* insofar as the State is 'democratic' – an instrument of a conception of the good established by some other method than by the power of the State. From the early modern days, right back to Hobbes, who did not yet argue for 'democracy' in the sense of 'popular government', such has been the 'democratic' view of State power.

Under Communism, the citizen is told that the State's power is good because it is the instrument by which the leadership creates the good and protects the citizen against 'reactionary' forces. (Under a mechanist conception of the good, for every power for 'progress' – having a normative direction – there is a 'reactionary' force. Speaking of 'reactionary' forces means conceiving of the good in terms of power, or else not thinking at all.)

When State power is a good because it is the only possible means towards the good (power itself) – but which entails a conception of a 'reactionary' power (such as democratic society) – it naturally allows any means towards the end whatsoever, for it is now power that defines the good and in effect *is* the good.

Finally, what defines the good under this circular definition? It has to be some expression of power. Which is – 'active measures', of course. They do not even have to be excused or rationalized, but can be spoken of quite openly.

Why the Term 'Disinformation'?

In the broadest sense, as the leading study on the subject tells us, disinformation is defined as any government communication (either overt or covert) containing intentionally false and misleading information which is designed to deceive and manipulate an opponent.[21] In Soviet usage, the term 'denotes a variety of techniques and activities to purvey false or misleading information, including rumours, insinuation and altered facts.'[22]

One of the reasons for using the word 'disinformation', which is the close English equivalent of the Russian word *dezinformatsia*, is to make it clear that we are not thinking of a political strategy such as that found in all political orders but of one peculiar to Communism, particularly of the Soviet variety. Disinformation is more to the point than the long-used term which embraces some of *dezinformatsia's* practices – propaganda. In the first place, the new term is not necessarily designed to propagate anything in particular; it is not so much a device of ideologists as of those having political power. (In the context of Soviet Communism, they may, of course, have been the same people.) This aspect becomes very important when the question of the applicability of the term to democracies is raised. The nature of political power in democratic States is such that they cannot make habitual use of 'disinformation', whereas they certainly can and do use 'propaganda'.

The concept of disinformation makes it possible to refer to techniques of misleading opinion and suppressing counterviews that 'propaganda' cannot cover, no matter how much we stretch the term.

There was need for a term that covered propaganda, censorship, forgeries, deliberate obfuscation, agent-of-influence operations and non-verbal types of deception generally. Until the adoption of the concept from the Russian, the English language had no such term.

As a number of authoritative studies of the subject have made evident,[23] Soviet disinformation – comprising a variety of active measures – was an essential part of political warfare. It was a fundamental instrument of power.

Active Measures and Disinformation

Premised on 'activism' – thereby implying an ideological basis – active measures –(*activnyye meropriyatiya*) constituted an armoury of weapons and devices used by the Soviet State. They included: disinformation, fostering discord among the Western allies, blackmail, discrediting political opponents, assisting 'liberation' revolts, and resorting to subversion, sabotage, assassinations, terrorism, etc. As a result, all – or nearly all – distinctions between war and peace disappeared. The West faced – although it was reluctant to admit it – a new form of cold war (or, more exactly, something between cold war and open war).

Within active measures, disinformation played a crucial role: it ensured that they were effective. This was done in a variety of ways:

1   Disinformation was designed to promote active measures short of open war; it succeeded when these measures – although at times indistinguishable from war – were not seen by the opponent's public as amounting to war. They may even have masqueraded as measures of 'peace'. A concomitant point: disinformation could effectively prevent an opponent from resorting to a strong, active response to active measures.

2   Disinformation allowed a greater degree of 'activism' within the sphere of active measures than would otherwise be possible. In the absence of disinformation, active measures would be dangerously close to open war.

3   Disinformation was also designed to confuse the analytical process with regard to ideology.

In themselves active measures were in a sense overt and attention-getting. Thus demonstrations are essentially designed to attract attention, assassinations are by nature dramatic events, insurrections are always likely to arouse general interest. Consequently, active measures were habitually accompanied by disinformation. If they were not, the active measures could be seen for what they are and traced to their source (if not suppressed or 'spiked' by the Western media). It was therefore a fundamental principle of disinformation to represent active measures which become apparent as internal issues – the product of circumstances, rather than the product of an international power struggle. Race conflict, for instance, would no doubt evoke very different responses when shown as a demand for justice rather than the work of political agitators. A major function of disinformation was to ensure that events that originated in some KGB *apparatchik's* mind be attributed to social conditions in the country where they occur.

This may all be rather obvious, but what is not so obvious is that the very framework within which disinformation and active measures operated was itself a triumph of Communist ideology. In the past, only materialist determinists attempted to explain social and political change by means of social 'wrongs' that could ostensibly be remedied only by granting political 'rights'. This position is certainly not part of the traditional concept of 'natural rights'. Now, however, it is the view taken by the behaviouralist science. Consequently, a Communist agitprop need only represent his active measures as a response to some social wrongs and he is literally free to act the way he wants.[24]

When one can work within such an intellectual framework, very little really clever deception is necessary. Soviet active measures worked within a pre-established condition of disinformation within the mind of the unreflecting common man, who was predisposed to accept the premises of Communism as a statement about society and its effects on human values.

There is some reason to believe that it was the policy of those promoting active measures to avoid raising issues that would suggest links between Communist theory and what serves the Soviet Union's interests. Active measures and disinformation seemed designed not so much to promote Communism directly – the ideology – as the power of the the Communist State (particularly the Soviet

Union). Hence some of those who analysed social and political developments in terms of their relationship to Communist ideology also became the victims of disinformation: why suppose that what is done in the interest of a State must also promote an ideology?

The framework of belief within which Communist active measures operated is (a) the materialist view held by non-Communists that 'activism' (anti-State behaviour) is first to be explained as the effect of a 'wrong' within society; and (b) any activity not so explicable must be directly traced to an attempt by ideologues to promote an ideology before it can be said to be 'Communist' in origin. With this intellectual framework operating in favour of Communist activists, it is small wonder that most people in the West did not believe that 'Communism' had anything to do with what happened outside the Communist bloc. In its heyday the greatest success of disinformation was to make 'Communism' seem significant only to those living in a Communist society, so that a personal rejection of the ideology was an adequate response to the might of the USSR.

The Politics of Evil

The realization that active measures and disinformation were not merely devices, some of which the West itself has had occasion to use, will become clearer if we keep in mind that one cannot understand the reality of evil by having some concept of the good. The issue is not one of contrast, like the difference between black and white. The question arises as a result of the concept of 'power', as in the fundamental problem of reconciling the omnipotence of God and God's benevolence with the fact of evil. The latter is the basis of Acton's principle that 'power tends to corrupt, and absolute power corrupts absolutely'. It is also the basis of the objection to totalitarianism as evil by nature, no matter what arguments are presented about the end justifying the means.

In a genuine ethical system, the doctrine that the end justifies the means – what some call 'Jesuitism' – expresses the fact that an ethical system is present in which some norms are more important than others. (Indeed, if you do not systematize, you get irreconcilable ethical problems as with euthanasia: nothing ethical can be done when absolutes clash.)

It is easy to shift from ethics to ideology, as when the Soviet 'active measures' are 'considered an element of "ideological work" to be waged relentlessly to ensure that, in Lenin's phrase, "word becomes deed" '.[25] This shift occurs when the view that the end justifies the means is an expression of instrumentalism. When this happens, we are facing power politics and an attempt to enforce totalitarianism.

When power is defined as good, as being a means to an end, it is not good, except under instrumentalism; because the latter system accepts power as a good rather than as raising the question of evil, it cannot be considered a legitimate ethical system.

So long as our society was conscious of the question of evil, it has sought to control power because it was felt that it is its very existence – not the existence of good or bad intentions – that raises the problem. This is why the political analyses of St Augustine and St Thomas Aquinas differ markedly from those of the ancient Greeks. References to 'Eastern despotism' traditionally invoked different attitudes to the concentration of political power. When religious conceptions began to decay, however, and the analysis of the relation of power and evil became obscure, the West lost the capacity to deal with such issues as emergent totalitarianism, except as something 'undemocratic'. We also lost the moral incentive to insist on a distinction between political orders; at times even to speak of a moral difference between Communism and democracy came close to appearing 'intolerant'. Consequently, insistence on the evidence for this difference – claiming, for example, that active measures are peculiar to the Communists – came to seem an act of hostility on our part, not theirs. This is a predicament likely to be faced by anyone who attempts to promote greater public awareness of the threat posed by active measures. The evidence is provided by behaviouralistically-inspired facts and figures. Unfortunately, behaviouralist assumptions are such that the purpose of raising the basic issues gets lost. There is no question that, according to the prevailing mood, to insist on the facts and figures – the evidence for active measures – is to betray 'hostility' on the part of the researchers. 'Hostility', one may add, is interpreted as 'prejudice' – the main reason for this interpretation being that in our society there are no defensible definitions of good and evil.

There was a further obstacle to regarding the existence of active measures as a part of long-term Soviet policy. Until there is irrefutable evidence that would stand up in our own courts of law, many people will think it 'unfair' to say that the Soviet Union engaged in activities such as terrorism and assassinations, the evidence notwithstanding. As even a preponderance of evidence is often not enough in our courts, the notion was extended to the sphere of world politics and coloured the outlook of those whose concept of 'tolerance' derives from the practice of democratic courts of law.

TERRORISM, INSTRUMENTALISM AND POWER

Terrorism belonged to the most salient of active measures. The assumptions and circumstances affecting the Soviet State-sponsored terrorism of our time differed from the earlier terrorism advocated by the anarchists.

In anarchist theory, the State is hopelessly corrupt and so is society (corrupted by the State). Any appeal to reason or principle is naïve. Terrorism is justified as the only possible way of initiating an anarchist millennium. (Thus, when represented as justifiable, terrorism has always been an aspect of instrumentalism.) Under anarchism, terrorism is expediential; the operating ethical system is 'naturist': man like all other animals can rely on his nature to supply him with a concept of the good. He needs no State, church or family. The revival of terrorism by political systems which defend State power as means towards a hypothetical anarchist end (the 'withering away of the State') is not expediential but is clearly an aspect of the power which is itself an aspect of instrumentalism.

The USSR's resort to terrorism signalized an abandonment of the long-standing fiction that Communism is part of the movement of 'history'; that in order to win, it does not need any special measures. When terrorism is defined as 'active measures' that can and 'ought' to be part of the policy of a Communist State, we see a shift to a frank acceptance by Communist ideologues that their system is based on power not reason or the forces of history.

As an active measure, terrorism has an enormous advantage over disinformation and propaganda: no one can cope with it by disbelief, indifference or a refusal to participate. Just as the difference between power and authority is that the fact of power offers no choice, so we do not have a choice with regard to terrorism. We are forced to participate in whatsoever terrorism is supposed to engineer. This is precisely why it is the essence of immorality when represented as part of some politico-ethical system – when we are not allowed a choice but are forced to become participants. Only a non-genuine ethical system – like Communist instrumentalism – that excludes choice (while pretending to be ethical) can condone such practices. Anarchism, to be sure, did not argue that terrorism is ethical, only that it is not blameworthy. The instrumentalism of Communism is quite different. The assumption on which it rests is that the power of a Communist government is good because it reputedly tends to the abolition of government. However, because such power is good, any form of coercion it chooses to use is good; its totalitarian arrogation of both the moral and the political authority makes coercion a good. In the sphere of genuine instrumentalist ethics, questions about the justification in terms of means towards an end are irrelevant. Terrorism is an expression of power as well as a means to power – which precludes any further debate.

State-sponsored Terrorism

A major problem political analysts face in analysing terrorism is that the group with the highest level of education, the greatest interest in public affairs and an awareness of intellectual issues – the people who normally constitute the 'public' that the analyst addresses, the 'sophisticates' – are committed to an interpretation of terrorism whose validity the analyst denies. Terrorism, by definition, is a political act, whereas nowadays the 'sophisticates' define all acts of violence as forms of aggression. The standard behaviouralist view about aggression reflects that of the frustration-aggression school. It claims that anyone who engages in an act of violence has been driven to it by built-up emotional pressures, as a result of frustrations induced by his society or environment.

One of the premises of this view is the psychoanalytic 'steam-boiler' theory, the other than Marxian tenet that 'capitalism' exploits everyone except capitalists; as a result, almost all people are frustrated and therefore given to violence. The 'sophisticates', ironically, cannot help agreeing with the Communist view that terrorism is a 'chronic and progressive disease afflicting bourgeois society, something that has become integral to that society'.[26] The predicament of a political analyst who attempts to establish a Soviet connection is that he thereby 'proves' that (a) he is not 'sophisticated' and (b) he is 'prejudiced'.

Arguing for the analyst's view, it is useless to point out that the 'sophisticates' are begging the question. Rather, it is a good idea to begin the way Jillian Becker's monograph *The Soviet Connection* does: 'Over the last decade, terrorist aggression has intensified rapidly all over the world outside the Soviet Communist bloc. Western researchers have found that much of it is state-sponsored and almost all of it is state-aided'.[27]

This position is important to our understanding of terrorism because it glosses over the factors involved in the motivation behind violence and focuses on why some kinds of violence – like terrorism – are of interest to the political theorist. What especially matters is the sponsor-ship and aid given to the terrorists, not their motivation.

A terrorist can be – and often is – mentally unbalanced. However as with Agca, who attempted to assassinate the Pope, the really important questions are: how did he get across borders with valid travel documents? Who supplied his weapon? Who was behind his training? Who planned it all? This is what matters, not issues of psychology and sociology, whether he was, medically speaking, a lunatic,[28] which should be the concern of his therapist, not the rest of us. 'Sophisticates' do not understand that they are ignoring matters of public interest in favour of private issues which should be beyond their concern.

The problem one faces in dealing with terrorism is similar to that of crime: we define crime, no matter what function it may serve for the individual, as anti-social behaviour. We define terrorism – like subversion and insurrection – as anti-State or political behaviour, although we know that those who engage in it may have no real understanding of what they are doing – may in fact be lunatics. Insofar as political theory is concerned, the mental state of political agents is irrelevant. The political theorist is not a physician who diagnoses a disease. Rather he is an analyst/investigator who dis-covers who does what and why, uncovers a conspiracy – if there is one – and suggests possible counter-measures. Until this is well understood, our ability to cope with the problem of terrorism will be impaired – a weakness of which Communists were no doubt aware. State-sponsored terrorism is a new kind of warfare which we are not equipped to counter effectively.

THE TOTALITARIAN CONNECTION

When a régime resorts to active measures on a systematic basis, this indicates that a totalitarian system is in opera-tion. What makes the capacity of a democracy inherently different in this respect? The key role is played by the attitude to authority. Under contractualism, the 'supreme authority' – the so-called sovereign power of the State – is limited by the function ascribed to authority. So long as we are members of society, we are compelled not to act on pure egoist principles. In a democracy, in which we are not compelled to act on any other principle, the authority of the 'sovereign power' is entirely negative: 'Don't!' is all that it is supposed to say. (The 'Don't' is limited to *modus vivendi* issues, as required by the contractual theory.)

But in non-contractual societies – which can be labelled 'ideological' – the contractual limitations do not exist. If there is no conceptual limit on the authority, it is hard to imagine how a legal limit can be effectively set by some constitutional enactment. Indeed, constitutional dispensations become mere formalities and the constitutions themselves worthless documents; as such, they are a regular feature of a totalitarian State.

Ideologically-based States, no matter how legalistic they may profess to be, do not have any restraints on the exercise of authority such as exist in democracies. They have no built-in 'ethico-political' brakes on the adoption of terrorism or other active measures as part of State policy. The question of whether to adopt them or not is decided by expediency: for example, what do circumstances require?

The true meaning of active measures as symptomatic of the system that generates them becomes apparent when they are considered *in toto*, as part of a larger scheme, with reference to the overriding ultimate goals of the totalitarian State. Let us look at some of the symptoms of totalitarianism at work.

Active Measures and *Angst*

Totalitarianism is not possible as an empirical fact unless it first creates a neurotic anxiety which it later relieves, causing an abiding sense of gratitude. Communism uses a technique similar to that employed by psychoanalysis: thus Marxian analysis creates a frame of mind which Communist ideology subsequently 'cures'. In the absence of total control – absolute confidence in one's psychoanalyst or party leader – the system of creating *angst* in order to exercise power inside the country will not work.

The Soviet Union extended the *angst*-producing measures to the outside world. The most notable example of anxiety in the world today relates to nuclear war.

The concern about nuclear war is not rational. No sane person could accept it as anything other than Armageddon. Indeed, the West's defence policy is premised on this view: nuclear war is unthinkable; therefore we will ensure that it remains so by maintaining a nuclear capability. However, those who say they are concerned about nuclear war are behaving in very strange ways. Much of what is done, such as going on peace marches and declaring cities 'nuclear free', is clearly ritualistic rather than rational. It is also neurotic.

This particular neurotic anxiety was fostered by Soviet disinformation. The USSR made the promotion of popular movements for peace a major part of its international policy for the 1980s.[29] There was no possibility, of course, of its doing so directly. Only a small percentage of the foreign public is sympathetic to or even interested in Communist views. However, by means of disinformation on a global scale it was possible to create a state of *angst* that serves Communist policy.

But a peace march? How could this serve Communism? Surely any government that allows its policy to be influenced by a demonstration does not deserve to be called a government. Although true, this is not the point. If the demonstration reflects *angst*, the failure of the democratic government to be influenced serves Communist policy. This is the point. In effect, one's own government becomes the 'enemy'; hence the enemy of the 'enemy' – the USSR – is looked on more favourably, no matter what it does. Although for many years there was not the slightest evidence that Soviet aggressive policy had in any way been reduced, most people in the West were convinced that the opposite was true; further, that democratic governments themselves were the main threat to peaceful coexistence. It is *angst* created by disinformation that did this, not some sudden increase in popular ignorance.

Disinformation – a Sign of Totalitarian Régimes

Being uninformed because of the deliberate policy of the government creates in citizens a state of anxiety that prevents organized resistance and promotes retreat into political apathy. One becomes preoccupied with oneself, one lives for the moment to extract as much pleasure as possible, no matter how little this may be.

Since such a result is possible only when there is total control as under totalitarianism – disinformation can fully serve as a tool of power only when the exercise of power is already total, when it is a method of perpetrating power rather than explaining the exercise of power in general. If so, systematic, full-scale disinformation is concomitant with a fully totalitarian régime. It is an *indicium* of such régimes: to prove that disinformation is being carried out is a major step towards showing that the régime is totalitarian.

Disinformation can take forms which are outside the usual, expected channels of propaganda. Consider, for instance, the Constitution of the USSR. Indeed, what it promises served as a principal form of disinformation, characteristic of the entire system. The document did not serve as a genuine 'constitution' in the way that the American Constitution sets forth the ethical premises of the State. The real constitution of the USSR, on the one hand, was the ideology of Communism, which could fill that role (serve as a constitution), precisely because it was totalitarian. On the other hand, it would not make sense to argue that the constitution of a democratic nation equals 'democracy', for democratic norms do not profess to supply a sufficient normative system for anybody. They are a 'rendering unto Caesar' and this is all. In consequence, at every point where clashes between democratic norms and other norms may arise we need clear, specific statements. Democratic constitutions have to be working systems. Not that people in democracies are more law-abiding than elsewhere. But insofar as the effect of the legal system is concerned, there is a major difference. Democratic constitutions have to work, whereas Communist constitutions are pieces of disinformation put together by the leaders.

COMMUNISM: THE HIGHEST STAGE OF TOTALITARIANISM

Totalitarianism can be defined as the organization of coercive power ostensibly to unify the function of political and moral authority so as to attain a needed order. Political authority serves the function described in the social contract theory; moral authority serves the function described in ethical theory; whereas the combination of the two in one body – a 'leader' who has a privileged insight into the requirements of both functions – serves only the interests of the leader or an oligarchic group. It becomes a synonym for tyranny.

Because totalitarianism originated as a unifying and ordering force, it was a rather favourable term when it was coined by Gentile. But since it is true that uniting moral and political authority entails tyranny, it is easy to see why totalitarianism has become a strictly pejorative concept.

It is not possible to combine political and ethical authority in one person without violating the principles on which both are based, for this combination confuses the function of being served. So long as we know that a political authority is only political, we can decide whether this authority is serving its function: either it is able to maintain law and order or it is not. Similarly we know whether a moral authority is hypocritical or not. But what is the criterion when the leader is both a political and a moral authority? What principles can he follow? No doubt, he must consult mainly himself and become a tyrant.

Is Communism totalitarian? Yes, and more obviously so than Fascism (or Nazism). It asserts that moral principles are relative; that there cannot be a logic to conceptions of the good and that the views of the leadership on all matters must prevail. The ruling group is constrained only by the amount of coercive power it can command.

Communists naturally deny that their system is totalitarian, for they wish to dissociate themselves from Fascism, but the denial is not enough. The logic of their position is such that Communism is necessarily the supreme expression of the totalitarian philosophy. As stated in the apposite thesis of Professor Leszek Nowak: 'Communism is the highest order of totalitarianism'.[30]

When speaking of totalitarianism, it is easy to forget that in discussions of the subject there is a tendency to confuse 'power' with 'authority'. Assertions that Communism is totalitarian do not merely reveal the efficiency of Communist systems in exercising power. What is asserted is that the nature of Communist ideology is such that those granted political authority are assigned an unlimited amount of it. Political authority – equalling the power of the sword – is such that, when it is in the interest of the rulers to extend their power, it can 'legitimately' move in any direction and cover all aspects of human behaviour. As Besançon puts it: 'The substance of the ideology, when it is in power, is that power itself'.[31]

It has been argued within the tradition of Western theory that sovereignty itself, if the concept is meaningful, is omnipotent, representing a totality of power. Sovereignty, however, provides an argument for acknowledging an authority that serves a limited function, an authority being limited to that function. The way to extend the authority of the sovereign power would be to enlarge the function (as by assigning jurisdiction over the norms of society) or to give to the sovereign power an ideological function (as by uniting Church and State).

In the Western tradition, Church and State are separated, for it is recognized that there are dangerous totalitarian implications in theocracy (though not necessarily in a State-supported Church, which is an entirely different idea). The tradition of the separateness of Church and State can be contrasted with Communist attempts to suppress the Church, which the Communist ideology sees as a rival system for making statements about human behaviour. What is established in clashes of this kind is that there are no limits to Communist jurisdiction. When the issue is totalitarianism, it is the jurisdiction claimed (and the extent of the claim made) – not the power exercised – that matters. Asserting universality, the ideology makes the system totalitarian.

Communism contends that it is a complete system; it claims to be 'scientific'; its concept of norms is such that it can tell all men what to believe. In our society, only scientism parallels this view of science's authority. Before World War II, it gave rise to a political movement called 'technocracy', a movement that was suppressed as 'Fascist' – totalitarian – because of its normative claims. True science, it should be noted, generally avoids making such claims because they would raise questions related to its jurisdiction – questions that for centuries troubled Church–State relations.

But when an ideology (which is by nature normative) claims to be scientific and when the claim is no longer considered to be the result of historical forces but – a crucial shift – as something brought about by believers in the ideology, the situation is different. It was this crucial shift, instituted by Lenin, that made Marxism a major political force.[32] Until Lenin made Communism politically important by arguing that adherents to its ideology 'ought' to have political power, Marxism was a theory about history that history had proved false.

What maintains it today is its totalitarian features. Purportedly, it is capable of explaining all human behaviour and of supplying men with a guide to norms. The supposedly normative completeness appeals to some pseudo-intellectuals[33] who think that a monistic materialist system of explanation is necessarily scientific. Many of them fail to realize that the nature of political authority is such that the system entails totalitarianism. Some of those who do realize this – so long as they do not have to endure it personally – seem not averse to having such power or being able to excuse having it on the ground of historical necessity.

Chapter 21

Facing the Soviet ideo-system

The problem the West faces with regard to Communist ideology is twofold: first, in a society which doubts whether ideology matters, how is one to understand what George Will called the 'ideologically marinated' Soviet mind?; second, what is one to make of those who, like Alexander Zinoviev, going beyond a mere insistence on the influence of ideology, distinguished between supporters of the orthodox theory (like Trotsky) and the more pragmatically-oriented (including Stalinists).

For the West to understand the 'ideologically marinated' Soviet mind was not easy. Democratic ideology is only part of the set of ideas considered relevant to behaviour or to the set opposed to what seems practicable. Even if we apply Zinoviev's 'nominal' versus 'practical' distinction as a tool of analysis (see below), we do not get any parallel distinctions relevant to democracy, for in the USSR 'ideology' implied a complete system – a true ideo-system. Adding the fact that the West has never really understood the Russian mind – it labels it 'Byzantine' – one is faced with possible speculations about intentions that make 'normal' international relations impossible. 'Talk softly and carry a big stick', Theodore Roosevelt said of similar situations. But to many statesmen in the West the best response was not clear.

Although Russia's ambition to be a European power goes back to the days of Peter the Great, it has been traditionally excluded from the councils of Europe. This was not because Russia was not important enough to deserve notice, but because of the problem Europe had in understanding its intentions – the question of trust and trustworthiness. This historical situation, of which both the West and the USSR were certainly conscious – and which was enhanced by the proverbial Russian suspicion of the West – was undoubtedly part of the long-standing situation, which Bertram Wolfe saw as one of the 'disparate and conflicting forces' that make it virtually impossible for us to 'deduce the twists and turns of Soviet policy by simple transposition from its ideology and totalitarian structure'.[34]

But if Russia has always been an enigma to the West, the superimposition on a Byzantine tradition of an ideology that is based on an outmoded economic theory has hopelessly confused the West's task of understanding the Soviet ideo-system. Indeed, it seemed so strange that an ideology with such an unrealistic basis could influence policy – or be anything other than an unrealizable ideal for its adherents – that the very existence of Communism as the official ideology of the USSR gave rise to the view that ideology in general could not be of any significance scientifically because what it postulates bears no resemblance to reality. This, in turn, helped promote the argument that consequently Communism and democracy are at odds only as much as national States are; hence the view that our concern should be limited to the capacity of States to make war and that the importance of Communist ideology on policy-making should be played down.

TYPOLOGICAL DIFFERENCES

There is a tendency for sovietologists to stress a typological difference between democratic theory and Communism – not in the truistic sense that as political ideologies they can be distinguished, but in the more fundamental sense that the two belong to different classes; hence they must be approached in wholly different ways. Thus A. Zinoviev, the sovietologue extraordinary, argues – as was noted earlier – that to understand Communism we must 'make a distinction between nominal and practical ideology'.[35] One should also note the expression coined by Alain Besançon: 'ideological pseudo-reality'.[36]

These distinctions are made on the empirical basis of the bewildering discrepancies between recently held party views and Marxist-Leninist theory; there is nonetheless a strong tendency to relate them to 'ideology'. Zinoviev further refers to the two-pronged nature of the concept: 'Ideology, I repeat, has two aspects, the philosophic and the pragmatic'.[37] Perhaps the reason why so much was made by Zinoviev and others of ideology as 'pragmatic' is that a fundamental distinction was drawn between Communism and democracy in terms of function.

If one speaks of a typological difference between Communism and democracy while focusing on the 'pragmatic', one should return to the fundamentals. Democracy is supposed to be 'good' or 'true' because of the assumptions it makes about the nature of man, whereas Communism is supposed to be 'true' because of the determined effect of material circumstances. This difference in provenance has a major effect on the comprehensiveness of the statements made by exponents of the two ideologies and on the way the latter function in society. They are not just two different ways of thinking about man's relations with the State but two fundamentally different ways of conceiving reality and the 'good'. The view projected by Communism is such that inevitably it comes into conflict with democratic society, no matter how peaceable its advocates are as individuals. Furthermore, whatever the argument of Marxist apologists with reference to the 'common roots' of the two ideologies, there is no real resemblance between them because Communism makes a comprehensive statement about the 'good', while democracy makes only a very limited pronouncement.

This difference is obscure because of the traditional interpretation of 'tolerance' as an aspect of 'enlightened sovereignty'. Thus the task of the sovereign power is simplified if it remains above normative disputes in the community. Although this stance served well enough so long as the State itself was not ideologically-based, it has now become untenable. Must a democratic State be 'tolerant' of Communism because the sovereign power should be 'above' normative disputes? The question is considered so fundamental that we tend to define democratic parties according to the answer they give: liberals say 'yes', conservatives say 'no'. The trouble is that neither party can relate its answer to democratic ideology.

Why is this so? Because democratic ideology evolved after the separation of Church and State. It essentially refers to the normative pronouncement made by the State – and only to that. When we speak of democratic tolerance we mean that democratic ideology is 'tolerant' of religion, philosophy, etc. because nothing that it says conflicts with other statements about what is 'true' and 'good'. Naturally, such tolerance does not extend to counter political statements, such as those made by radical ideologies. To argue that it does, would be as absurd as arguing that Catholicism must teach Buddhism so as to demonstrate its universality ('catholicism'). Basically, then, 'tolerance' follows from the fact that democratic ideology is limited ontologically, not by a relativistic attitude to values or some mystical restriction on behaviour induced by the legal system. Under a totalitarian ideology, the situation is entirely different.

Communism is not an advancement on democracy or its permutation: it is ideologically independent. Like science, it originated as an epistemological, not a normative, system. Speaking of ideology with reference to Communism, one speaks not of norms but of a way of interpreting reality as a whole. (The title of Zinoviev's book *The Reality of Communism* is particularly telling.) Within this reality, it is nonsense to speak of tolerance. Democratic norms such as tolerance, equality and liberty are out of place.

DOCTRINE OF A SUPERPOWER

Books which focus on ideology and try to uncover its true role in the Soviet Union and in its foreign policies are rare in the West. The seriousness with which the problem of ideology is analysed in the monograph by R. Judson Mitchell, *Ideology of a Superpower*, entitles this study to closer scrutiny. Because it has a stated purpose that seems both plodding and limited,[38] there is a danger that its thesis will be given inadequate attention. It is perhaps best understood through an historical comparison.

Just as the European powers badly misunderstood the threat posed by Napoleon because they thought of France as projecting a revolutionary ideology and posing a social threat when it was a military threat, so today Communism is being confronted as subversion by an alien ideology when the issue is a 'transition from revolutionary ideology to the ideology of a superpower'.[39] This transition has two elements. First, there has been a shift of emphasis from the systematic to the doctrinal aspects of belief. As a result, internationally the issue is no longer that of gaining adherents to Communist ideology but of encouraging 'fellow travellers', who may even be indifferent to the ideology as an organized system of belief. Second, the consciousness of being a 'superpower' – a major military power – is an important determinant of the doctrinal content of the ideology. In point of fact, Mitchell contends, it no longer matters whether Communism is revolutionary or not.

The reference to 'doctrine' stems from Mitchell's adaptation of A. Ross Johnson's version of Huntington and Brzezinski's analysis of 'three levels of political ideas found in Communist ideology': general philosophic assumptions (like dialectical materialism); doctrinal elements 'indicating the general direction of political action' (like the dictatorship of the proletariat); and specific programmes of political action (like Stalin's 'socialism in one country').[40]

Quoting Johnson, Mitchell notes that 'action programmes are often indistinguishable from policies in a Communist political system' but differ from 'policy' (as our society understands the term) in being specifically related by means of 'doctrine' to the ideology's philosophic elements. 'Doctrine' is defined as the 'politically

crucial link between dogmatic assumptions and pragmatic action'.[41]

The sequence of the terms used – 'politically'; 'dogmatic'; 'pragmatic' – is important: what Mitchell has to say
about the ideology of a superpower rests upon it. The
point he makes is that, first, the revisionism which is
taking place in Communist theory reflects the fact that
the USSR is now a 'superpower' (a concept that refers to
its international relations); and second, that at least some
of this status is attributable to the political advantages
conferred by its capacity to adapt the ideology to current
conditions – so that the 'unchanging' ideology seems to
be always relevant and in the forefront of 'progress'.

Many commentators on Soviet attitudes to ideology
regard the process of theoretical revision cynically, as
evidence that Communists do not believe in their ideology. This view, of course, raises the question of what it is
that they do believe in if they do not believe in Communism. Are we to suppose that at heart Communists are
democrats? Those who hold this cynical view are bound
to assume that ideology does not really matter and are
reduced to thinking in terms of crude behaviouralism.
Mitchell, however, avoids being drawn into such issues
and uses the behavioural evidence of Communist theoreticians themselves: 'Today Leninism is not merely a
theory; it is a doctrine practiced by millions of people'.[42]

As Mitchell observes: 'As described by Yepishev [the
source of the quotation] and other Soviet spokesmen, the
task of theory is the clarification of the linkage between
underlying causative factors and actual patterns of
behavior'.[43]

The word 'doctrine' – as in 'doctrine practiced by
millions' – is useful for it relates ideology to actual
behaviour and both of them to 'causative factors', which
is what behaviouralists want to speak about. But 'doctrine'
is not the same as 'ideology': to understand their mutual
relationship other quotations are needed. Thus: 'Leninism is a theory dealing with the acquisition, uses, and
purposes of political power';[44] it 'is not simply a theory of
force';[45] and further: 'The significance of . . . Soviet

theoretical methodology. . . is that a clear separation between Soviet thought on domestic politics and Soviet thought on international relations is impossible'. Most significant is Mitchell's view that 'there is no Soviet theory of international relations as such; rather. . . the Soviets apply their general theory on social relationships to a range of external phenomena'.[46]

What does this all mean ideologically and in terms of future international relations? Mitchell concludes that 'Soviet policy formation has two bedrocks: the irreducible, minimum goal of survival of the régime (that is, avoidance of bourgeois restoration) and the assumption of the ultimate unification of the world under Soviet leadership'.[47]

CHANGE – 'YES', IDEOLOGY – 'NO'

Mitchell's concern for ideology seems alien to the spirit of the social sciences today. Thus, in his new study that received professional acclaim, Timothy Colton has practically eliminated the concept.[48]

To be sure, Colton does refer to ideology, as on p. 13, where he speaks of the Brezhnev Politburo as using the Marxist ideology for 'legitimation of the status quo'. But such usage is significant: 'legitimation' is the sociologist's equivalent of the psychologist's idea of 'rationalization'. Basically, it means a denial that ideology has a significant political and social function.

Colton's other references to ideology are minimal. Though the first paragraph of Chapter 2 refers to it implicitly, his attitude is most clearly expressed by the formula he uses to analyse what ails the Soviet Union, in the Section 'Old formulas lose their effectiveness' (pp. 39–43). Here Colton speaks of 'the party's system of political education' (presumably, of ideology), but it is clear from the way he does it that he is primarily speaking of 'technology', and of Soviet ineptitude: 'although it did a serviceable job in the early days, it has a good deal less impact on today's better educated. . . public, and it makes stunningly inept use of modern electronic technology'. The argument has shifted from ideology to technology.

How did this happen? Earlier, Colton makes a statement with which it would be hard to disagree: 'The Soviet Union, probably to a greater extent than most countries, lives by time-tested practice. It addresses its major problems with remarkably stable formulas and approaches'. Although it may seem that Colton is saying that Soviet ideologues are doctrinaire, his very next sentence shows that he is not thinking of ideology but of 'formulas' and that his own thinking is formula-oriented. 'The catch,' he says, 'is that sooner or later all old habits generate diminishing returns'.

There is, of course, no 'law of neology', which would make Colton's assertion true. It is not true, for instance, that after a century or so the rule 'Keep to the right' ceases to regulate traffic. This is a case of what one might call the liberal-neoteric fallacy. It rests on the argument that adaptation to change is a good and that therefore change is a good. Since Darwin, it has been impossible to convince anyone that this is a fallacious argument; further, that other ways of arriving at the same conclusion – such as Colton's absurd 'Old habits generate diminishing returns' – are equally misguided. These ways are also quite useless as formulas for analysing the consequences of being a doctrinaire Marxist.

Thus the role of ideology in the USSR – a history-proven factor in Soviet behaviour – has been swept away. One senses the implication that it is aberrant even to acknowledge that ideology may be important. In the end, reading Colton's report proves to be a strange experience. Political science takes on the appearance of a cult which allows its practitioners to worship a new deity called 'Change'.

THE 'HOMOSOS' SYNDROME

What lesson can be derived from Zinoviev's writings, in particular from his book *Homo Sovieticus*? In offering his extraordinary satire to the West, is he not missing his target because he does not fully understand the current Western mind?

He can hardly know, for instance, that we no longer make an intelligible distinction between satire and ridicule. (What is called 'political satire' can become a representation of an American politician as grotesquely aged. But why should a distortion of physical characteristics be considered political satire?)

In genuine satire, caricature is based on graphic presentation of the *reductio ad absurdum* principle of logic, in which it is the logic of viewpoints – not appearances – that is attacked. By nature, although satire is based on logic, it is not confined by the requirement of logic that each step in the analysis be presented. The essential message of all satirists is: 'Do not be misled by the apparent logic of appearances; apply the *reductio ad absurdum* principle and you will see the inherent absurdity'.

Our society stopped distinguishing between appearance and reality when it was decided that 'reality' *is* appearance – the empiricist viewpoint. It was then that the capacity to understand satire was lost. The fact that Zinoviev uses satire suggests he is unaware that most members of our society can no longer understand it. He may also not be aware that it is the empiricist viewpoint that enabled us to be so readily taken in by disinformation by (and about) the Soviet Union.

Zinoviev interprets our credulity by assigning a 'homosos' type of mentality to our society. Speaking of books which 'fuddle the brains of the Western man-in-the-street about Soviet society'[49] he says that they are aimed at 'ignoramuses with a particular mind-set' and that the intellectual level of these ignoramuses is 'no higher than that of a run-of-the-mill Party *apparatchik*'. If many people in the West can be taken in by books and ideas that Zinoviev, among others, recognizes as 'rubbish', this is because there are powerful forces which blur the distinction between appearance and reality. This phenomenon is inspired not by any official ideology (as in the USSR) but by logical positivism. There is now a sort of universal *homo ignoramus* who has replaced the previous species *homo sapiens*. What the man-in-the-street in the West has in common with the run-of-the-mill *apparatchik* is the view that reality is the same as appearance; and that disinformation and lies are 'truth', just because they are disseminated.

But since the gulf between the Soviet and Western man was always wide, one must ask how this can be made clear to the Westerner who remains confused about the nature of 'homosos' and the effects of Communist ideology. It is possible that Western man's ignorance of the former 'homosos' reinforces his habitual underestimation of the role played by the latter.

We make a bad mistake if we adopt the behaviouralist view that observation can show us the factors that make up *homo sovieticus*. The reason is that when adopting behaviouralist procedures we are confronted with an indeterminate number of factors which we have no means of analysing. For the same reason, a behaviouralist type of analysis of the political situation in the Soviet Union was almost certain to lead us astray.

As a general proposition, behaviouralist analysis of a situation of which human beliefs and values are elements, can result only in the view that such beliefs and values are not a factor; that an assertion to the contrary by those who think they do play a part, is an act of 'hypocrisy'. The general nature of this proposition about behaviouralist analysis is due to the circumstance that behaviouralism deals only with observable facts, whereas value systems are about 'ideals'. To the behaviouralist, ideals are not present except as 'fictions' or acts of hypocrisy.

Assuming that there is no point in establishing that people who live under Communism and reputedly act in accord with its ideology are not in fact doing so but, from a behaviouralist point of view, are hypocrites, what exactly is it that a political philosopher can contribute to understanding the 'homosos' syndrome? He can establish that 'homosos' was the opposite of a hypocrite: traditionally and ideologically he was an authoritarian with an inherent tendency to succumb to despotism, and also lacking a genuine sense of liberty – a fact of great importance to an understanding of Communist policy.

COMMUNISM AS COSMOLOGY

Marx's prediction that under Communism the State will wither away is not currently given its original prominence. The matter deserves attention: if we do not grasp its significance, we shall not be able to understand why a Soviet citizen could 'believe in' Communism but also believe that his State was not attempting to put it into practice; or that leaders of the Communist Party could be utterly cynical in their behaviour yet show evidence of thinking like true believers. One should not forget that, for instance, Stalin – the ruthless psychopath – believed sufficiently in the Marxist-based biological theories of Lysenko seriously to endanger the State and, consequently, his own position as head of State. For decades any genuine reform of the system was rendered impossible by the fact that attempts to do so ran counter to Communist theory and were opposed by literally millions of faceless bureaucrats.

The Marxian prediction about the future of Communism can provide the needed explanation: in effect Marx was predicting that even if the State withers away, Communism will remain (more precisely, it will then have been fully achieved). How could he believe such a thing? Putting Marxism aside, in a democracy everyone is convinced that if the democratic State disappeared – or changed into something else – the operative political system could no longer be called 'democratic'. This is because democratic ideology is about the State, society and the individual, and little else. Communist ideology, however, is a cosmology, or an ontology. It is not set forth in a statement about the individual's relation to the State – is not parallel to contractual theory, liberalism, etc. – but is about 'existence' itself, all of it. This being so, the State can of course 'wither away' and Communism remain. It is this position which Communists believe in, no matter how inept, self-seeking and corrupt members of the Party may be.

Thus Communism does not need to be manifested in the State in order to appear 'true'. Such a view grants to the State and ruling party a degree of power that not even Fascism achieved. Under Communism, it was hard to become truly disillusioned with the State's performance, or go beyond a wish for better days ahead. An ideological stance of this type is so foreign to democratic societies that they seemed inclined to think that Soviet Communists were all hypocrites, who professed to be ideologues, yet were longing to escape to capitalism, or awaiting an opportunity to overthrow their oppressive régime.

During the long decades of Communist orthodoxy no such event was likely to occur. This was not because the authorities failed to be vigilant but because the outcome was conceptually impossible. Except for staunch Catholics, Jews and others whose ontological conceptions cut Communism down to size as an economic theory with political overtones, there was no alternative to Communism for anyone raised to believe in its validity as an account of man's position in the universe.

GORBACHEV: POWER AND THE RELEVANCE OF IDEOLOGY

The Soviet system was the 'offspring of an historical concept' (Marxism) and an 'ideological society'. In the words of Vladimir Bukovsky, 'You cannot change any part of it without offering an internally consistent set of ideological and historical reasons'.

Did Gorbachev refer his action to ideology? During his first three or four years in office there were indications that he favoured the restitution of some early, 'pure' values of Marxism; that he was for the promotion of a 'sophisticated' form of international class struggle through 'all human' dialectics;[50] and that he rejected Stalinism but respected Leninism.[51] He thus gave a nod to ideology but made no attempt to use it as a vehicle of reform. Thus, initially he showed no sign of breaking away from the ideological tradition; Gorbachevism did not mean a rejection of ideology but rather its purification – which could have entailed a new kind of orthodoxy.

What made it difficult to obtain a clear perception of the Gorbachev phenomenon?

1   While, under Communism, strategy is rooted in ideology, regular reassertions of strategic goals have a deep entrenching impact on ideology itself. Before *perestroika* upset it all, the continuing role of ideology had traditionally been assured; it was unremittingly kept alive in men's minds. Nothing comparable exists in the West. As a rule, governments have no long-range strategy or ideological prescriptions that can direct action. To be sure, they can (and occasionally do) focus on a set of democratic principles and values – of a general and abstract nature – that can justify a certain action but can seldom offer a clear choice.

2   The sceptical Western attitude to ideology made it possible to accept Gorbachev's words while disregarding his deeds (or lack of them). It was also an important factor in his popularity in the West. The fact that until 1990 he refrained from renouncing Marxism-Leninism outright did not seem to worry most Westerners. It was consonant with their turn of mind to dismiss something which, in their opinion, did not have any real existence in the first place.

3   The Brezhnev doctrine entrenched the USSR in the role of an ideological guardian of its satellites. In July 1989 Gorbachev renounced the Brezhnev doctrine; subsequently he did not interfere with the demise of Communist régimes in East Central Europe. But this abandonment of the ideological grip was not total: it did not extend to the Third World. The result was an ideological empire 'with a hole in the middle'. In the words of the American analyst Charles H. Fairbanks, Jr., 'the Soviet Empire [was] more and more assuming the doughnut form latent in ideological empires'.[52] There was no consistency in Gorbachev's attitude to ideology.

4   There were other examples of inconsistency. Thus his article on 'The Idea of Socialism and the Revolutionary *Perestroika*' (*Pravda*, 26 November 1989) reaffirmed: (a) the goal of 'humane socialism' consistent with Marxism-Leninism and (b) the importance of the October Revolution. It also refused to reject (a) the primacy of public property and (b) the importance of 'centralism' and planning. Earlier, in a speech to students he spoke of preserving the Marxist-Leninist ideology cleansed of 'dogmatism, scholasticism and arbitrary interpretation'. (*Pravda*, 16 November 1989). He saw the role of the Communist Party as crucial: 'The party was and remains the main organizing and coordinating force . . . playing an integrating and rallying role in society and . . . preventing an undesirable . . . turn of events'. (Party meeting of 28 September 1989 reported in *The New York Times* 8 February 1990.)

Yet, unexpectedly, in 1990 *perestroika* was used to pull down the ideological structure. What followed can be seen as moves to dismantle the official ideology: (a) At the meeting of the CP's Central Committee it was decided that the primacy of the Party should be abolished (Presumably the issue of ending the CP's monopoly of power was to be settled at the next Party Congress.) Thus Gorbachev: 'We should abandon the ideological dogmatism that became engrained during past decades, outdated stereotypes in domestic policy and outmoded views on the world revolutionary process and world development'. (Speech of 5 February 1990, reported by *The New York Times* of 6 February 1990.) (b) A few days later, on 13 February, the principle of class struggle was dropped. (c) In March it was decided to restore the citizen's right to obtain land from the State. Legalization of citizens' ownership of factories and other means of production was enacted quickly: it was approved by the Supreme Soviet on 6 March and ratified by the Congress of People's Deputies on 13 March. Yet, as was quickly pointed out, the new legislation was not a fundamental reform. It stopped short of introducing 'ordinary' private property and augured no radical change in society. (Adam Kruczek, '*W sowieckiej prasie*' ['In Soviet Press'], *Kultura*, April 1990, p. 110).

5   In considering the Western reaction to Gorbachev in terms of ideology, the question that should have been asked was: 'Do we interpret *glasnost* and *perestroika* as democratization?' Straightforward as the question may seem, it is quite ambiguous for democratic society to hold two different concepts of democracy (and apply them inconsistently in appraising the 'democratic' nature of other societies). In formalist democracy, the emphasis is on majority rule, limits to the franchise, the presence of more than one party, fixed terms of office, and so forth. In conceptions of ideological democracy, on the other hand, the emphasis is on the effect on social and political institutions of the abstract norms 'equality' and 'individualism' (as in debates about equal schooling, distribution of income, freedom of speech, etc.). We have never integrated these two conceptions of democracy – this hardly matters insofar as the direction of democratic societies is concerned; however, it makes it difficult and even misleading to apply the concepts 'democracy' and 'democratization' outside our own societies. The problem arises when we try to understand *glasnost, perestroika,* and Gorbachev's behaviour. Are we looking at form, ideology or something else?

What must raise doubts about Gorbachevism as some kind of democratization is that nothing he did or said was represented by him or anyone else as 'democratization' in terms of the democratic *ideology*. (Since we ourselves have no clear notion of the relationship between formalist and ideological democracy, we deceived ourselves by being optimistic about the future direction of the USSR.) Even if Gorbachev was sincere, and saw *glasnost* and *perestroika* as solutions to the very obvious problems the USSR was facing, there was no reason to suppose that the Soviet Union was moving towards 'democracy', the ideological concept.

Ideology as an instrumental device

Gorbachev's attitude to dialectics was ambivalent and the instrumentalism which guided his politics added a measure of unpredictability. Yet, instrumentalism is essential in a discussion of the interrelationship between ideology and power. Under Soviet Communism its ideology had always to be realized pragmatically; the 'scientific' element in Marxism reinforced instrumentalism, which served those in power.

Instrumentalism is not a label attached to Communist policy-makers by Western analysts as a matter of course. One of the reasons may be that instrumentalism – Dewey's version of pragmatism – has been seen as so typically American that many European philosophers often ignore the question it raises, and even the function it has served. Pragmatism, for instance, has been of major importance in adjusting classical education to contemporary conditions. In view of the 'knowledge explosion', those raised as scholars would in fact, under the classical conception, be dilettantes if it were not for the pragmatist requirement that knowledge as a good be related to how one earns a living, or – in other words – to one's specialization.

It is absurd, of course, that we define good and truth in terms of the 'cash value' – to use Dewey's daring phrase – and in order to retain philosophic detachment, most philosophers have found it necessary to reject such a view. So has our society-at-large. However, its appropriateness to Communism – especially to those in power under its régime – is obvious, for the concepts of 'true' and 'good' are for them definable in terms of advantage. Instrumentalism is an ideal working philosophy for the activist and the arrogant, for those who are seeking power or having power and are not too particular about the means. It does not deal with the existentialist question: 'What am I doing here, a mere cog in the machine who is somehow aware he is a cog?' It does not work for those constrained by 'rule of law' conceptions.

For this reason, in the American setting, instrumentalism never moved very far from the market-place: it was relevant to the notion of science as a good or 'the good', as well as the conversion of many American universities into what in effect are trade schools. When in the 1960s its principles were adopted by hippies to defend an artificial leisure class (people on welfare), hippies and their version of instrumentalism were persecuted with a ferocity similar to that formerly reserved for heretics.

Instrumentalism remained a philosophy of the workplace because it is too relativistic to allow even for democratic ideology. If 'democracy' is but a set of institutions – regular elections, majority rule, adult suffrage, etc. – instrumentalism accords with practice; but if 'democracy' is thought of as having an ideological base such that individualism as a norm constrains 'equality' in its institutional form (majority rule) and equality constrains individualism in an institutionalized form (*laissez-faire*), it is not clear what one is supposed to do with regard to instrumentalism.

Suppose, however, that the society we are examining has always regarded its principles as forms – a 'party' as determining 'truth' (policy), a 'constitution' etc. – or as a 'system' for arriving at truth (the dialectic). Under such conditions, the workplace which is being served is that of officialdom and the determining factor is, of, course, retaining office (power).

Events in East Central Europe in the winter of 1989–90 provided some striking examples of rationalization by some East German *apparatchiki* who were voted out of office. 'The people' – they argued – do not know their own interests; they need assistance from a party truly committed to their interests – the CP'. Their stance was hardly surprising. What we now propose to explain by instrumentalism has long been called 'hypocrisy'. (The latter, incidentally, may be an inappropriate term to apply to an ideological situation, for it implies an 'ought' in respect to the belief: ought Communists to believe in Communism?) An incidental benefit of using instrumentalism in this situation is to get rid of, first, the (absurd) implication that most people 'ought' to be Communists, second, the belief that critics of Communism respect the ideology when it is orthodox.

But rationalizing our own past errors in analysis is of no real significance when what we really want to know is the direction of real *glasnost* (cum *perestroika*) which would involve an abandonment of notions of 'orthodoxy' in favour of a dynamic conception of truth. This is precisely what the 'dialectic' was supposed to supply: 'truth' within a framework of flux, as a way of defining 'progress' in the absence of a definable goal. This is also what instrumentalism is when the mystical elements of the dialectic are removed. Gorbachev's action was 'realistic' – a Lysenko affair was no longer conceivable – but, because some of the Marxian goals, such as the classless society and distributive justice seemed to have been abandoned, it was also unpredictable. (When ideology reigned supreme, what the Party – or government – would do was fairly predictable.) Gorbachev has thus taken the weakest element in Marx, the dialectic, and converted its mysticism into opportunism, or turned it into instrumentalism.

Was Gorbachev himself able to foresee the future? Hardly. We confused ourselves when sneering at Marx for defining as the good a particular end to the dialectical process – the classless society in which the State has withered away. Marx, however, must have realized that the dialectic needs a goal if it is to be defined as the means to an end ('truth') or a statement about the nature of the truth. Gorbachev freed his hand by getting rid of some orthodox goals and left potential enemies at a loss, for they had no real way of deciding exactly what he was up to. There was abundant evidence of contradictory moves on his part. Despite the frequent claims by observers – both internal and external – that the changes were 'irreversible', the issue was by no means clear in the summer of 1991.

Gorbachevism and After

Gorbachevism did not at first presage the abandonment of Marxism-Leninism but a cautious ideological renewal. Marxist-Leninist 'praxis' (the dogma of the 'unity of theory and practice') had been discredited by the mid-1980s.[53] Gorbachev moved gingerly, careful not to blur the image of Lenin-the-Guru, while spouting libertarian slogans. Predictably, the position became untenable: the ideology entrenched since the October Revolution had long ago lost its ironclad quality and its immunity to challenge; the door to dissent was ajar. The coup of August 1991 confirmed that Gorbachev was intent on saving the system while taking it out of the totalitarian shell. But the system, as we know it, is not reformable.

The Communist system is not reformable because of ideology. Once ideology is taken out or is allowed to wither away – as it was in most of Eastern Europe in the 1980s – the system becomes dysfunctional and is ready to collapse. This is why the Soviet Union as it was known for seven decades ceased to exist in 1991. (This is also why all former Communist States are having such a hard time transforming themselves into free market democracies.) A Communist State is like a cast-iron artifact: if you try to chip off some of its parts, the whole disintegrates. Gorbachev, the pragmatist, tinkered with ideology opportunely, using it selectively in support of his actions, which were designed to keep him in power: a tactic of political survival. By the time of the August 1991 putsch, ideology was eliminated from the parlance of all and sundry:[54] no references were made either to 'Marxism' or even to the 'abandonment of Marxism'. Pure pragmatism prevailed. Writing only a few days before the coup, Gorbachev noted: 'Society is rapidly freeing itself from ideology'.[55] He emphatically renounced the totalitarian past: 'A system created according to the rules of tyranny and totalitarianism could no longer be tolerated'.[56]

But statements like these were as grossly belated as his actions were indecisive. Thus, the banning of the Communist Party was largely due to the impact of Yeltsin's stance and leadership. It was the force of events that led to the disintegration of the Communist political and economic structures and terminated the viability of the Soviet Union as a State. After the August coup visitors noted a non-ideological mood prevailing in the country, which was about to witness the dissolution of the USSR by the end of the year and the eclipse of Gorbachevism.

To conclude, in the past the official ideology continued to exist in a recognizable form only when linked with the power structure: it must personally have mattered to vested interests of the *apparat* that the ideology should continue as it did. It is the importance of Communism to the power structure that made it relevant (or irrelevant) in the USSR. Gorbachev hesitated too long to renounce the doctrine and gave the *coup de grâce* to the Party much too late for his own benefit; in all likelihood, he was unable to discard his deep-seated belief in the instrumental link between ideology and power. When he began to doubt the existence of such a link – as he must have – his power evaporated.

A note is needed concerning some comments on what has been happening in relation to the collapse of Communism and the reaction of those on the left who cannot come to terms with that collapse.

Most of the recent comments by authors of all persuasions reflect reasoning from the 'pragmatic' point of view: Communism has not 'worked', therefore it is not 'true', and that is that. Of course, no 'true' Communist whose outlook has remained unchanged believes anything of the sort. But there are others – let us call them the 'millenarians' – who think likewise. The actual collapse of Communist régimes is of no real importance to those who value 'classlessness' (a lack of social order and authority) and look forward to a fuzzy sort of millennium, harbouring a conviction that things could be better than they are, though just how is not all that clear. Communism to them (or an ideology disguised as 'socialism') still offers the promise of being in accord with that vague sense of social good and promise of something 'better'. Until people are compelled to recognize that for more than two millennia political philosophy has been trying to make human beings more specific about what they are assuming and what they are desiring, there is little reason to conclude that the Communist faith has been defeated and obliterated. Its bits and pieces appeal to some 'millenarians' who may have rejected the original theological part of the concept while accepting its materialist incarnation as a possibility.

The demise of Communist power does not mean an 'end of ideology'. The future of orthodoxy – as in China – is still uncertain. But at least two ideological trends should be noted: first, we have witnessed in the West a radicalism surfacing in a new form such as 'political correctness', a sort of Trojan horse that the Communist besiegers of liberal democracy left behind, prior to their retreat; second, within the former USSR – a shift of ideological focus to the quasi-ideology of nationalism.

An alarming legacy of Communism is the combination of self-righteousness and violence that manifests itself (primarily) in North America as 'political correctness', for this is likely to be reinforced by the collapse of the power structure in the former Soviet Union. Advocates of 'political correctness' are not likely to miss the obvious message that an ideology loses ground when it cannot be enforced.

Western societies repudiated the use of coercive measures to enforce beliefs long ago as a result of the Wars of Religion, imbuing the relations between State and society with the norm 'tolerance' and evolving the concept of the separation of Church and State. Communism, by professing to be 'scientific' – and offering the 'whole truth' – was unable to accept such a division of authority; hence, when instituted, it has seen nothing wrong with enforcing its ideology.

Viewed from outside the results seemed impressive: the combination of power and ideology appeared to produce a degree of unity and unanimity that no democracy ever achieved. Although this 'unity' now appears to have been an illusion, there can be no doubt that some advocates of 'political correctness' (not to speak of their early doctrinaire radical mentors) were impressed; and that their opinion is not likely to change as a result of the collapse of the enforcing agencies. Lately, the vigour of political correctness has increased together with the weakening of the power structure that enforced Communism. Thus, one feels that advocates of political correctness are using events in Europe to justify their own increasing coerciveness (and violence) much as if they were saying to themselves: 'You see what weakness and loss of power entail? They mean the loss of ideals!'

Within the Communist empire, however, the breakdown of power to enforce the ideology has allowed nationalism to surface and – at least for the moment – to serve as a sort of interim ideology, as it did in the nineteenth century when it served as a precursor of democracy.

Nationalism is a concept of 'society' rather than a genuine political ideology. It tells us which national or ethnic group we identify with, but cannot itself perform the function of ideology. Indeed, if one tries to make it function like this, one is likely to move in the direction of Fascism rather than democracy. What we have to keep in mind – what the emerging nation-States of the former Communist empire must remember – is that modern democracy is not just a 'rule of the people' (nation, presumably) but a set of principles and political institutions adapted to the expression of principles (or norms). It does not have a great deal to do with 'majority rule'.

Obviously the members of the former Communist empire have to insist on 'nationalism' – and to repudiate the doctrine which contended that nationalism was of no ideological importance; but this repudiation will not be enough to ensure anything that could be called democracy or that will enable the emerging nations to function as States. The absence of an adequate ideology (where one is badly needed) is another troubling legacy of Communism and is liable to cause very serious international problems for years to come owing to the emergency of a cluster of unstable and perhaps nonviable States.

Chapter 22

Sources of Western incomprehension

PHILOSOPHICAL HERITAGE: THE ELIMINATION OF 'MIND' AND 'ORDER'

Political theory still represents an intellectual tradition which other disciplines have discarded under the influence of empiricism. Except in periods of 'cold war', the theorist's argument that Communism constitutes a threat is usually greeted with frank disbelief. The stance adopted is that now the facts do not clearly show Communism to be a threat; hence 'peace lovers' (those who do not like the *angst* induced by threats) regard political theorists as troublemakers and spokesmen for reaction.

There are two ways of dealing with such an attitude. One is to show – by means of factual analysis of events and situations (e.g. the invasion of Afghanistan or the attempt to assassinate the Pope) or through historical analysis of the Communist policy of aggression and of life in Communist countries – that the belief that all is now well and the cold war behind us is an illusion fostered by Communist disinformation. This approach, while of interest to specialists, does not have much effect on the general public; findings of this type require a scholar's attention to detail and the average reader cannot be expected to understand them.

Another approach would make a case for the ideological view: the immediate facts – or what appear to be such – are not the determining factors; disinformation is effective because most people are empiricists and hope for the best about the validity of what they regard as facts. Unless this view is changed, it is hard to see how its adherents are likely to regard Communism as a threat so long as Communists want them to think otherwise (even to look on Communism favourably). Control of the situation should be taken out of the hands of Communists and placed where it belongs, that is, in the minds of the believers: an intelligent person ought to be able to decide for himself what the truth about Communism is.

This is not the case today – not because of the intrinsic power of Communism or disinformation, but because a few centuries ago our society initiated a line of thought that ultimately led to the view that there is no such thing as 'mind'. (It is a 'ghost in a machine', says Ryle.) Hence things that mind manipulates – e.g. ideologies – must appear equally 'illusory' and of 'no consequence'.

(It is implied that only behaviouralists can have anything important to say about Communism, and if Communists mislead them by disinformation it is very mean of them; what else can be done except perhaps inform them that spreading disinformation is unscientific?)

The philosophical roots of the present incomprehension are in the *tabula rasa* concept as revived by Locke: at birth, the mind is a clean slate or does not exist. In itself, the concept is designed only to get rid of simplistic 'explanations' of human behaviour which beg the question – such as 'conscience' as an explanation of morality, and 'instinct' as an explanation of whatever one is too lazy to analyse, as when using 'gregariousness' to explain State and society. The *tabula rasa* hypothesis disallowed such 'explanations' and promoted 'reason'.

Reason as a concept presupposes 'mind'; hence the idea that even if we are not born with a 'mind', we develop one as the result of experience. Furthermore, 'mind' will be (a) unique to the individual and thus entails respect for the individual (a basic democratic and Christian view) and (b) unique to our species (man is the 'rational' animal; our behaviour, such as the use of language and morals, is also unique).

Then came Hume and – shortly after him – even

stricter and narrower empirical views. Hume argued against the influence of 'reason' ('Reason is the slave of the passions'), in effect saying that we do not develop a 'mind' as a result of experience but remain always on exactly the same level as other animals. A century later, this led to Pavlov's experiments with 'conditioned response' and the assumption that what is true of dogs is also true of human beings; also to the further assumption that 'animal behaviourism' and 'behaviourism' have a common basis and that any doubts about this – such as those of political theorists who are convinced that there is no such thing as a Communist dog or cat – are 'unscientific'.

In terms of rationality, order, and ideology, Hume is important because his views eliminated not only 'mind' from the species *homo sapiens* but order from the universe: if 'mind' reflects a learnable order then there must be an order to be learned. But if man acts on, and is 'successful' as a result of acting on disorder – 'passion' – then obviously there is no such order to be learned. Man does not have a 'mind' and does not need one because the universe itself lacks order (and presumably a source of order such as 'God').

This view led directly to (is indistinguishable from) 'associationism' – the dominant psychological (ethical and rational) theory. It states that human beings are completely dependent on chance associations acquired by experience; this is purportedly not disadvantageous because there really is nothing else. Whatever is, is; to speak of something else is to be merely 'speculative': a deadly sin to empiricists.

Speaking about 'something else' – about, for instance, ideologies, which by definition are mental contents rather than things as they are – characterizes the philosophically-minded who thus (a) assume there is a mind; (b) supply it with a content; (c) assert that the content affects behaviour (what 'is'); (d) assert (usually) that the mind's content is more important than current behaviour because it is about past, present and future, whereas 'behaviour' (and behaviouralism) is only about immediate circumstances.

The above view does not rest on some curious pre-occupation with 'ideology', but on a view about 'mind' and 'reason' that has not been overthrown by 'science', 'philosophy' or anything else. Rather it has got lost by the wayside as a result of attempts to simplify the problems of developing a scientific methodology.

IDEOLOGY AND HYPOCRISY

If in Western Europe the consequence of eighteenth-century analysis has been doubt about ideologies as a force in human affairs, the consequence of not having such a tradition has been much more serious. In a work written in the 1930s,[57] Basil Willey suggested that the trouble with Russia was that it never had an eighteenth century. The implication is that if it is not a part of one's intellectual tradition to doubt one's own motives, the opportunities for self-deception are enormously increased; when this happens, hypocrisy, deceit and double-dealing can become a policy which overshadows the ideology that reputedly motivates us.

If such was the implication, a similar comment can be made about the political views of those (liberals and others) who seem to think democratic conceptions originated with J.S. Mill. In Western tradition Hume's analysis requires us to question our motives. Hume's views are not statements about what we should do but how we should think about our thinking: we can think about Hume but cannot act on what he says. This is why Burke, using Hume's analysis of human motivations, argued that we should rely on what social experience has established as valid, and be very wary of what 'reason' asserts to be the good. Reason and logic make sense but not when defined as such by people who are justifying their actions. This is what Burke got out of Hume. He was right in believing that failure to hold such views is likely to encourage hypocrisy and deceit. Eighteenth-century ideas are necessary to understand what is happening in the twentieth century.

J.S. Mill argued for a 'liberty' based on doubt about

belief rather than doubt about the motive for belief – which ignored what Hume said and Burke believed. Basically, this is why today's liberals and conservatives do not understand each other although their fundamental attitude to democracy is much the same. When we speak about liberals, conservatives and democratic socialists, we usually mean they are agreed about the democratic ideology – though not agreed about human psychology – whereas when speaking of non-democratic socialists – Communists – we mean they hold to a different ideology.

Those who assume that Communism is like any other ideology – that it is an accident of circumstance that makes one a Marxist, rather than a conservative or a democratic socialist – are unconsciously using their own ideology to understand another ideology. The viewpoint is that of a liberal democrat and is not acceptable even to a democratic socialist. Liberals conceive of democratic tolerance as requiring them to place all ideologies on the same level (differences being a matter of individual psychology). Consequently, the liberal mind produces an attitude to Communism that serves the interests of Communist countries.

The liberal misconception about the 'equality' of ideologies is particularly naïve in view of the demands made upon the individual by institutionalized Communism. When institutionalized – when it is an established ideology (what one renders unto Caesar in terms of belief) – Communism most certainly is not like other ideologies. It is all-devouring: the assertion it makes about belief is such that one is required to render unto Caesar not only what is Caesar's but what have traditionally been the prerogatives of taste, manners, piety, science and so forth. Everything becomes subject to positive law: the State becomes totalitarian. Communism is totalitarian because it not only provides a 'complete' normative system, but also controls the way in which it is to be interpreted. The decision as to what the ideology says is taken away from the individual believer and given to the head of the Party. Consequently, there is no possible way of making a valid objection to what is said or done in the name of Communism. Anyone who raises an objection deserves, by that very fact, to be treated as insane or guilty of treason.

According to a statement (made in 1986) attributed to the sovietologist Jerry Hough, 'ideology is a set of ideas through which people affirm their loyalty', and in the USSR it serves the political leader as a 'form of policy guidance'.[58] The assertion that ideology still played a crucial role under Communism has been questioned by many critics of Communist régimes (both internal 'dissidents' and others living under Communism, and external observers). Why did Hough appear at times to take the position that this controversial issue had been definitely settled? What matters is the definition given to ideology; also, why a particular definition is used at a particular time.

Here is what Hough had to say about ideology a few years ago:

> The word 'ideology' is no longer defined as it once was by the theorists of totalitarianism ('a reasonably coherent body of ideas concerning practical means of how to change and reform a society'), but has reverted to the meaning used by Karl Mannheim and many others: the rationalizations that legitimate and support the dominant interests in a society.[59]

The significant difference between these two definitions is that the first one (by the 'theorists of totalitarianism') adopts the position rejected by Hume's analysis of motivations, while the second is an attempt to give meaning to ideology while taking into account (consciously or unconsciously) the analysis made by Hume (and those who followed the Humean view, such as the Freudians). If man is not a 'rational animal' in the sense of being rationally motivated, then what is represented as capable of serving as a rational motivation – an ideology – must serve some other function. Consequently, one of the tests for both behaviouralists and political theorists is deciding what this function is. Many theorists today tend to behave like behaviouralists: when discussing theory they think it incapable of functioning in the way conceived by classical philosophers. They do not think man has the psychological characteristics formerly attributed to him. Most people today think of man as a 'naked ape' rather than as *homo sapiens*. They approach the political scene accordingly: a 'naked ape' can employ knowledge in the service of his drives – as Hume said – but his actual motivation cannot differ from that of the hairy apes, who, as is well known, have no ideologies.

These issues were widely – though confusingly – discussed in the 'end of ideology' debates and after, but it looks as if the basic issues were left unresolved. With reference to Communist ideology, some writers speak of 'hypocrisy' whilst other speak of 'affirming loyalty'; amazingly enough, both are speaking of the same thing. These seemingly inconsistent viewpoints are expressions of the same basic proposition: that an ideology does not determine the behaviour of those professing it. I suspect the basic issues will not be resolved, for they ultimately raise the question of whether we are part of a mechanistic system, which is not the kind of question that can be resolved. The best one can do is decide which stance is congenial to one's outlook.

In his study *The Soviet Union and Social Science Theory*, Hough discusses the Soviet Union as an attempt to put into practice the theories of Communism – their use in policy guidance. Such a position implies that ideas do affect behaviour, or it presents a pre-Humean position; yet it is clear from Hough's other statements – when he speaks of 'affirming loyalty' – that the principal influence on his views about the function of ideas is post-Humean. Could it be that he has not resolved for himself what the function of an ideology can be and is therefore very vague about what the function actually is?

It could be argued that, as a working system of government, Communism is inherently cynical because as an ideology it presupposes a logically impossible psychological state – co-operation, not just co-operativeness – and consequently ensures that in practice someone will have to enforce the necessary cooperation and be a dictator. (If you believe in Communism as a workable system, you must have a totalitarian personality.) However, this view misses the fundamental issue, which is a version of the chicken and egg problem: which comes first, an ideology or an actual system of government?

Pragmatically this question matters a great deal, for one is bound to ask whether by now Communists in office should differ from ideological Communists. More generally, however, the question is about 'mind' and the definition of man: is he *homo sapiens* or a 'naked ape'?

If we are naked apes, the question is one of how we managed to put on clothes at a time when there was no such thing as clothes; if on the other hand we belong to the species *homo sapiens*, the answer is obvious. What political theorists have been trying to say is that putting on one's clothes is not really a problem; that if behaviouralists do not understand it, then it is because they begin with the Humean view – that there is no such thing as 'mind' (and therefore no major difference between man and ape, or between 'big ape' and 'head of State'). Political philosophers think there is a difference, but they have had problems in convincing the kind of people who have doubts about the thinking process and the motivation preceding the putting on of clothes. Such people have doubts about 'mind', as well as about ethics and commonsense – two concepts that political theorists regard as central to what the members of State do.

THE CONSEQUENCES OF INCOMPREHENSION

Critics of Communism naturally do not expect to be patiently listened to by Communists, but they expect adherents of democracy to listen. If however their attack is fundamental, they are likely to be shunned, for their strong objection is taken as proof of threatened self-interest rather than of a desire to point out a logical or ethical flaw. The basic assumption is that only moderate criticisms of Communism can be valid. All others are 'paranoid'. The practical consequence is that only liberal objections are given a fair hearing; conservative views are rejected. The explanation for this now common fact of politics is that a basic element in Communist belief is part of Western thinking: one's values reflect one's class position; only those fundamentally threatened will feel strongly about Communism as a 'menace'. The stronger the voices of critics of Communism, the more stridently they are accused of self-interest; the more cogent their reasoning, the more skilful the rationalization offered by their opponents. Since democracy does not believe in entrenched privilege, it follows that the most severe critics of Communism become (in the eyes of the liberal-minded) more of a threat to the democracy they claim to be defending than to the Communism they profess to be attacking.

This paranoid view of reality in which genuine criticism is seen as hypocritical – and only trivial and innocuous objections considered valid – has led to a general withdrawal of conservatives from public affairs. We are back to the belief of many eighteenth-century Christian stoics: when everyone is crazy, the best plan is to retire to one's study. Although this may have been the proper response in the eighteenth century (though Burke did not think so), such an attitude is imprudent. It is democratic societies that have become 'paranoid' about objections to Communism.

Despite appearances, Communist reasoning is relativistic rather than normative: what is later in time is superior, even when a materialist conception of what is taking place excludes teleology; the concept of 'progress' becomes a materialist's method of giving a normative direction to change. What is later in time is 'better', provided it accords with the authority of what someone like Marx says 'logically' follows. (Thus if Marx said that 'logically' the contradictions in capitalism will lead to its elimination, then the seizure of private property by the State is 'progress'.) In this sense, under Communism, ultimately the 'ought' statements do *not* derive from facts.

Our society would be both materialist and relativist even if Marx had never existed. The ultimate source of

Marxian and scientismic relativism and materialism is Hume. However, it is the Communist method of representing their political and normative order as a 'scientific' solution to the axiological problems posed by empiricism that makes the method attractive to some people (both thinking and unthinking), who like to suppose that anyone who resists the 'latest thing' is by definition misguided (or a 'reactionary').

If anyone doubts that Communism has had a major impact on our normative thinking, let him consider the fact that in North America 'conservative' is a 'boo' word today. When people are reluctant to be so labelled, we can be certain that Marxian thought has been at work. The democratic ideology itself does not rate conservatism either as an error or a dubious form of democracy.

Because we have incorporated elements of Marxian ideology into our own conceptions of ideology, it is impossible for most people to think of Communism as a threat of any kind. They may think of the former USSR or China as a threat, or even little Cuba, but not 'Communism'. This is because almost everyone thinks of an ideology in the way Communists do – as something reflecting conditions within a society. Following that line of thought, people assume Communism cannot be a 'threat' to democratic States; instead, it is a 'remedy' for bad social and economic conditions.

For this reason, many of the staunchest supporters of the democratic way of life are also the most complacent. It seems impossible to convince the beneficiaries of democratic capitalism that there is, or could be, a threat to their way of life from anything so tenuous as an 'ideology'. Paradoxically, the greater the amount of evidence available showing that Communism is an absurd and impractical social and economic system, the more certain most people are that Communism could not pose a threat.

This incomprehension of ideology has serious implications which the citizens of Western societies ought to face. They should take notice of the message coming repeatedly from those who have lived under Communism. It is: do not believe the theory which says that there cannot be anything really wrong with Communist societies so long as their members (of the 'homosos' type) profess support; do not suppose you need no defence against Communism just because your own system is clearly superior.

Part V

Conclusion

Chapter 23

Towards a definition of ideology

From the perspective of this study, ideology is seen as a *system of ideas used to comprehend socio-political reality*. Why is one more definition offered when so many exist? What are the assumptions behind such a general definition and what precisely should be excluded from it?

The concept of ideology, which historically could be defined as the study of systems of thought (a connotation now obsolete), arose at a time when simple acceptance of elaborate systems of ideas (religious faith) or the practice of a methodology dependent on a set of ideas (science) or the advocacy of new political and social systems as if they were truths (one current sense of ideology), were considered irrational. Ideas were known to influence behaviour and thought to be 'rational' because they were systematized. Ideology differed from epistemology in being limited to ideas affecting behaviour, and to those that were part of a conscious system. In effect, ideology came to exclude both religious and scientific concepts and became a statement about political and social behaviour. As such, however, it has not proved amenable to behaviouralist study, for it presupposed (a) that ideas influence behaviour and (b) that the systematic element implies a 'rational' rather than an 'emotional' influence, so that ideology can be better dealt with by the theorist's analysis than by behaviouralist methodology.

These factors account for a variety of attitudes to – and definitions of – ideology that must bewilder the layman: there seem to be as many definitions as definers. Many of the latter offer statements that make one wonder why they attempt a definition. Ideology seems to them to be an 'illusion' or 'superstition' of some kind rather than an influence on behaviour – an effect rather than a cause.

Such 'behavioural' definitions differ from person to person because they derive from their authors' outlooks and personalities and are not in fact about other people's beliefs (their ideologies). Under the impact of behaviouralism, these authors deny that 'mind' – as something necessary to systematize ideas into an ideology – actually exists (only personalities exist), or if it does, that the resulting system can affect behaviour in the way necessary to a concept of ideology.

Trying to understand human behaviour in non-determinist terms implies accepting the evidence that human beings are capable of acting on teleological principles, of which ideology is one form. Accordingly, let us slightly modify the early sense of ideology that evolved from Destutt de Tracy's 'science of ideas' to imply that there is enough of a separation between mind and body for us to entertain the idea that what happens in the 'mind' affects behaviour. Instead, then, of saying that ideology is 'about' social and political reality, let us say that it is 'used to comprehend' such reality.

What can be said in favour of the word 'comprehend'? If we were all clear about the scientific meaning of 'explain' as opposed to popular meanings, a better word than 'comprehend' would be 'explain'. In science an 'explanation' can function as a prediction: it is not an 'explanation' unless it does so; the 'proof' of the validity of 'explanation' is that it makes prediction possible. Unfortunately, in popular usage an 'explanation' is the correlative of 'understanding': someone has explained, if someone else can say 'I understand'. There is no necessary relationship between such explanations and any other situation, including the situation the explanations are supposed to explain. Such explanations are not about an objective reality but about the mental states of human beings. So long as this confusion exists, some other way of expressing a relationship between 'explanations' and 'action' is necessary. Vague as the word 'comprehend' may be, in the given context it conveys the idea that ideologies both explain situations and create them. Thus, socialists and conservatives are not only the products of certain circumstances (just as behaviouralists say) but also create them because of their ideology (just as theorists say).

How can one justify the brevity of the proposed definition? Definitions of ideology tend to be complicated by qualifications such as 'action-oriented' and 'symbol-directed' – qualifications that are not patently required by the evidence. If we are not to be misled by such definitions, we must remember that Hume argued that 'ideas' cannot determine behaviour. Consequently, when speaking about systems of ideas – ideologies – many authors feel it necessary to specify that ideologies do in fact do so. The result is a misleading distinction between ideology and other systems of thought, such as science and religion, which are also intended to influence behaviour, i.e. are 'action-oriented'. Let us not forget that the pragmatists argued that if ideas are not 'action-oriented' – do not have a cash value – they are not 'true'.

The nature of Hume's argument is such, however, that 'intention' – or 'orientation', as current usage has it – is not enough. Inasmuch as ideologies do in fact influence behaviour, they have to be capable of evoking the factor in human beings – emotion – which Hume said 'causes' behaviour. This means that ideologies must be 'emotive' or have a characteristic of certain words and symbols that Hume's adherents use to explain why – despite what Hume said – 'propaganda', 'advertising', 'rhetoric' and 'poetry' do affect behaviour. Hence definitions of ideology often refer to the 'emotivity' of ideologies and the presence of symbols, images and the like.[1]

IDEOLOGY AND ACTION

Should any reference to 'action' be included in the definition of ideology? Consider the following text: 'A political ideology is a system of beliefs that explains and justifies a preferred political order, either existing or proposed, and offers a strategy (institutions, processes, programs) for its attainment'.[2] The above definition seems more like a definition of a party platform than of ideology. Herbert Waltzer's leading sentence in the paragraph that follows suggests: 'A political ideology is intended to unite people in a political organization capable of effective action'. But it surely cannot be said that *Das Kapital* is not ideological because it is not a revolutionary's handbook, and that consequently Lenin was the first Communist ideologue.

The applicability of the definition, however, is not the point at issue. What matters is the relation between ideology and action. When we speak about ideology in terms of political action, are we speaking about party politics? Is this the reason why behaviouralists, once contemptuous of the topic of ideology, seem to have shifted their ground in recent years? If it is, political theorists and 'positivists' (including behaviouralists) are as far apart as ever on the issue of ideology: to a theorist, party platform and ideology are only tenuously related. Undue emphasis on this relationship reduces the significance of ideology in human affairs.

Ideological issues can be misunderstood if one's attention is confined to the way a government is arrived at, and to the type of legislation passed. Party politics are ideologically irrelevant, as are the personal values of political leaders. It is to the issue of freedom – as understood by Burke and his contemporaries – that one should look for the essence of ideology. To give a modern example, an understanding of Communism cannot be gained by merely studying Five Year Plans (the Communist equivalent of party platforms) or the personalities of Communist leaders.

The same applies to democratic politics and ideology. If this fact were understood by behaviouralists, some of the issues they now find so baffling would be clarified. Why did many Republicans not desert the party when Nixon was shown to be both dishonourable (not a true Republican) and dishonest? Why do many leftists tolerate a right-wing government and vice versa? What is it about ideology that makes this possible when, if ideology were what behaviouralists think it is, such behaviour would be completely out of the question?

Given that what we now call ideology was formerly discussed under the concept 'liberty', Burke's explanation seems the best. When speaking about liberty, we speak about a way of life: the argument cannot be reduced to a mere slogan or platform. For this reason, an adequate definition of ideology must be of a general nature: a system of ideas used to comprehend socio-political reality.

FUNCTIONAL AND NON-FUNCTIONAL DEFINITIONS OF IDEOLOGY

Definitions of ideology, like ethical theories, fall into two categories: functional and non-functional; consequently, when assessing such definitions one must ask whether they assume a function or not.

When appraising definitions of ideology we need to keep in mind the history of the concept – that it followed upon contractualism, which in the minds of many people it virtually replaced, with the result that a common argument against contractualism today is that it says nothing of the normative issues dealt with by ideology. Political ideologies need to be appraised in the same way as ethical propositions.

Contractualism served the historic function of defending the State's authority when all authority was being questioned (during the Reformation) by arguing that the State is not a purely coercive institution, since rational human beings choose to accept such coercion. This position ceased to be an adequate account of man's relation to the State when the moral authority of the Church was beclouded by the 'Enlightenment' and the rise of science. Willy-nilly, the State had to take over a good deal of the moral authority of the Church: ideologies represent various attempts to do so, being 'totalitarian' when they attempt to replace the Church entirely, as under Fascism and Communism, and 'democratic' when they adopt to a varying degree the 'charitable' – or social – functions of the Church.

The purpose of the above capsule history of the last four hundred years of political theory is to provide a basis for the appraisal of ideologies in the way that ethical systems are appraised, as well as a framework for an assessment of definitions of ideology.

A difficulty arises: do ideologies serve a function, or are they merely a reflection of something else? This problem is seldom recognized as such; philosophers dismiss it complacently as unworthy of their attention: they are out to discover and appraise 'truth' and have no time for pragmatic issues.

Political theorists cannot be so high-handed. For them, it is beside the point to debate the 'truth' of Communism when the real issue is its propagation and promotion, usually by irrational means such as subversion. But Communism is not entirely dependent on coercion and manipulation since it provides its own specific system of instrumentalist ethics. Any definition of Communism has to take such facts into account.

Modern behavioural relativists lack the tradition that makes function an integral part of the concept of ideology. They may incorporate in their definitions observed facts about the relationship between human behaviour and ideological views, but their commitment as behaviouralists is to the influence of material circumstances such as economic conditions, party factions, personalities; their references to ideological function come as an afterthought. They may see this function as 'rationalization'.

Such indeed is the case with Herbert Waltzer's discussion (in a political theory text, to be sure) of 'Functional Theories of Ideology',[3] in which the emphasis is on some 'psychological need' for ideology – basically as a rationalization of 'real' motives, which according to psychoanalysts are not know to the rationalizer. There is ample precedent for such a view in modern relativism, most of whose theories are also non-functional, based on the assumption that man could do without ethics. Indeed, any theory of the State, ideology or ethics which presents opinion about them as reflections of 'something else' – either sociological or psychological factors – is a non-functional theory. Accordingly, it is a waste of time to debate whether an ideology or an ethical theory affects, or is meant to affect, behaviour.

Normative theorists are conscious of ideology in terms of function: to them the concept of ideology does serve a function in political theory. The theory of sovereignty, for example, has supplied the sovereign power with a *raison d'être* – security – but not a detailed policy so that, if political theory were meant to be not only explanatory but also predictive, it had to move into the area of ideology. The latter emerged as the 'morality' of the sovereign power and the basis for policy (whenever that policy was to consist of something more than acts of expediency or adjustment to passing circumstances). Such a view was neither necessary nor even possible until the emergence of an ideological mentality. The early ideological State – which preceded the rise of modern 'isms' – was a mental image created by those who mulled over arguments for and against the possibility of the 'people' being sovereign. It was realized that, whatever 'democracy' meant, it could not refer to the sovereignty of the governed but to a set of ideas – such as 'political morality' or 'governing principles' – which fall within the compass of 'ideology'.

THE NEW DEFINITION AND THE 'ISMS'

The new definition proposed here is not meant to be a catch-all to accommodate all ideologies; it focuses on democracies and serves as a yardstick to be applied mainly to democratic ideologies. Treating non-democratic systems as exceptions, it reverses the attitude that was prevalent for several decades, whereby totalitarian ideologies were regarded as fully-fledged while democracy and its political creeds were denied the label of true 'ideology'. Too often in the past, theorists who described liberalism or conservatism as 'ideologies' had to face scepticism and incomprehension. The new definition 'repatriates' the concept of ideology to democracy.

Among the obvious merits of the proposed mode of understanding ideology is that it solves the problem of the presence of alien ideologies in a democratic system. Thus, as non-democratic ideologies, Fascism and Communism cannot provide the basis for parties acceptable to democracy.

Furthermore, terms such as 'liberal' and 'conservative' make sense only within a democratic framework. Proponents of non-democratic ideologies find these terms unintelligible. Their outlook is such that there can be no differences of opinion – no 'loyal opposition', in the Western parliamentary tradition. To define 'ideology' without taking account of such matters and, as a result, concluding that a 'democracy' not only can but 'should' include totalitarian parties as well as liberal and conservative ones, violates elementary logic.

When conservatism, liberalism and democratic socialism are discussed in terms of the new definition, they are – as ideologies – made part of the more comprehensive ideology, viz. 'democracy'. Neither a socialist who is prepared to admit that when his beliefs are implemented the result will assist Communism, nor a liberal capable of imagining that his views may lead to the acceptance of a Communist régime, is a democratic thinker.

To speak of democratic 'isms' as ideologies does not mean that we are thinking of 'habits of mind', which might lead anywhere, but rather of systems of ideas which must fit into the framework of democratic ideology. If they do not, it is not that they have 'evolved' into something else but that they were not democratic in the first place.

The issue is of particular importance to conservatives, who have always found it difficult to define themselves. When trying to do so, they seem to make a case for democracy not as some absolute good but as about the best that human beings can do under the circumstances. This vagueness is understandable when we realize that their definitions of conservatism as an ideology and of democracy coincide. What they are trying to 'conserve' is in fact 'a system of ideas used to comprehend socio-political reality'.

This is, of course, not to say that only conservatives believe in the latter definition. It would be more accurate to say that conservatives think that belief in 'a system of ideas used to comprehend social and political reality' is a good. They do not believe that by not having such a system we are somehow made 'free', or more open to understanding ultimate 'truth'. (To the conservative, anti-authoritarian views and scepticism – often labelled as liberalism – are not the same as being 'tolerant', 'open-minded', or 'progressive': the traditional 'liberal' goods.)

If conservatism tends to imply acceptance of the new definition as 'good', liberalism entails a sceptical view. Under the definition, a liberal views set ways of comprehending social and political reality as limitations on human potential. He therefore resists such ways, even though the real nature of his objection may not be clear either to himself or others. Thus liberals tend to become 'rebels without a cause'. They demand amendments to regulations that often stultify the intent of the legislation. Laws limiting the powers of the police, for instance, are not related by the liberals to evidence that a democratic police force is a menace to the citizens' liberty, but seem based on the vague idea that it would be much better if we did not have a police force; they also believe that if we do not limit its powers every time we see a need to expand it, the police force itself – rather than criminals – will destroy democratic liberties. Thus liberals are far from clear about their objectives.

How does one fit socialism into the new definition of ideology? The answer is not easy to give. This is because adherents of socialism fail to understand the significance of the definitional restriction placed on reality: 'social and political reality'. There is, by implication, another kind of reality dealt with by something other than political ideology. When socialists make 'distributive justice' the *whole* of justice, they ignore the fact that a large number of people – perhaps the majority – do not agree that everything defined as a good can be distributed equally or, alternatively, that a compensatory system for what cannot be so distributed can be agreed on. Rawls went badly astray in supposing that one could have a new kind of social contract based on the socialist conception of justice.

There is a weakness in today's discussions of 'isms' which can be shown by focusing on a contemporary author's comment on the prescriptive element of ideology: 'If ideal and existing society are depicted as more-or-less harmonious, [the prescriptive element] will consist of minor remedies to preserve, amend or restore the status quo'.[4] From what he and his co-authors say, they do not appear to have any clear notion that, by definition, the three democratic isms assert that 'the ideal and existing society are depicted as more-or-less harmonious'. (Awareness of this will help to explain, first, why democratic societies have been called non-ideological and, second, why most definitions of the three isms are vague and misleading.)

Liberalism, socialism and conservatism can be presented as difficult to distinguish from one another, or misleadingly said to be incompatible, if one forgets that they have a common premise such as: 'Given that democracy is the best possible political order, here is what needs specifically to be done or at least recognized'. (It is the 'given' part of these ideologies that makes Communists assert that democratic parties are fictions because they hold exactly the same views; and it is the absolute certainty of liberals, conservatives and socialists that they do not hold the same views that makes them feel that Communists do not understand democracy and democratic processes.)

It would be reassuring to be able to say that democratic theorists and commentators have a clear conception of democratic ideology. But is this the case? 'Liberalism', says Eccleshall, is 'a more integrated ideology than many academic commentators acknowledged it to be'.[5] By 'integrated' does he mean 'integrated into the overall democratic ideology'? He does not; he means something more like 'coherent and independent of other ideological possibilities'. Similarly, for him 'Conservatism is a deceptively simple ideology . . . because its meaning seems plain. . . . The adjective "conservative" has denoted a tendency to preserve'.[6] The question is: preserve what? Absolutely anything? This is what some who have tried to give the political concept of conservative a psychological meaning – to see it as a mental bent – have said: 'Conservatism, on this view, is less an explicit, ideological conception of society than a subjective preference for a settled way of life'. Does Eccleshall see what is wrong with this position and reject it? Here is what he says: [As a tool of analysis] 'it confuses recurrent patterns of human behaviour with the emergence . . . of a particular conception of society. . . . To suggest that conservatism is rooted in the stuff of life obscures the fact that it is an historical phenomenon: a set of beliefs which certain social groups began to articulate at a specific historical moment. Conservatism . . . is no less ideological than either liberalism or socialism'.[7] Had Eccleshall really understood the relation between democracy and conservatism he would have said so, perhaps in as 'deceptively simple' a statement as 'Conservatism is committed to the preservation of democracy as an ideology'. This statement would of course need developing, but it would not be as vague as was his pronouncement about 'a set of beliefs which certain social groups began to articulate'.

Does his co-author, Vincent Geoghegan, do better with his integration of socialism and democracy? Unfortunately not, for he seems not to understand that democratic socialism cannot be made 'democratic' by the simple device of accepting application of the majority rule principle to the process of competing for political office. He sets socialism in opposition to capitalism: 'In capitalist societies, socialists argue, equality exists only at the formal constitutional level'.[8] If anyone should be criticized for talking about 'formal constitutional levels' rather than realities, it should be Geoghegan. If what is called socialism does not begin with the 'given' about democracy as ideology, it is not democratic socialism. There is something wrong with a definition of ideology that does not make this clear.

Evidently, liberalism, conservatism and socialism cannot be called democratic ideologies unless they presuppose the overarching democratic ideology as a good. To recognize this point of view, rather than ignore it (as is usually the case), should be the task of political analysts who are intent on clarifying the 'definitional' issues that have so often aroused controversy. Given that all three isms are aspects of democratic ideology, it makes little sense to define democracy in terms of its forms and procedures (such as attaining political office through majority rule) or its behavioural processes. The existence of parties with different ideologies must lead to the conclusion that the essence of democracy lies elsewhere. Democratic parties are of course necessary because democracy is an ideology which allows diverse opinions about what should be done.

REPATRIATION OF IDEOLOGY

According to the view that was established in the 1930s and prevailed for half a century, 'democracy' referred to a set of political institutions peculiar chiefly to Western European countries and their colonies. Although the common fact shared by modern democracies was clearly 'ideological' – institutional forms differed from State to State – the term 'ideology' was assumed to be inapplicable. Ideology was considered a propaganda device peculiar to States with a recent history of totalitarian despotism. The misleading nature of this view seems to have been largely ignored. Nor was it recognized that excluding 'democracy' from the concept of ideology was not only unhistorical and intellectually untenable but reflected a serious split between the philosophical and the positivist orientations within the discipline. The idea of political science as a unified study became more fictitious than ever. If, to a behaviouralist mind, an 'ideology' is so vague and so uncertainly related to political behaviour that it cannot be intelligibly defined, what is one to think of behaviouralist views of political theory in general? Are we not right in supposing that the vague and tendentious definitions of ideology by the positivists are a good indication of their real views about political theory?

The simplified definition of ideology hereby proposed – a denial that there is anything vague or outlandish about the concept – is meant to encourage the 'repatriation' of ideology or bringing it back onto the democratic track. To deny that the term 'ideology' is applicable to liberal democracies – which differ from each other institutionally – is to deny that democracies have much in common.

'Repatriation' can be accomplished by insisting that there is a continuity in both political theory and history: for, of course, democracy existed before our century in quite a real sense; moreover, that there is a continuity linking democracy as ideology with contractualism. The study of government and the State is by its nature concerned with continuities. All significant aspects of those continuities must themselves be continuities: if political scientists find ideology of increasing interest, this can only be because ideology is a necessary feature of the modern State. What is not ideology, is policy – the area of traditional concern to behaviouralists (decision-making, policy-making, etc.). Ideology and policy must not be confused; and a definition should make that clear.

To repatriate ideology would be to assert that the notion of ideology preceded the birth of modern democracy and take cognizance of the fact that later – in the 1930s – it was applied exclusively to non-democratic societies. Repatriation is necessary if we are to make sense of the history of democracy. The hiatus between classical Greek and modern democracies is too great for any genuine connection between them to be claimed; also, statements referring to formal organization, although they are in harmony with modern democracies, can be inappropriate if applied to classical democracy. Thus, in modern times Britain and many members of the Commonwealth have not had a revolution. As a result, these countries can still be called 'monarchies'; but Britain is also the founder of modern democracy which, unlike that of the ancient Greeks, is compatible with different types of political organization. Today, the presence or absence of democracy depends on the observance of democratic norms rather than forms. Indeed, if we apply the concept of 'form' to modern States – as C.B. Macpherson did – such current democratic systems as those of the UK and the USA will appear quite different from one another: the British Constitution, for instance, being unwritten, while the American is an actual operating document. On the other hand, a commentator focusing his attention on a formal structure may find that a democracy like the USA and a non-democracy like the former USSR, have a similarity suggested by their respective 'federal' frameworks. However, what democracy and Communism do not have in common is also what modern and classical democracies happen not to have in common: ideology.

Analysts who concentrate on forms are apt to minimize the role of norms or even ignore them altogether. What particularly troubles the theorist is that the emphasis on form has led to a distortion of democratic norms, which have now been adapted to fit the 'form' concept of democracy. One of the 'form' concepts, the 'majority rule' which entails relativism as the fundamental normative view of a democratic society, has made 'liberty' appear to be an argument for anarchism, a form suitable for a pluralist democracy. The graffiti on slum walls calling for 'Anarchism now!' may seem naïve but are very real to the policeman on the beat. Crime in the streets and meaningless violence are anarchism now, and emanate from a relativism which follows from representing modern democracy as form rather than norm.

As a part of the repatriation of ideology, the recognition that democracy is not a mere form will not be a cure-all for our problems. For one thing, preoccupation with the relationship between form and norm has existed ever since Plato set out the problem in the *Republic* – and blurred the distinction by speaking of his State in terms of form only. We have no modern theory of that relationship. In practice, we have mere ritual and hypocrisy. The call to bridge the gap between norm and form, theory and practice, to return ideology to the democratic path could herald the return to political principles, but much more needs to be done.

Postscript

Although definitions of 'ideology' are likely to remain as controversial as those of 'religion', attempts to do without the concept – as in the 'end of ideology' debate of the 1960s – betray a rejection of political theory itself; discussion of ideology (and ideologies) constitutes a continuation into modern times – or reflection – of the issues which originally led to a separation between the 'natural' and 'social' sciences. For every political theory still deserving attention – every 'classical' theory – begins with some observation or point about the human condition which makes it necessary to analyse organized group behaviour in terms of 'mind'. The opposition between political theory and behaviouralism is not the product of the modern behavioural persuasion, but can be found whenever the point is made that human behaviour differs from that of social insects. Political theory is about individual and group behaviour which is subject to 'will' and is not determined by kinship, sexual instinct, etc.; ideologies are about the most 'desirable' of these factors – the non-determined political relations.

If the question 'How can the need for scrutinizing ideologies in philosophic terms be justified?' must be answered, the reply could proceed as follows. The attention paid to ideology by philosophically-minded theorists represents a continuation of the contractualist tradition of 'choice' with regard to organized social behaviour. The central issue is 'freedom' versus 'materialist determinism'. Political theory, theorists say, is about the options open to us in respect of organized group behaviour; behavioural-ism is about what is determined. Thus political theory deals with freedom; within political theory, ideologies are ranked in terms of this issue. Ideology, theorists say, is one of the non-determined elements, even though some ideologies – Communism, for instance – assert that they are based on deterministic factors.

WHY 'PHILOSOPHY OF POLITICAL IDEOLOGIES'?

The problem faced by proponents of the philosophic approach is that ideologies conceived as political factors presuppose the influence of 'mind' on human behaviour, whereas even so eminent and staid a philosopher as Gilbert Ryle has gone so far as to mock such a thing as 'mind'. Ryle refers to it as the 'ghost in the machine'. His view, of course, is deterministic: if the cosmos is a mechanism, any unmechanistic element, such as 'mind', may well be dismissed as a sort of superstition smiled at by the sophisticated.

The problem faced by the political theorist is not that there exists an overwhelming body of evidence in favour of determinism but that the social sciences have to be more deterministic than the physical sciences. The reason is that the physical sciences deal with observable regularities from which they can make deductions: for example, when the weighing of samples of various elements and compounds led to concepts of atomic weight and ultimately the current search for and analysis of atomic particles. The social sciences, on the other hand, are still searching for regularities; to facilitate the search, they have to assume a determinism which physicists in their field now find to be a puzzle rather than a help.

The consequence of adopting determinism as a methodology rather than making an initial assumption is that 'mind' and influence on 'mind' – ideologies – have to be discounted as political factors, or else given a materialist basis. Even very 'conservative' behaviouralists adopt a kind of materialist determinism in their interpretation of political behaviour that is very close to the Marxian.

When the political theorist asserts that ideology as understood by behaviouralists represents a commitment to determinism and that he, the theorist, must continue to make a case for ideology as a part of theory, he is insisting on 'mind' as a meaningful factor in human behaviour. He is not trying to prove that 'mind' is meaningful: he does not have to do so any more than a behaviouralist has to prove determinism in order to be a behaviouralist. The theorist's assumption about ideology is just one of two possibilities, neither of which is provable. For a theorist, it would be philosophically indefensible to allow determinism to control the field, for by itself it is not a sound view. If there are two possibilities, both must be presented.

It is possible that soon the 'philosophic' position on ideology will not seem to be a 'mere' continuation of a tradition that began with the ancient Greeks. The 'ghost in the machine' school is making itself increasingly ridiculous as the implications of its view become apparent. The public, for instance, tends to get excited over the idea that a single cell from the bone of Neanderthal man could be cultured and turned into a new Neanderthal, or that Shakespeare might perhaps be dug up and start writing more plays. Some people are attracted by the idea that one day there will be a pill to cure everything – malevolence, stinginess and undemocratic tendencies.

Ideas of this type are based on the assumption called 'somatism', which implies that there is no 'mind' but only bodily dispositions. As such ideas are propagated by somatist enthusiasts, a resistance develops on the part of those who are more reflective and critical than the average man. Surely there must be a 'mind' that characterizes Plato or Shakespeare, irrespective of their individual 'constitution'. What can appeal to mind – ideology – must also affect behaviour entirely apart from materialist factors. One day proponents of the 'philosophic approach' will be vindicated for upholding the age-long tradition that mind is meaningful and can therefore be influenced by ideas and ideology.

Current discussions – and definitions – of political ideologies usually consist of an extraordinary mixture of ideas, occasionally offered with an apology that the subject-matter is difficult. In simpler formulations, there is a narrowness induced by the positivist-inspired analyses of ideologies of which social scientists masquerading as theorists are unaware.

Unlike the positivistic approach, the philosophic approach to ideology is multi-dimensional. It is commonplace to say that the theorist brings to bear the evidence of history and economics, the analysis of philosophy and jurisprudence and even the findings of behaviouralism. But he also looks at the mentalities of individuals and groups in their roles of adherents to particular ideologies. He has to do so, for according to his premise about the importance of 'mind', all the factors he considers – including the insights of various disciplines – must affect our behaviour. By the exercise of his own mind, he attempts to anticipate what will eventually happen as a result of the behaviour induced by other minds. He thus keeps to the old tradition that 'science' (in the sense of 'knowledge' and 'understanding') is valuable insofar as it is predictive, rather than merely descriptive.

Behaviouralism with its ostensible assumption that only 'facts' matter (what 'is'), has the unfortunate effect of preventing multi-dimensionality – the very kind of analysis that the social sciences consider necessary to 'true' science. Whatever sociology or economics establish as a factor must apply to what psychology discovers, and vice versa. Behaviouralists are well aware of this problem, as witness their frequent references to the 'interdisciplinary' approach. Whether they practise it is another matter. Interdisciplinarity often becomes a verbal device – the behaviouralist's stab at the theorist's multi-dimensionality. The behavioural approach in politics is essentially unilinear.

A multi-dimensional interpretation has certain implications. The various themes – such as the content of ideologies, their influence on each other, the way they are perceived, the role of Western mentality, the cultures which gave rise to the isms (and which enfold them), the philosophic insights – must all be confronted *in toto*, simultaneously. Hence the author's task is to phrase his argument both directly and indirectly, approach his subject-matter openly as well as obliquely, reveal a variety of aspects which form his own outlook, and provide a unified point of view even when dealing with the ideas and theories of others.

Notes

INTRODUCTION

1 R.N. Berki, *Socialism* (J.M. Dent, London, 1975), pp. 9–10.
2 Charles L. Stevenson, *Ethics and Language* (Yale University Press, New Haven, 1962), p. 34.
3 Noël O'Sullivan, *Conservatism* (J.M. Dent, London, 1976), p. 9.
4 *Encounter*, Vol. LI, No. 4 (October 1978), pp. 46–7.
5 Jean-François Revel, *La Connaissance inutile* (Bernard Grasset, Paris, 1988), pp. 91ff.

PART I

1 Commonsense in this context means that the perceptions of members of the class human being are interchangeable, and that a failure to be able to perceive in common – as with colour blindness or a paranoid's hallucinations – represents a defect in the individual rather than evidence of the untrustworthiness of human perception. If we do not agree and cannot be brought to agree that this is the case, the experimental method collapses. It works only because the testing and confirming of empirical 'truths' is based on the assumption that the sensory experience of all 'normal' people (a concept which is itself defined in terms of 'common-sense') is interchangeable because of the self-other class we are conceptually employing. Without it we cannot escape solipsism. On the basis of the observer-observed distinction that science professes to be using, all statements based on experiment would have to be preceded by the assertion 'I assume solipsism is invalid when maintaining the validity of the experimental method'. Since we do not do this, we are evidently arguing from a self-other-it position. In effect we are asserting we believe in 'commonsense' not as something that for reasons unknown arrives at or is 'the truth' but as something that enables us to approach the truth because it excludes solipsism and individual aberrations of perception. The experimental method, in other words, is a refined

and very exacting statement about the validity of 'commonsense' not a statement about the validity of a self-it conception of reality or the reliability of sensory data.

2 Clinton Rossiter, *Conservatism in America* (Alfred A. Knopf, New York, 1955), p. 61.

3 Williams F. Buckley, Jr., 'Notes Towards an Empirical Definition of Conservatism' in Frank S. Meyer (ed.), *What is Conservatism?* (Holt, Rinehart and Winston, New York, 1964), pp. 211–26.

4 Russell Kirk, Lewis Lapham, Philip M. Crane and others, *Objections to Conservatism*, The Heritage Lectures, No. 3 (The Heritage Foundation, Washington, DC, 1981), p. 82.

5 The argument that no human being can anticipate all possible situations (create a perfect rule book) and that therefore a decision-maker is ultimately necessary, can be forestalled by including in the rule-book a rule to the effect that disputes not covered are disallowed and that the disputants are to be disqualified.

6 Roger Scruton, *The Meaning of Conservatism* (Penguin, Harmondsworth, 1980), p.16.

7 Roger Scruton, *The Meaning of Conservatism* (Penguin, Harmondsworth, 1980), pp. 18–19.

8 Thus, in the book by William R. Harbour, an American conservative, although the author devotes a whole chapter to the conservative view of human reason, the latter's limitations and inadequacies are brought into focus (*The Foundations of Conservative Thought: An Anglo-American Tradition in Perspective*, University of Notre Dame Press, Notre Dame, 1982, ch. 3). Although some of his points will be acceptable to European conservatives, on the whole they will regard the exercise as misguided: we are not living in a period of history when anyone with a respect for man should lend his support to attacks on reason. The issues were thrashed out at the close of the eighteenth century when Americans broke with the European tradition. Many American conservatives managed at that time to flee to the wilds of Canada. It is there that the European tradition of conservatism has persisted, despite the similarities in social conditions between Canada and the USA.

9 The term continuity, more than 'tradition', defines the conservative, for the latter term makes the conservative a mystic who yearns only for stability in a world in flux.

10 Although there is no 'desire theory', the following distinctions can be made: (a) *Desire*: a general term for motivation considered in the light of Hume's argument that we are moved by 'emotion' rather than 'reason'; (b) *Desirable*: a term applicable to what we otherwise call norms. Without it, a desire theory, such as it is, would merely be a statement about motivation – a psychological theory; (c) *Desired*: a term for specific desires. Conceivably, it could include what is called 'the desirable'. Traditional philosophy, to be sure, does not like distinctions which are not mutually exclusive, but the discussion of 'desire' did not originate there.

11 If this is the 'conservative' view, conservatives have not clearly

articulated it. The view is not mentioned by the Law Reform Commission of Canada in its report *Fear of Punishment: Deterrence* (Ottawa, 1976) which reviews a vast body of literature on deterrence. The Commission comes closest to it when referring to 'making an example' of the criminal by ferocious penalties. The conservative is likely to say that the gradation of penalties reflects society's hierarchy of norms and that a democratic government has no right to take a stand on what that should be or interfere with its operation by introducing ways of deterrence. After all, in early nineteenth-century England infliction of the death penalty for shoplifting or sheep-stealing made them almost non-crimes, for juries refused to convict. The penalties violated their concept of justice.

12 Anthony Quinton, *The Politics of Imperfection* (Faber and Faber, London, 1978), p. 13.

13 There is no trace of it, for instance in Peter Viereck's wide-ranging essays reflecting the conservative personality in America. See his *Shame and Glory of the Intellectuals* (1953) or *The Unadjusted Man* (1956).

14 Anthony Quinton, *The Politics of Imperfection* (Faber and Faber, London, 1978), p. 60.

15 Anthony Quinton, *The Politics of Imperfection* (Faber and Faber, London, 1978), p. 60.

16 Edmund Burke, *Reflections on the Revolution in France* [1790] (Oxford University Press, World's Classics, London, 1958), p. 23.

17 Edmund Burke, *Reflections on the Revolution in France* [1790] (Oxford University Press, World's Classics, London, 1958), p.64.

18 Edmund Burke, *Reflections on the Revolution in France* [1790] (Oxford University Press, World's Classics, London, 1958), p. 67.

19 Edmund Burke, *Reflections on the Revolution in France* [1790] (Oxford University Press, World's Classics, London, 1958), p. 67.

20 Quoted by Thomas Mahoney in the Library of Liberal Arts edition of Edmund Burke, *Reflections on the Revolution in France* (Bobbs-Merrill, Indianapolis, 1955), p.297.

21 Edmund Burke, *Reflections on the Revolution in France* (Oxford University Press, World's Classics, 1958), p.65.

22 Edmund Burke, *Reflections on the Revolution in France* (Oxford University Press, World's Classics, 1958), p.65.

23 Edmund Burke, *Reflections on the Revolution in France* (Oxford University Press, World's Classics, 1958), p.65

24 Edmund Burke, *Reflections on the Revolution in France* (Oxford University Press, World's Classics, 1958), p. 68.

25 George Will, *Statecraft as Soulcraft: What Government Does* (Simon & Schuster, New York, 1983), p. 20.

26 The associationist theory, which considers man a non-rational animal (or at least no more 'rational' than any other animal), represents the conservative as someone whose personal experience has been such that he dislikes change. Such people do exist, of course, and some of them call themselves conservatives. Others do not – among them are the few Fabian socialists still around, who

have no intention of changing their views. Remaining steadfast to their tradition is their brand of conservatism. Obviously, it is confusing to call all those resistant to change 'conservatives' when some of them are politically left-wing.

27 Roger Scruton, *The Meaning of Conservatism*, (Penguin, Harmondsworth, 1980), p. 44.

PART II

1 John Stuart Mill, *On Liberty* (World's Classics edition of *On Liberty, Representative Government & The Subjection of Women*, Oxford University Press [1912], repr. 1954), p. 5.

2 John Rawls, *A Theory of Justice* (Harvard University Press, Cambridge, Mass., 1971), p. 202.

3 L.T. Hobhouse, *Liberalism* [1911] (Oxford University Press, New York, 1964), p. 116.

4 L.T. Hobhouse, *Liberalism* [1911] (Oxford University Press, New York, 1964), p. 120.

5 L.T. Hobhouse, *Liberalism* [1911] (Oxford University Press, New York, 1964), p. 119.

6 L.T. Hobhouse, *Liberalism* [1911] (Oxford University Press, New York, 1964), p. 115–16.

7 L.T. Hobhouse, *Liberalism* [1911] (Oxford University Press, New York, 1964), p. 30.

8 L.T. Hobhouse, *Liberalism* [1911] (Oxford University Press, New York, 1964), p. 31.

9 L.T. Hobhouse, *Liberalism* [1911] (Oxford University Press, New York, 1964), p. 63.

10 L.T. Hobhouse, *Liberalism* [1911] (Oxford University Press, New York, 1964), p. 63.

11 Some 'liberals' today may even be included to find room for the radical notion of 'repressive tolerance'. The latter is discussed in my *Approaches to Democracy* (pp. 103–6).

12 Maurice Cranston, *Freedom: A New Analysis* [1953] (Longmans, Green, London, 1954), p. 66.

13 Maurice Cranston, *Freedom: A New Analysis* [1953] (Longmans, Green, London, 1954), p. 65. Quoting John Locke, *Essay Concerning Human Understanding*, vol. II, pp. xxxiii, 19.

14 Maurice Cranston, *Freedom: A New Analysis* [1953] (Longmans, Green, London, 1954) pp. 67–71.

15 Maurice Cranston, *Freedom: A New Analysis* [1953] (Longmans, Green, London, 1954), p. 65.

16 Maurice Cranston, *Freedom: A New Analysis* [1953] (Longmans, Green, London, 1954), pp. 74–5.

17 Maurice Cranston, *Freedom: A New Analysis* [1953] (Longmans, Green, London, 1954), p. 85.

18 Maurice Cranston, *Freedom: A New Analysis* [1953] (Longmans, Green, London, 1954), p. 86.

19 Thus, in a symposium edited by Douglas MacLean and Claudia

Mills, *Liberalism Reconsidered* (Rowman and Allanheld, Totowa, N.J., 1983), Theda Skockpol says 'The United States, as Louis Hartz argues in *The Liberal Tradition in America*, may have been born liberal' (p. 87); Walter Berns: 'The United States was the first nation to found itself on liberal principles' (p. 51); and Christopher Lasch: 'Those who insist that American liberal democracy has always rested on the frontier. . . have grasped something of central importance' (p. 106).

20 This is what Berns does. 'Thomas Hobbes' he says, 'can be credited with being liberalism's founding father.' Walter Berns, 'Taking Rights Frivolously' in *Liberalism Reconsidered* (Rowman and Allanheld, Totowa, N.J., 1983), p. 52.

21 Ronald Dworkin, *Taking Rights Seriously* (Harvard University Press, Cambridge, 1977), p. 4.

22 Ronald Dworkin, *Taking Rights Seriously* (Harvard University Press, Cambridge, 1977), p. 5.

23 Walter Berns, 'Taking Rights Frivolously' in *Liberalism Reconsidered* (Rowman and Allanheld, Totowa, N.J., 1983), p. 57.

24 Mark Sagoff, 'Liberalism and Law' in *Liberalism Reconsidered*, (Rowman and Allanheld, Totowa, N.J., 1983), p. 12.

25 Ronald Dworkin, *Taking Rights Seriously*, (Harvard University Press, Cambridge, 1977), p. 290.

26 Ronald Dworkin, 'Neutrality, Equality, and Liberalism' in *Liberalism Reconsidered*, (Rowman and Allanheld, Totowa, N.J., 1983), p. 2.

27 Ronald Dworkin, 'Neutrality, Equality, and Liberalism' in *Liberalism Reconsidered*, (Rowman and Allanheld, Totowa, N.J., 1983), p. 2.

28 Sagoff, 'Liberalism and Law' in *Liberalism Reconsidered* (Rowman and Allanheld, Totowa, N.J., 1983), p. 18.

29 Sagoff, 'Liberalism and Law' in *Liberalism Reconsidered* (Rowman and Allanheld, Totowa, N.J., 1983), p. 15.

30 Sagoff, 'Liberalism and Law' in *Liberalism Reconsidered* (Rowman and Allanheld, Totowa, N.J., 1983), p. 21.

31 Sagoff, 'Liberalism and Law' in *Liberalism Reconsidered* (Rowman and Allanheld, Totowa, N.J., 1983), p. 22.

32 Take, for instance, the posture adopted by Carole Pateman in her book *The Problem of Political Obligation* (John Wiley, Chichester and New York, 1979). What is characteristic of her style is the substitution of feminine pronouns in contexts where the masculine form is conventionally used to cover the common gender, as in the sentence 'Each individual will be able to decide for herself what ought to be done'. (p. 138) Why was the author reluctant to resort to a form of compromise, as through pluralization: 'Individuals will be able to decide for themselves'? What has happened to the common-sense embodied in convention? In such context, as a rule, the conventional 'him' and 'himself' are called by grammarians 'common gender', not masculine gender. Even if they did not, even if they were all 'Male chauvinist theorists' – the term which Pateman applies to Rousseau (p. 157) – what difference would it make with regard to the status of women in our society? How much

'freer' are women as a result of Pateman's defiance of what is still standard practice?

33 Pateman, *The Problem of Political Obligation* (John Wiley, Chichester and New York, 1979), p. 24.

34 Pateman, *The Problem of Political Obligation* (John Wiley, Chichester and New York, 1979), p. 18.

35 Pateman, *The Problem of Political Obligation* (John Wiley, Chichester and New York, 1979), p. 25.

36 Lincoln Allison, *Right Principles: A Conservative Philosophy of Politics* (Basil Blackwell, Oxford, 1984), p. 76.

37 Lincoln Allison, *Right Principles: A Conservative Philosophy of Politics* (Basil Blackwell, Oxford, 1984), p. 158.

38 See Postscript to my *Politics and Religion in Seventeenth-Century France* (University of California Press, Berkeley and Los Angeles, 1960).

39 Roland H. Bainton, *The Reformation of the Sixteenth Century* (The Beacon Press, Boston, 1952; paperback edition 9th printing 1963), pp. 214 ff.

40 K.R. Minogue, *The Liberal Mind* (Methuen, London, 1963), p.46.

41 K.R. Minogue, *The Liberal Mind* (Methuen, London, 1963), p. 14.

42 K.R. Minogue, *The Liberal Mind* (Methuen, London, 1963), p. 17.

43 K.R. Minogue, *The Liberal Mind* (Methuen, London, 1963), p. 25.

44 K.R. Minogue, *The Liberal Mind* (Methuen, London, 1963), p. 65.

45 K.R. Minogue, *The Liberal Mind* (Methuen, London, 1963), p. 67–8.

46 K.R. Minogue, *The Liberal Mind* (Methuen, London, 1963), p. 73.

47 K.R. Minogue, *The Liberal Mind* (Methuen, London, 1963), p. 75.

48 K.R. Minogue, *The Liberal Mind* (Methuen, London, 1963), p. 23.

49 K.R. Minogue, *The Liberal Mind* (Methuen, London , 1963), p. 204.

50 John Rawls, *A Theory of Justice*, (Harvard University Press, Cambridge, Mass., 1971), p. 15.

51 John Rawls, *A Theory of Justice*, (Harvard University Press, Cambridge, Mass., 1971), p. 15.

52 John Rawls, *A Theory of Justice*, (Harvard University Press, Cambridge, Mass., 1971), pp. 72–3.

53 John Rawls, *A Theory of Justice*, (Harvard University Press, Cambridge, Mass., 1971), p. 575.

54 Gerald F. Gaus, *The Modern Liberal Theory of Man* (Croom Helm, London, St Martin's Press, New York, 1983), p. 2.

55 The fact that Mill used only the term 'individuality' can now make the issues rather confusing. In keeping with the strong tendency for words ending in 'ism' to refer to belief systems having a normative element ('ism' is now itself an English word), individualism is distinguished from individuality in the way anarchism is from anarchy. To us, questions about individuality are epistemological, while those about individualism are normative. We become needlessly entangled in 'is-ought' problems when we fail to differentiate between these two words.

In Mill's day, or at least in Mill's usage, the distinction was not observed. In Chapter III of his book *On Liberty* ('Of Individuality') he discusses whether 'men should be free to act upon their opinions' (p. 69). By using the word 'should', he makes it clear that he is speaking about a norm equivalent to our individualism (though the term he uses is individuality). His norm is defined as 'liberty' conceived as a right to think of norms in terms of the dictates of one's own conscience. In other words, Mill discusses what we today call 'relativism' as a possible norm. Thus Chapter III confronts us with the curious problem of how an epistemological view – relativism – can be treated as if it were normative. Mill can be said to have introduced this problem although he was not a philosophic relativist. He denies that we can treat norms as truths and argues that this view should be institutionalized by means of the norm 'individuality', or as we would say 'individualism'.

56 Gerald F. Gaus, *The Modern Liberal Theory of Man* (Croom Helm, London, St Martin's Press, New York, 1983), p. 6.

57 John Rawls, *A Theory of Justice* (Harvard University Press, Cambridge, Mass., 1971), p. 30.

58 John Rawls, *A Theory of Justice* (Harvard University Press, Cambridge, Mass., 1971), p. 31.

59 John Rawls, *A Theory of Justice* (Harvard University Press, Cambridge, Mass., 1971), p. 101.

60 John Rawls, *A Theory of Justice* (Harvard University Press, Cambridge, Mass., 1971), p. 100–1.

61 Robert Nozick, *Anarchy, State, and Utopia* (Basic Books, New York, 1974), p. ix.

62 Robert Nozick, *Anarchy, State, and Utopia* (Basic Books, New York, 1974), p. xi.

63 Robert Nozick, *Anarchy, State, and Utopia* (Basic Books, New York, 1974), p. 35.

64 John Rawls, *A Theory of Justice* (Harvard University Press, Cambridge, Mass., 1971), p. 100.

65 John Rawls, *A Theory of Justice* (Harvard University Press, Cambridge, Mass., 1971), p. 106.

66 John Rawls, *A Theory of Justice* (Harvard University Press, Cambridge, Mass., 1971), p. 105.

67 Walter Kaufmann, *Without Guilt and Justice* [1973] (Dell, New York, 1975), p. 82.

68 Walter Kaufmann, *Without Guilt and Justice* [1973] (Dell, New York, 1975), p. 85.

69 Rare indeed are statements like that of Yves R. Simon: 'With proper attention given to the social aspects of personal destinies, the principle of equal opportunity loses the absolutism which would make it a first-class factor of atomization and a formidable wrecker of democratic communities'. *Philosophy of Democratic Government* [1951] (University of Chicago Press, 1961), p. 230.

70 Yves R. Simon, *Philosophy of Democratic Government* [1951] (University of Chicago Press, 1961), pp. 222 ff.

71 Herbert J. Muller, *Issues of Freedom* (Harper, New York, 1960), pp. 17–18, referring to Adler's *The Idea of Freedom* (Doubleday, Garden City, 1958). 'The wording', says Muller, 'is Adler's'. The same

typology is offered in Mortimer J. Adler, *Six Great Ideas* (Macmillan, New York, 1981), ch. 19.

72 J.J. Rousseau, *The Social Contract* (World's Classics, Oxford University Press, London [1947], repr. 1956), p. 263.

73 John A. Hall, *Liberalism* (Paladin/Grafton Books, London, 1988), p. 184.

74 E.F. Carritt, 'Liberty and Equality', *Law Quarterley Review*, Vol. 56 (1940), pp. 61–74. Reprinted in Anthony Quinton (ed.), *Political Philosophy* (Oxford University Press, London, 1967), p. 133.

75 George F. Will, *Statecraft as Soulcraft: What Government Does* (Simon and Schuster, New York, 1983), p. 66.

76 D.D. Raphael, *Problems of Political Philosophy* (Pall Mall Press, London, 1970), pp. 115, 142.

77 J.S. Mill, *On Liberty* (World's Classics, Oxford University Press [1912], repr. 1954), p. 18.

78 'I do believe in freedom and reason', says Popper, 'but I do not think that one can construct a simple, practical and fruitful theory in these terms. They are too abstract, and too prone to be misused; and, of course, nothing whatever can be gained by their definition'. Karl Popper, 'The open society and its enemies revisited', *The Economist*, 23 April, 1988, p. 19.

79 This assertion may appear obscure to those who use the concepts 'liberty' and 'freedom' interchangeably. It is a reference to the logic of determinism. Determinism entails the view that there is one (and only one) cause–effect system and no other factor operating in the universe. (If there is such a factor, or if there is such a thing as chance, free will, or even a separate system of causality, such as Bergson's vitalism, determinism is logically impossible.) The question of 'freedom' is a question about the exclusivity of a postulated causal order; it is also a necessary postulate underlying any norm whatsoever, including, of course, the norm 'liberty', for norms by nature presuppose a choice that is possible only if we are not living under a determinist order.

80 Mill (as a utilitarian, of sorts) rejected contractualism, but argued for the normative value that contractualist theory evokes. He saw in 'liberty' a normative way of attacking contractualism, or, specifically, of limiting the normative consequences of contractualist theory. It is this basic fact about 'liberty' as a concept that makes it now so confusing as a norm but also makes it so utterly 'political': we have to distinguish it from the issue of 'freedom'.

81 John Plamenatz, *On Alien Rule and Self-Government* (Longmans, London, 1960), p. 1.

82 Alexander Passerin d' Entrèves, *The Notion of the State* (Clarendon Press, Oxford, 1967), p. 201.

83 Adopted by the General Assembly of the United Nations, 10 December 1948. The title, incidentally, contains a misplaced modifier: are we not talking about a UN declaration of 'universal rights' rather than a 'universal declaration' of human rights?

PART III

1 R.N. Berki, *Socialism* (J.M. Dent, London, 1975), p. 25.
2 R.N. Berki, *Socialism* (J.M. Dent, London, 1975), pp. 25–6.
3 Among scientists there is now growing criticism of Alfred Binet's point of view – which for the last few decades superseded Galton's – and of his methods of measuring intelligence. See H.J. Eysenck's article referring to his own research: 'After Binet, Back to Galton', *Encounter*, Vol. LX, No. 2 (February 1983), pp. 74–9.
4 See: Sidney Hook, *Political Power and Personal Freedom* (Collier Books, New York 1962), pp. 397–437.
5 Sidney Hook, *Political Power and Personal Freedom* (Collier Books, New York, 1962), p. 401.
6 Sidney Hook, *Political Power and Personal Freedom* (Collier Books, New York, 1962), p. 410.
7 In saying that 'Communism imposes slavery', the concept slavery is extended to cover not only those individuals regarded as property, but also those not legally capable of becoming 'independent', of working for themselves – a condition peculiar to Communist societies. This extension is necessary if we are to understand how historically slaves could purchase their freedom by accumulating enough money to purchase themselves. In Tsarist times, slaves had that right. Thus Pushkin, 'first national poet of Russia', was the grandson of Peter the Great's pillow. (Peter discovered, Heaven knows how, that resting the imperial head on the belly of his black slave allayed the imperial insomnia.) But such a spectacular change of status – from bedding to literary lion – could only occur under what Marx would define as feudalism. Since then the opportunities for gaining independence have been eliminated by making private property something one cannot accumulate but can only consume in the economist's sense of the word, so that under a command economy it was impossible for a Soviet citizen to invest his private property so as to achieve some kind of independence. Like the slaves of old, the average Soviet citizen had only two courses open to him: to work for the State – which acts like the overseer of a gigantic estate – or to be punished for not doing so.
8 C.A.R. Crosland, *The Future of Socialism* (Schocken Books, New York, 1963), p. 224.
9 C.A.R. Crosland, *The Future of Socialism* (Schocken Books, New York, 1963), p. 354.
10 C.A.R. Crosland, *The Future of Socialism* (Schocken Books, New York, 1963), p. 356.
11 In the revised version of his Inaugural Lecture 'Two Concepts of Liberty' (Clarendon Press, Oxford, 1958) included in his *Four Essays on Liberty* (Oxford University Press, London, New York, 1969).
12 Roy Hattersley, *Choose Freedom: The Future of Democratic Socialism* (Michael Joseph, London, 1987), p. 129.
13 Roy Hattersley, *Choose Freedom: The Future of Democratic Socialism* (Michael Joseph, London, 1987), p. 129.

14 Keith Dixon, *Freedom and Equality: The Moral Basis of Democratic Socialism* (Routledge and Kegan Paul, London, 1986), p. 3.
15 See: 'Compulsory rational freedom is the conception of freedom advanced by Spinoza, Rousseau (sometimes), Hegel and Bosanquet (and most British Hegelians)'. Maurice Cranston, *Freedom: A New Analysis* [1953] (Longmans, Green, London, 1954), p. 29.
16 Roy Hattersley, *Choose Freedom: The Future of Democratic Socialism* (Michael Joseph, London, 1987), pp. 23, 53, respectively.
17 John Dunn, *The Politics of Socialism* (Cambridge University Press, Cambridge, 1984), p. 9.
18 The fact that Communist prisons are not nearly so pleasant as ours does not prove that we are not being influenced by Marxian ideas. Paradoxically, democratic society may in some ways be more Marxian than we think and Communist societies less Marxian than we are.
19 Jean-François Revel, *The Totalitarian Temptation* (Doubleday, Garden City, NY, 1977), p. 23.
20 Jean-François Revel, *The Totalitarian Temptation* (Doubleday, Garden City, NY, 1977), p. 29.
21 Revel's account of the intellectual process involved is not entirely felicitous and obscures the nature of the process. References to 'class struggle', for instance, are a mark of obeisance to his intellectual background and early development rather than an objective analysis of who believes what and why.
22 Revel is very clear on this shibboleth. 'The liberal left', he says, 'backed up by many "conservatives", long believed that there was only one kind of imperialism: American imperialism. When it finally had to resign itself to recognizing the existence of Soviet imperialism, it immediately developed a purification ritual: calling a plague on both their houses'. Jean-François Revel, *How Democracies Perish* (Doubleday, Garden City, NY, 1983) p. 306.
23 Jean-François Revel, *The Totalitarian Temptation*, (Doubleday, Garden City, NY, 1977), p. 146.
24 Michael Harrington, *Socialism: Past and Future* (Little, Brown and Company, Boston, 1989), p. 4.
25 Michael Harrington, *Socialism: Past and Future* (Little, Brown and Company, Boston, 1989), p. 1.
26 Michael Harrington, *Socialism: Past and Future* (Little, Brown and Company, Boston, 1989), p. 3.
27 Michael Harrington, *Socialism: Past and Future* (Little, Brown and Company, Boston, 1989), p. 3.
28 Michael Harrington, *Socialism: Past and Future* (Little, Brown and Company, Boston, 1989), p. 3.
29 Michael Harrington, *Socialism: Past and Future* (Little, Brown and Company, Boston, 1989), p. 4.
30 Michael Harrington, *Socialism: Past and Future* (Little, Brown and Company, Boston, 1989), p. 7.
31 Michael Harrington, *Socialism: Past and Future* (Little, Brown and Company, Boston, 1989), p. 253.

32 Michael Harrington, *Socialism: Past and Future* (Little, Brown and Company, Boston 1989), p. 265.
33 Michael Harrington, *Socialism: Past and Future* (Little, Brown and Company, Boston, 1989), p. 273.
34 Michael Harrington, *Socialism: Past and Future* (Little, Brown and Company, Boston, 1989), p. 274.
35 Michael Harrington, *Socialism: Past and Future* (Little, Brown and Company, Boston, 1989), p. 275.
36 Michael Harrington, *Socialism: Past and Future* (Little, Brown and Company, Boston, 1989), p. 277.
37 Gavin Kitching, *Rethinking Socialism* (Methuen, London, 1983), p. 30.
38 Gavin Kitching, *Rethinking Socialism* (Methuen, London, 1983), p. 55.
39 Gavin Kitching, *Rethinking Socialism* (Methuen, London, 1983), p. 30.
40 Note especially his *Class and Economic Change in Kenya: the Making of an African Petite-Bourgeoisie 1905–70 (1980)*.
41 F.A. Hayek, *The Fatal Conceit: the Errors of Socialism* [1988] (The Collected Works of F.A. Hayek, Vol I, The University of Chicago Press, Chicago, 1989), p. 127.
42 F.A. Hayek, *The Fatal Conceit: the Errors of Socialism* [1988] (The Collected Works of F.A. Hayek, Vol I, The University of Chicago Press, Chicago, 1989), p. 100.
43 F.A. Hayek, *The Fatal Conceit: the Errors of Socialism* [1988] (The Collected Works of F.A. Hayek, Vol I, The University of Chicago Press, Chicago, 1989), p. 27.
44 F.A. Hayek, *The Fatal Conceit: the Errors of Socialism* [1988] (The Collected Works of F.A. Hayek, Vol I, The University of Chicago Press, Chicago, 1989), p. 10.

PART IV

1 Edited by W.J. Stankiewicz (The Free Press of Glencoe, New York, 1964).
2 William Delany, 'The Role of Ideology: A Summation' in Chaim I. Waxman (ed.), *The End of Ideology Debate* (Simon and Schuster, New York, 1969), p. 292.
3 Chaim I. Waxman, (ed.), *The End of Ideology Debate* (Simon and Schuster, New York, 1969), p. 5.
4 Michael Harrington, 'The Anti-Ideology Ideologues' in Chaim I. Waxman (ed.), *The End of Ideology Debate* (Simon and Schuster, New York, 1969), p. 346.
5 Joseph M. Bochenski, 'Marxism in Communist Countries' in Milorad M. Drachkovitch (ed.), *Marxist Ideology in the Contemporary World – Its Appeals and Paradoxes* (Hoover Institution, Stanford, and Frederick A. Praeger, New York, 1966), p. 74.
6 Daniel Bell, 'The "End of Ideology" in the Soviet Union?' in Milorad M. Drachkovitch (ed.), *Marxist Ideology in the Contemporary*

World – Its Appeals and Paradoxes (Hoover Institution, Stanford, and Frederick A. Praeger, New York, 1966), p. 109.

7   Daniel Bell, 'The "End of Ideology" in the Soviet Union?' in Milorad M. Drachkovitch (ed.), *Marxist Ideology in the Contemporary World – Its Appeals and Paradoxes* (Hoover Institution, Stanford, and Frederick A. Praeger, New York, 1966), p. 108.

8   Daniel Bell, 'The "End of Ideology" in the Soviet Union?' in Milorad M. Drachkovitch (ed.), *Marxist Ideology in the Contemporary World – Its Appeals and Paradoxes* (Hoover Institution, Stanford, and Frederick A. Praeger, New York, 1966), p. 108.

9   Milovan Djilas, 'Christ and the Commissar' in the G.R. Urban (ed.), *Stalinism: Its Impact on Russia and the World* (Temple Smith, London, 1982), p. 208.

10 Milovan Djilas, 'Christ and the Commissar' in the G.R. Urban (ed.), *Stalinism: Its Impact on Russia and the World* (Temple Smith, London, 1982), p. 207.

11 In his *1984* Orwell, who well understood the issue, represented adherence to ideology as a matter of being able to give the 'correct' answer – that of authority – to a question about perception: how many fingers were being held up to view. To think that what is being portrayed is the consequence of torture or coercion is to misunderstand Orwell's analysis of totalitarianism. The point is the relation between authoritarianism and irrationalism which results in an entrenchment of power.

12 Hobbes argued that the only possible basis for the continuance of political power is not power *per se* but a perpetuation (in those who acknowledge it) of a readiness to acknowledge power as functional. He maintained that political power exists over time – the emphasis is the key point – because it deals with a problem that only those capable of conceiving of themselves as continuing in time can think of; hence they can suffer from '*angst*' and desire 'security'. (Thus political power is not a matter of dominance-submission.)
    Political authority, then, characteristically persists over time – lasts longer than anyone's lifetime – because it is a way of dealing with a persistent problem: the system exists because the problem persists. Political authority has to be a system rather than an expedient.

13 Alexander Zinoviev, *The Reality of Communism* (Paladin Books, London, 1985), p. 292.

14 Alain Besançon, *Les Origines intellectuelles du Léninisme* (Calmann-Lévy, Paris, 1977), p. 9. [My translation].

15 Alfred G. Meyer, *Leninism* (Frederick A. Praeger, New York, 1962), p. 291.

16 Alfred G. Meyer, *Leninism* (Frederick A. Praeger, New York, 1962), p. 291.

17 Bertram D. Wolfe, *Communist Totalitarianism: Keys to The Soviet System* (Beacon Press, Boston, 1961 [revised ed]), p. 314.

18 Leszek Kolakowski, 'The Devil in History' in G.R. Urban (ed.), *Stalinism: Its Impact on Russia and the World*, p. 251.

19 Leszek Kolakowski, 'The Devil in History' in G.R. Urban (ed.),

Stalinism: Its Impact on Russia and the World, p. 251.

20 Thus establishing once and for all that the concept 'democracy' cannot legitimately be applied to both political orders – liberal democracy and Communism – since they do not justify the same thing, or that they have the same ideals no matter how similar their political institutions are made to seem. To do otherwise, as in the notorious example of C.B. Macpherson, is to perpetuate a lie.

21 Richard H. Shultz and Roy Godson, *Dezinformatsia: Active Measures in Soviet Strategy* (Pergamon-Brassey's, Washington DC, 1984), pp. 37–8.

22 'Active Measures', *Survey,* Vol. 27 (118/119), Autumn–Winter 1983, p. 53.

23 Such as Richard H. Schultz and Roy Godson, *Dezinformatsia: Active Measures in Soviet Strategy* (Pergamon-Brassey's, Washington DC, 1984); Ladislav Bittman, *The KGB and Soviet Disinformation* (Pergamon-Brassey's, Washington DC, 1985); Chapman Pincher, *The Secret Offensive* (Sidgwick & Jackson, London, 1986); and Thierry Wolton, *Le K.g.b. en France* (Grasset, Paris, 1986).

24 Indeed, preposterous though it may seem, the 'wrong' need not even be represented as a current one. It could have happened in the distant past, as in the case of the Armenians who became suddenly aware of the injuries suffered by their ancestors under Turkish pashas and accordingly 'retaliated' against modern Turkey in a way that undermines its position in NATO. It may be thought that no one in his senses could suppose that he is seeing the effects of a genuine sense of grievance among a formerly oppressed people. Nonetheless, the implausible argument was generally accepted by the media without question. The actual facts of the situation – that the interests of the USSR were being served – was considered to be merely a coincidence.

25 *Disinformation: Soviet Active Measures and Disinformation Forecast* (Washington, DC), No. 1, Fall 1985, p. 8.

26 The Soviet view is quoted in Jillian Becker, *The Soviet Connection: State Sponsorship of Terrorism* (Institute for European Defence & Strategic Studies, London, 1985), p. 24.

27 Jillian Becker, *The Soviet Connection: State Sponsorship of Terrorism* (Institute for European Defence & Strategic Studies, London, 1985), p. 13.

28 'He was not mentally deranged. If he had been, he would not have been selected for the key role in this most serious international conspiracy'. Paul Henze, Introduction to his *The Plot to Kill the Pope* (Charles Scribner's Sons, New York, 1985). Page 1 (unnumbered).

29 See 'The Soviet Peace Programme for the 1980s'; *International Affairs* (Moscow), October 1981.

30 See Marek Ciesielczyk, 'Komunizm jako najwyższy stopień totalitaryzmu [Communism as the highest order of totalitarianism], *Kultura* (Paris), No. 4/451, April 1985, pp. 115–22.

31 'La substance de l'idéologie, lorsqu'elle est au pouvoir, est ce pouvoir lui-même.' Alain Besançon, *Les Origines intellectuelles du Léninisme,* p. 296.

32 Although, as a political theory it was so obscure that as eminent a scholar as the Danish philosopher, Harald Höffding (1843–1931), does not mention it in his monumental study *A History of Modern Philosophy* (first English ed. 1900).

33 Speaking of his own society, Zinoviev maintains that Marxism is 'the quintessence of mediocrity'; that it is a 'boring, unaesthetic ideology. An ideology of oppressors created for oppressors. And for the oppressed as well'. Alexander Zinoviev, *The Radiant Future* (Random House, New York, 1980), p. 125.

34 Bertram D. Wolfe, *An Ideology in Power: Reflections on the Russian Revolution* (Stein & Day, New York, 1969), p.346.

35 Alexander Zinoviev, *The Reality of Communism* (Paladin Books, London 1985), p. 299.

36 Alain Besançon, *The Soviet Syndrome* (Harcourt Brace Jovanovich, New York and London, 1978), p. 16.

37 Alexander Zinoviev, *The Reality of Communism* (Paladin Books, London, 1985), p. 301.

38 In his own words: 'To identify and evaluate the major components of the doctrinal reformulation of the Brezhnev era' R. Judson Mitchell, *Ideology of a Superpower: Contemporary Soviet Doctrine on International Relations* (Hoover Institution Press, Stanford, 1982), p. 14.

39 R. Judson Mitchell, *Ideology of a Superpower: Contemporary Soviet Doctrine on International Relations* (Hoover Institution Press, Stanford, 1982) p. 115.

40 R. Judson Mitchell, *Ideology of a Superpower: Contemporary Soviet Doctrine on International Relations* (Hoover Institution Press, Stanford, 1982), p. 3.

41 R. Judson Mitchell, *Ideology of a Superpower: Contemporary Soviet Doctrine on International Relations* (Hoover Institution Press, Stanford, 1982), p. 3.

42 R. Judson Mitchell, *Ideology of a Superpower: Contemporary Soviet Doctrine on International Relations* (Hoover Institution Press, Stanford, 1982), p. 9 quoting A.A. Yepishev, *Some Aspects of Party-Political Work in the Soviet Armed Forces* (Progress Publishers, Moscow, 1975), pp. 5–6.

43 R. Judson Mitchell, *Ideology of a Superpower: Contemporary Soviet Doctrine on International Relations* (Hoover Institution Press, Stanford, 1982), pp. 5–6.

44 R. Judson Mitchell, *Ideology of a Superpower: Contemporary Soviet Doctrine on International Relations* (Hoover Institution Press, Stanford, 1982), pp. 5–6.

45 R. Judson Mitchell, *Ideology of a Superpower: Contemporary Soviet Doctrine on International Relations* (Hoover Institution Press, Stanford, 1982), p. 10.

46 R. Judson Mitchell, *Ideology of a Superpower: Contemporary Soviet Doctrine on International Relations* (Hoover Institution Press, Stanford, 1982), p. 10.

47 R. Judson Mitchell, *Ideology of a Superpower: Contemporary Soviet Doctrine on International Relations* (Hoover Institution Press, Stanford, 1982), p. 118.

48 Timothy J. Colton, *The Dilemma of Reform in the Soviet Union* (Council on Foreign Relations, Revised edition, New York, 1986).

49 Alexander Zinoviev, *Homo Sovieticus* (Paladin Grafton Books, London, 1986), p. 225.

50 See Gerhard Wettig, *Soviet Policy under Gorbachev* (Alliance Publishers, London, 1988).

51 'It is no revelation that I regularly read Lenin.' Mikhail Gorbachev in *The Issyk-Kul Forum* (Novosti, Moscow, 1987), p. 17.

52 Charles H. Fairbanks, Jr., 'Gorbachev's Global Doughnut', *The National Interest*, Spring 1990, p. 30.

53 This was duly noted – in his book *The Grand Failure* (1989) – by Zbigniew Brzezinski, who foresaw the future and boldly predicted the consequence of the events he had previously observed: the coming demise of Communism.

54 Mikhail Gorbachev's memoir *The August Coup* (HarperCollins, New York, 1991), completed immediately after the putsch, is a testimony to the new style: a de-ideologized newspeak. It is not free, however, from a trace of nostalgia for 'socialism': 'I am convinced that the discrediting of socialism in the eyes of the masses is a passing phase'. (p. 109).

55 Mikhail Gorbachev, *The August Coup* (HarperCollins, New York, 1991), p. 101.

56 Mikhail Gorbachev, *The August Coup* (HarperCollins, New York, 1991), p. 102.

57 Basil Willey, *The Eighteenth Century Background* [1940] (Chatto and Windus, London, 1961), p. 111.

58 Kennan Institute for Advanced Russian Studies, 'Meeting Report' (9 April, 1986), Washington DC.

59 Jerry F. Hough, *The Soviet Union and Social Science Theory* (Harvard University Press, Cambridge, 1977), p. 20.

CONCLUSION

1 Thus to Mostafa Rejai 'Political ideology is an emotion-laden, myth-saturated, action-related system of beliefs and values about people and society, legitimacy and authority that is acquired to a large extent as a matter of faith and habit'. *Comparative Political Ideologies* (St. Martin's Press, New York, 1984), p. 9. So defined, an ideology is the antithesis of rationality. inasmuch as it affects human behaviour – is 'action-related' – it apparently does so in the way that the delusions and hallucinations of the madman lead him into the kind of irrational behaviour that enables the rest of mankind to recognize his madness. What happened to the reasoning that any advocate of an ideology presents? Rejai does not say. He justs asserts that the 'Myths and values of ideology are communicated through symbols'. He thereby implies that they do not get communicated.

2 Reo M. Christenson, Alan S. Engel, Dan N. Jacobs et al., *Ideologies and Modern Politics* (Harper & Row, New York, 1981), p. 4.

3 Reo M. Christenson, Alan S. Engel, Dan N. Jacobs et al., *Ideologies and Modern Politics* (Harper & Row, New York, 1981), pp. 11ff.
4 Robert Eccleshall, 'Introduction: the world of ideology' in Robert Eccleshall, Vincent Geoghegan, Richard Jay and Rick Wilford, *Political Ideologies* (Hutchinson, London, 1984), p. 7.
5 'Liberalism', in Robert Eccleshall, Vincent Geoghegan, Richard Jay and Rick Wilford, *Political Ideologies* (Hutchinson, London, 1984), p. 37.
6 'Conservatism', in Robert Eccleshall, Vincent Geoghegan, Richard Jay and Rick Wilford, *Political Ideologies* (Hutchinson, London, 1984), p. 80.
7 Richard Eccleshall, Vincent Geoghegan, Richard Jay and Rick Wilford, *Political Ideologies* (Hutchinson, London, 1984), p. 81.
8 Vincent Geoghegan, 'Socialism', Robert Eccleshall, Vincent Geoghegan, Richard Jay and Rick Wilford, *Political Ideologies* (Hutchinson, London, 1984), p. 115.

Bibliographical references

Adler, Mortimer J. *Six Great Ideas*, (Macmillan, New York, 1981).

Allison, Lincoln. *Right Principles: A Conservative Philosophy of Politics* (Basil Blackwell, Oxford, 1984).

Bainton, Ronald H. *The Reformation of the Sixteenth Century* [1952] (The Beacon Press, Boston, 1963).

Becker, Jillian. *The Soviet Connection: State Sponsorship of Terrorism* (Institute for European Defence & Strategic Studies, London, 1985).

Berki, R.N. *Socialism* (J.M. Dent, London, 1975).

Berlin, Isaiah. *Four Essays on Liberty* (Oxford University Press, London & New York, 1969).

Besançon, Alain. *Les Origines intellectuelles du Léninisme* (Calmann-Lévy, Paris, 1977)

—— *The Soviet Syndrome* (Harcourt Brace Jovanovich, New York and London, 1978).

Bittman, Ladislav. *The KGB and Soviet Disinformation* (Pergamon-Brassey's, Washington DC, 1985).

Brzezinski, Zbigniew. *The Grand Failure: The Birth and Death of Communism in the Twentieth Century* (Charles Scribner's Sons, New York, 1989).

Burke, Edmund. *Reflections on the Revolution in France* [1790] (Oxford University Press, World's Classics, London, 1958).

Christenson, Reo M., Alan S. Engel, Dan N. Jacob *et al. Ideologies and Modern Politics* (Harper & Row, 3rd. ed., New York, 1981).

Colton, Timothy J. *The Dilemma of Reform in the Soviet Union* (Council on Foreign Relations, Revised edition, New York, 1986).

Cranston, Maurice. *Freedom: A New Analysis* [1953] (Longmans, Green, London, 1954).

Crosland, C.A.R. *The Future of Socialism* (Schocken Books, New York, 1963).

d'Entrèves, Alexander Passerin. *The Notion of the State* (Clarendon Press, Oxford, 1967).

Dixon, Keith. *Freedom and Equality: The Moral Basis of Democratic Socialism* (Routledge and Kegan Paul, London, 1986).

Drachkovitch, Milorad M. (ed.). *Marxist Ideology in the Contemporary*

World – Its Appeals and Paradoxes (Hoover Institution, Stanford and Frederick A. Praeger, New York, 1966).

Dunn, John. *The Politics of Socialism* (Cambridge University Press, Cambridge, 1984).

Dworkin, Ronald. *Taking Rights Seriously* (Harvard University Press, Cambridge, 1977).

Eccleshall, Robert, Vincent Geoghegan, Richard Jay and Rick Wilford. *Political Ideologies* (Hutchinson, London, 1984).

Fukuyama, Francis. 'The End of History?' *The National Interest*, No. 16 (Summer 1989).

Gaus, Gerald F. *The Modern Liberal Theory of Man* (Croom Helm, London, St. Martin's Press, New York, 1983).

Gorbachev, Mikhail. *The August Coup: The Truth and the Lessons* (HarperCollins, New York, 1991).

Hall, John A. *Liberalism* (Paladin/Grafton Books, London, 1988).

Harbour, William R. *The Foundations of Conservative Thought: An Anglo-American Tradition in Perspective* (University of Notre Dame Press, Notre Dame, 1982).

Harrington, Michael. *Socialism: Past and Future* (Little, Brown and Company, Boston, 1989).

Hattersley, Roy. *Choose Freedom: The Future of Democratic Socialism* (Michael Joseph, London, 1987).

Hayek, F.A. *The Fatal Conceit: the Errors of Socialism* [1988] (The Collected Works of F.A. Hayek, Vol.I, The University of Chicago Press, Chicago, 1989).

Henze, Paul. *The Plot to Kill the Pope* (Charles Scribner's Sons, New York, 1985).

Hobhouse, L.T. *Liberalism* [1911] (Oxford University Press, New York, 1964).

Hook, Sidney. *Political Power and Personal Freedom* (Collier Books, New York, 1962).

Hough, Jerry F. *The Soviet Union and Social Science Theory* (Harvard University Press, Cambridge, 1977).

The Issyk-Kul Forum: A New Way of Thinking (Novosti, Moscow, 1987).

Kaufmann, Walter. *Without Guilt and Justice* [1973] (Dell, New York, 1975).

Kirk, Russell, Lewis Lapham, Philip M. Crane and others. *Objections to Conservatism*, The Heritage Lectures, No.3 (The Heritage Foundation, Washington, DC, 1981).

Kitching, Gavin. *Rethinking Socialism* (Methuen, London, 1983).

Kolakowski, Leszek. 'The Devil in History' in G.R. Urban (ed.), *Stalinism: Its Impact on Russia and the World* (Temple Smith, London, 1982).

—— 'How to be a Conservative–Liberal-Socialist,' *Encounter*, Vol. LI, No. 4 (October 1978).

MacLean, Douglas and Claudia Mills (eds). *Liberalism Reconsidered* (Rowman and Allanheld, Totowa, NJ, 1983).

Meyer, Alfred G. *Leninism* (Frederick A. Praeger, New York, 1962).

Meyer, Frank S. (ed.). *What is Conservatism?* (Holt, Rinehart and Winston, New York, 1964).

Mill, John Stuart. *On Liberty* (The World's Classic edition of *On Liberty* [1859], *Representative Government* [1861] *& The Subjection of Women* [1869] (Oxford University Press, Oxford [1912], repr. 1954).

Minogue, K.R. *The Liberal Mind* (Methuen, London, 1963).

Mitchell, R. Judson. *Ideology of a Superpower: Contemporary Soviet Doctrine on International Relations* (Hoover Institution Press, Stanford, 1982).

Muller, Herbert J. *Issues of Freedom* (Harper, New York, 1960).

Nozick, Robert. *Anarchy, State and Utopia* (Basic Books, New York, 1974).

O'Sullivan, Noël. *Conservatism* (J.M. Dent, London, 1976).

Pateman, Carole. *The Problem of Political Obligation* (John Wiley, Chichester and New York, 1979).

Plamenatz, John. *On Alien Rule and Self-Government* (Longmans, London, 1960).

Quinton, Anthony (ed.). *Political Philosophy* (Oxford University Press, London, 1967).

—— *The Politics of Imperfection* (Faber and Faber, London, 1978).

Raphael, D.D. *Problems of Political Philosophy* (Pall Mall Press, London, 1970).

Rawls, John. *A Theory of Justice* (Harvard University Press, Cambridge, Mass., 1971).

Rejai, Mostafa. *Comparative Political Ideologies* (St. Martin's Press, New York, 1984).

Revel, Jean François. *La Connaissance inutile* (Bernard Grasset, Paris, 1988).

—— *How Democracies Perish* (Doubleday, Garden City, NY, 1983).

—— *The Totalitarian Temptation* (Doubleday, Garden City, NY, 1977).

Rossiter, Clinton. *Conservatism in America* (Alfred A. Knopf, New York, 1955).

Rousseau, J.J. *The Social Contract* [1762] (World's Classics, Oxford University Press, London [1947], repr. 1956).

Scruton, Roger. *The Meaning of Conservatism* (Penguin, Harmondsworth, 1980).

Shultz, Richard H. and Roy Godson. *Dezinformatsia: Active Measures in Soviet Strategy* (Pergamon-Brassey's, Washington, DC, 1984).

Simon, Yves R. *Philosophy of Democratic Government* [1951] (University of Chicago Press, Chicago, 1961).

Stankiewicz, W.J. *Approaches to Democracy: Philosophy of Government at the Close of the Twentieth Century* (Edward Arnold, London, 1980).

—— (ed.). *Political Thought Since World War II: Critical and Interpretive Essays* (The Free Press of Glencoe, New York, 1964).

—— *Politics & Religion in Seventeenth-Century France* (University of California Press, Berkeley and Los Angeles, 1960).

Stevenson, Charles L. *Ethics and Language* (Yale University Press, New Haven, 1962).

Urban, G.R. (ed.). *Stalinism: Its Impact on Russia and the World* (Temple Smith, London, 1982).

Viereck, Peter. *Shame and Glory of the Intellectuals* [1953] (Capricorn Books, New York, 1965).

—— *The Unadjusted Man* [1956] (Capricorn Books, New York, 1962).

Waxman, Chaim I. (ed.). *The End of Ideology Debate* (Simon and Schuster, New York, 1969).

Wettig, Gerhard. *Soviet Foreign Policy under Gorbachev* (Alliance Publishers, London, 1988).

Will, George. *Statecraft as Soulcraft: What Government Does* (Simon and Schuster, New York, 1983).

Willey, Basil. *The Eighteenth Century Background* [1940] (Chatto and Windus, London, 1961).

Wolfe, Bertram D. *Communist Totalitarianism: Keys to the Soviet System* (Beacon Press, Boston, 1961).

—— *An Ideology in Power: Reflections on the Russian Revolution* (Stein & Day, New York, 1969).

Wolton, Thierry. *Le K.g.b. en France* (Grasset, Paris, 1986).

Zinoviev, Alexander. *Homo Sovieticus* [1982] (Paladin Grafton Books, London, 1986).

—— *The Radiant Future* (Random House, New York, 1980).

—— *The Reality of Communism* (Paladin Books, London, 1985).

Index

420–1; and Communism 410;
capsule history of 409–10;
need for scrutinizing ideology
420–1; and individualism
164–5; on liberty and freedom
196; insistence on 'mind' 422;
differing from philosophy
105; on scepticism 110;
'pragmatic' philosophy of 67;
and rights 80, 88
*Political Thought Since World War
II* (W. J. Stankiewicz, ed.) 309
Pontecorvo, Bruno 289
Popper, Karl 197
power: as ability and dominance
334; and authority 229, 334,
336; coercive 59, 62–3; and
Communist and democratic
ideology 337; of democratic
government 341–2; as means
to an end 358–9; and property
230; sovereign 335; and
Communist State 344
pragmatic evils: and sequential
goods 269
pragmatism: and education 329,
330; and Gorbachev 385, 387,
388; its function and
instrumentalism 385; Hayek's
303–5; Lenin's 348
Pravda 383
progress: Hayek on 302–4; trial-
and-error basis 36; and
Western civilization 93
propaganda: and disinformation
355
property: concept of 271–2; and
disinformation 355–6;
distribution of 241–2; and
equality 243–4; and equality
of opportunity 182–3; and
freedom 230; as primary good
212; and source of inequality
211; 'natural law' view of 214;
and power 230; redistribution
of 30; and self 182, 222; and
socialism 222; and traditional
ethics 236; and work ethic 213
Protestant Reformation 162,
207, 293

Protestantism: work ethic of 213,
226, 237, 241
prudence: prudential behaviour
and society 72; as touchstone
of conservative thought 64; as
contractual factor 107, 108;
and the good 66–7; as
normative component of
political authority 68; as
normative principle 65; and
the self 70
psychoanalysis: and Burke's idea
on restraint 84; on human
behaviour 141
Puritanism 149
putsch (August 1991) 388, 389

Quinton, Anthony: on
conservatism 73–4; and Burke
75

Raphael, D.D.: on freedom 192
Rawls, J. 119, 157, 159, 173; on
social contract 161–2, 414;
and contractualism 118, 161;
Dunn on 273, 274; on
education 170; on distributive
justice 161–3; on 'justice as
fairness' 169–71, 177; on
liberty 118–19; on equality of
opportunity and fraternity
177–9; on rights 168; on the
under-privileged 167
Reagan, Ronald 12
Reality of Communism, The
(Alexander Zinoviev) 373
*Reflections on the Revolution in
France* (Edmund Burke) 83
relativism 22, 161; and authority
68–9; Burke on 77; and
Communist reasoning 400;
and conservatism 24, 25, 68;
and conservatives 18, 23–4;
and concept of crime 76;
cultural 219; desire and the
desirable 68; and equality
217; and equality of
opportunity 183–4; ethical
284; and fraternity 246–7; and
the good 158; Hayek on 302;